COUNTY
STREET ATLAS

BERKSHIRE

CW00607372

Ordnance Survey

COUNTY
STREET ATLAS

BERKSHIRE

1st edition

COUNTY STREET ATLAS
BERKSHIRE

First Edition published 1993 by

Ordnance Survey   and **George Philip**
Romsey Road   an imprint of Reed Consumer Books Limited
Maybush   Michelin House, 81 Fulham Road, London SW3 6R
Southampton SO9 4DH   and Auckland, Melbourne, Singapore and Toronto

ISBN 0 540 05835 1 (George Philip)
ISBN 0 319 00374 4 (Ordnance Survey)

To the best of the Publishers' knowledge, the information in this atlas
was correct at the time of going to press. No responsibility can be
accepted for any errors or their consequences.

The representation in this atlas of a road, track or path is no evidence
of the existence of a right of way.

COUNTY STREET ATLASES
available in hardback (3½ inches to 1 mile)

Berkshire	**East Kent**
Buckinghamshire	**West Kent**
East Essex	**Oxfordshire**
West Essex	**Surrey** (3 inches to 1 mile)
North Hampshire	**East Sussex**
South Hampshire	**West Sussex**
Hertfordshire	**Warwickshire**

POCKET STREET ATLASES
available in paperback (2½ inches to 1 mile)

Berkshire	**Hertfordshire**
Buckinghamshire	**Surrey** (2 inches to 1 mile)

Printed in Great Britain

CONTENTS

Key to map pages   vi-vii
Administrative boundaries   viii
Street maps   1-153
Index explanation and abbreviations   154
Index of towns, villages and rural localities   155
Index of street names   156-179

KEY TO MAP SYMBOLS

British Rail Station		Motorway and Dual Carriageway		
London Transport Station		Main or through road		
Private Railway Station	A27(T)	Road numbers (Dept of Transport)		
Bus or Coach Station		Gate or obstruction to traffic		
(H) Heliport		(restrictions may not apply at all times and to all vehicles)		
Police Station (may not be open 24hrs)	- - - - -	Footpath		
Hospital with Casualty Facilities (may not be open 24hrs)	- - -	Bridleway		
	- - -	Path	The representation in this atlas of a	
Post Office		Track	road, track or path is no evidence of the existence of a right of way.	

Place of Worship	Amb Sta	Ambulance Station	LC	Level Crossing
Important Building	Coll	College	Liby	Library
	FB	Foot Bridge	Mus	Museum
P Parking	F Sta	Fire Station	Sch	School
120 Adjoining Page Indicator	Hospl	Hospital	TH	Town Hall

The large letters and numbers around the edge of the maps are the referencing system.
An explanation of how to use the system for locating the position of street names appears on
page **154**. The small numbers identify the 1 kilometre National Grid lines.

Scale of Maps is 2.6 inches to 1 mile

0		¼		½		¾		1 mile
0	250m	500m	700m	1 Kilometre				

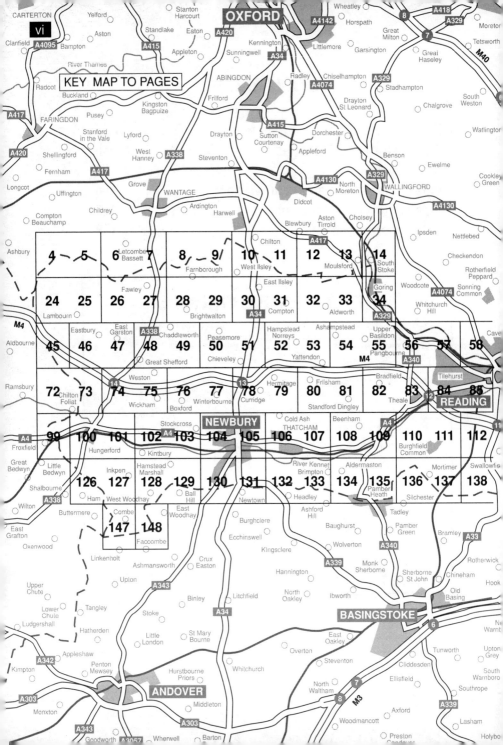

KEY MAP TO PAGES

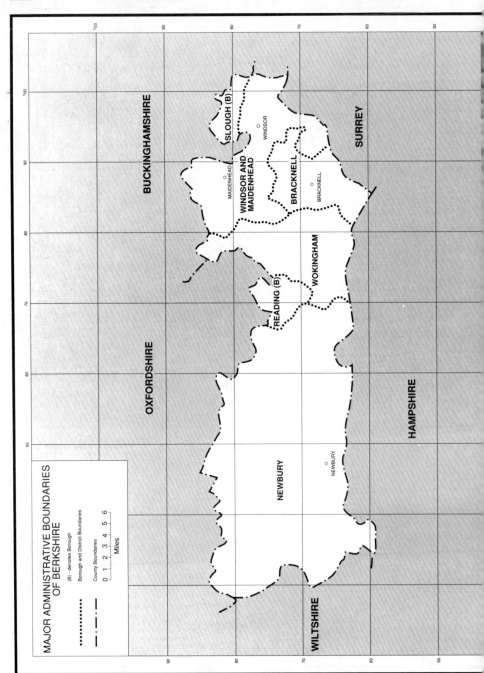

MAJOR ADMINISTRATIVE BOUNDARIES
OF BERKSHIRE

(B) : denotes Borough

Borough and District Boundaries

County Boundaries

0 1 2 3 4 5 6
Miles

BUCKINGHAMSHIRE

SURREY

SLOUGH (B)

WINDSOR

MAIDENHEAD

WINDSOR AND
MAIDENHEAD

BRACKNELL

BRACKNELL

WOKINGHAM

READING (B)

OXFORDSHIRE

HAMPSHIRE

NEWBURY

NEWBURY

WILTSHIRE

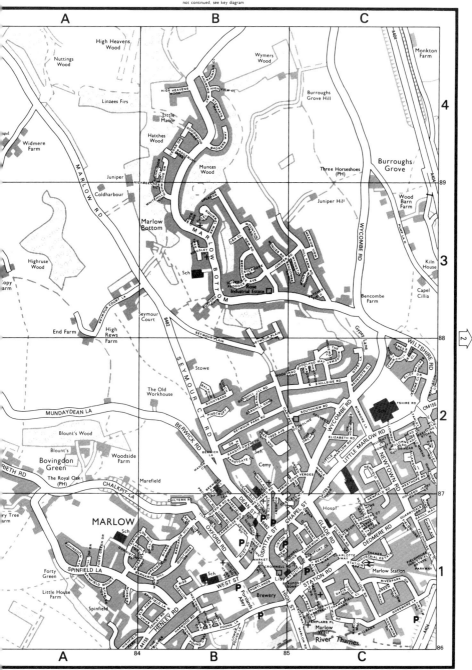

not continued, see key diagram

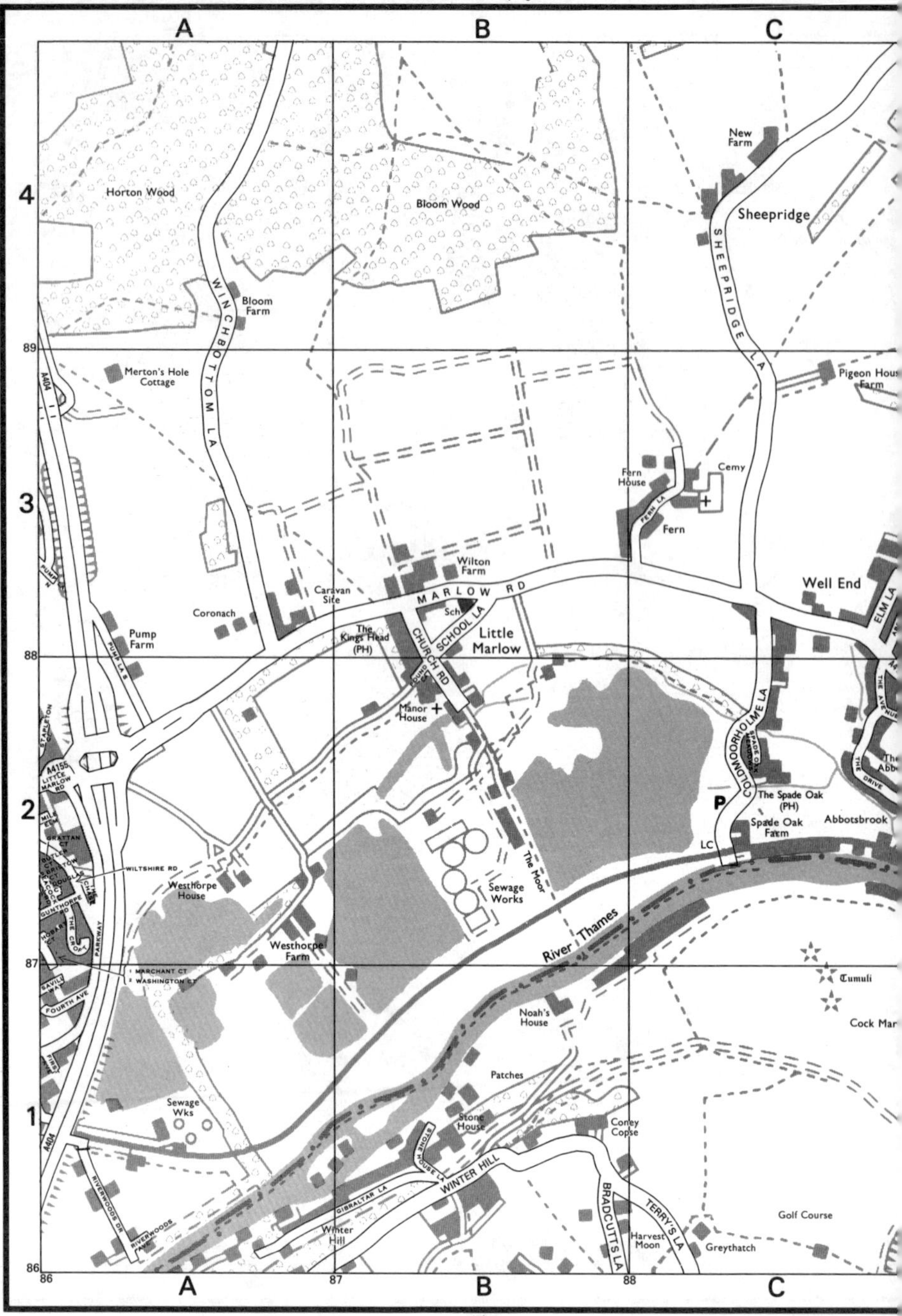

1

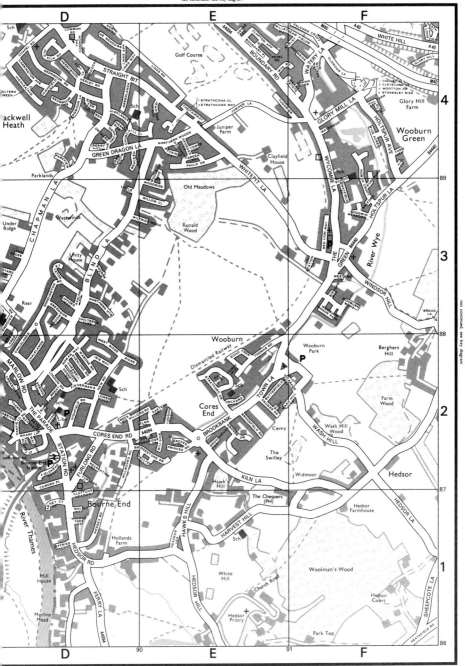

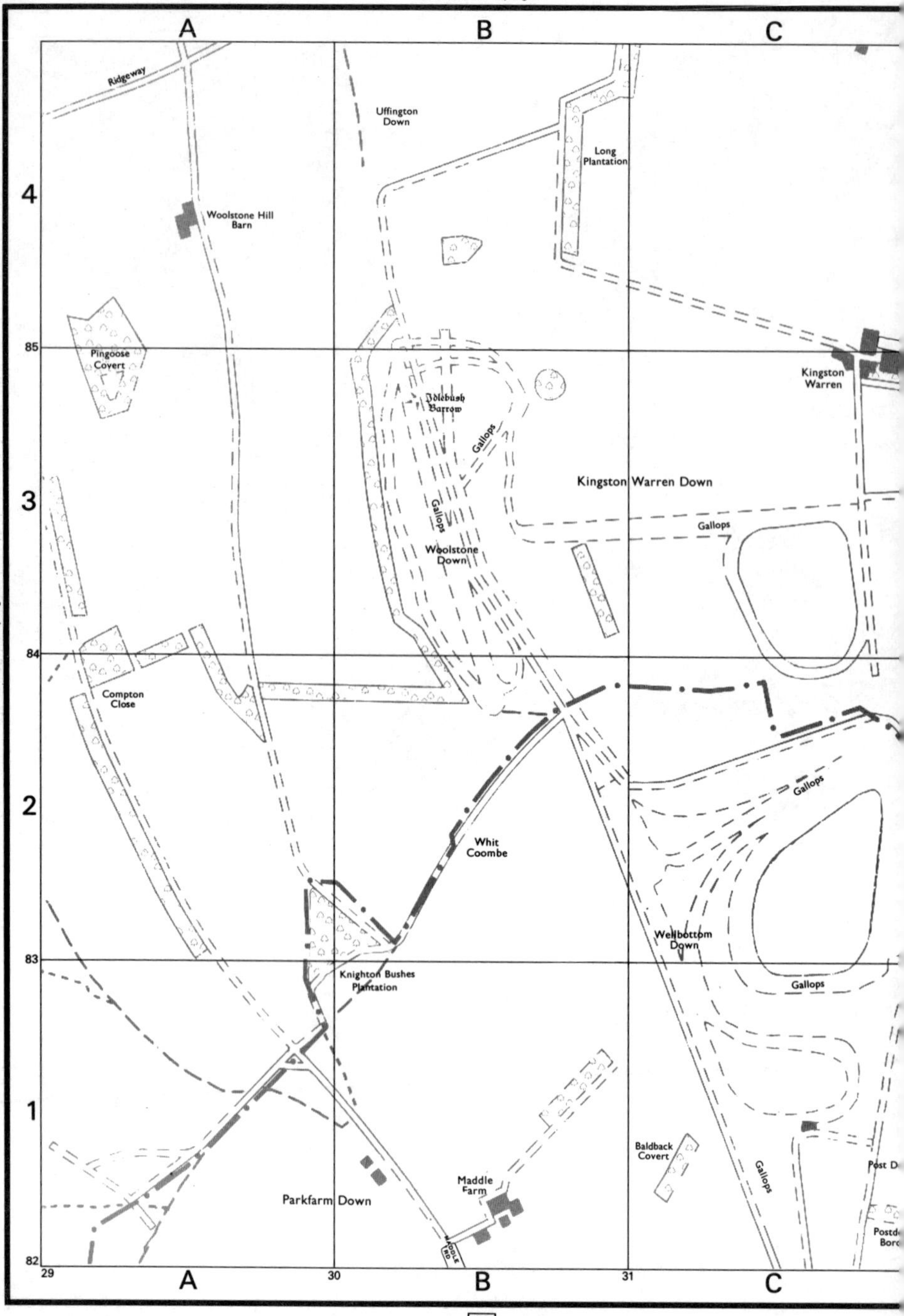

not continued, see key diagram

A   B   C

Ridgeway

Uffington
Down

Long
Plantation

4

Woolstone Hill
Barn

85

Pingoose
Covert

Kingston
Warren

Idlebush
Barrow

Gallops

Kingston Warren Down

3

Gallops

Gallops

Woolstone
Down

84

Compton
Close

2

Gallops

Whit
Coombe

Wellbottom
Down

83

Knighton Bushes
Plantation

Gallops

1

Baldback
Covert

Gallops

Post D

Parkfarm Down

Maddle
Farm

Postd
Bore

82

29   30   31

A   B   C

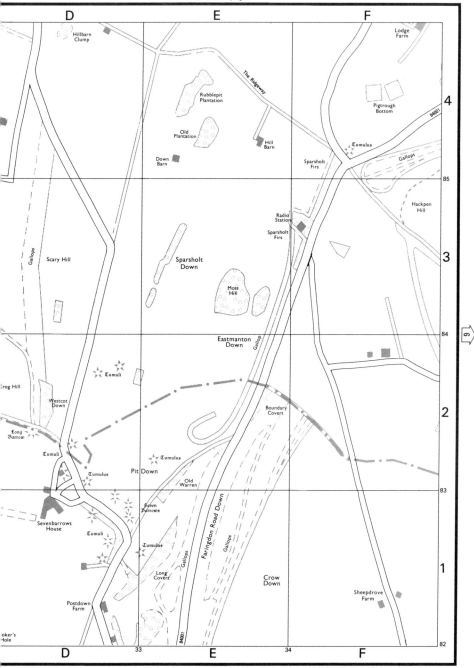

D   E   F

Hillbarn
Clump

Lodge
Farm

The Ridgeway

Rubblepit
Plantation

Pigtrough
Bottom

4

B4001

Old
Plantation

Hill
Barn

Tumulus

Down
Barn

Sparsholt
Firs

Gallops

85

Radio
Station

Hackpen
Hill

Sparsholt
Firs

Gallops

Scary Hill

Sparsholt
Down

3

Moss
Hill

84

6

Eastmanton
Down

Gallop

Crog Hill

Tumuli

Westcot
Down

Boundary
Covert

2

Long
Barrow

Tumuli

Tumulus

Pit Down

Old
Warren

83

Faringdon Road Down

Sevenbarrows
House

Syben
Barrows

Tumuli

Tumulus

Gallops

Gallops

Long
Covert

Crow
Down

1

Sheepdrove
Farm

Postdown
Farm

oker's
ole

B4001

82

D   33   E   34   F

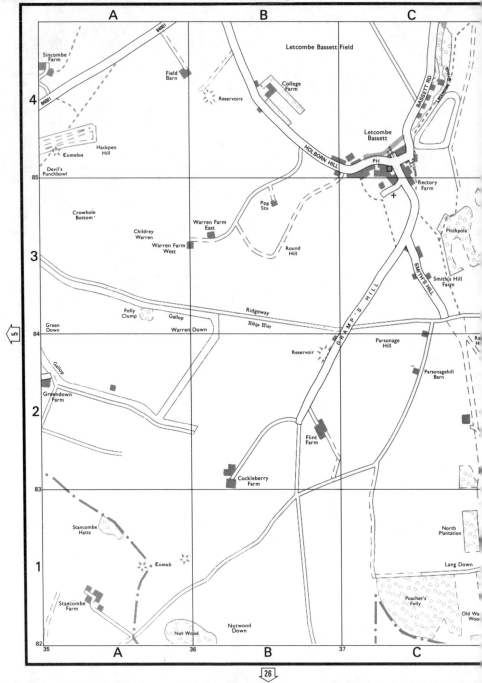

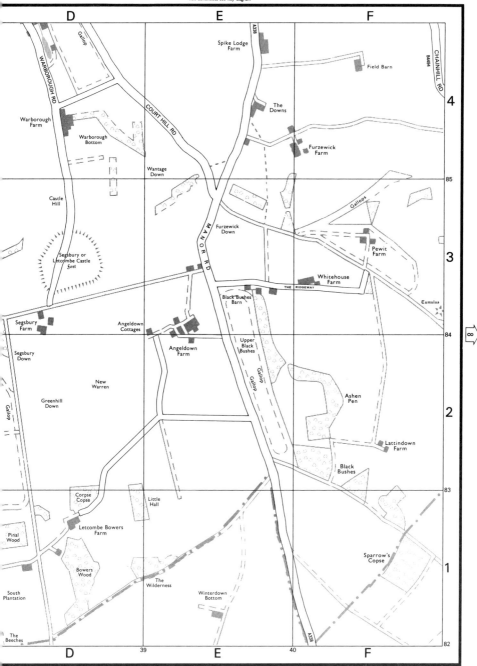

D

Gallop

WARBOROUGH RD

Warborough
Farm

Warborough
Bottom

COURT HILL RD

Wantage
Down

Castle
Hill

Segsbury or
Letcombe Castle
Fort

Segsbury
Farm

Segsbury
Down

New
Warren

Greenhill
Down

Gallop

Corpse
Copse

Letcombe Bowers
Farm

Pinal
Wood

Bowers
Wood

South
Plantation

The
Beeches

D

39

E

Spike Lodge
Farm

The
Downs

Furzewick
Farm

A338

MANOR RD

Furzewick
Down

Angeldown
Cottages

Angeldown
Farm

Upper
Black
Bushes

Gallop
Gallop

Little
Hall

The
Wilderness

Winterdown
Bottom

E

40

F

Field Barn

CHAINHILL RD

B4494

4

85

Gallops

Pewit
Farm

3

Whitehouse
Farm

THE RIDGEWAY

Black Bushes
Barn

Cumulus

84

Ashen
Pen

2

Lattindown
Farm

Black
Bushes

83

Sparrow's
Copse

1

A338

82

F

8

A
B
C

CHAINHILL RD
B4494

Gallop

Chalkhill
Barn

Long Valley Down

Coldharbour Road (Track)

Birch
Wood

4

Goddard's Roads (Track)

Corsica Pine
Wood

Jew's
Harp

The
Sycamores

85

Ardington Down

BITHAM RD

Midsummer
Wood

Ridgeway

Gallop

3

Middlehill
Down

Grim's Ditch

The Ridgeway Path (Oxfordshire Circular Walk)

Ridgeway
Down

Monument
on site of
Tumulus

Wether
Down

Old Street (Track)

Betterton
Down

84

Yew Down

Mead
Platt

The Warren

2

Triangle
Wood

Lattin Down

Wireless
Station

Lockinge Kiln
Farm

Lockinge
Down

83

Farnborough Furze
Down

1

Little Coombe
Farm

Moonlight
Barn

Farnborough

COPPERAGE RD

82

Coombe
Lodge

B4494

41
A
42
B
43
C

D   **E**   **F**

Diamond Jubilee Wood

White Way

Tile Barn

MEADHILL WAY
PLANTATION
GORSE WAY
DIDS RD

Knob Down

Grim's Ditch

4

Grim's Ditch

Oldharbour Rd

Fore Down

Foredown Plantation

Sidlevdy Road (Track)

East Ginge Down

The Ridgeway Path (Oxfordshire Circular Walk)

Cuckhamsley Hill

East Hendred Down

85

Ridgeway Barn

Tumulus

O C Walk

ew's Barn

Johnson's Farm

Upper Plantation

3

Down Barn

Abbot's Heath

Gallops

Gallop

Middle Plantation

Sheep Down

West Ginge Down

Big Allens

Kilman Knoll Down

84

Gallops

Gallops

Little Allens

O C Walk

ew

2

Knollend Down

Lands End

Lower Barn

COPPERAGE RD

Old Street (Track)

83

Old Down

Starveall Farm

1

Harcourt Farm

Hernehill Down

CATMORE RD

82

D   45   **E**   46   **F**

10

29

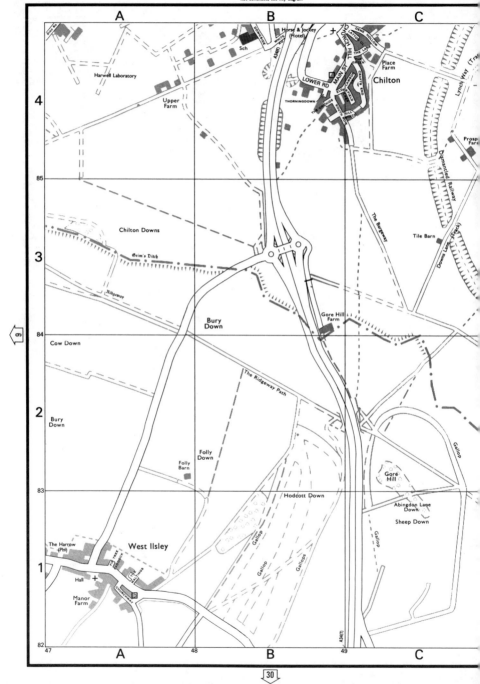

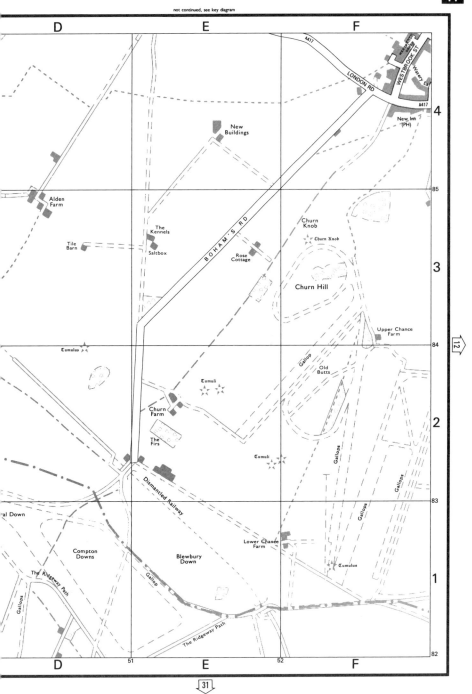

11

D **E** **F**

A417

WESTBROOK ST

Wantry La

HEATH ROW

LONDON RD

A417

New Inn
(PH)

4

New
Buildings

85

Alden
Farm

The
Kennels

Churn
Knob

Churn Knob

Tile
Barn

Saltbox

BOHAM'S RD

Rose
Cottage

Churn Hill

3

Upper Chance
Farm

84

Tumulus

Gallop

Old
Butts

112

Tumuli

Churn
Farm

Gallops

2

The
Firs

Tumuli

Gallops

Dismantled Railway

83

al Down

Gallops

Compton
Downs

Lower Chance
Farm

Blewbury
Down

The Ridgeway Path

Gallop

Tumulus

1

Gallops

The Ridgeway Path

82

D 51 **E** 52 **F**

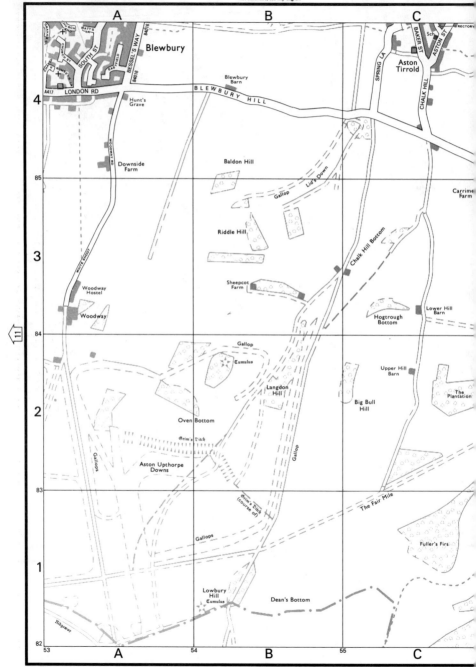

Blewbury

Aston Tirrold

Blewbury Barn

BLEWBURY HILL

Hunt's Grave

Baldon Hill

Carrime Farm

Downside Farm

Lid's Down

Gallop

Riddle Hill

Chalk Hill Bottom

Sheepcot Farm

Woodway Hostel

Lower Hill Barn

Hogtrough Bottom

Woodway

Gallop

Tumulus

Upper Hill Barn

The Plantation

Langdon Hill

Big Bull Hill

Oven Bottom

Grim's Ditch

Aston Upthorpe Downs

Gallop

Gallops

Grim's Ditch (course of)

The Fair Mile

Gallops

Fuller's Firs

Lowbury Hill Tumulus

Dean's Bottom

Ridgeway

13

D E F

Abbey
(site of)

Cholsey and Moulsford
Station

Westfield
Farm

4

Moat
Lollingdon Farm

WESTFIELD RD

The
Lynch

Lollingdon Hill

85

Bowslade

HALFPENNY LA

Offlands
Farm

3

Sheephouse

Breach
House

Sch

Ticknell Path

Westfield
Nursery

GLEBE CL

84

[14]

SHORTLANDS HILL

Moulsford

Cholsey Downs

Kingstanding
Hill

North Rd

NORTH UNHILL BANK

2

Starveall
Farm

North Unhill Bank

Moulsford Bottom

COW LA

83

...ll Bottom

Pump
House

Greenlands
Farm

Lingley Knoll

Earthwork

Moulsford
Downs

Well Barn

1

Devil's Ditch

WANTAGE RD

...hill Wood

Ridge
Roads

M11

82

D 57 E 58 F

14

A   B   C

4

85

3

2

84

2

83

1

82

Cholsey

PAPIST WAY
1 CELSEA PL
2 CHARLES RD

Hospital

Hospl

READING RD

PAPIST WAY

A329

The
Gables

Littlestoke
Manor Farm

Ash
Cottages

Barracks
Farm

B4009

Middle
Barn

Viaduct

The Ridgeway Path

THE STREET

School

The
Oak

WALLINGFORD RD

White Hill

Watch
Folly

Freedom
Cottages

Lower
Farm

WOODCOTE RD

Ivol
Barn

FERRY LA

Ferry

FERRY RD

South Stoke

FERRY LA

UNDERHILL

River Thames

CROSS KEYS RD

Glebe
Cottages

Lower Cadley's
Farm

Sowberry
Court

THE STREET

South
Bank

Grove Farm
House

Grove
House

The Ridgeway Path

Runsford Hole

Grove
Farm

WALLINGFORD RD

Ye Olde
Leathern Bottel
(PH)

Spring
Farm

Spring Farm
Cottages

ICKNIELD RD

BEECH LA

A329

B4009

59   A   60   B   61   C

13

not continued, see key diagram

D E F

Crockmore Farm
Fawley
Benhams Wood
BENHAMS LA
Oaken Grove
A4155
4
Round Hill Farm
Roothouse Wood
Rowe Wood
Fawley Court Farm
85
Round Hill
The Golden Ball (PH)
Lower Assendon
Great Hill
Henley Park
New Cottages
BIX HILL
BIX
Cemy
No Man's Hill
Deer Park
Fawley Court
Henley Reach
3
Lambridge Hill
Hospital
The Grove
College
Little Wood
84
Lambridge Wood
FAIR MILE
The Mount
South Lodge
River Thames
16
2
LAMBRIDGE WOOD RD
BARN LA
Caravan & Camping Site
REMENHAM LA
Badgemore End
Badgemore Stables
Swiss Farm
Remenham Court
Golf Course
Badgemore House
Beechwood
NORTHFIELD END
Court
MARLOW RD
PHYLLIS
Phyllis Court
LAMBRIDGE LA
CH
RUPERT CL
RUPERT ST
BELL ST
Wilminster Park
83
Sch
Friar Park
COUNT VIEW
NEW ST
THAMES
Sch
Lower Hernes
Hospl
LAURENCE RD
YORK RD
BELL ST
Church
Parkside
PACK AND PRIME LA
WEST ST
MARKET PL
HART ST
DUKE ST
SIDE
MATSON DR
WHITE HILL A423(T)
A321
1
Pack and Prime Lane
GRAVEL HILL
FRIDAY ST
STATION RD
WARGRAVE RD
College
DEANFIELD AVE
MILTON
Coll
READING RD
Henley-on-Thames Station
HENLEY-ON-THAMES
1 VALLEY RD
2 GAINSBOROUGH RD
3 GAINSBOROUGH HILL
GREYS RD
UPTON CL
A4131
A321
Greenfield Cottages
HARCOURT CL
GROVE RD
MARMION RD
Hernes
HAYWARDS CL
Sch
82

D 75 E 76 F

A   B   C

Greenlands
Dairy Farm

Greenlands

North Cot Wood

Burrow
Farm

4

A4155

DAIRY LA

Chalkpit
Wood

Mill End

Binfields
Wood

Hambleden
Lock
Weir

Mill

Millend
Farm

85

Killdown
Bank

Temple
Island

Towing Path

River Thames

FERRY LA

Hambleden
Place

WESTFIELD
COTTS

3

Remenham

REMENHAM LA

ASTON FERRY LA

Westf
Far

Hotel

Aston

15

84

Culham
Farm

Towing Path

REMENHAM CHURCH LA

ASTON LA

Culham
Court

Culham
House

Lower Culham
Farm

2

Woodside
Farm

Remenham
Wood

Common
Barn

83

Remenham
Place

Remenham
Hill

Middle Culham
Farm

Rosehill
Wood

A423(T)

WHITE HILL

1

Branfords

Parkplace
Farm

Wild's
Belt

CH

Aspects Park
Golf Centre

Upper Culham
Farm

A321

MARGRAVE
RD

Park Place

Piggots
Corner

82

77   78   79

A   B   C

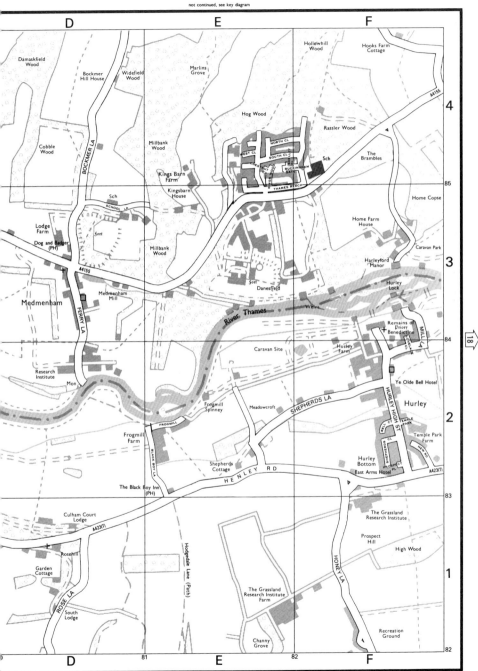

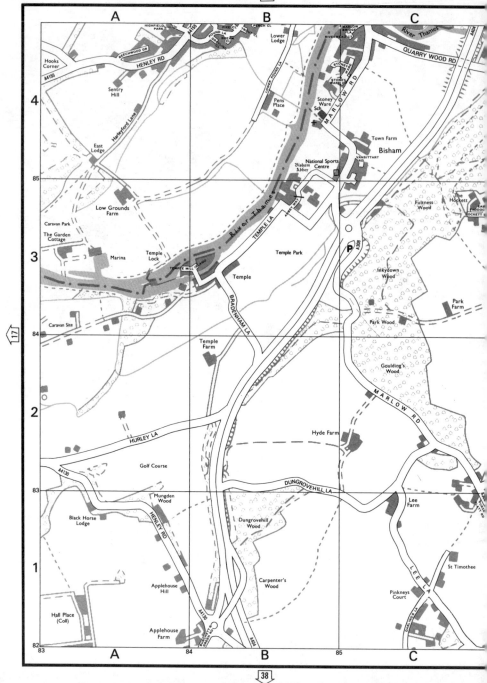

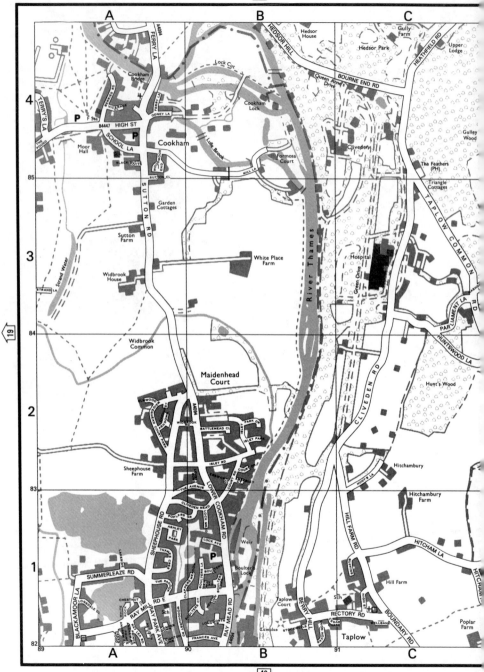

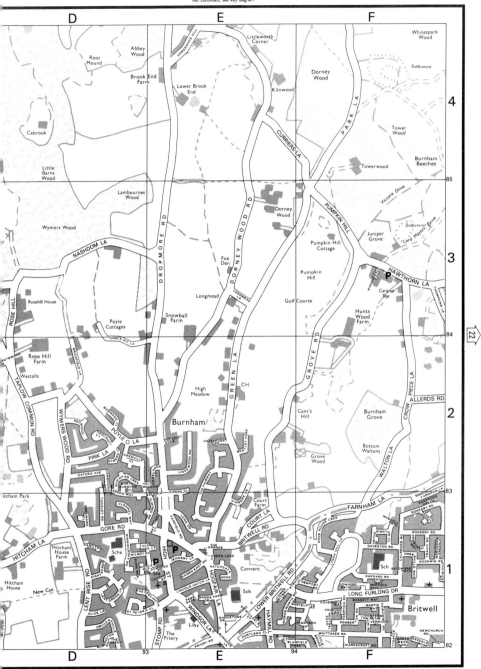

not continued, see key diagram

D **E** **F**

The Pickeridge

Fox and Pheasant (PH)

Fulmer

FULMER RD

M40

Furzeney Wood

STOKE COMMON RD

HAY LA

Sch

ALLHUSEN GDNS

Fulmer House Farm

4

PH

Church Farm

ALDERBOURNE LA

Alder Bourne

Stoke Common

Watersplash Farm

Fulmer Rise Manor

WINDMILL RD

CHERRY TREE LA

GERRARDS CROSS RD

Penn Wood

Fernacres Farm

85

Frame Wood

FULMER COMMON RD

PINE RD

Mill House Farm

Langley Corner

EVEHURST

Sch

FRAMEWOOD RD

LEIGMARE CL

Hollybush Hill

GREEN

BLUES RD

Fairfield Lodge

Fulmer Grange

Upton Lake

Upton Farm

3

CHERRY TREE

HILL RD

Lib

SEFTON PADDOX

ROGERS LA

HOLLYBUSH HILL

Upton Wood

Upton Wood

CAMELLA

P

Sch

SCHOOL LA

HOLLYBUSH HILL

The Stag (PH)

84

BELLS HILL

BROOKLEY RD

Sefton Park

Twin Trees Farm

BLACK PARK RD

Queen's Drive

PARK

PLOUGH LA

TURNERS RD

FARTHING GREEN LA

ST ANS

Wexham Street

Rowley Wood

ROWLEY LA

Iver Heath

2

WEXHAM ST

Golf Course

Galleons Lane

P

GRAY'S PARK RD

B416

Grange Farm

Golf Course

Blackpark Lake

Gallions Wood

83

PARK RD

Berry Farm

Cattle Market

Spring Wood

Rowley Farm

Avenue Drive

Rowley Lake

Bell Farm

1

Red Lion (PH)

Hospital

STOKE RD

STOKE GREEN

WEXHAM PARK LA

UXBRIDGE RD

A412

A412

CHURCH LA

WEXHAM RD

Stoke Place

Stoke Green

82

D **E** **F**

'99 00

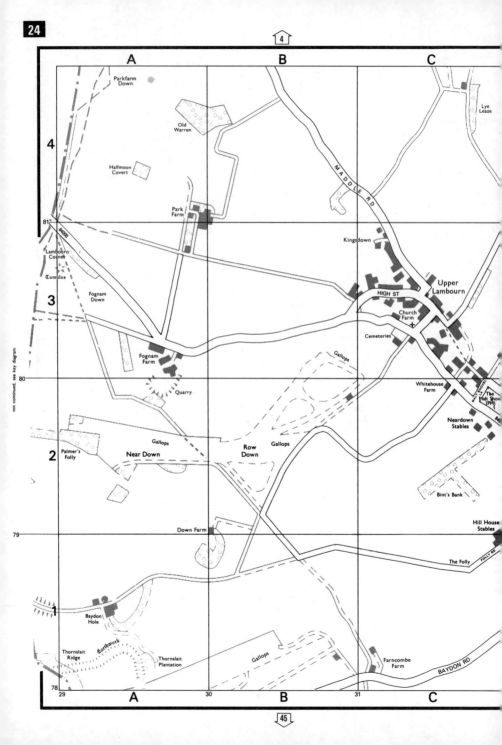

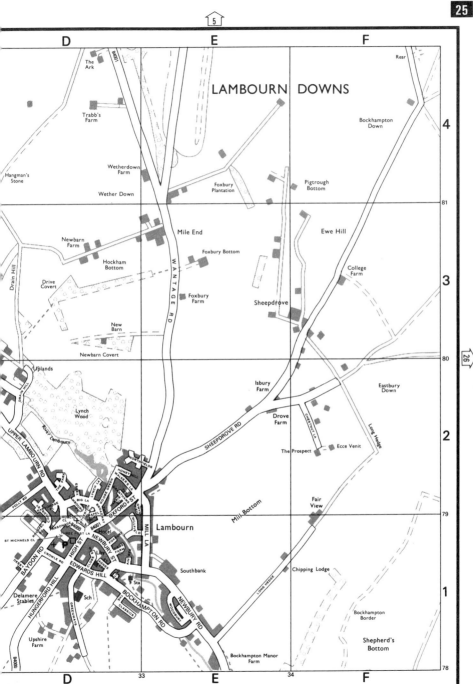

D E F

The Ark

B4001

Trabb's
Farm

Hangman's
Stone

LAMBOURN DOWNS

Resr

Bockhampton
Down

4

Wetherdown
Farm

Wether Down

Foxbury
Plantation

Pigtrough
Bottom

81

Drain Hill

Newbarn
Farm

Hockham
Bottom

Drive
Covert

New
Barn

Newbarn Covert

Mile End

W
A
N
T
A
G
E

R
D

Foxbury Bottom

Foxbury
Farm

Ewe Hill

College
Farm

Sheepdrove

3

Uplands

UPPER LAMBOURN RD

DRAIN HILL

Lynch
Wood

River Lambourn

Isbury
Farm

SHEEPDROVE RD

Drove
Farm

The Prospect

CHESTNUT LA

Ecce Venit

Eastbury
Down

Long Hedge

80

2

FOLLY RD

BAYDON RD

OXFORD'S ST

POSTFIELDS

HONEY
HILL

WALKER'S LA

LYNCH LA

BIG LA

THREE POST LA

B4000

B4001

ST MICHAELS CL

P

HIGH ST

CROWLE RD

NEWBURY ST

MILL LA

Lambourn

Hotel

Fair
View

Mill Bottom

79

Delamere
Stables

HUNGERFORD HILL

EDWARDS HILL

Sch

GREENWAY

BOCKHAMPTON RD

Southbank

Sta

NEWBURY RD

WOODSPEEN

CLARRICKS

Chipping Lodge

LONG HEDGE

Bockhampton
Border

1

Upshire
Farm

B4000

Bockhampton Manor
Farm

Shepherd's
Bottom

78

D

33

E

34

F

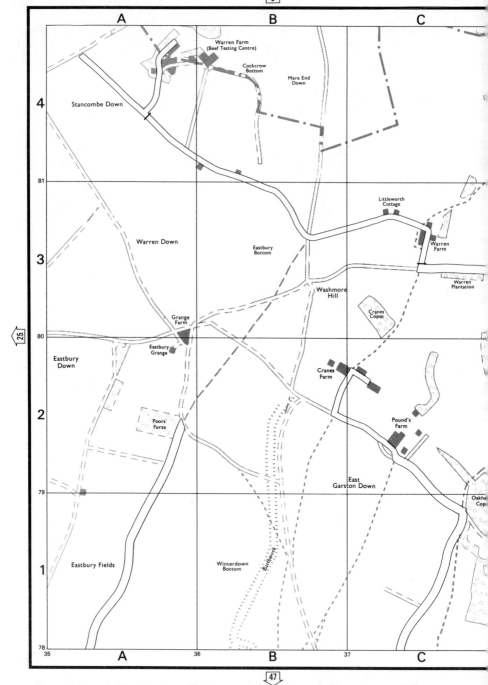

A　　　　　　　　B　　　　　　　　C

Warren Farm
(Beef Testing Centre)

Cockcrow
Bottom

Mere End
Down

4

Stancombe Down

81

Littleworth
Cottage

3

Warren Down

Eastbury
Bottom

Warren
Farm

Washmore
Hill

Warren
Plantation

Cranes
Copse

Grange
Farm

25　80

Eastbury
Grange

Eastbury
Down

Cranes
Farm

2

Poors'
Furze

Pound's
Farm

East
Garston Down

79

Oakhe
Cop

1

Eastbury Fields

Winterdown
Bottom

78
35　　　　　　　A　　　　36　　　　　B　　　　37　　　　　C

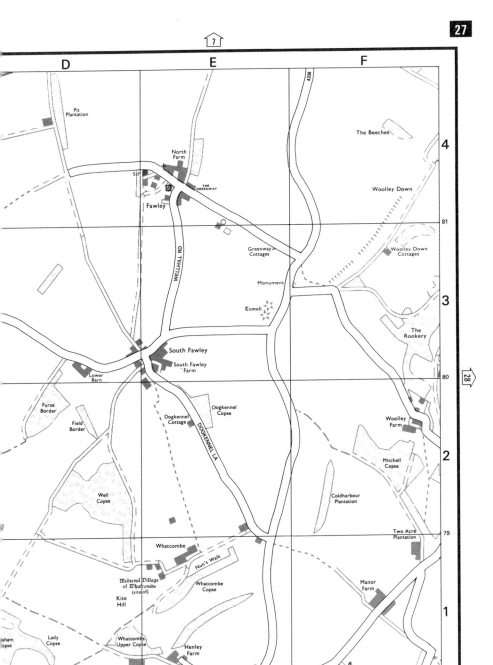

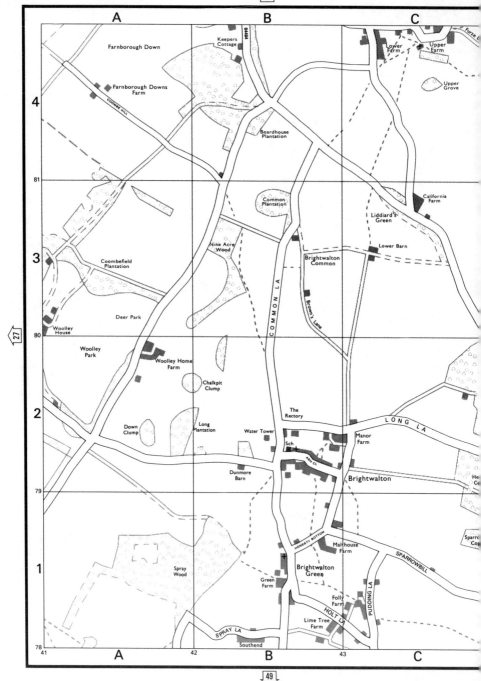

A   B   C

Farnborough Down

Keepers
Cottage

B4494

Lower
Farm

Upper
Farm

Upper
Grove

Farnborough Downs
Farm

COOMBE HILL

4

Boardhouse
Plantation

California
Farm

81

Common
Plantation

Liddiard's
Green

Coombefield
Plantation

Nine Acre
Wood

Lower Barn

3

Brightwalton
Common

COMMON LA

Brown's Lane

Deer Park

Woolley
House

80

Woolley
Park

Woolley Home
Farm

Chalkpit
Clump

The
Rectory

LONG LA

2

Down
Clump

Long
Plantation

Water Tower

Sch

Manor
Farm

Dunmore
Barn

ASH CL.

Brightwalton

Heath
Cel

79

HONESTY BOTTOM

Sparro
Cop

Spray
Wood

Malthouse
Farm

SPARROWBILL

1

Brightwalton
Green

Green
Farm

Folly
Farm

PUDDING LA

SPRAY LA

HOLT LA

Lime Tree
Farm

78

41   Southend   **42**   **43**

A   B   C

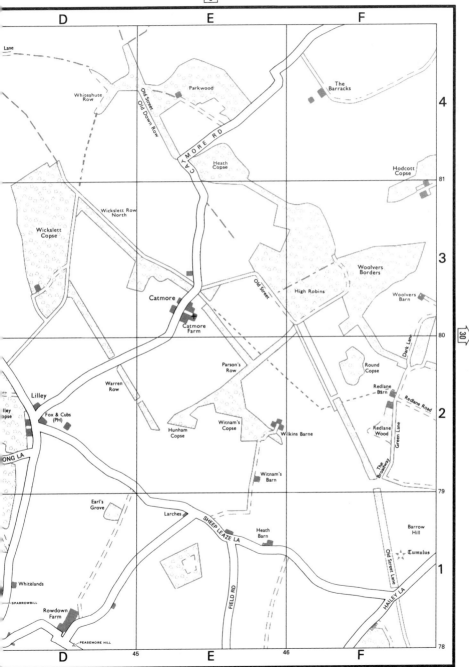

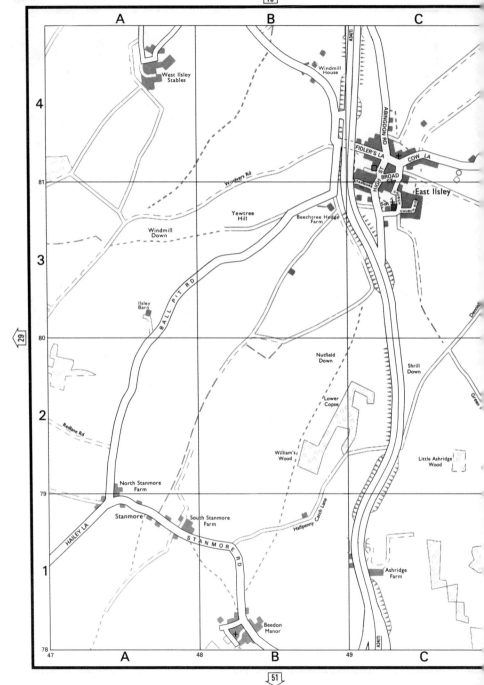

A   B   C

West Ilsley
Stables

Windmill
House

ABINGDON RD

FIDLER'S LA

COW LA

BROAD ST

HIGH ST

East Ilsley

Woolvers Rd

STANMORE

Yewtree
Hill

Beechtree Hedge
Farm

Windmill
Down

Denn

BALL PIT RD

Ilsley
Barn

Nutfield
Down

Shrill
Down

A34(T)

Green

Lower
Copse

Redlane Rd

William's
Wood

Little Ashridge
Wood

North Stanmore
Farm

HAILEY LA

Stanmore

South Stanmore
Farm

Catch Lane

STANMORE RD

Halfpenny

Ashridge
Farm

A34(T)

Beedon
Manor

A   B   C

47 48 49

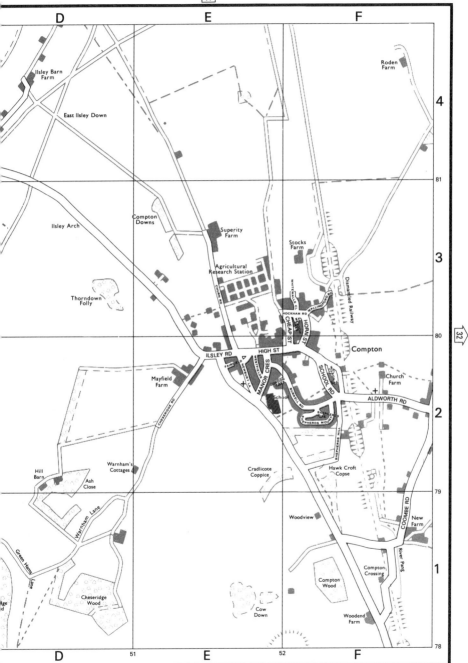

D   E   F

Ilsley Barn
Farm

Roden
Farm

East Ilsley Down

4

81

Compton
Downs

Ilsley Arch

Superity
Farm

Stocks
Farm

3

Agricultural
Research Station

Dismantled Railway

Thorndown
Folly

WHITE WALK LA

HOCKHAM RD

WALLINGFORD RD

HORN ST

CHEAP ST

80

ILSLEY RD HIGH ST

Compton

FAIRFIELD RD

SCHOOL RD

Mayfield
Farm

MANOR CRES

Church
Farm

CHESERIDGE RD

School

SHEPHERDS MOUNT

ALDWORTH RD

2

SUNFIELD RD

THE SHEPHERDS

Warnham's
Cottages

Hill
Barn

Ash
Close

Cradlicote
Coppice

Hawk Croft
Copse

79

COOMBE RD

Woodview

New
Farm

Warnham Lane

River Pang

Compton
Crossing

1

Green Hamd Lane

Cheseridge
Wood

Compton
Wood

Cow
Down

Woodend
Farm

78

D 51 E 52 F

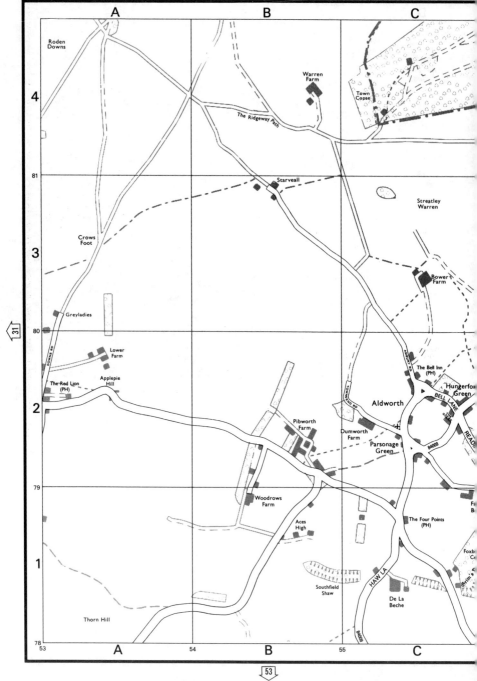

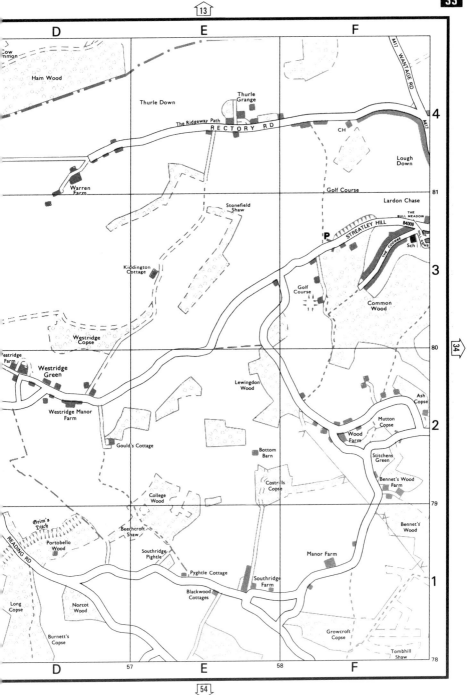

D E F

4

81

3

80

34

2

79

1

78

D 57 E 58 F

Ham Wood

Thurle Down

Thurle Grange

The Ridgeway Path

RECTORY RD

CH

Lough Down

Warren Farm

Golf Course

Lardon Chase

Stonefield Shaw

THE BULL MEADOW

STREATLEY HILL

B4009

P

Sch

Kiddington Cottage

Golf Course

Common Wood

Westridge Copse

estridge Farm

Westridge Green

Lewingdon Wood

Ash Copse

Mutton Copse

Wood Farm

Westridge Manor Farm

Gould's Cottage

Bottom Barn

Stitchens Green

Bennet's Wood Farm

College Wood

Costrills Copse

Grim's Ditch

Beechcroft Shaw

READING RD

Portobello Wood

Southridge Pightle

Pyghtle Cottage

Southridge Farm

Manor Farm

Bennet's Wood

Blackwood Cottages

Long Copse

Norcot Wood

Growcroft Copse

Burnett's Copse

Tombhill Shaw

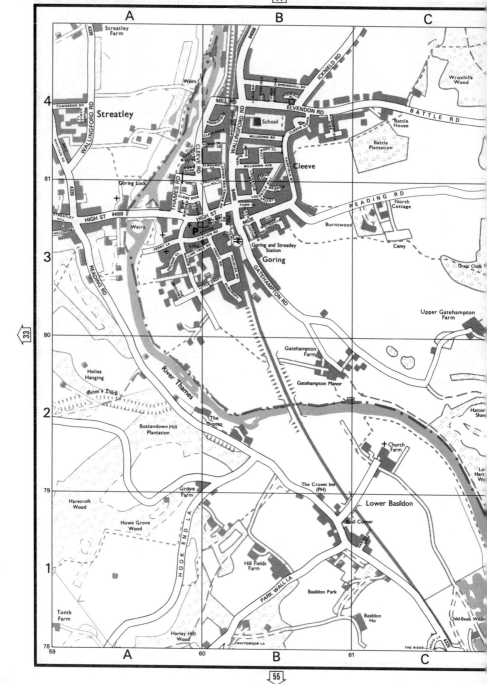

33

A   **B**   **C**

Streatley Farm

Weirs

4

Streatley

TOWNSEND RD

WALLINGFORD RD

A329

MILL RD

SPRINGHILL RD

ICKNIELD RD

ELVENDON RD

School

Wroxhills Wood

BATTLE RD

Battle House

Battle Plantation

81

Goring Lock

THAMES RD

CLEEVE RD

HIGH ST

MILLDOWN RD

GFT CL

MILLDOWN AVE

Cleeve

READING RD

North Cottage

A329

HIGH ST

B4009

Weirs

STATION RD

FERRY LA

Goring and Streatley Station

Goring

Burntwood

Cemy

Great Chalk

3

READING RD

GATEHAMPTON RD

Upper Gatehampton Farm

80

River Thames

Gatehampton Farm

Gatehampton Manor

Hattor Shaw

2

Holies Hanging

Grim's Ditch

Rottendown Hill Plantation

The Grotto

Church Farm

Lo Hart We

79

Grove Farm

Harecroft Wood

Howe Grove Wood

HOOK END LA

The Crown Inn (PH)

Lower Basildon

Bull Corner

1

Tomb Farm

Harley Hill Wood

Hill Fields Farm

PARK WALL LA

WHITEMOOR LA

Basildon Park

Basildon Ho

THE RIDGE

Child-Beale Wildli

A329

78

59   **A**   **60**   **B**   **61**   **C**

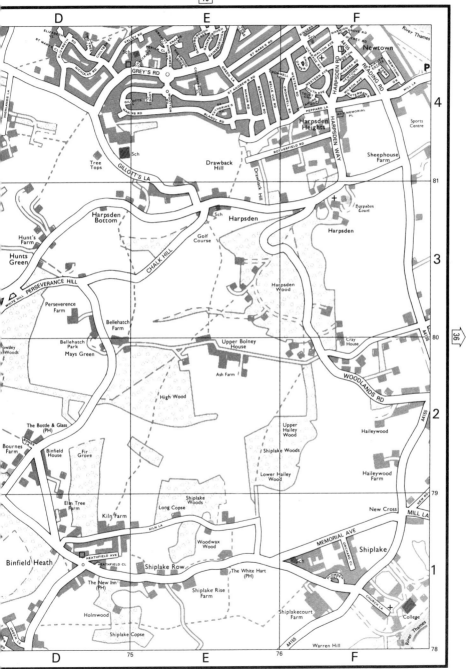

A   B   C

4

81

3

80

2

79

1

78

Mill
Bank

WARGRAVE RD

MILL LA

A321

Lock

Happy Valley

Temple Coombe
Farm

Temple
Combe

The Druids Temple
Danesg Grove

Hatchgate
House

White Cottages

Kenton's Corner
Cottage

KENTON'S LA

Worley's
Farm

Cockpo
Green
The Old Ha
(PH)

ASHLEY HILL

Hatchgate
Farm

Scho

Bolney Court
Farm

Bolney
Court

Kilnpits

BOLNEY RD

River Thames

MANOR WOOD GATE

Hennerton
House

Penny's Lane

Fairman's
Wood

Crazies
Hill

Maple Croft

Gibstroude
Farm

Hennerton Backwater

Wargrave
Marsh

Lower Rivermead
Farm

Golf Course

STATION RD

NORTHFIELD AV   BYEFIELD RD

Lower
Shiplake

Shiplake
Station

LC

BASMORE
PARK

MILL RD

Lashbrook

Ash Brook

Towing Path

WILLOW LA

Napier
Place

Wargrave
Manor

A4155

FIVE
CHESTNUTS

BADGERS WLK

BASKERVILLE LA

OAKS RD

SHIPLAKE
BOTTOM RD

WOODLANDS RD

MEAD

NEW RD

BLAKES RD

HIGHFIELD PA

White
Gables

MILL LA

Lock

Andrew
Duncan
House

Phillimore's
Island

River Loddon

Borough Lake

CORDON DR

STATION RD

Wargrave
Station

Ferry F

Ferry

A321

HIGH ST

WARGRAVE RD

CHURCH
ST

DARK LA

SCHOOL LA

B477

B477

RIDGE WAY

VICTORIA RD

Upper
Wargrave

SCHOOL HILL

SILVERDALE

Sch

BLISS RD

Wargrave

MUMBERY HILL

B477

A   B   C
77   78   79

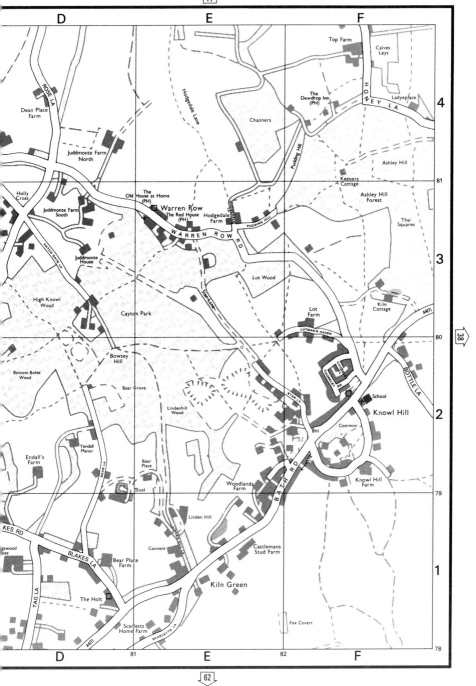

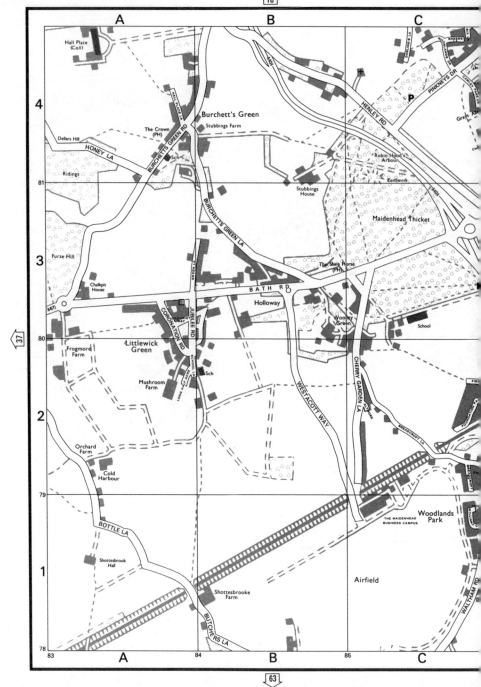

A B C

Hall Place
(Coll)

4

Burchett's Green

The Crown
(PH)
Stubbings Farm

Dellars Hill

HONEY LA

Sch

BURCHETTS GREEN RD

Ridings

81

BURCHETTS GREEN LA

Stubbings
House

HENLEY RD

Robin Hood's
Arbour

Earthwork

P

PINKNEYS DR

BAKERS

WOODLANDS DR

DARLINGS LA

CANTLEY

Gray

Maidenhead Thicket

3

Furze Hill

Chalkpit
House

BATH RD

The Shire Horse
(PH)

Holloway

Woolley
Green

School

FIRE

CORONATION RD

JUBILEE RD

Littlewick
Green

Frogmore
Farm

Mushroom
Farm

Sch

CHERRY GARDEN LA

WESTACOTT WAY

BREADCROFT LA

FOUNDATION

80

37

2

Orchard
Farm

Cold
Harbour

79

BOTTLE LA

Shottesbrook
Hall

1

Shottesbrooke
Farm

BUTCHERS LA

THE MAIDENHEAD
BUSINESS CAMPUS

**Woodlands
Park**

Airfield

WALTHAM RD

78

83 A 84 B 85 C

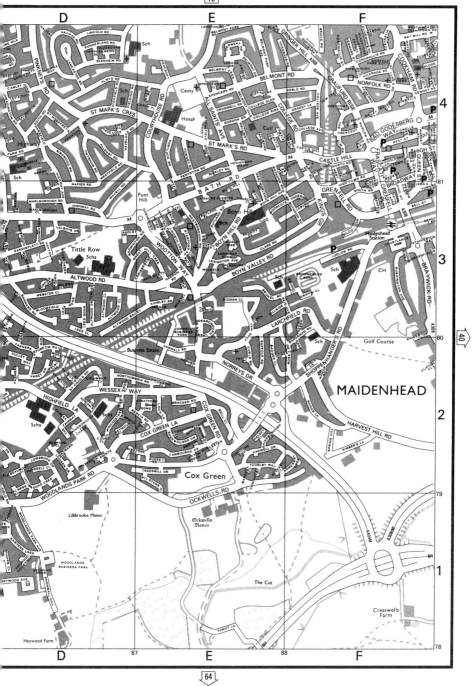

MAIDENHEAD

21

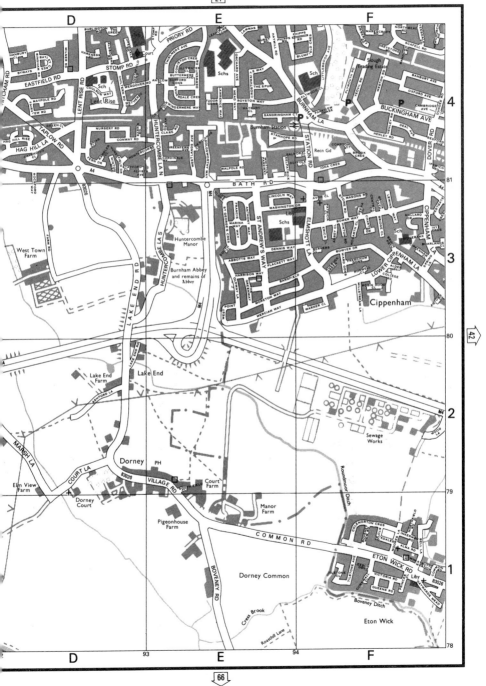

66

142

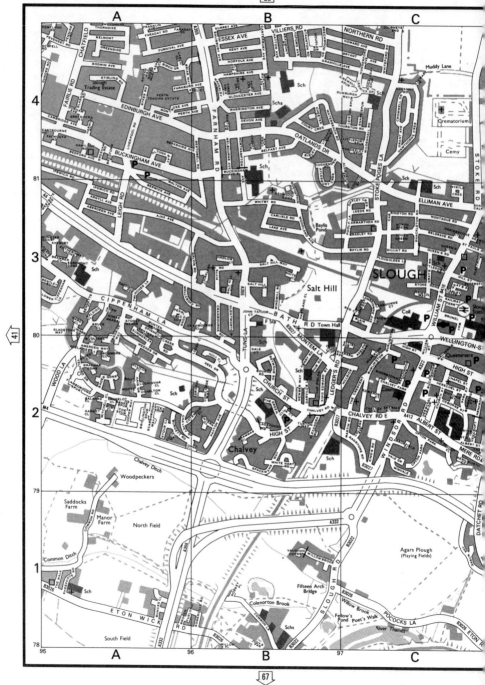

SLOUGH

Chalvey

Salt Hill

Agars Plough
(Playing Fields)

Crematorium

Cemy

Muddy Lane

Saddocks
Farm

Manor
Farm

North Field

Common Ditch

South Field

Woodpeckers

Chalvey Ditch

Fifteen Arch
Bridge

Colenorton Brook

Willow Brook

Fellow's
Pond

Poet's Walk

River Thames

Pococks La

Slough Trading Estate

Perth Trading Estate

ETON WICK

BATH RD

Town Hall

Queensmere

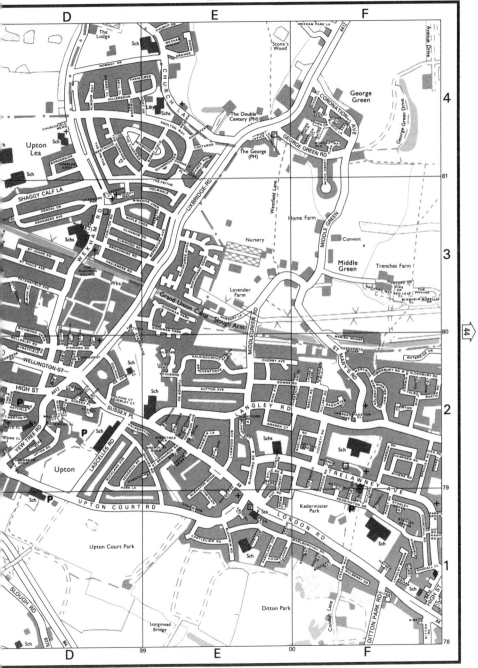

A B C

Sch · Nursery · Coppins
Coppins · Coppins Farm

St Johns
Ashen Cross
BELLSWOOD LA
SWALLOW ST
LOVE GREEN LA
Bangors
BANGORS RD S

Langley Park · Treal Farm · WOOD LA · Heath Lodge · Love Green · Love Green Farm · Hospl · HIGH ST · Iver

4

Shreding Green
HOLLYBUSH LA
Shredding Green Farm
GILLIATT CL
VICTORIA CRES
MARINA WAY

81

Love Hill House Farm
LANGLEY PARK RD
B470
LOBBS
IVERDALE

Devon Court
TRENCHES LA
MANSION LA
Ridgeway Trading Estate
RIDGE WAY

3

TRENCHES LA
Moat · Parsonage Farm · Golf Course
HOLLOW HILL LA
PICKFORD DR
CH
COURT LA

Grand Union Canal
Caravan Park

80

WATERSIDE DR
Langley Station
Iver Station
THORNEY LA SOUTH

ALDERBURY RD
STATION RD
CANAL WHARF
LANGLEY BUSINESS CENTRE
MEAD AVE
MEAD RD
MARKET LA
Withy Bridge
Richings Park
BATHURST WLK
Lib
ST JAMES WLK
SYKE CLUM
SYKE RD
SOMERSET WLK

2

Col
MEADFIELD RD
HEADFIELD RD
NEW RD
WREN CT
ELDER RD
KENNET RD
Schs
Wood
RICHINGS WAY
ST LEONARDS
Thorney Ho
Langley Rd
WILLOUGHBY RD
ELMHURST RD
BURROWAY RD
IVES RD
RAYMOND RD
THAMES
SEACOURT RD
NORTH PARK
POTINGS

79

HIGH ST
PARLAUNT RD
College
Home Farm
Old Slade Farm

P
Harvey Park
SUTTON LA
Home Wood
Weir

1

School
GRAMPIAN
Sutton
Oak Plantation

LONDON RD
A4
M4
SEVERN CRES
Old Wood
Sewage Works

78
01 A 02 B 03 C

43

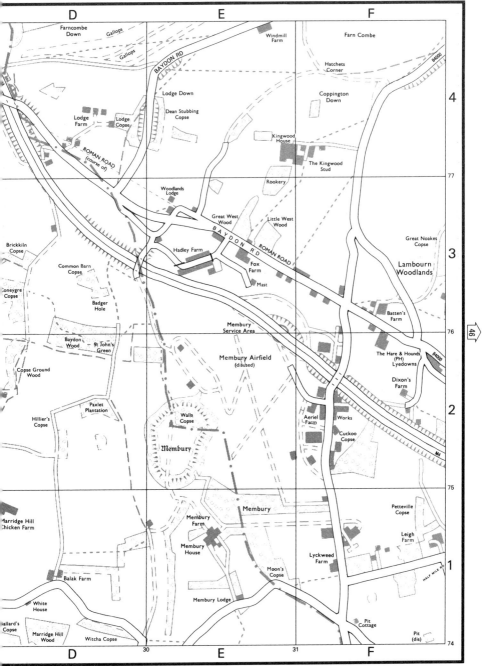

D

E

F

Farncombe
Down

Gallops

Gallops

Windmill
Farm

Farn Combe

Hatchets
Corner

BAYDON RD

Lodge Down

Dean Stubbing
Copse

Coppington
Down

4

Lodge
Farm

Lodge
Copse

Kingwood
House

ROMAN ROAD
(course of)

The Kingwood
Stud

77

Woodlands
Lodge

Rookery

Brickkiln
Copse

Great West
Wood

Little West
Wood

Great Noakes
Copse

Common Barn
Copse

Hadley Farm

BAYDON RD

ROMAN ROAD

Lambourn
Woodlands

3

Coneygre
Copse

Badger
Hole

Fox
Farm

Mast

Batten's
Farm

Baydon
Wood

St John's
Green

Membury
Service Area

76

Copse Ground
Wood

Membury Airfield
(disused)

The Hare & Hounds
(PH)
Lyedowns

46

Paxlet
Plantation

Walls
Copse

Aeriel
Farm

Works

Dixon's
Farm

Hillier's
Copse

Membury

Cuckoo
Copse

2

Marridge Hill
Chicken Farm

Membury

Petteville
Copse

75

Membury
Farm

Lyckweed
Farm

Leigh
Farm

Balak Farm

Membury
House

Moon's
Copse

1

White
House

Ballard's
Copse

Marridge Hill
Wood

Witcha Copse

Membury Lodge

Pit
Cottage

HALF MILE RD

Pit
(dis)

74

D

30

E

31

F

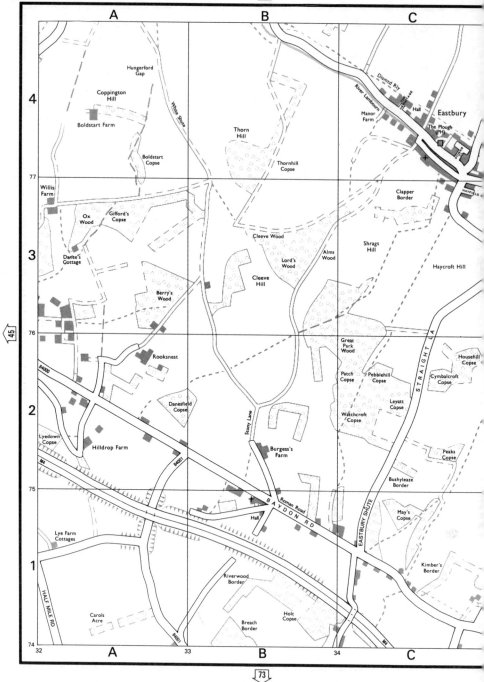

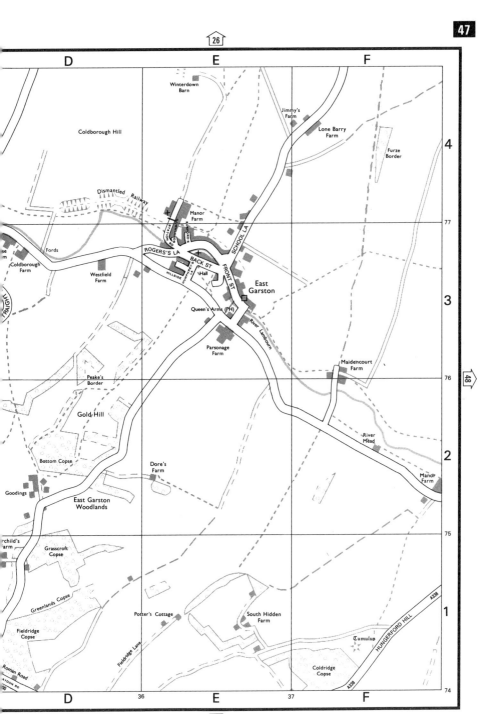

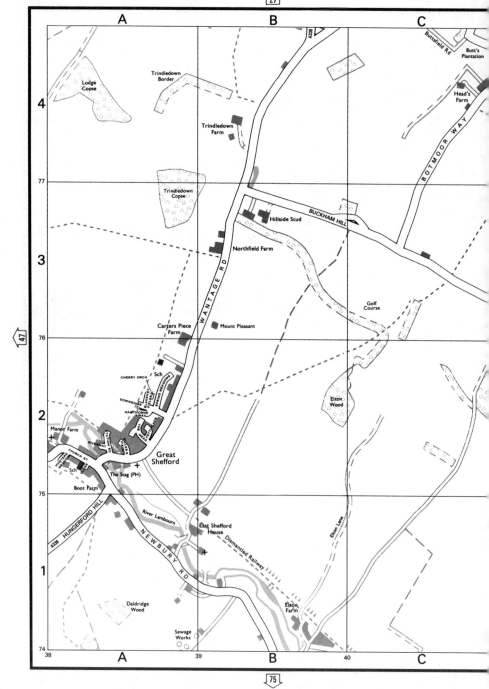

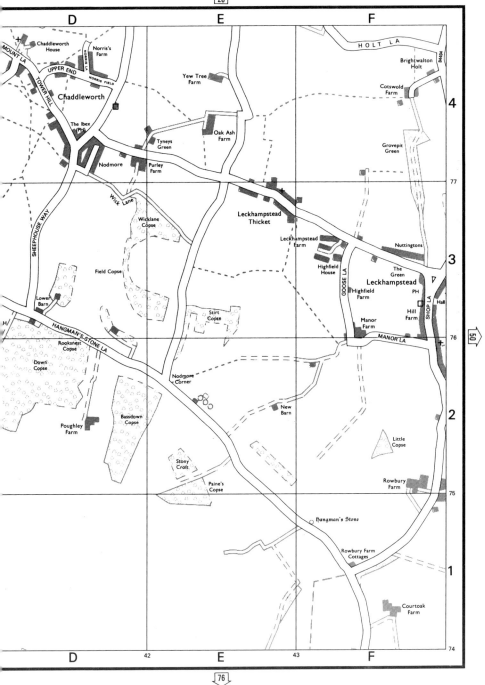

D E F

MOUNT LA
Chaddleworth House
Norris's Farm
UPPER END
NORRIS LA
NORRIS FIELD
TOWER HILL
Chaddleworth
Yew Tree Farm
HOLT LA
Brightwalton Holt
B4494
Cotswold Farm
4
The Ibex (PH)
Oak Ash Farm
Tyneys Green
Grovepit Green
Nodmore
Purley Farm
77
SHEEPHOUSE WAY
Wick Lane
Wicklane Copse
Leckhampstead Thicket
Leckhampstead Farm
Nuttingtons
Field Copse
Highfield House
GOOSE LA
The Green
Leckhampstead
3
Highfield Farm
PH
Lower Barn
Stirt Copse
Hill Farm
Hall
SHOP LA
Manor Farm
HANGMAN'S STONE LA
MANOR LA
76
H/
Rooksnest Copse
50
Down Copse
Nodmore Corner
New Barn
2
Poughley Farm
Bassdown Copse
Little Copse
Stony Croft
Rowbury Farm
Paine's Copse
75
Hangman's Stone
Rowbury Farm Cottages
1
Courtoak Farm
74

D E F

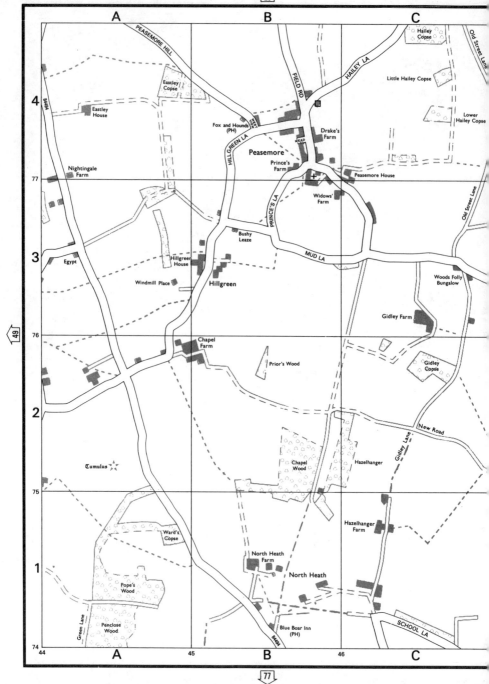

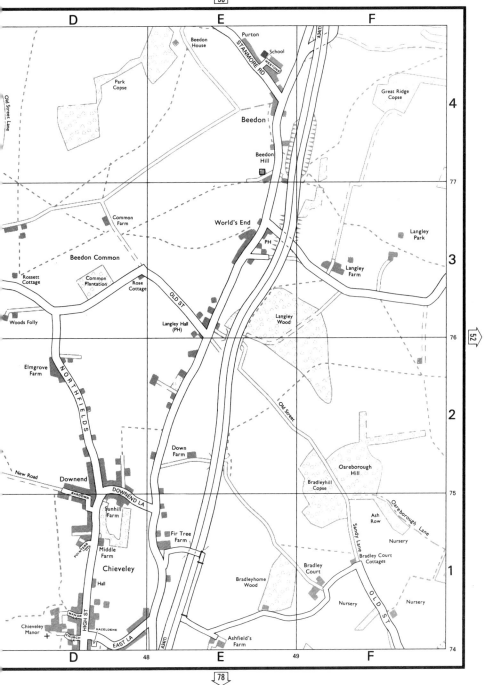

D   E   F

Old Street Lane

Beedon House

Purton

School

STANMORE RD

A34(T)

Park Copse

Great Ridge Copse

4

Beedon

Beedon Hill

77

Common Farm

World's End

Langley Park

Beedon Common

PH

Langley Farm

3

Rossett Cottage

Common Plantation

Rose Cottage

OLD ST

Langley Wood

Woods Folly

Langley Hall (PH)

76

52

Elmgrove Farm

NORTHFIELDS

Old Street

2

New Road

Down Farm

Oareborough Hill

Downend

Bradleyhill Copse

75

BARDOWN

DOWNEND LA

Oareborough Lane

Sunhill Farm

Ash Row

Nursery

POUND LA

Fir Tree Farm

Sandy Lane

Bradley Court Cottages

Middle Farm

Bradley Court

OLD ST

1

Chieveley

Hall

Bradleyhome Wood

MANOR

HIGH ST

HAZELDENE

Nursery

Nursery

Chieveley Manor

CHURCH

EAST LA

A34(T)

Ashfield's Farm

74

D   48   E   49   F

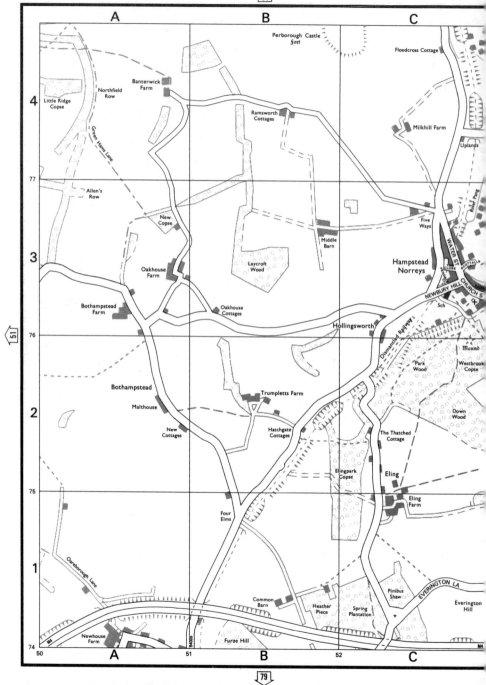

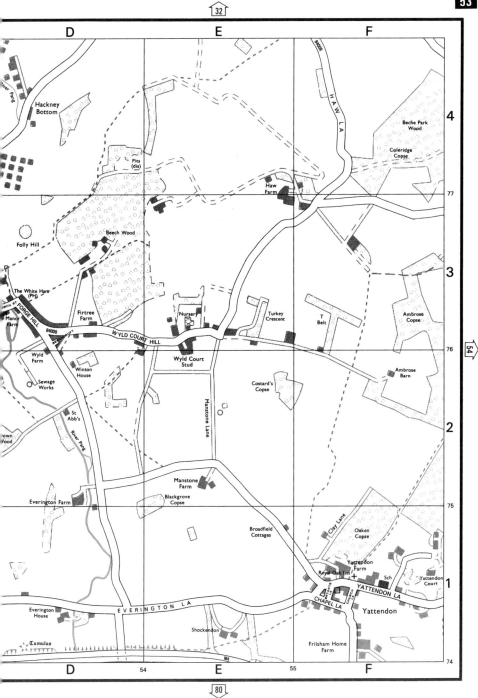

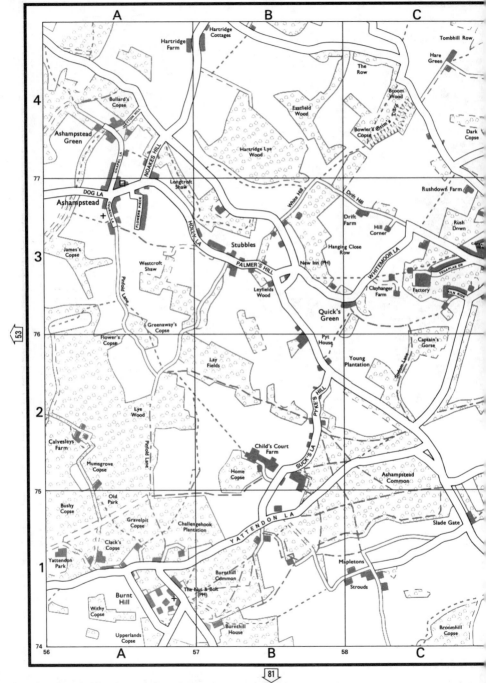

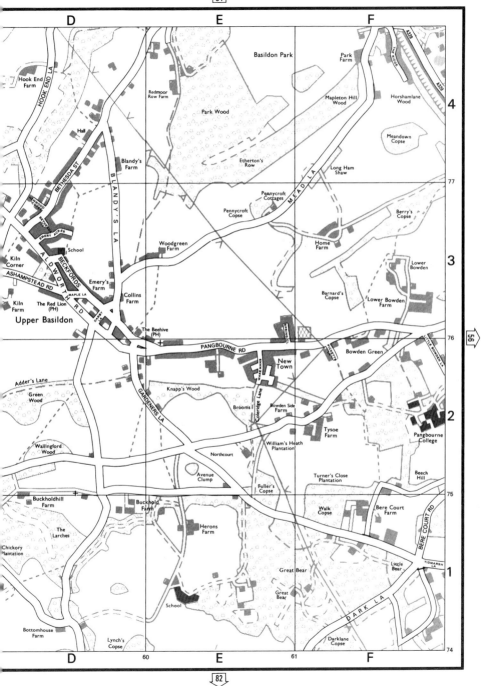

D   E   F

Basildon Park

Park Farm

Hook End Farm

Redmoor Row Farm

Mapleton Hill Wood

Horshamlane Wood

4

Park Wood

HOOK END LA

THE RIDGE

A329

A329

Hall

Blandy's Farm

BETHESDA ST

BLANDY'S LA

Etherton's Row

Long Ham Shaw

Meandown Copse

77

Pennycroft Cottages

Pennycroft Copse

MEAD LA

Berry's Copse

BEECHWOOD

BEECH

EMERY ACRES

School

ALDWORTH

BECKFORDS

RD

Woodgreen Farm

Home Farm

3

Kiln Corner

Lower Bowden

ASHAMPSTEAD RD

Emery's Farm

MAPLE LA

Collins Farm

Barnard's Copse

Lower Bowden Farm

Kiln Farm

The Red Lion (PH)

Upper Basildon

OXFORD

The Beehive (PH)

PANGBOURNE RD

76

56

New Town

Bowden Green

MILL BOARD LA

POCKETS

Adder's Lane

Knapp's Wood

GARDENERS LA

YEW MANS

Coleridge Lane

Brooms

Bowden Side Farm

Tysoe Farm

2

Green Wood

Pangbourne College

Wallingford Wood

Northcourt

William's Heath Plantation

Avenue Clump

Fuller's Copse

Turner's Close Plantation

Beech Hill

Buckholdhill Farm

75

Buckhold Farm

Walk Copse

Bere Court Farm

BERE COURT RD

The Larches

Herons Farm

Chickory Plantation

Little Bear

TIDMARSH

1

Great Bear

Great Bear

School

DARK LA

Bottomhouse Farm

Lynch's Copse

Darklane Copse

74

D   60   E   61   F

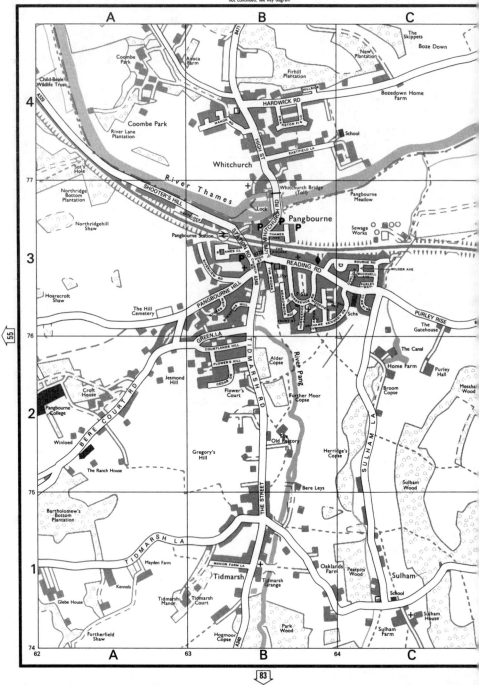

D   E   F

4

Hardwick
Stud Farm

Straw
Hill

Westfordhill
Copse

Bottom
Shaw

Blackwell
Copse

Hardwick
House

East Lodge

Bottom
Farm

Huntley
Wood

77

The
White House

Westbury
Farm

Mapledurham
Lock

Mapledurham

Springs Farm

Home
Farm

Park Wood

Mapledurham
House

3

Purley on Thames

Park Farm

GLEBE RD

PURLEY VILLAGE

PURLEY RISE

BEECH RD

NURSERY GDNS

PURLEY LA

NEW HILL

MAPLEDURHAM

WOKINGHAM WAY

River Thames

58

Wks

HUCKLEBERRY

Purley Gardens
Marina

76

Sch

HIGHFIELD RD

Purley
Park

HAZEL RD

New Farm

ORCHARD CL

APPLE CL

SKERRIT WAY

OXFORD RD

LONG LA

WHITE LODGE

ALDISCOMBE

Schools

A329

Kentwood
Deeps

2

ROSEMEAD AVE

School

MARTIN

CLAYDON

FULLBROOK

Tilehurst Station

LONGLEAT DR

OVERLANDERS
END

75

BARBARA'S MEADOW

Sch

OVERDOWN RD

OAK TREE RD

GRAMER AVE

SANDGATE

CONIFER DR

OAK TREE

Western
Darks

A329

Stoneham
Farm

HILLVIEW

The Arthur
Newbery Park

KENTWOOD HILL

FOREST

Vicarage
Copse

DARK LA

SOUTHERN

Sch

RINGWOOD RD

1

Vicarage
Wood

School

ARMOUR HILL

McIlroy
Park

Mud
House

Back Lane

TRELAWNEY
DR

PIERCE'S HILL RD

WESTWOOD RD

ARMOUR RD

WEDGEWOOD WAY
DRESDEN WAY
STAFFORDSHIRE CL

POTTERY RD

Romany
Lane

74

D   66   E   67   F

not continued, see key diagram

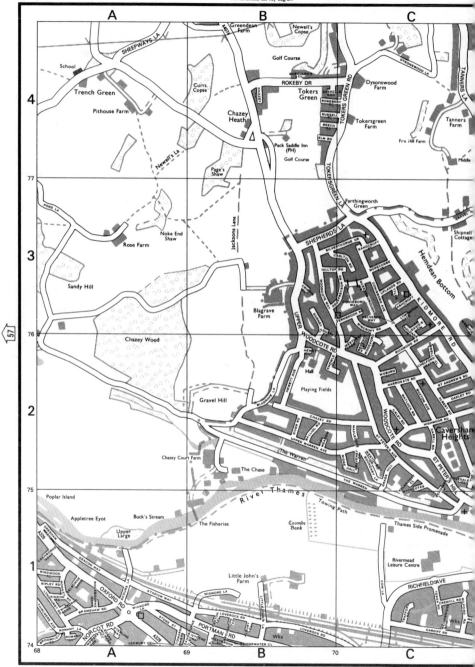

D   E   F

Chalkhousegreen Farm

Chambers Copse

B481

ALDEBURGH CL
Bryant's Farm

Cork's Farm

Sandpit Lane

Tagg Lane

RIDINGS
TOWER CL
CRANBROOKGREEN

Chapman's Farm

Rowlane Farmhouse

Dunsden Green

4

KIDMORE END RD

CRAWSHAY
ROSEHILL PARK
SPINNEY
COURTENAY DR

Cucumber Wood

ghdown ottom

PEPPARD RD

KILN RD

Clayfield Copse

Blackhouse Wood

Littlestead Green

77

Golf Course

Emmer Green

Club House

GORSELANDS
PINETREE CT
The Common

TWIN OAKS
CHALGROVE

HERTFORD CL

Caversham Park

Sch

CAVERSHAM PARK RD

Foxhill Farm

3

VEL HILL
ERLEGH AVE

GROVE RD
ST BARNABAS RD
KNIGHTS WAY
EVESHAM RD

BUCKINGHAM DR

NORTHBROOK RD

MILESTONE RD

UPPINGHAM GDNS

CHATSWORTH CL

LOWFIELD RD

Play Hatch

Playhatch Farm

SURLEY ROW

School

Hall

Caversham Park
1 QUANTOCK AVE
2 REDBERRY CL
3 SHAKESPEARE CL

Sch

1 ILCHESTER MEWS
2 ILLINGWORTH AVE
3 KELSO MEWS
4 GIFFORD CL
5 FARLEIGH MEWS

Milestone Wood

76

ROTHERFIELD WAY

ELIOT CL

PEPPARD RD

Caversham

Allot Gdns

Reading Crematorium

Cemetery

School

A4155

00

Cemy

VICTORIA RD
QUEEN

School

LADY JANE
COLL
DERBY FIELD

School

LONGHURST CL

KILDARE

NORMAN

HENLEY RD

Lowfield Farm

2

PRIEST HILL
ANNE'S RD

WESTFIELD RD
B481

Lower Caversham

OXFORD ST
CROMWELL RD

SOUTH VIEW AVE
WARSACK ST
NELSON RD

DONKIN HILL

LOWER HENLEY RD

ANNES CL
KESTON
LISCOMBE

AMERSHAM RD

75

BRIDGE
VASTERN RD

CHURCH ST
A4155

GOSBROOK RD
CARDINAL

WILLOWS

Caversham Bridge

Fry's Island

B3349
KING'S RD
QUEEN'S RD

CHAMPION

Marina

Nature Reserve

1

CAVERSHAM RD

B479

Reading Bridge

GEORGE ST

P
Lock

View Island

King's Meadow

River Thames

Dean's Farm

74

D   72   E   73   F

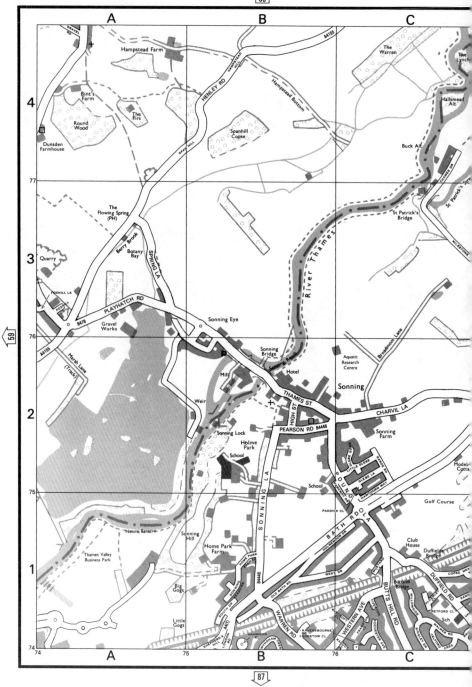

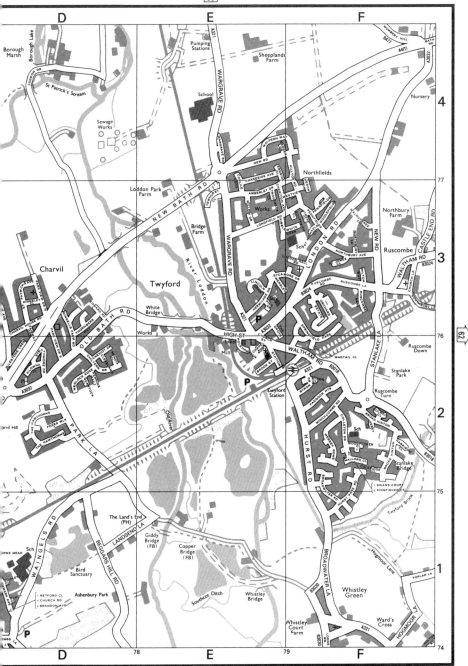

D   E   F

Borough Marsh

Borough Lake

St Patrick's Stream

Sewage Works

Pumping Stations

Sheeplands Farm

HUMBERY HILL

BATH RD

A4(T)

Nursery

4

School

WARGRAVE RD

A321

NEW BATH RD

NEW RD

MALVERN WAY

CHASESIDE AVE

Northfields

77

Loddon Park Farm

Bridge Farm

River Loddon

AMBERLEY RD

Works

LONDON RD

WHITE GROVE

Walnut Tree

Northbury Farm

Ruscombe

Northbury

CASTLE END RD

3

Charvil

Twyford

WARGRAVE RD

A321

White Bridge

Sch

BICYCAMORE DR

NORTHBURY AVE

RUSCOMBE LA

WALTHAM RD

B3024

Sch

Works

P

HIGH ST

Mill

WALTHAM RD

WAGTAIL CL

Ruscombe Down

Stanlake Park

76

OLD BATH RD

PARK LA

BROOK ST

B3018

STANLAKE LA

Ruscombe Turn

Charvil Hill

THE HAWTHORNS

Old River

P

Twyford Station

PADDOCK HTS

HURST RD

WINCHCOMBE RD

Sch

Stanlake Bridge

B3018

2

Swans Court

Kingfisher Ct

75

The Land's End (PH)

LANDSEND LA

Giddy Bridge (FB)

Copper Bridge (FB)

BEGGARS HILL RD

WAINGELS RD

Bird Sanctuary

Ashenbury Park

1 RETFORD CL
2 CHURCH RD
3 BRANDON AVE

Southcot Ditch

Whistley Bridge

BROADWATER LA

B3030

Whistley Green

Hogmoor Lane

POPLAR LA

HOGMOOR LA

Ward's Cross

1

Whistley Court Farm

A321

B3030

74

P

D   E   F

78   79

62

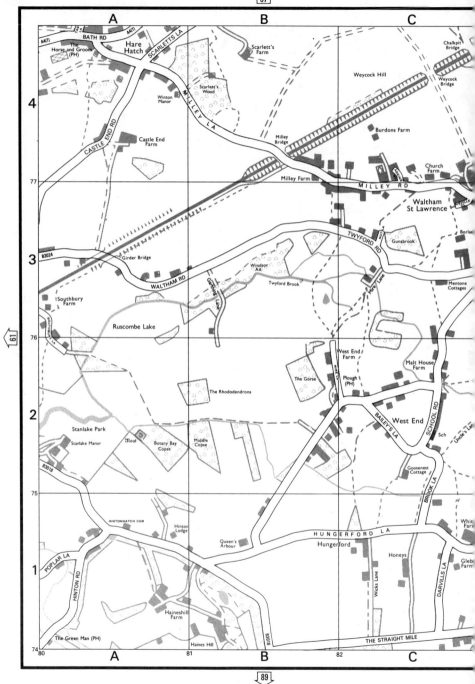

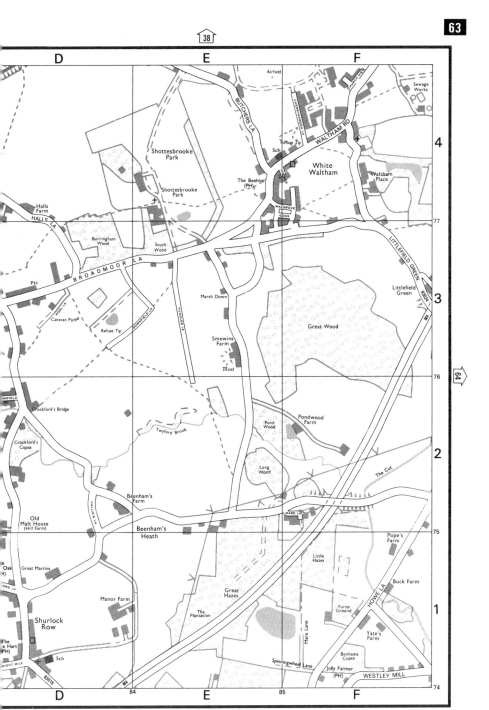

D E F

4

77

3

76

64

2

75

1

74

D E F

84 85

Airfield

Sewage Works

CHERRY ORCHARD LA

WALTHAM RD

Sch
Refuse Tip

White Waltham

Waltham Place

The Beehive (PH)

WALGROVE GDNS

Shottesbrooke Park

Shottesbrooke Park

LITTLEFIELD GREEN

B3024

M4

Halls Farm

HALLS LA

Burringham Wood

South Wood

BROADMOOR LA

PH

POOL LA

TOWNFIELD LA

FURZE LA

Marsh Down

Littlefield Green

Caravan Park

Refuse Tip

Smewins Farm

Great Wood

Moat

Crockford's Bridge

WNFIELD

Twyford Brook

Pond Wood

Pondwood Farm

The Cut

Crockford's Copse

Long Wood

Beenham's Farm

CALLINS LA

MARE LA

Old Malt House (Hill Farm)

Beenham's Heath

Pope's Farm

Oak

Great Martins

ORD LA

Little Hazes

Buck Farm

HOWE LA

Manor Farm

The Plantation

Great Hazes

Furze Ground

Shurlock Row

Mare Lane

Yate's Farm

e Hart (PH)

Sch

AIGHT MILE

B3018

M4

Spinningwheel Lane

Benhams Copse

Jolly Farmer (PH)

WESTLEY MILL

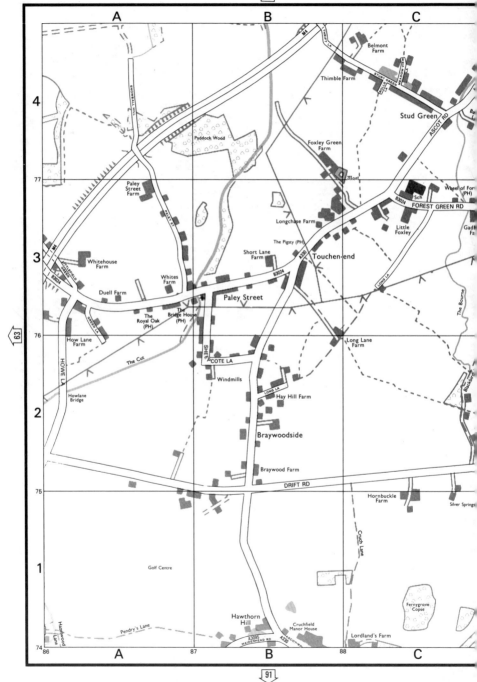

39

A   B   C

M4

THRIFT LA

Belmont
Farm

Thimble Farm

STUD GREEN LA

DELLS LA

MELDON LA

4

Stud Green

ASCOT RD

Foxley Green
Farm

Paddock Wood

Moat

77

Paley
Street
Farm

Wheel of For
(PH)

Sch

B3024

FOREST GREEN RD

Longchase Farm

Little
Foxley

Gad
F2

The Pigsty (PH)

HALEY LA

Short Lane
Farm

B3024

Touchen-end

The Bourne

3

Whitehouse
Farm

LONG LA

M4

FORESTFIELD

B3024

Whites
Farm

Duell Farm

Paley Street

The
Royal Oak
(PH)

The
Bridge House
(PH)

76

How Lane
Farm

Long Lane
Farm

HOWE LA

SHEEPCOTE LA

The Cut

Blackbird

Howlane
Bridge

Windmills

LONG LA

Hay Hill Farm

2

Braywoodside

Braywood Farm

DRIFT RD

75

Hornbuckle
Farm

Silver Springs

Cruch Lane

1

Golf Centre

Fernygrove
Copse

Hazelwood Lane

Pendry's Lane

Hawthorn
Hill

Cruchfield
Manor House

Lordland's Farm

74

86   A   87   B   88   C

A 3095 MAIDENHEAD RD A330 ASCOT RD

91

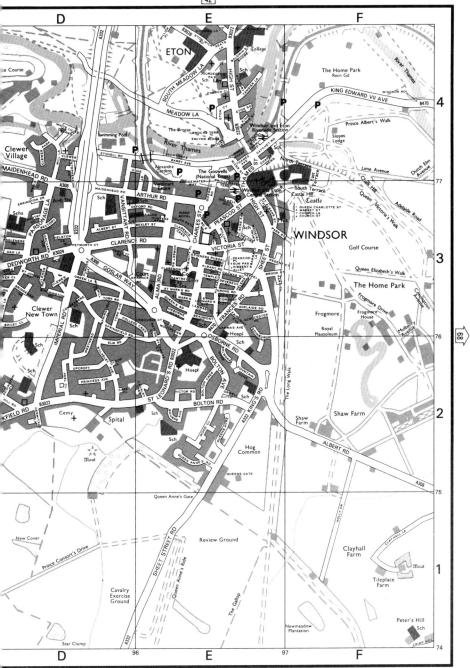

D   E   F

ETON

The Home Park
Recn Gd

River Thames

College

Sch

KING EDWARD VII AVE

B470

4

Prince Albert's Walk

SOUTH MEADOW LA

HIGH ST

MEADOW LA

Slopes
Lodge

The Brocas

BROCAS TERR

Swimming Pool

EMLYNS BLDGS

River Thames

Windsor and Eton
Riverside Station

Lime Avenue

Dutch Elm
Avenue

Clewer
Village

STOVELL RD

BROMLEAF

North Terrace

BARRY AVE

Alexandra
Gardens

The Goswells
(National Trust)

Chalk Hill

77

MAIDENHEAD RD

A308

Vansittart
Estate

BRIDGEWATER

South Terrace
Castle Hill

Queen Victoria's Walk

Adelaide Road

Windsor and Eton
Central Station

Castle

MAIDENHEAD RD

ARTHUR RD

Sch

OXFORD RD

VANSITTART RD

A332

Sch

Schs

PARSONAGE LA

ALBERT ST

BEXLEY ST

CLARENCE RD

CHARLES ST

PEASCOD ST

HIGH ST

QUEEN CHARLOTTE ST
MARKET ST
CHURCH LA
CHURCH ST

WINDSOR

1
2
3
4

RELSTON

PETWORTH CT

VICTORIA ST

SHEET ST

REGENT

Golf Course

3

DEDWORTH RD

B3024

OAK LA

CLARENCE RD

GOSLAR WAY

A308

CLAREMONT

CAWTREY

ST MARK'S RD

ALMA RD

FRANCES RD

PEASCOD ST
SUN PAS
HIBBERT'S
ALLEY

ALBANY RD

BROOK ST

Queen Elizabeth's Walk

Coronation Avenue

Clewer
New Town

IMPERIAL RD

Sch

COLLEGE CRES

YORK RD

QUEENS RD

GROVE RD

CON

TEMPLE RD

DEVEREUX RD

BEAUMONT RD

LANNAS

OSBORNE RD

ADELAIDE SQ

THOMAS AVE

GLOUCESTER

EDINBURGH

The Home Park

Frogmore Drive

Frogmore

Frogmore
House

Sch

Hospl

76

Royal
Mausoleum

Mulberry Avenue

Sch

ELM RD

UPCROFT

Sch

PRINCESS AVE

PEEL CL

B3022

ST LEONARD'S RD

BOLTON AVE

Hospl

VICTOR RD

BOLTON RD

ORKEL

Sch

FOUNTAIN

The Long Walk

Shaw
Farm

Shaw Farm

2

HILL RD

B3022

Cemy

Spital

Moat

Sch

QUEEN ANNE'S RD

Hog
Common

ALBERT RD

A308

75

QUEENS GATE

Queen Anne's Gate

New Cover

Prince Consort's Drive

SHEET STREET RD

Review Ground

Queen Anne's Ride

HOLLY RD

Clayhall
Farm

Moat

Tileplace
Farm

1

CLAYHALL LA

Cavalry
Exercise
Ground

The Gallop

Newmeadow
Plantation

Peter's Hill

Sch

Star Clump

CRIMP HILL

74

D   96   E   97   F

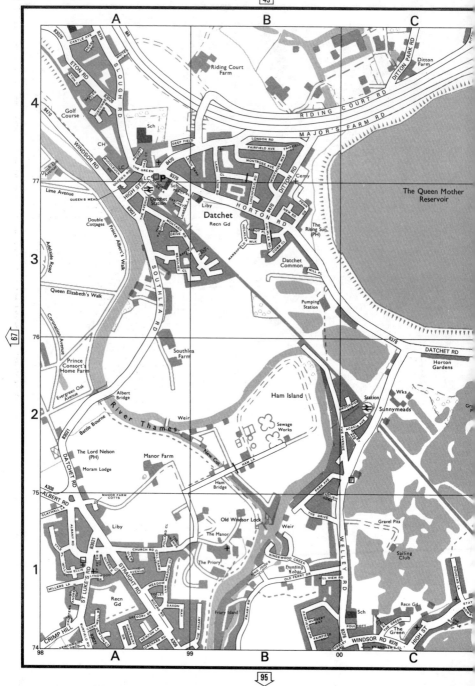

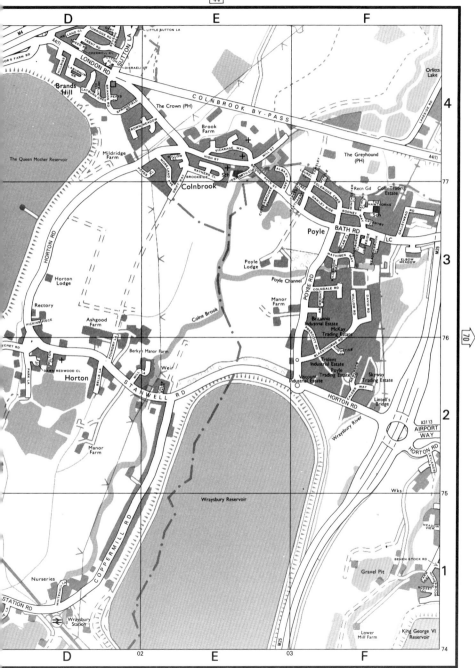

D   E   F

M4

OR'S FARM RD

A4(T)

LAND CL

TORRIDGE RD

CHERWELL CL

LONDON RD

LITTLE BUTTON LA

DISRAELI CT

Orletts
Lake

Brands
Hill

COLNBROOK BY-PASS

4

The Crown (PH)

Brook
Farm

A4(T)

The Greyhound
(PH)

Mildridge
Farm

VICARAGE WAY

HIGH ST

The Queen Mother Reservoir

Sch

RAYNERS CL

BROOKSIDE CL

Colnbrook

Recn Gd

Coln Trading
Estate

77

OLERIDGE CRES

Sch

BATH RD

Poyle

LC

ELBOW
MEADOW

3

HORTON RD

Poyle
Lodge

Poyle Channel

POYLE RD

M25

Horton
Lodge

COLNDALE RD

Rectory

PICKINS PIECE

Colne Brook

Manor
Farm

Britannia
Industrial Estate
McKay
Trading Estate

76

Ashgood
Farm

Berkyn Manor Farm

Weir

Trident
Industrial Estate
Poyle
Trading Estate

Skyway
Trading Estate

CHET RD

DAWN REDWOOD CL

Horton

STANWELL RD

Industrial Estate

HORTON RD

Lintell's
Bridge

2

A3113
AIRPORT
WAY

Manor
Farm

Wraysbury River

HORTON RD

Wks

75

Wraysbury Reservoir

MEADOW
VIEW

COPPERMILL RD

BENEN STOCK RD

1

Nurseries

Gravel Pit

STATION RD

Wraysbury
Station

Lower
Mill Farm

King George VI
Reservoir

74

D   02   E   03   F

not continued, see key diagram

A   B   C

Harmondsworth

HARMONDSWORTH LA

HOLLOWAY LA

LAKESIDE RD

Works

Tithe Barn

High St

ACCOMMODATION LA

Moor Farm

Sch

CANDOVER

Home Farm

Heathrow Boulevard

Government Buildings

Hotel

SKYPORT DR

ZEALAND AVE

Summit Centre

HATCH LA

TARMAC RD

Moor Roundabout

A4(T)

COLNBROOK BY-PASS

ORCHARD CT

BATH RD

NORTHOLT

NEWTON RD

NEWBURY RD

Longfordmoor

Longford Bridge

Mad Bridge

Moor Bridge

Longford

Hotel

P   P

NORTHERN PERIMETER RD (W)

P

BATH RD

Longford Roundabout

River Colne

WESSEX RD

WESSEX RD

PERRY OAKS DR

Longford River

Perry Oaks Sewage Works

S T A N W E L L   M O O R   R D

WESTERN PERIMETER RD

BEDFONT CT

Nurseries

BURROWS HILL CL

WESSEX RD

SPOUT LA N

HORTON RD

P

Weir

SPOUT LA

AIRPORT WAY A3113

Duke of Northumberland's River

SOUTHERN PERIMETER RD

Cargo Terminal

RIVERSIDE RD

LOWLANDS RD

RIVERSIDE RD

SOUTHAMPTON WAY

STRANRAER RD

SOUTHAMPTON RD

SOLENT RD

MEADOW VIEW

THORNBANK CL

HORTON RD

Gravel Pits

OAKS RD

LINDSAY CL

HIGH ST

BEDFONT RD

LONG LA

WHATMORE CL

NAWS LA

Stanwell Moor

STANWELL MOOR RD

B378

GIBSON PL

PARK RD

HAVILLAND

Court Farm Industrial Estate

Blackburn Trading Estate

King George VI Reservoir

STANHOPE HEATH

ATHERTON LA

TRINITY

Stanwell

HADFIELD RD

Sch

A   B   C

04   05   06

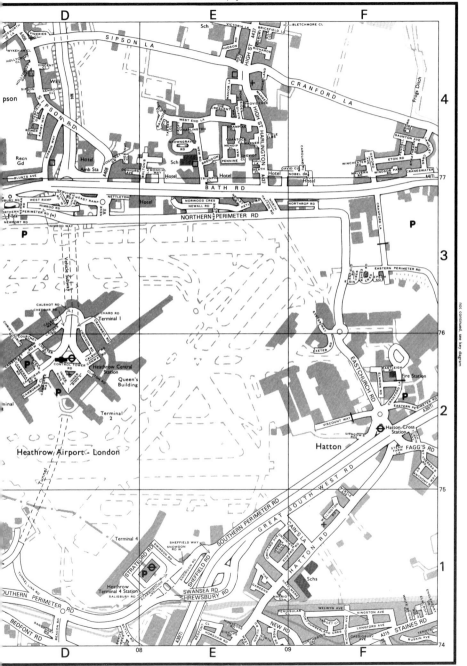

Heathrow Airport - London

Hatton

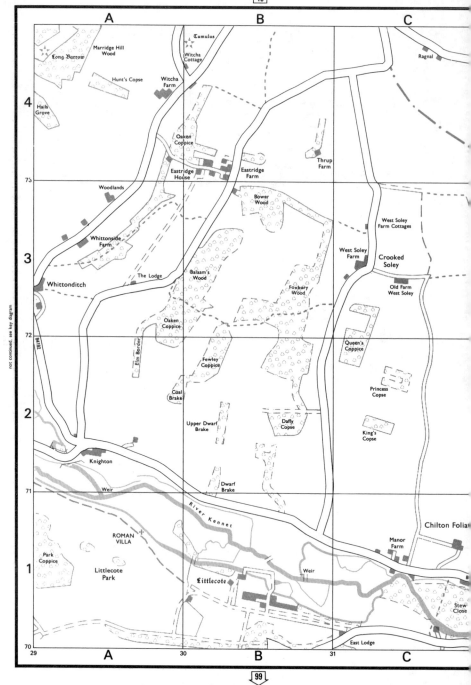

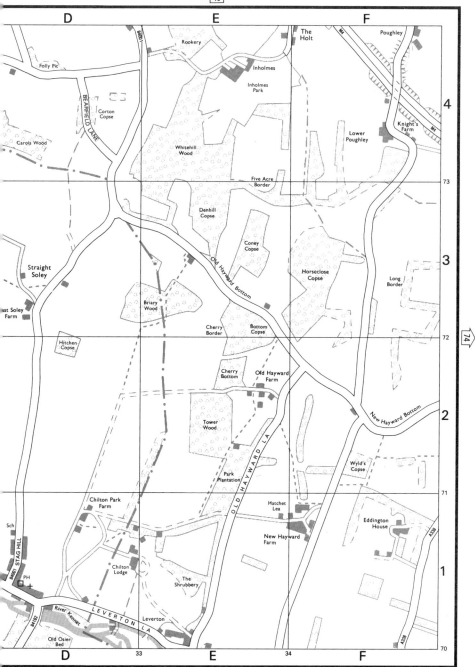

47

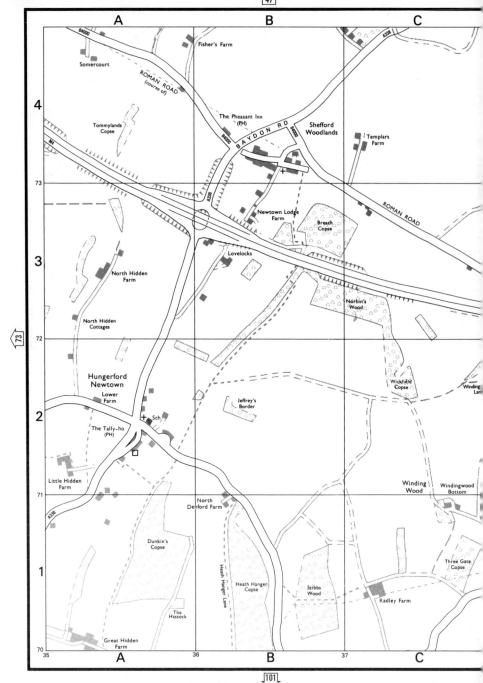

73

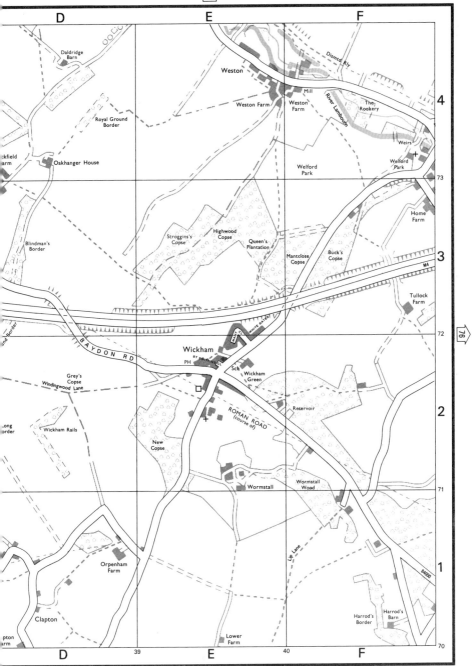

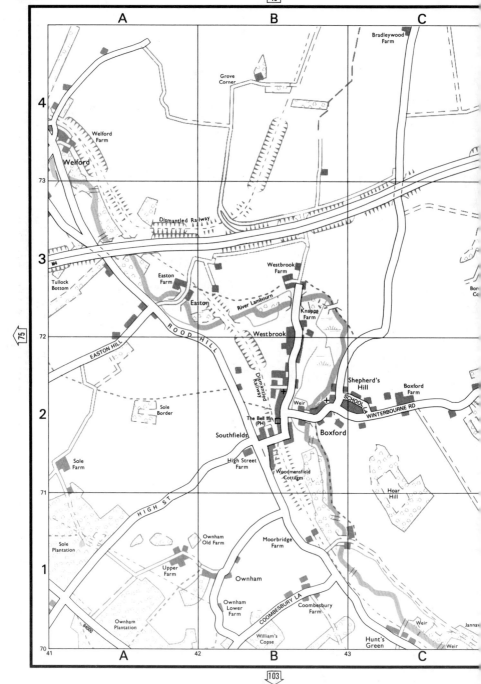

75

50

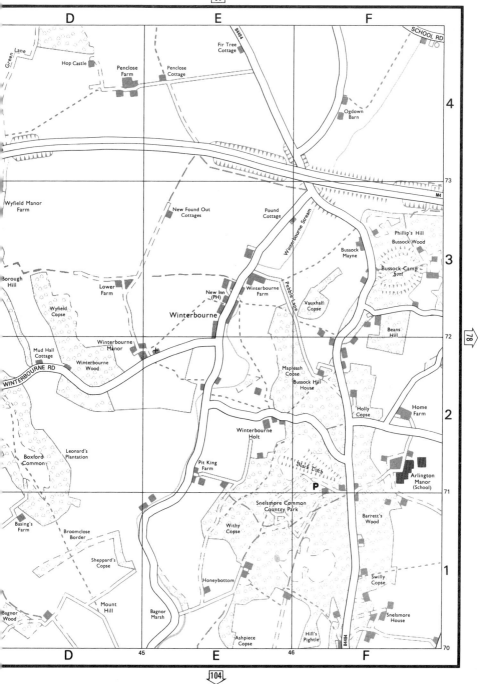

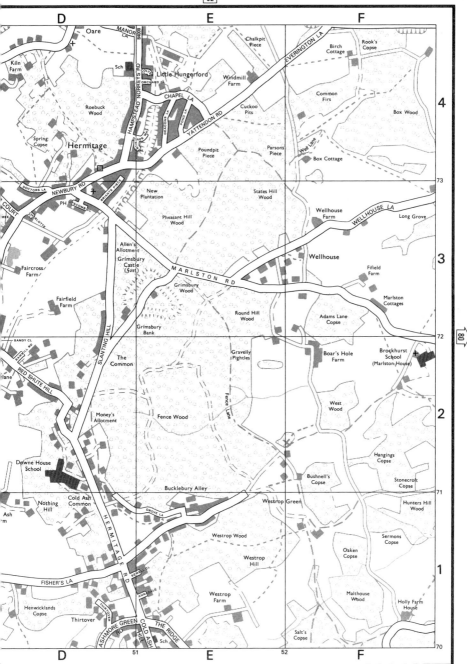

D   E   F

Oare

Kiln
Farm

MANOR LA

Sch

Little Hungerford

ORCHARD CL

Chalkpit
Piece

Windmill
Farm

EVERINGTON LA

Birch
Cottage

Rook's
Copse

HAMPSTEAD NORREYS RD

CHAPEL LA

Common
Firs

Box Wood

Roebuck
Wood

YATTENDON RD

Cuckoo
Pits

4

Spring
Copse

Hermitage

Poundpit
Piece

Parsons
Piece

Well Lane

Box Cottage

73

DOCTORS LA

NEWBURY RD

PH

New
Plantation

States Hill
Wood

Wellhouse
Farm

WELLHOUSE LA

Long Grove

COURT

CHARLOTTE

Pheasant Hill
Wood

Wellhouse

3

Fifield
Farm

Faircross
Farm

Allen's
Allotment

Grimsbury
Castle
(fort)

MARLSTON RD

Grimsbury
Wood

Adams Lane
Copse

Marlston
Cottages

Fairfield
Farm

Round Hill
Wood

72

80

SANDY CL

SLANTING HILL

Grimsbury
Bank

The
Common

Gravelly
Pightles

Boar's Hole
Farm

Brockhurst
School
(Marlston House)

RED SHUTE HILL

Fence Lane

West
Wood

lane

Money's
Allotment

Fence Wood

2

Hangings
Copse

Downe House
School

Bushnell's
Copse

Stonecroft
Copse

71

Cold Ash
Common

Nothing
Hill

HERMITAGE RD

GROVE LA

Bucklebury Alley

Westrop Green

Hunters Hill
Wood

Ash
m

Sermons
Copse

FISHER'S LA

Westrop Wood

Westrop
Hill

Oaken
Copse

1

ANNADALE

Henwicklands
Copse

Thirtover

ASHMORE GREEN

COLD ASH

THE RIDGE

Sch

Westrop
Farm

Salt's
Copse

Malthouse
Wood

Holly Farm
House

70

D   51   E   52   F

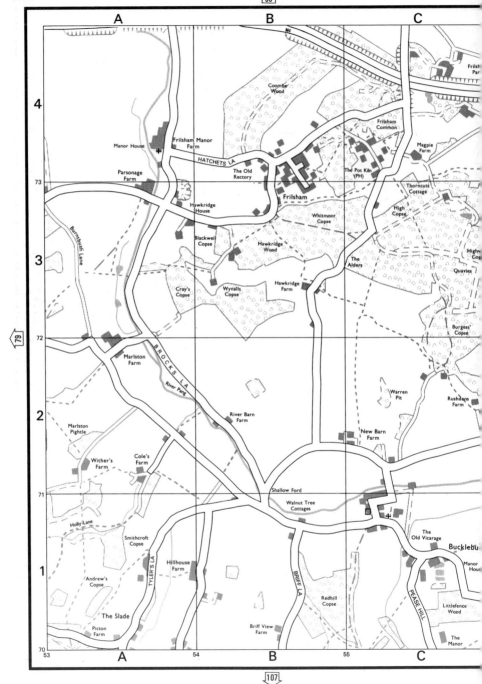

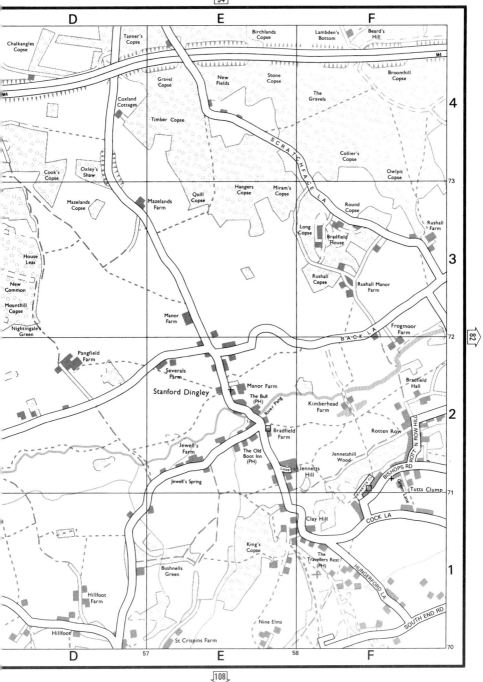

D   E   F

Chalkangles Copse

Tanner's Copse

Birchlands Copse

Lambden's Bottom

Beard's Hill

M4

Gravel Copse

New Fields

Stone Copse

Broomhill Copse

Coxland Cottages

The Gravels

4

Timber Copse

Cook's Copse

Oxley's Shaw

SCRATCHFACE LA

Collier's Copse

Owlpit Copse

73

Mazelands Copse

Mazelands Farm

Quill Copse

Hangers Copse

Miram's Copse

Round Copse

Rushall Farm

Long Copse

Bradfield House

House Leas

Rushall Copse

Rushall Manor Farm

3

New Common

Mounthill Copse

Manor Farm

Nightingale's Green

BACK LA

Frogmoor Farm

72

Pangfield Farm

Severals Farm

Bradfield Hall

Stanford Dingley

Manor Farm

The Bull (PH)

River Pang

Kimberhead Farm

Rotten Row

BISHOPS RD

ROW 'N ROW HILL

2

Jewell's Farm

Bradfield Farm

The Old Boot Inn (PH)

Jennetshill Wood

Tutts Clump

Green Lane

Jewell's Spring

Jennetts Hill

COCK LA

71

Clay Hill

King's Copse

Bushnells Green

The Travellers Rest (PH)

HUNGERFORD LA

1

Hillfoot Farm

Nine Elms

SOUTH END RD

Hillfoot

St Crispins Farm

70

D   57   E   58   F

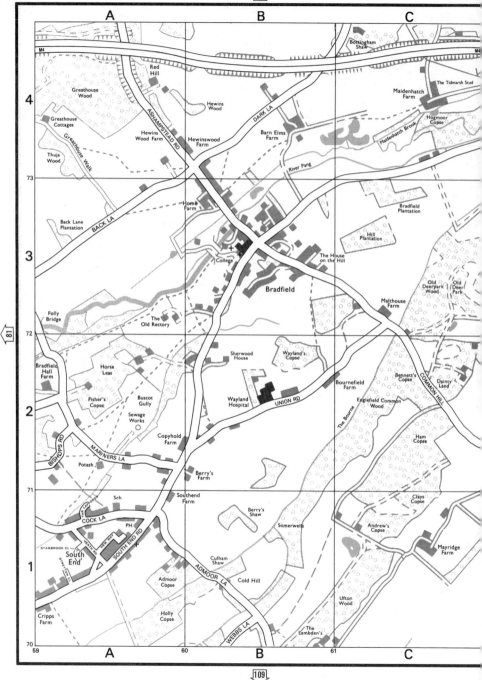

A   B   C

M4

Bottingham
Shaw

Red
Hill

The Tidmarsh Stud

Greathouse
Wood

Maidenhatch
Farm

4

Hewins
Wood

DARK LA

Hogmoor
Copse

Greathouse
Cottages

Hewins
Wood Farm

Hewinswood
Farm

Barn Elms
Farm

Maidenhatch Brook

ASHAMPSTEAD RD

Thuja
Wood

Greathouse Walk

River Pang

73

Home
Farm

Bradfield
Plantation

Back Lane
Plantation

BACK LA

Hill
Plantation

College

3

Bradfield

The House
on the Hill

Old
Deerpark
Wood

Old
Deer
Park

Folly
Bridge

Malthouse
Farm

The
Old Rectory

72

Bradfield
Hall
Farm

Sherwood
House

Wayland's
Copse

Bournefield
Farm

Bennett's
Copse

COMMON HILL

Dainty
Land

Horse
Leas

Buscot
Gully

UNION RD

Wayland
Hospital

Englefield Common
Wood

The Bourne

Fisher's
Copse

2

Sewage
Works

Copyhold
Farm

Ham
Copse

BISHOPS RD

MARINERS LA

Potash

Berry's
Farm

71

Sch

Southend
Farm

Clays
Copse

COCK LA

PH

Berry's
Shaw

Somerwells

Andrew's
Copse

STANBROOK CL

SOUTH END RD

NEW WAY

Mayridge
Farm

1

South
End

Admoor
Copse

ADMOOR LA

Culham
Shaw

Cold Hill

Ufton
Wood

Cripps
Farm

Holly
Copse

The
Lambden's

WEBBS LA

70

59   A   60   B   61   C

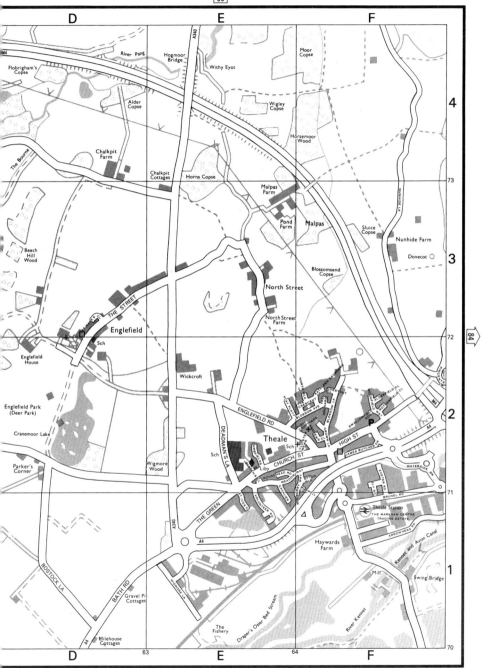

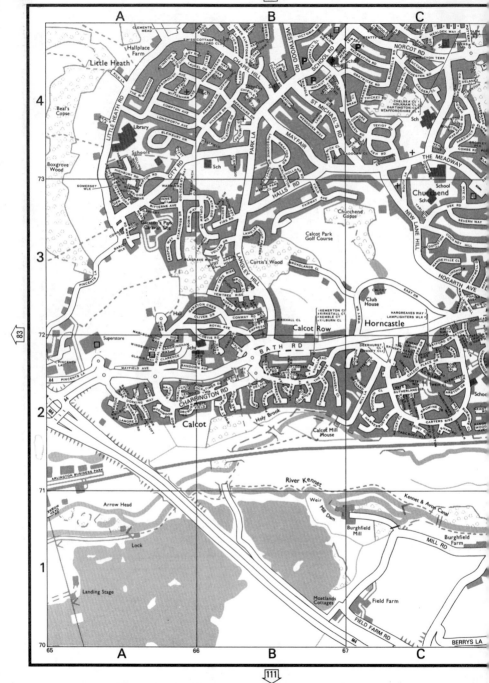

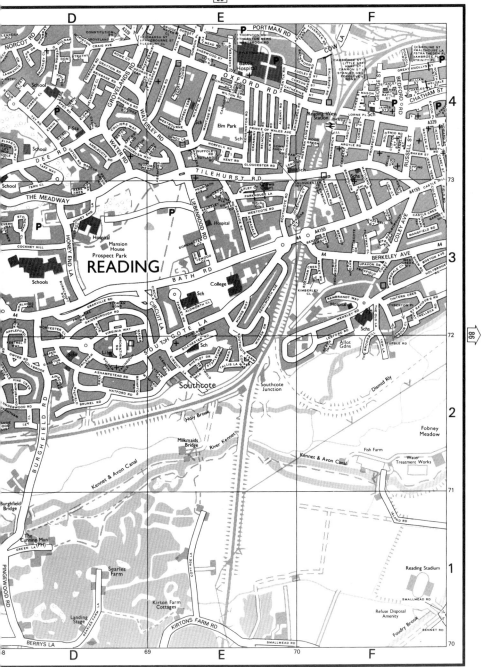

59

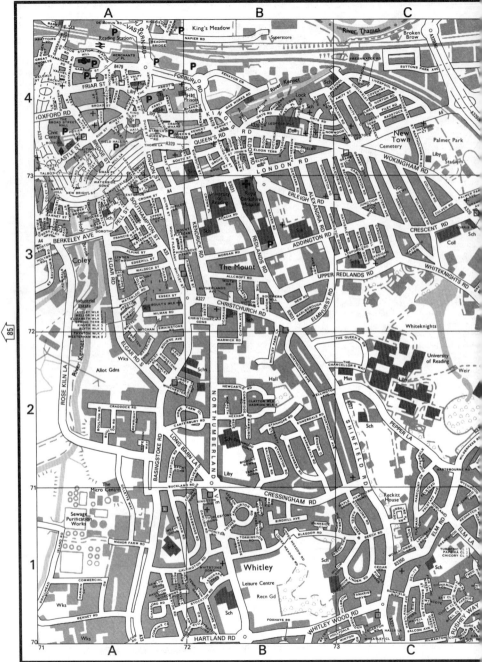

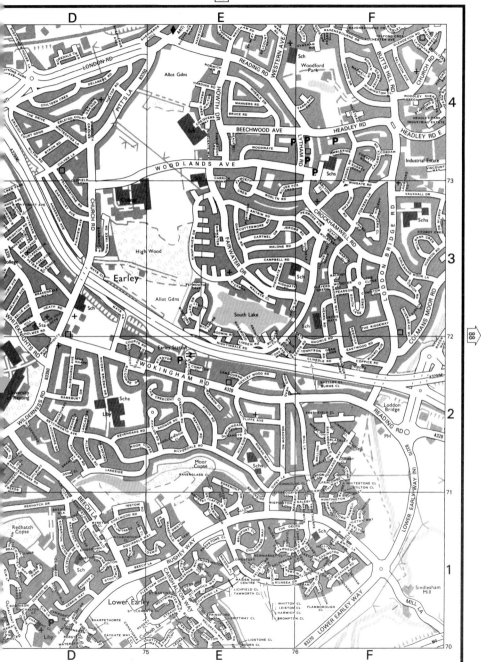

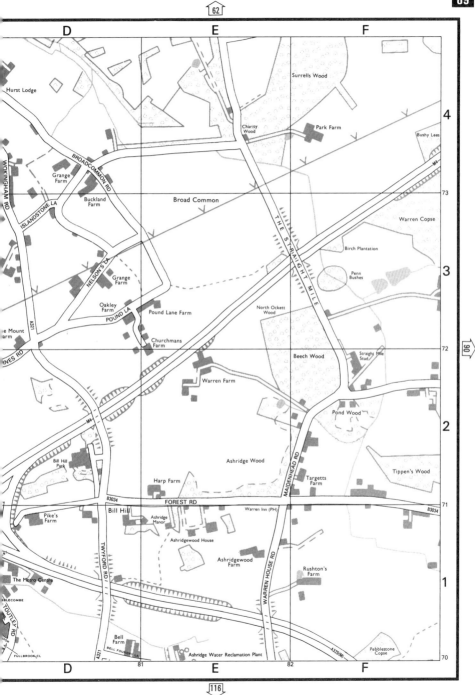

D E F

Hurst Lodge

Surrells Wood

Charity Wood

Park Farm

Bushy Lees

4

BROADCOMMON RD

WOKINGHAM RD

Grange Farm

Buckland Farm

ISLANDSTONE LA

Broad Common

73

Warren Copse

THE STRAIGHT MILE

Birch Plantation

NELSON'S LA

Grange Farm

Penn Bushes

3

Oakley Farm

POUND LA

Pound Lane Farm

North Ockett Wood

A321

Churchmans Farm

Beech Wood

Straight Mile Stud

72

90

e Mount arm

INES RD

Warren Farm

MAIDENHEAD RD

Pond Wood

Bill Hill Park

Ashridge Wood

Tippen's Wood

2

Harp Farm

Targetts Farm

B3034

FOREST RD

Warren Inn (PH)

71

B3034

Pike's Farm

Bill Hill

Ashridge Manor

WARREN HOUSE RD

TWYFORD RD

Ashridgewood House

Ashridgewood Farm

Rushton's Farm

1

The Metro Centre

BLECOMBE

TOUTLEY RD

Bell Farm

A321

BELL FOUNDRY LA

Ashridge Water Reclamation Plant

A329(M)

Pebblestone Copse

70

FULLBROOK CL

D 81 E 82 F

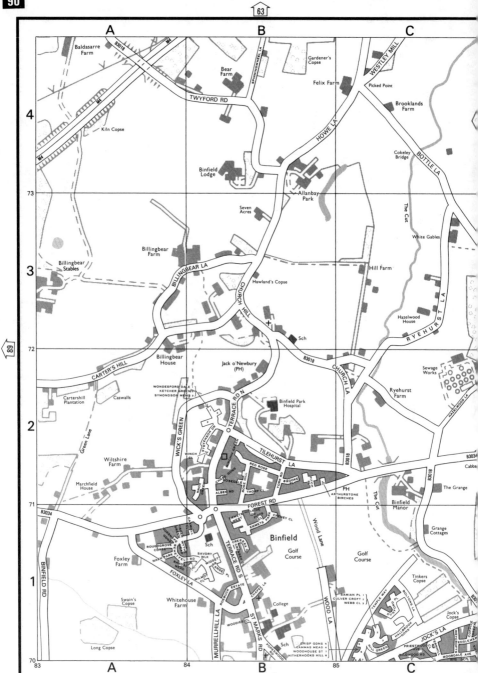

A   B   C

Baldasarre Farm
Bear Farm
Gardener's Copse
Felix Farm
Picked Point
WESTLEY MILL
Brooklands Farm
TWYFORD RD
B3018
M4
Kiln Copse
HOWE LA
Cokeley Bridge
BOTTLE LA
4

Binfield Lodge
Allanbay Park
Seven Acres
The Cut
White Gables
73

Billingbear Farm
BILLINGBEAR LA
CHURCH HILL
Hawland's Copse
Hill Farm
Hazelwood House
RYEHURST LA
Billingbear Stables
Billingbear House
3

CARTER'S HILL
Billingbear House
Jack o'Newbury (PH)
Sch
B3018
CHURCH LA
Ryehurst Farm
Sewage Works
72

Cartershill Plantation
Caswalls
WONDESFORD DALE
KETCHER GREEN
SYMONDSON MEWS
Binfield Park Hospital
Green Lane
WICK'S GREEN
TERRACE RD N
B3018
The Grange
Cabba
2

Wiltshire Farm
WINCH
TILEHURST LA
RED ROSE
BROOKES
PH
ARTHURSTONE BIRCHES
Binfield Manor
B3034
Marchfield House
ALBEN
THORP CL
FOREST RD
Binfield
Golf Course
Golf Course
Grange Cottages
71

BINFIELD RD
ROUGHGROVE COPSE
Foxley Farm
FOXLEY LA
Sch
SAVORY WLK
CHENEY CL
EMMETS PARK
TERRACE RD S
Wood Lane
Binfield
Golf Course
WOOD LA
Tinkers Copse
SAMIAN PL
CULVER CROFT
WEBB CL
TEMPLE WAY
Jock's Copse
JOCK'S LA
1

Swain's Copse
Whitehouse Farm
MURRELLHILL LA
ST MARKS RD
WOODIES CL
College
Sch
CRISP GDNS
CAMMAS HEAD
WOODHOUSE ST
HITHERHOOKS HILL
MOORDALE AVE
Long Copse
70

83   A   84   B   85   C

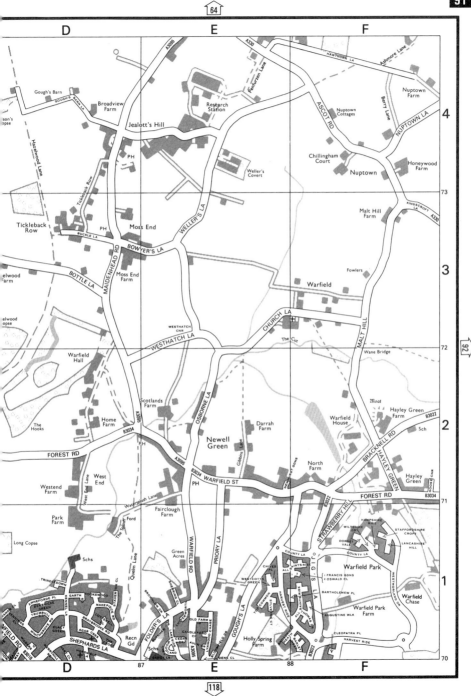

65
91

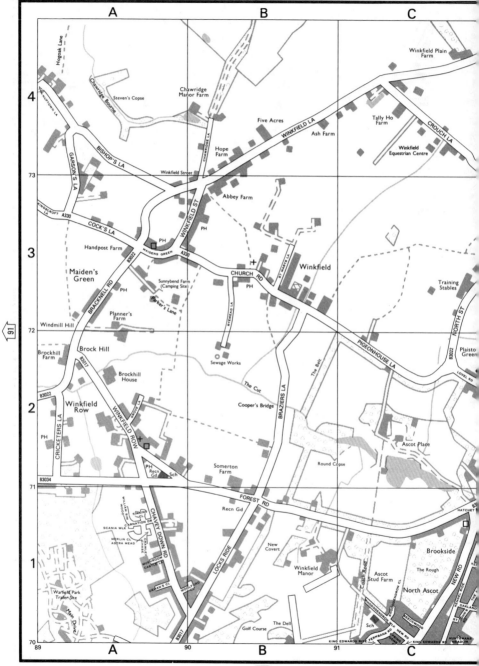

119

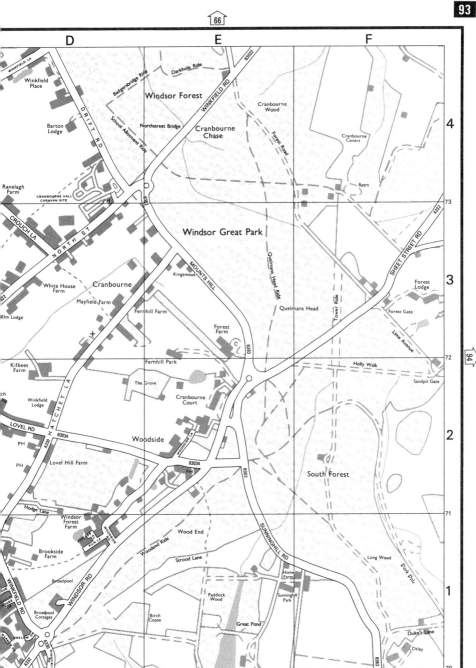

D   E   F

Winkfield Place

Windsor Forest

Badgersbridge Ride

Darkhole Ride

Cranbourne Wood

Cranbourne Covert

4

Barton Lodge

Northstreet Bridge

Cranbourne Chase

Forest Road

DRIFT RD

WINKFIELD RD

B3022

School Allotment Ride

Ranelagh Farm

CRANBOURNE HALL CARAVAN SITE

PH

Resrs

73

A332

CROUCH LA

NORTH ST

Windsor Great Park

SHEET STREET RD

White House Farm

Cranbourne

Kingsmead

MOUNTS HILL

Quelmans Head Ride

Forest Lodge

3

Elm Lodge

Mayfield Farm

Fernhill Farm

Quelmans Head

Tower Ride

Forest Gate

Line Avenue

Kilbees Farm

Forest Farm

C

B383

Fernhill Park

Holly Walk

72

94

The Grove

Cranbourne Court

Sandpit Gate

Winkfield Lodge

HATCHET LA

LOVEL RD

A330

B3034

Woodside

MOORHOUSE LA

2

PH

Lovel Hill Farm

B3034

PH

South Forest

PH

Hodge Lane

Windsor Forest Farm

71

Brookside Farm

Wood End

Woodend Ride

Strood Lane

SUNNINGHILL RD

B383

Long Wood

Park Dale

1

WINDSOR RD

Broadpool

Home Farm

WINKFIELD RD

Broadpool Cottages

Birch Copse

Paddock Wood

Sunninghill Park

A332

Great Pond

Duke's Lane

B383

Otley

70

D   E   F

93   94

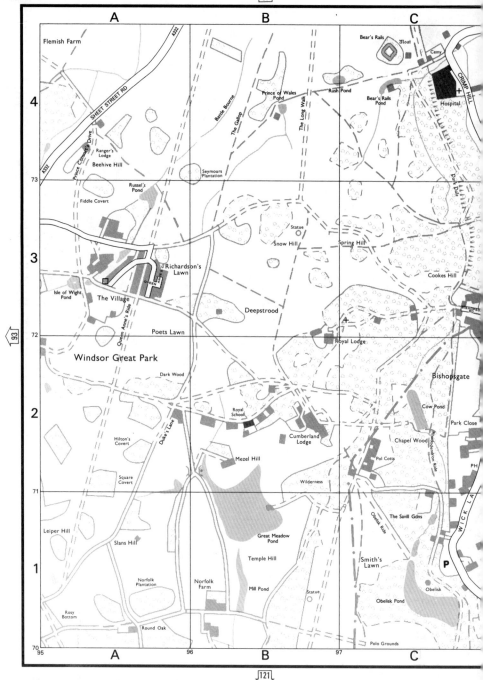

93

A

Flemish Farm

SHEET STREET RD

A332

Prince Consort's Drive

A332

Ranger's
Lodge

Beehive Hill

73

Russel's
Pond

Fiddle Covert

3

QUEEN ANNE'S RIDE

Richardson's
Lawn

Isle of Wight
Pond

The Village

Queen Anne's Ride

Poets Lawn

72

Windsor Great Park

Dark Wood

2

Hilton's
Covert

Duke's Lane

Square
Covert

71

Leiper Hill

Slans Hill

1

Norfolk
Plantation

Rosy
Bottom

Round Oak

70

95

A

96

B

B

Battle Bourne

The Gallop

Seymours
Plantation

Prince of Wales
Pond

The Long Walk

Statue

Snow Hill

Deepstrood

Royal
School

Cumberland
Lodge

Mezel Hill

Wilderness

Great Meadow
Pond

Temple Hill

Norfolk
Farm

Mill Pond

Statue

B

97

C

Rush Pond

Bear's Rails

Moat

Cemy

CRIMP HILL

Bear's Rails
Pond

Hospital

Dark Dale

Spring Hill

Cookes Hill

+

Royal Lodge

Bishopsgate

Cow Pond

Park Close

Rhododendron Ride

Chapel Wood

Pol Cotts

PH

Obelisk Ride

The Savill Gdns

WICK LA

Smith's
Lawn

P

Obelisk

Obelisk Pond

Polo Grounds

C

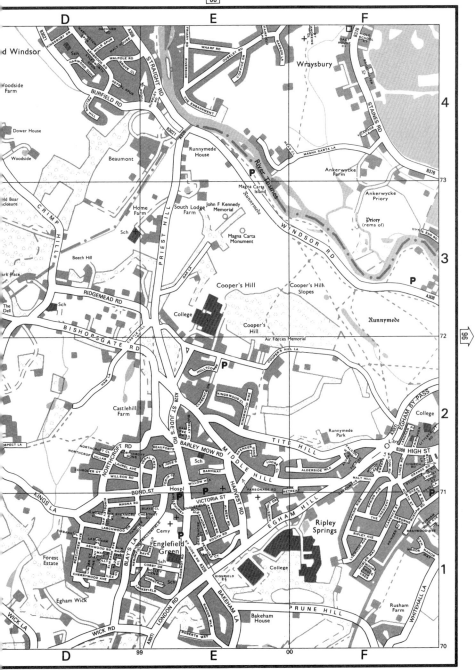

69

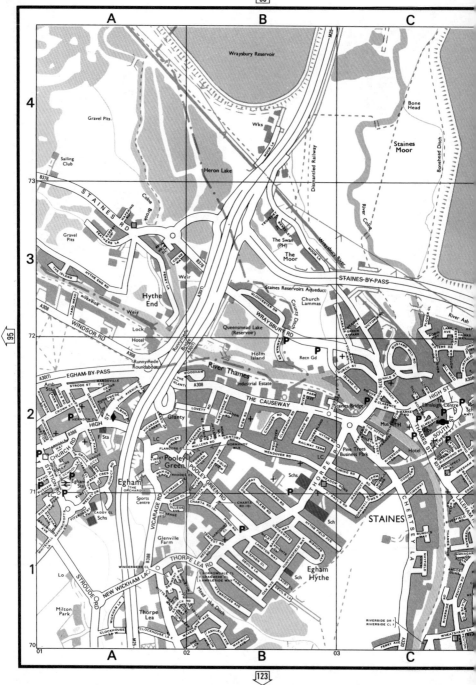

95

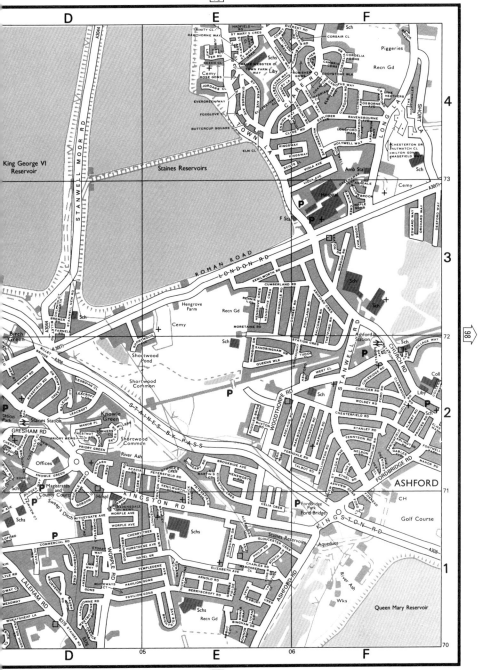

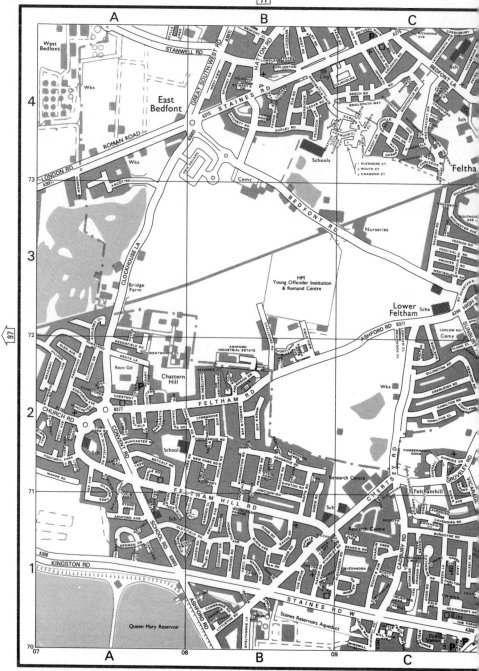

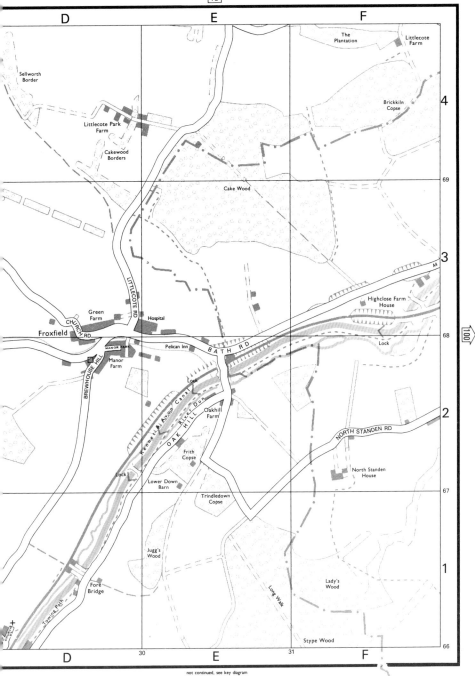

| D | E | F |

Sellworth
Border

Littlecote Park
Farm

Cakewood
Borders

Cake Wood

The
Plantation

Littlecote
Farm

Brickkiln
Copse

4

69

3

Highclose Farm
House

M4

Green
Farm

Hospital

Froxfield

CHURCH RD.

LITTLECOTE RD

Manor
Farm

MANOR PARK

BREWHOUSE HILL

Pelican Inn

BATH RD.

Lock

Lock

68

100

Kennet & Avon Canal

OAK HILL

Oakhill
Farm

River Dun

NORTH STANDEN RD

2

Frith
Copse

North Standen
House

Lock

Lower Down
Barn

Trindledown
Copse

67

Jugg's
Wood

Fore
Bridge

Long Walk

Lady's
Wood

1

Towing Path

Stype Wood

66

| D | E | F |

30   31

not continued, see key diagram

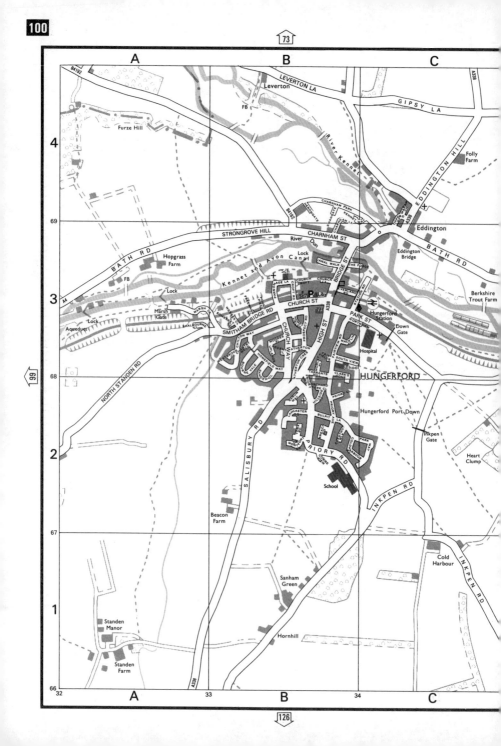

74

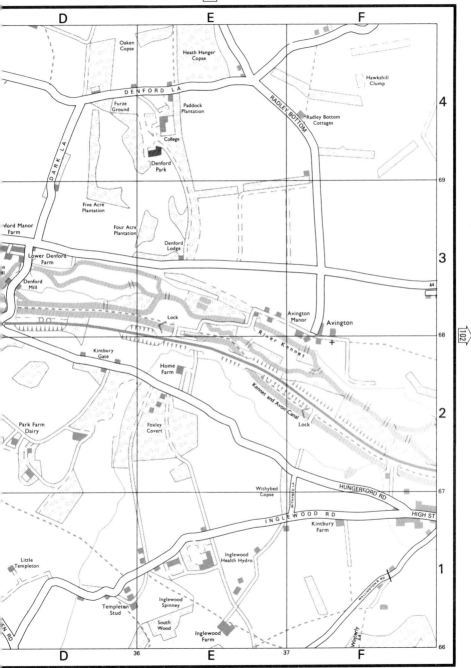

102

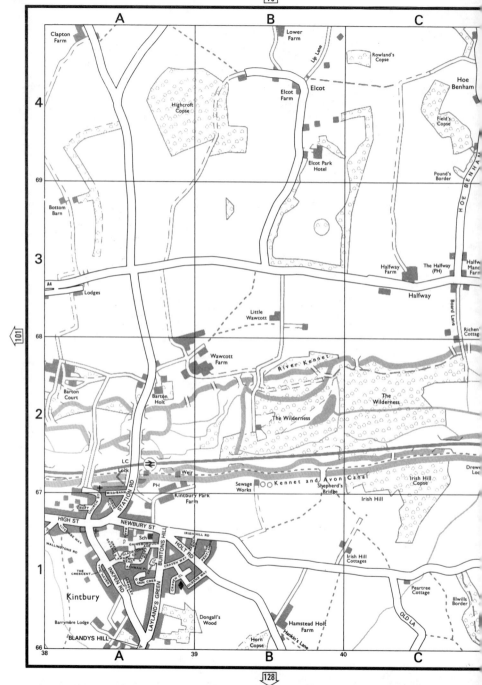

A   B   C

Clapton Farm

Lower Farm

Lip Lane

Rowland's Copse

Elcot

Hoe Benham

Highcroft Copse

Elcot Farm

4

Field's Copse

Elcot Park Hotel

69

Pound's Border

Bottom Barn

HOE BENHAM

3

Halfway Farm

The Halfway (PH)

Halfway Manor Farm

A4

Lodges

Halfway

Board Lane

Little Wawcott

Richen Cottage

101

68

River Kennet

Wawcott Farm

Barton Court

Barton Holt

The Wilderness

The Wilderness

2

Drewe Loc

LC
Lock

Weir

Kennet and Avon Canal

Irish Hill Copse

PH

Sewage Works

Shepherd's Bridge

Irish Hill

67

Kintbury Park Farm

STATION RD

MILL BANK

THE CROFT
CHURCH ST

HIGH ST

NEWBURY ST

IRISH HILL RD

Irish Hill Cottages

Sch

BURTONS HILL

HOLT RD

WALLINGTONS RD

THE CRESCENT

INKPEN RD

LAWRENCE

CRAVEN WAY

OUTLANE WAY

Peartree Cottage

Illwills Border

1

Kintbury

LAYLAND'S GREEN

OLD LA

Barrymore Lodge

Dongall's Wood

BLANDYS HILL

Hamstead Holt Farm

66

Hankin's Lane

Horn Copse

38   A   39   B   40   C

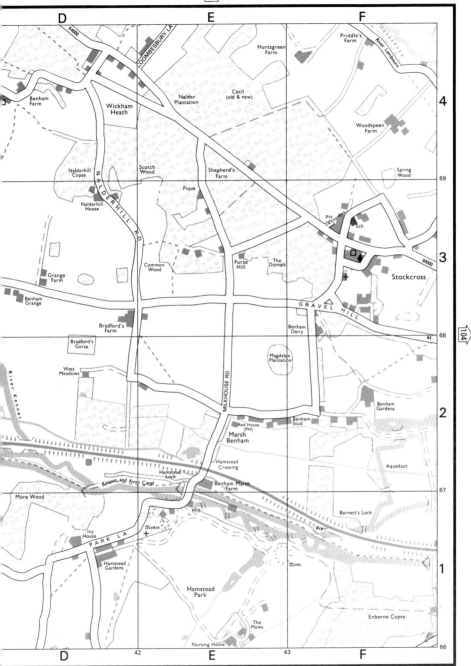

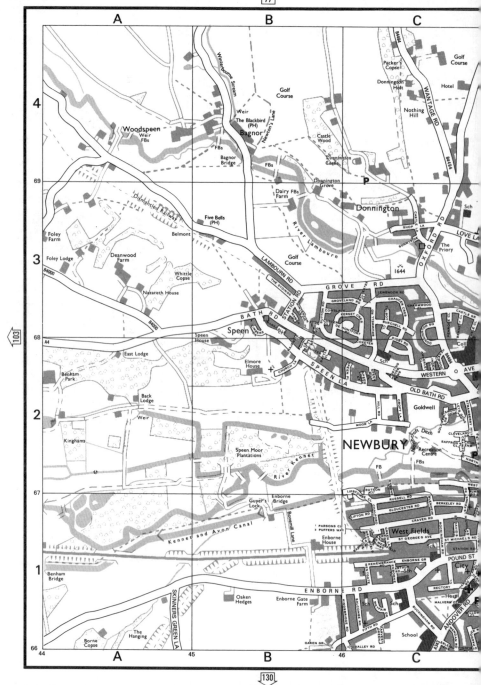

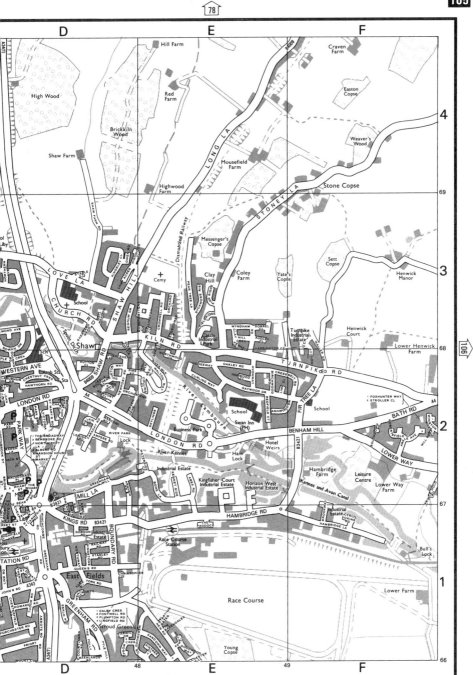

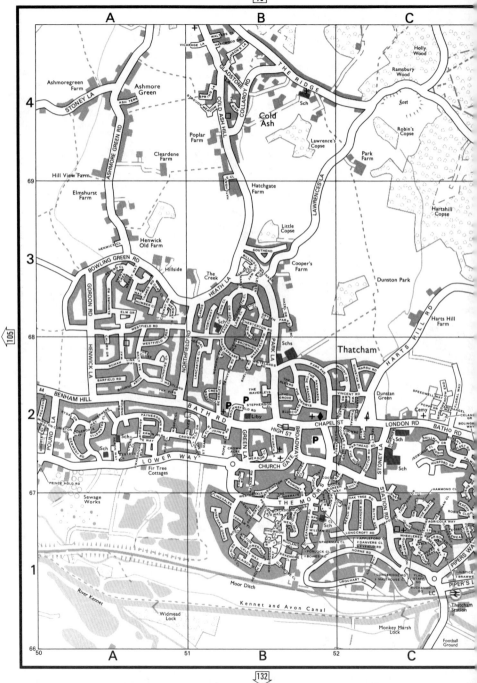

105

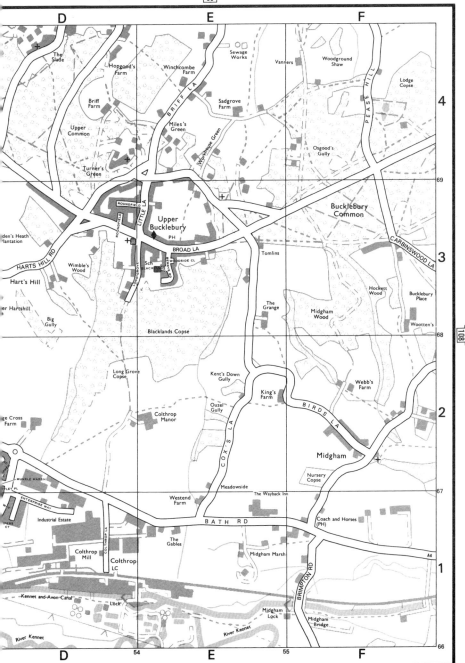

D   E   F

The Slade
Hopgood's Farm
Winchcombe Farm
Sewage Works
Vanners
Woodground Shaw
Lodge Copse
Briff Farm
BRIFF LA
Sadgrove Farm
Upper Common
Miles's Green
Workhouse Green
Osgood's Gully
PEASE HILL

4

Turner's Green

69

Bucklebury Common

CARBINSWOOD LA

ROUNDFIELD
LITTLE LA
Upper Bucklebury
PH
eden's Heath lantation
ROUNDFIELD
BROAD LA
Tomlins

3

HARTS HILL RD
Wimble's Wood
WOODSIDE CL
LONGGROVE LA
Sch
BLACKLANDS RD
Hart's Hill
Hockett Wood
Bucklebury Place
er Hartshill
Big Gully
The Grange
Midgham Wood
Wootten's

68

Blacklands Copse
Long Grove Copse
Kent's Down Gully
Webb's Farm

ge Cross Farm
King's Farm
BIRDS LA

2

Colthrop Manor
Ouzel Gully
COX'S LA
MUNKLE MARSH
Midgham
LEY PL
ENTERPRISE WAY
Nursery Copse

N D
PERS CT
Industrial Estate
Meadowside
Westend Farm
The Wayback Inn

67

BATH RD
Coach and Horses (PH)
COLTHROP LA
The Gables
A4
Colthrop Mill
Colthrop LC
Midgham Marsh
BRIMPTON RD

1

Kennet-and-Avon Canal
Lock
Midgham Lock
Midgham Bridge
River Kennet
River Kennet

66

D   54   E   55   F

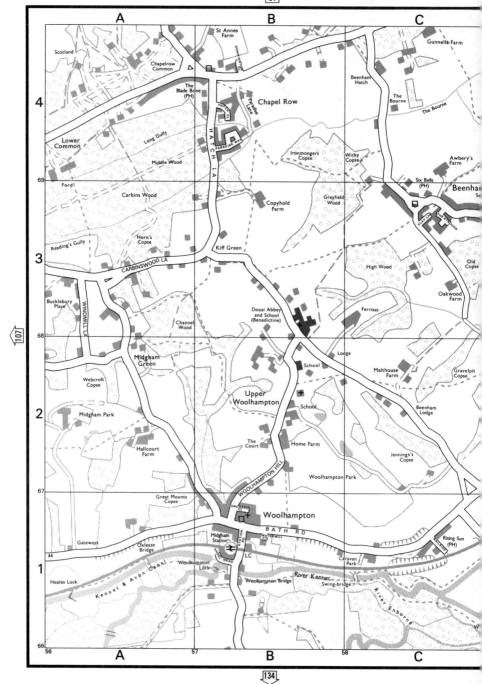

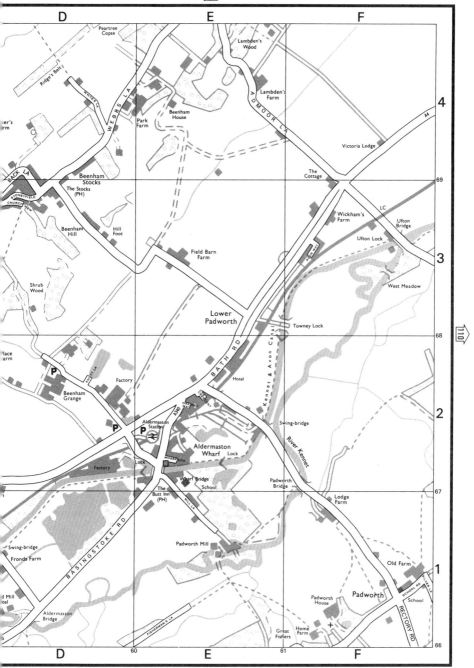

D E F

4

Peartree
Copse

Lambden's
Wood

Ridge's Belt

WEBBS LA

WHITE ST LA

Lambden's
Farm

A 4

Park
Farm

Beenham
House

Victoria Lodge

BACK LA

STONEFIELD
CHURCH VIEW

Beenham
Stocks

The Stocks
(PH)

The
Cottage

69

Wickham's
Farm

LC

Ufton
Bridge

Beenham
Hill

Hill
Foot

Field Barn
Farm

Ufton Lock

A 340 (M)

West Meadow

3

Shrub
Wood

Lower
Padworth

Towney Lock

68

110

Place
Farm

P

RIGHT LA

Factory

BATH RD

Hotel

Kennet & Avon Canal

2

Beenham
Grange

P

Aldermaston
Station

P

A340

OXLEY WAY

WHARF RD

Aldermaston
Wharf

Lock

Swing-bridge

River Kennet

Factory

Lock

WHARFSIDE

Wharf Bridge

School

The
Butt Inn
(PH)

MILLS LA

Padworth
Bridge

Lodge
Farm

67

Swing-bridge

Fronds Farm

BASINGSTOKE RD

Padworth Mill

Old Farm

1

d Mill
el

Aldermaston
Bridge

FISHERMAN'S LA

Padworth
House

Home
Farm

Great
Fishers

Padworth

School

SCHOOL RD

+

RECTORY RD

66

D 60 E 61 F

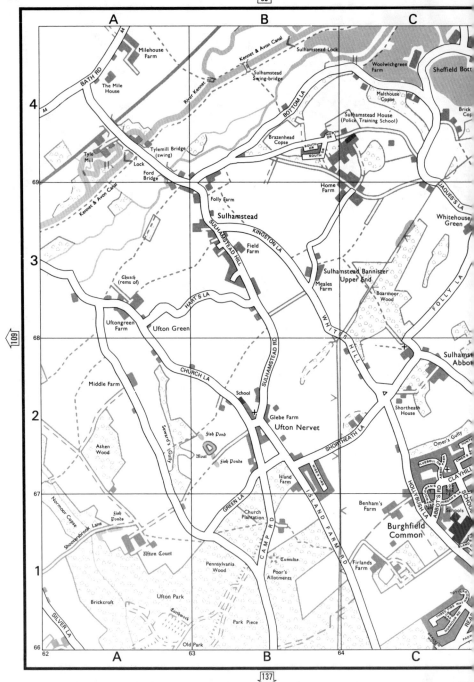

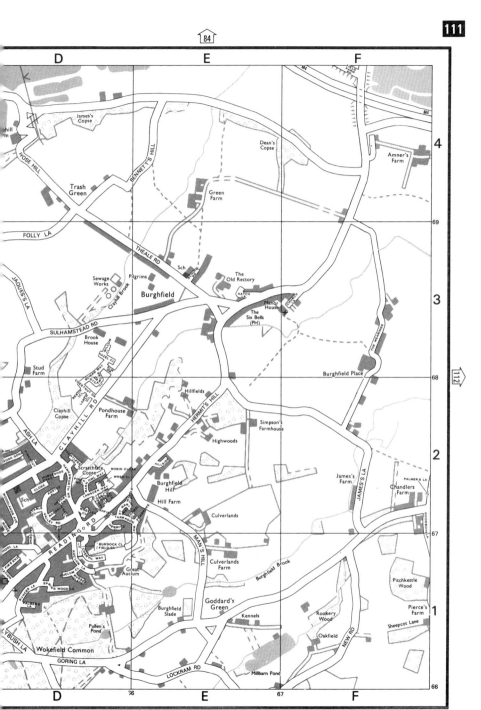

112

85

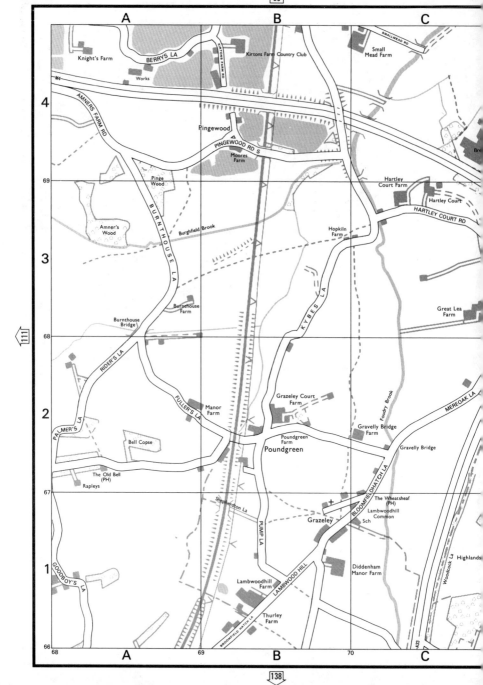

111

138

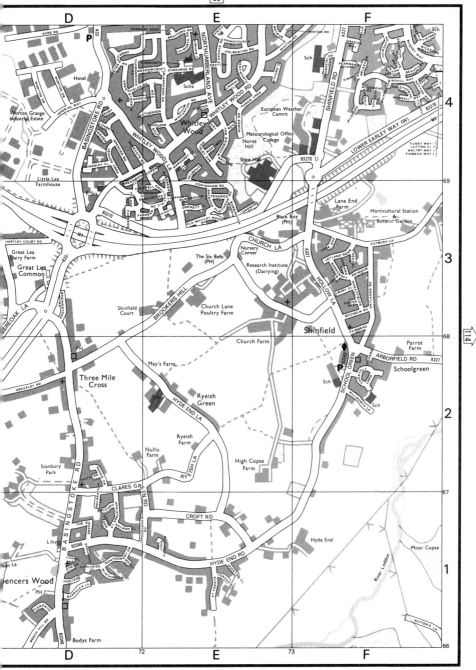

A

TILNEY WAY
CHEVIOT WAY
RUSHEY WAY
CLYDE ODELL
BRADMORE WAY
FAREHAM
MALTBY WAY
ASHWORTH
PRESTON
FELTHORPE CL
FINFECK WAY
LOWER EARLEY WAY (W)
B3270
MA

B

GRAFFHAM CL
PREMIER
CUTBUSH LA
DANEHILL
WIMBLE
REG DELL
CHAPEL
MERRIFIELD CL
B3270

C

MA
GIPSY LA
Loddon's La
Carter's Hill
JULKES LA
The Holt
Carter's Hill Farm
PARKCORNER LA
GORSE BARNHILL LA
MOLE RD

LOWER EARLEY WAY

4

Upperwood House

Upperwood Farm

St John's Copse

Rushy Mead

69

Shinfield Grange

Oldhouse Farm

Research Centre

The Grove

River Loddon

Barett's La

Newlands

3

Hall Farm

CARTERSHILL LA

ELLIS'S HILL

Weirs

Church (remains of)

68

ARBORFIELD RD

A327

Arborfield Bridge

Arborfield Grange

CHURCH LA

Newlands

+

Ellis's Hill

Hazeltons Copse

Sewage Works

2

Bridge Farm

MILKINGBARN LA

Riding Sch

Arborfield

READING RD

WALSH GATE

Cross Lanes Farm

SINDLESHAM RD

Newland Farm

COLE LA

Rounds Copse

Pound Copse

GREENSWARD LA

B3030

The Bull (PH)

B3349

Schs

SCHOOL RD

67

Nursery

PUDDING LA

ANDERSON

EMBLEN

Arborfield Cross

Langleypond Cross

1

SWALLOWFIELD RD

Arborfield Court

EVERSLEY RD

Targetts Farm

LANGLEY COMMON RD

BAIRD RD

Moat

White's Farm

Ducks Nest Farm

Kenney's Farm

Bartlett's Farm

BRAMSHILL CL
VALON RD

A327

66

74   **A**   75   **B**   76   **C**

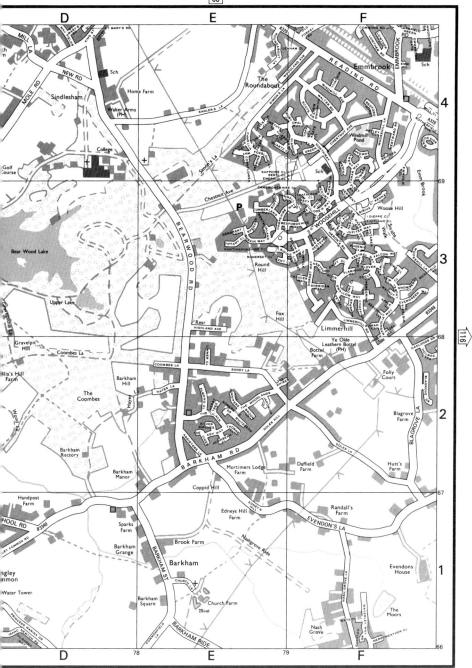

89

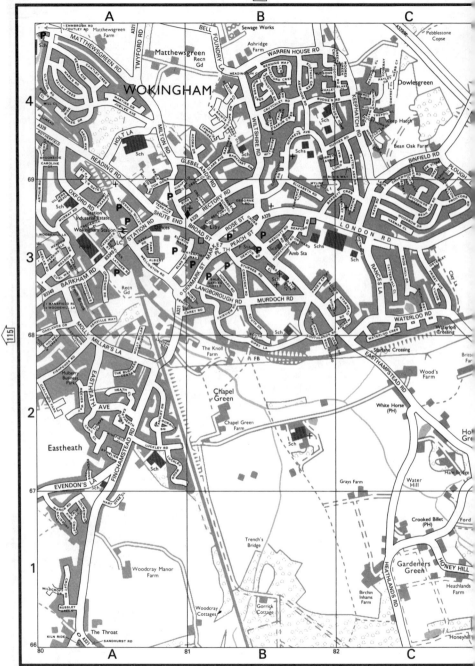

115

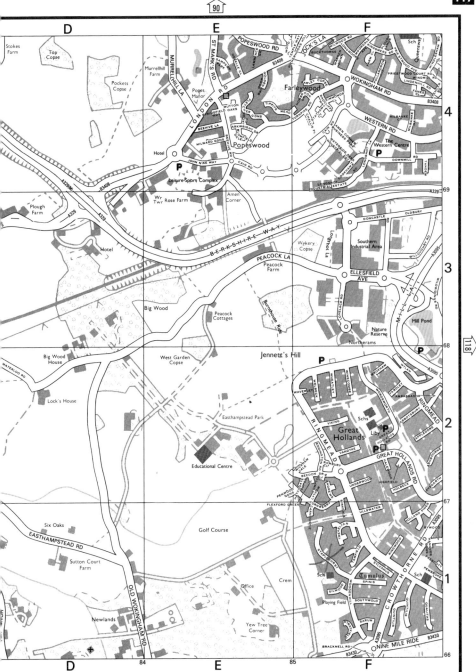

91

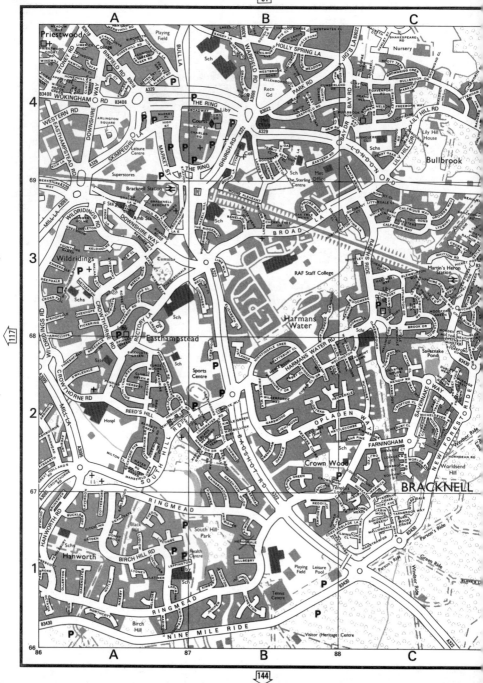

117

144

120

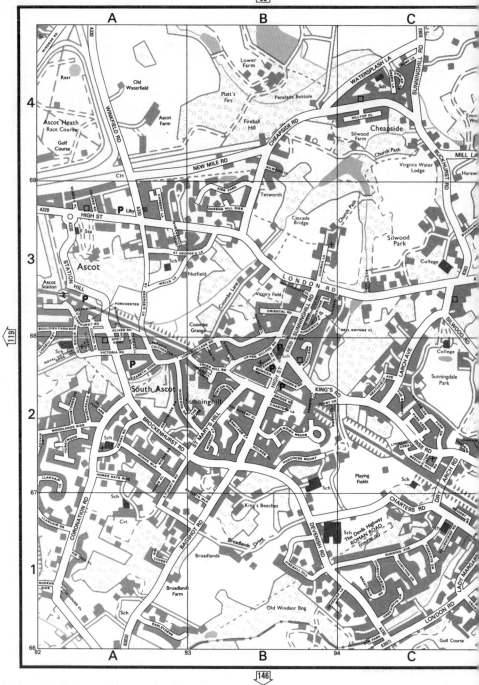

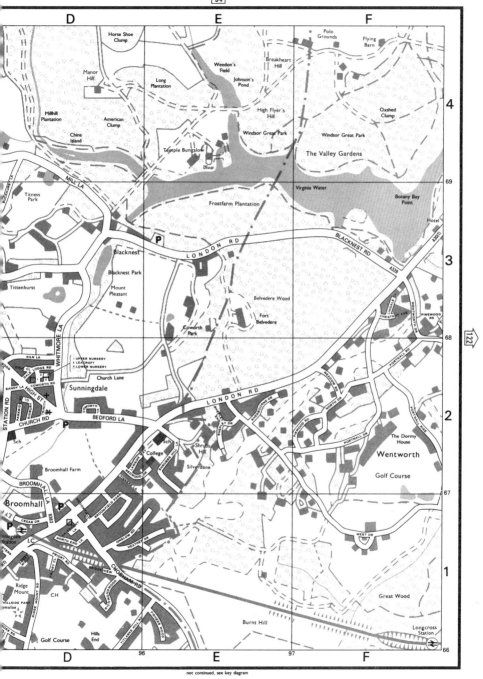

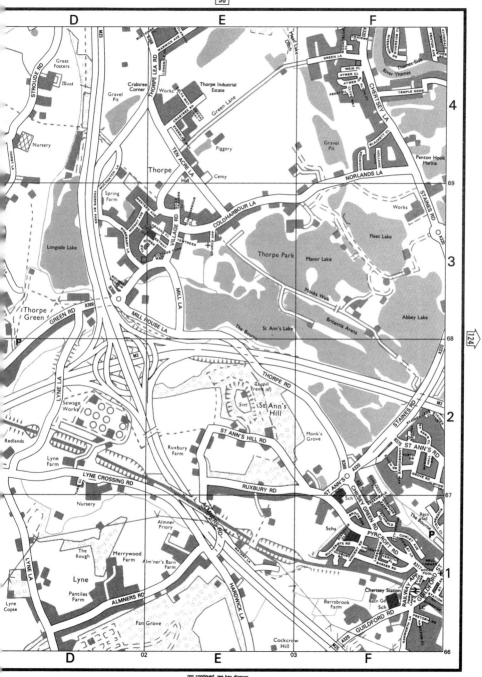

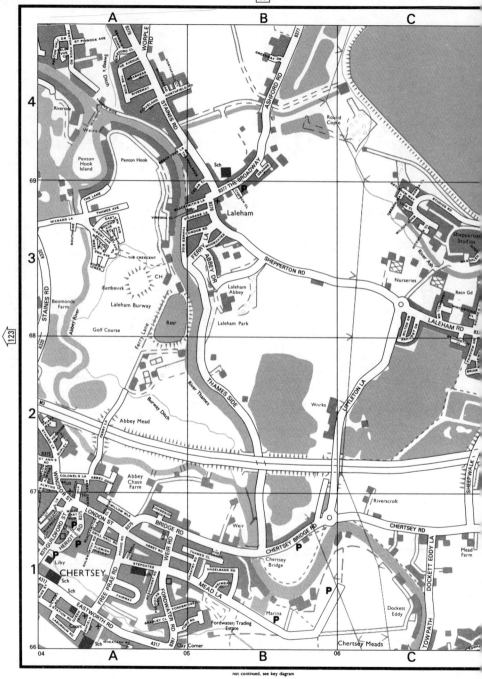

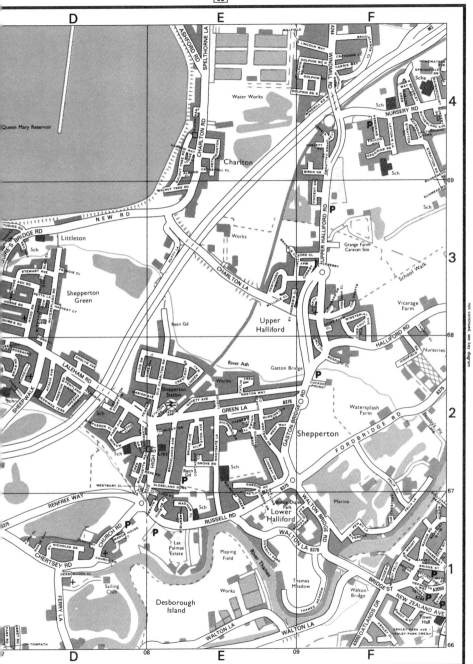

D   E   F

Queen Mary Reservoir

Water Works

Charlton

Littleton

NEW RD

Works

Shepperton Green

Grange Farm
Caravan Site

School Walk

CHARLTON LA

Upper
Halliford

Vicarage
Farm

Recn Gd

River Ash

Nurseries

Gaston Bridge

Works

Watersplash
Farm

Shepperton
Station

GREEN LA

Shepperton

FORDBRIDGE RD

LALEHAM RD

SHEPPWALK

HIGH ST

Liby

Recn
Gd

Sch

Marina

RENFREE WAY

WESTBURY CL

GLEBELAND GDNS

Bishop Duns

Lower
Halliford

WALTON LA

CHERTSEY RD

CHURCH RD

Las
Palmas
Estate

RUSSELL RD

WALTON BRIDGE RD

WALTON LA

Playing
Field

River Thames

Thames
Meadow

Walton
Bridge

BRIDGE ST

NEW ZEALAND AVE

Town
Hall

FERRY LA

Sailing
Club

Desborough
Island

TOWPATH

Works

WALTON LA

WALTON LA

D   08   E   09   F

4

69

3

68

2

67

1

66

not continued, see key diagram

A   B   C

A339

Anvilles

Hightree
Copse

Elm
Copse

Moat

Totterdown
House

4

Upper Slope End
Farm

The
Gully

Middle
Copse

65

Prosperous
Home Farm

Lower Slope End
Farm

Kiln
Copse

The
Heath

Anville's Copse

Great Sadler's
Copse

A338

3

Six Acre

Daniel's La

Mount
Prosperous

Bitham La

A338

64

BITHAM LA

not continued, see key diagram

CUTTING HILL

CUTTING HILL

2

Happy Valley
Nursery

Cowley's
Copse

Lower Spray
Farm

Lower Spray
Copse

SPRAY RD

HAM RD

Dove's
Farm

Ham Spray
Farm

Field La

Crown & Anchor
(PH)

63

Sch

Ham

Ham Spray
House

Manor
House

LYNCH RD

Eastcourt
Farm

The Lynch

Inwood
Copse

1

Manor
Farm

62

32   A   33   B   34   C

Ham Hill

101
128
147

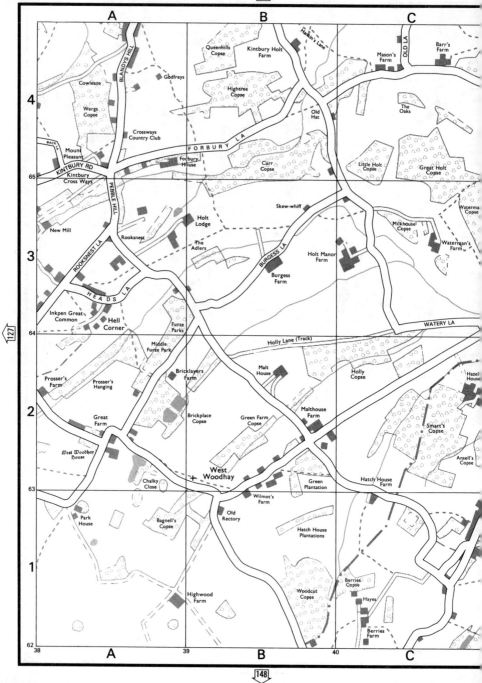

127

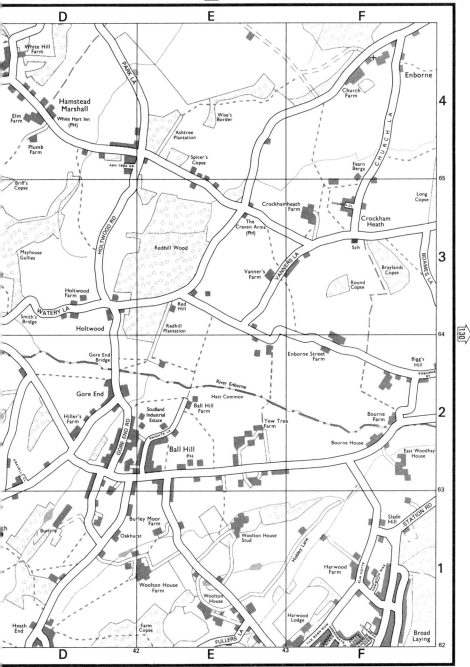

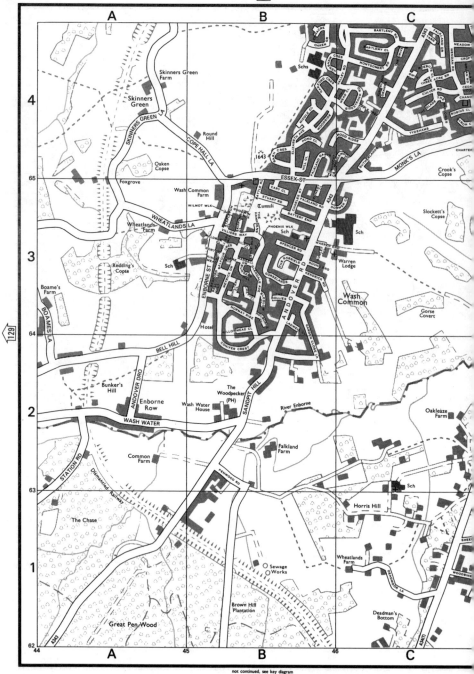

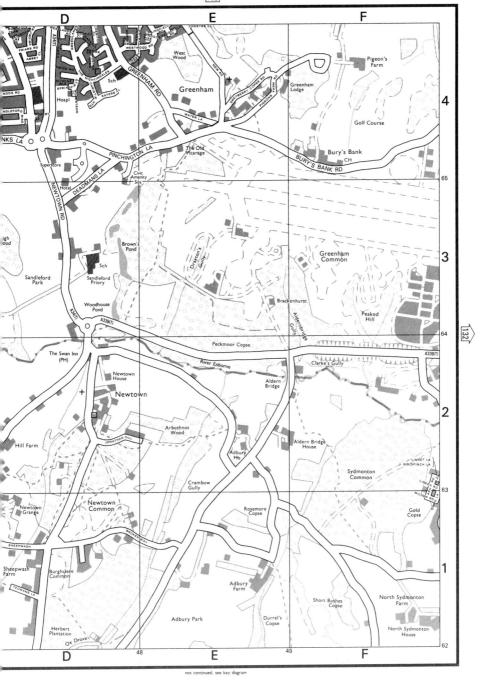

D   **E**   **F**

MONKSHANK LA
FRIARS RD
ABBEY
CHESTER CL
WESTWOOD RD
West Wood
NEW RD
GREENHAM RD
Sch
Greenham
GREYBERRY COPSE RD
PIGEONS FARM RD
Pigeon's Farm
Greenham Lodge
Golf Course

4

NDOS RD
NDLEFORD
Hospl
WATER LA
PINCHINGTON LA
The Old Vicarage
BURY'S BANK RD
Bury's Bank
CH

KS LA
Superstore
DEADMANS LA
NEWTOWN RD
Hotel
Civic Amenity Site

65

igh ood
Brown's Pond
Sch
Sandleford Priory
Drayton's Gully
Greenham Common

3

Sandleford Park
Woodhouse Pond
A339(T)
Brackenhurst
Aldermbridge Gully
Peaked Hill

132

The Swan Inn (PH)
A339(T)
Peckmoor Copse
River Enborne
Clarke's Gully

64

Newtown House
Newtown
Aldern Bridge
Aldern Bridge House

2

Hill Farm
JONATHAN HILL
Arbuthnot Wood
Adbury Ho
Sydmonton Common
LINNET LA
GOLDFINCH LA
LINDEN RD
WILLOW RD

63

Newtown Grange
Newtown Common
BROKEN WAY
Crambow Gully
Rosemore Copse
Gold Copse

Sheepwash Farm
Burghclere Common
SHEEPWASH
TEGMANS LA
Adbury Farm
Short Bushes Copse
North Sydmonton Farm

1

Herbert Plantation
OX DROVE
Adbury Park
Durrel's Copse
North Sydmonton House

62

D   48   **E**   49   **F**

not continued, see key diagram

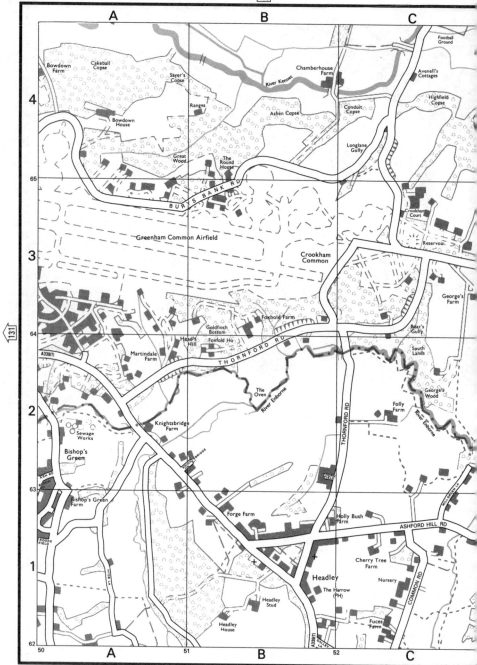

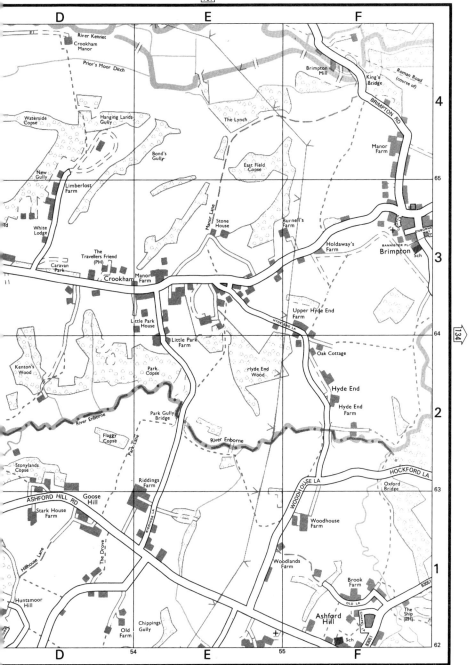

D E F

4

65

3

Brimpton

64

2

134

63

1

62

D 54 E 55 F

not continued, see key diagram

108
133

not continued, see key diagram

D E F

4

Aqua Vitae Copse

Padworth Pig Farm

Upper Lodge

The Old Rectory

Fisherman's Cottage

Upper Church Farm

RECTORY RD

FISHERMAN'S LA

age rks

Aldermaston
Church Farm

Springhill Farm

Rays Farm

Padworth Gully

65

CONGREVE OF

CHURCH RD

SPRING LA

The Birches

Court Farm

Raghill Farm

REDLANE HILL

RAGHILL

3

Foot Bridge

Black Pightle

Harbourhill Copse

PAICES HILL

RED LA

Quarry (dis)

Old Warren

CHAPEL LA

WELSHMAN'S RD

64

136

Aldermaston Park

Birch Copse

ROMAN ROAD
(course of)

Little Heath

Keeper's Belt

SOKE RD

2

Waterman's Pightle

Park Farm

63

Upper Moor Copse

Soke Pig Farm

WINKWORTH LA

The Falcon (PH)

PELICAN RD

FALCON FIELDS

PH

1

ALMSWOOD RD

Liby

PAMBER HEATH RD

SPENCER

BRACKENWOOD

Pamber Heath

FRANKLIN AVE

CHURCH

Sta

SILCHESTER RD

MILLFORDS HILL

Stacey's Industrial Estate

TADLEY COMMON RD

Tadley Court

Tadley Common

VALLEY WAY

THE GLEN

Liby

Sch

SILVERDALE

BURNEY BIT

62

D 60 E 61 F

not continued, see key diagram

A   B   C

Brent's Gully

Oval Pond

SILVER LA

Camp Rd

Roundoak Piece

Gibbet Piece

Four Houses Corner

Cowpond Piece

Water Tower

Five Oa

LONGMOO

PADWORTH RD

The Croft

Holden's Firs

Tumuli

65

RECTORY RD

The Round Oak (PH)

Fifty Acre Piece

Hundred Acre Piece

VICTORIA RD

Padworth Common

ROMAN ROAD (course of)

Pond Bay

Pickling Yard Plantation

ST CATHERINE'S HILL

STEPHEN'S RD

3

RAMPTONS LA

Stockwell's Piece

Chaplin's Copse

Turners Arms (PH)

WEST END RD

Burnt Common

Budd's Firs

Summerlug

Welshman's Pond

WELSHMAN'S RD

West End Farm

64

THE BRIDGES

Mortimer West End

Simms's Copse

TURN O LA

Fox Hill

Lovegrove's Farm

Simms Stud Fa

Benyon's Inclosure

Red Lion (PH)

West End Brook

ROMAN ROAD (course of)

Nine Acre Copse

Simms's Plant

2

Hungry Hill

Pond Farm

Kiln Pond

Stone Hill

63

Sort

ROMAN ROAD (course of)

Catthawl Lands Copse

WALL LA

Earthwork

Earthwork

Kiln Yard Copse

SOKE RD

Catthawlands Farm

AMPHITHEATRE

1

SILCHESTER RD

KINGS RD

The Drove

Manor Farm

The Devil's Highway
ROMAN ROAD (course of)

School

Museum

CALLEVA ATREBATVM
ROMAN TOWN
(remains of)

CHURCH LA

P

BRAMLEY RD

Silchester Common

Calleva Arms (PH)

Silchester

ROMAN ROAD (course of)

Park Dale

62

THE LANE

Silchester Hall

62   A   63   B   64   C

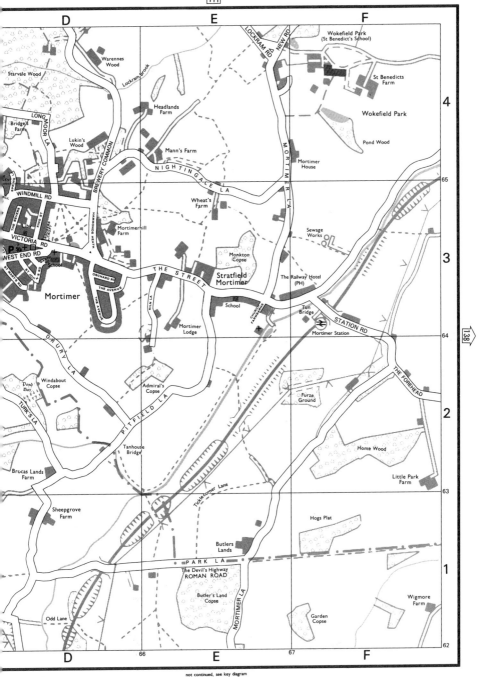

D   E   F

4

Warennes Wood

Starvale Wood

Lockram Brook

Wokefield Park
(St Benedict's School)

St Benedicts Farm

Wokefield Park

Headlands Farm

Pond Wood

LONG MOOR LA

Bridge's Farm

Lukin's Wood

Mann's Farm

BREWERY COMMON

NIGHTINGALE LA

MORTIMER LA

Mortimer House

65

WINDMILL RD

Wheat's Farm

Mortimerhill Farm

HAMMOND'S HEATH

Sewage Works

VICTORIA RD

WEST END RD

Monkton Copse

Stratfield Mortimer

The Railway Hotel (PH)

3

School

THE STREET

THE AVENUE

ORCHARD RD

Mortimer

KILN LA

School
CHURCH / FARMHOUSE

Tun Bridge

STATION RD

Mortimer Station

64

DRURY LA

Mortimer Lodge

Admiral's Copse

Furze Ground

THE FOREHEAD

Pond Bay

Windabout Copse

PITFIELD LA

TURK'S LA

Home Wood

2

Tanhouse Bridge

Brocas Lands Farm

Little Park Farm

63

Sheepgrove Farm

Tickle Corner Lane

Hogs Plat

Butlers Lands

PARK LA

1

The Devil's Highway
ROMAN ROAD

MORTIMER LA

Odd Lane

Butler's Land Copse

Wigmore Farm

Garden Copse

62

D   E   F

66   67

138

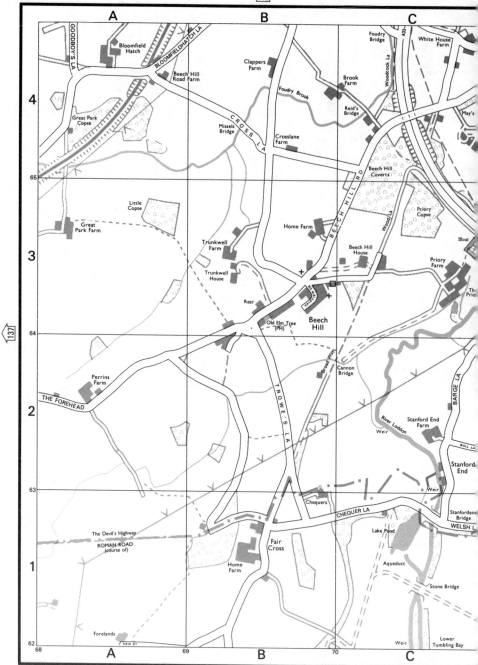

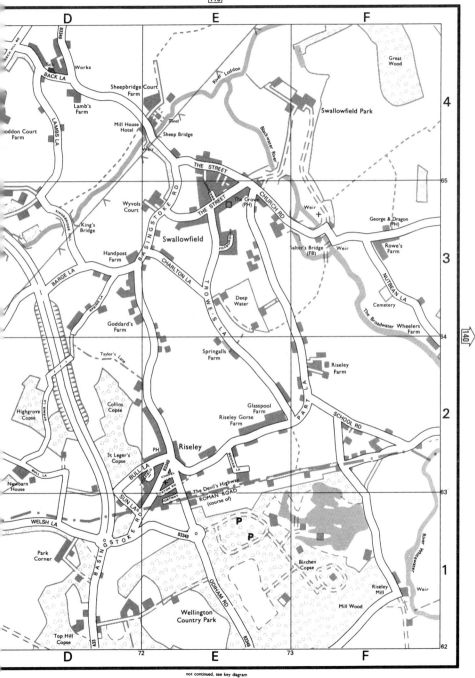

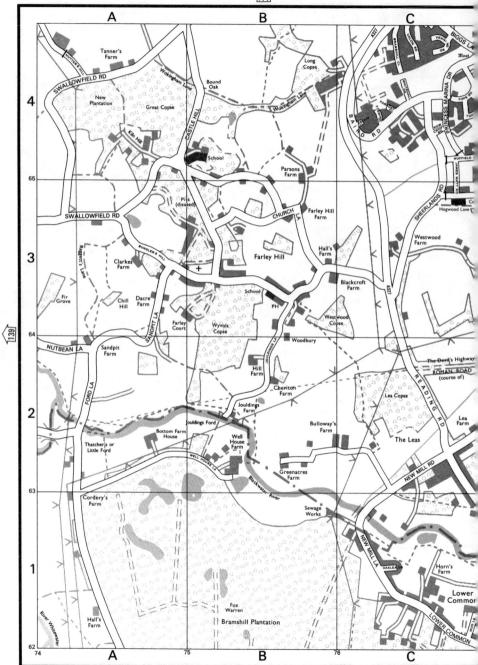

115

142

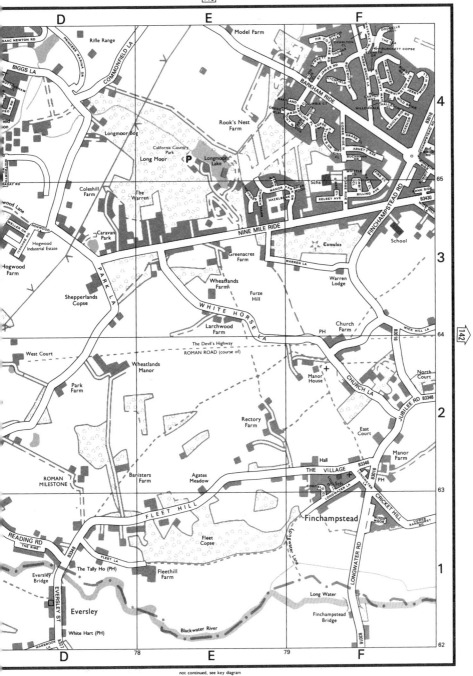

not continued, see key diagram

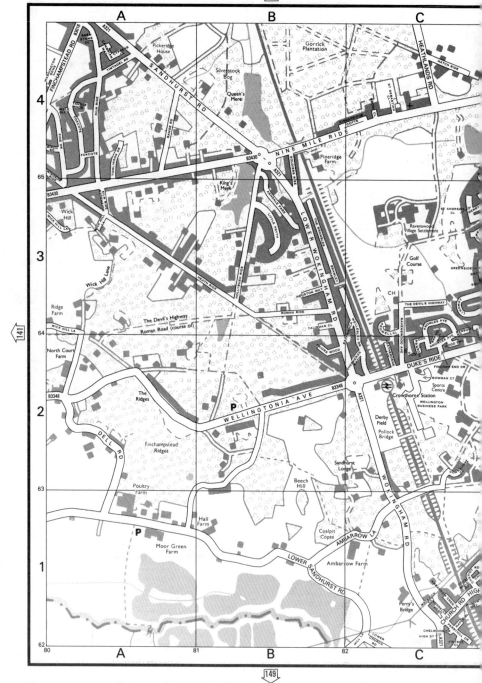

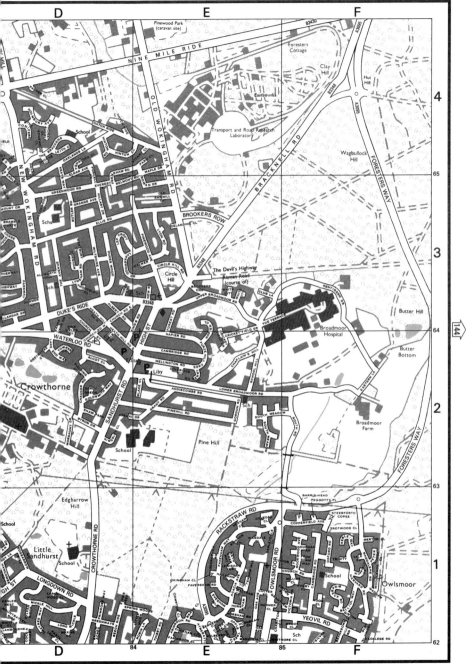

D   E   F

B3430

Pinewood Park
(caravan site)

Foresters
Cottage

NINE MILE RIDE

Clay
Hill

Hut
Hill

4

School

Earthworks

Transport and Road Research
Laboratory

Wagbullock
Hill

OLD WOKINGHAM RD

BRACKNELL RD

FORESTERS WAY

65

BROOKERS ROW

B3348

Celandine Cl

3

NEW WOKINGHAM RD

The Devil's Highway
Roman Road
(course of)

Circle
Hill

Butter Hill

DUKE'S RIDE

B3348

UPPER BROADMOOR RD

KENTIGERN DR

THE TERRACE

Broadmoor
Hospital

64

144

WATERLOO RD

HIGH ST

RAPIER RD

CRICKETFIELD GR

CLUB LA

Butter
Bottom

P

CAMBRIDGE RD

CHAPLAIN'S HILL

P

WELLINGTON RD

Liby

ADDISCOMBE RD

LOWER BROADMOOR RD

2

Crowthorne

SANDHURST RD

PINEHILL RD

Sch

SOUTH MEADOW

Broadmoor
Farm

FORESTERS WAY

School

Pine Hill

63

Edgbarrow
Hill

BARRIS HEAD
PEGGOTTS PL

CROWTHORNE RD

RACKSTRAW RD

STEERFORTH
COPSE

COPPERFIELD AVE

TROTWOOD CL

School

Little
Sandhurst

OWLSMOOR RD

MERTON CL

School

CHURCH

School

1

LONGDOWN RD

OKINGHAM CL

FAVERSHAM

A3095

Owlsmoor

SPRING WOODS

GREENWAYS

YEOVIL RD

Sch

COLLEGE RD

62

D   84   E   85   F

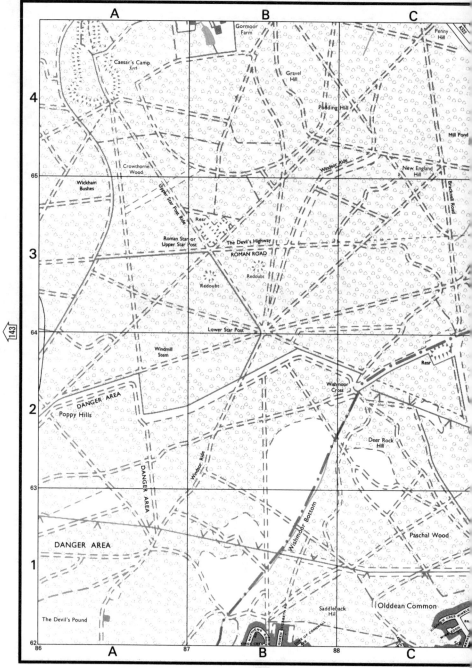

A   B   C

Gormoor Farm

Caesar's Camp
Fort

Penny Hill

A321

Gravel Hill

4

Podding Hill

Mill Pond

Crowthorne Wood

Windsor Ride

New England Hill

65

Wickham Bushes

Bracknell Road

Upper Star Post Ride

Resr

Roman Star or Upper Star Post

The Devil's Highway

3

ROMAN ROAD

Redoubt

Redoubt

64

Lower Star Post

Windmill Stem

Resr

Wishmoor Cross

DANGER AREA

2

Poppy Hills

Deer Rock Hill

DANGER AREA

Windsor Ride

63

Paschal Wood

DANGER AREA

Wishmoor Bottom

1

Olddean Common

Saddleback Hill

The Devil's Pound

62

86   87   88

A   B   C

119

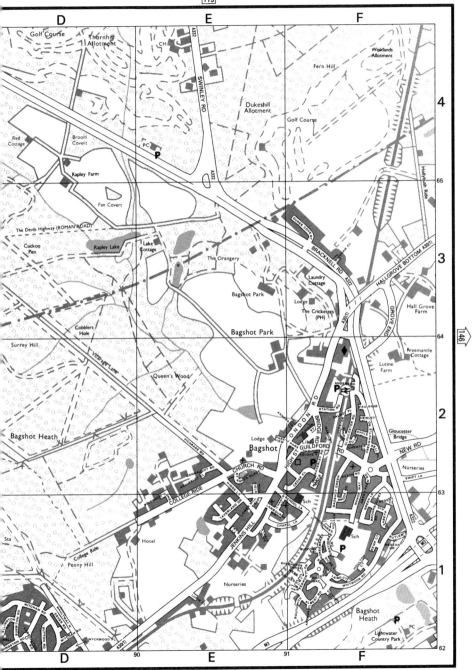

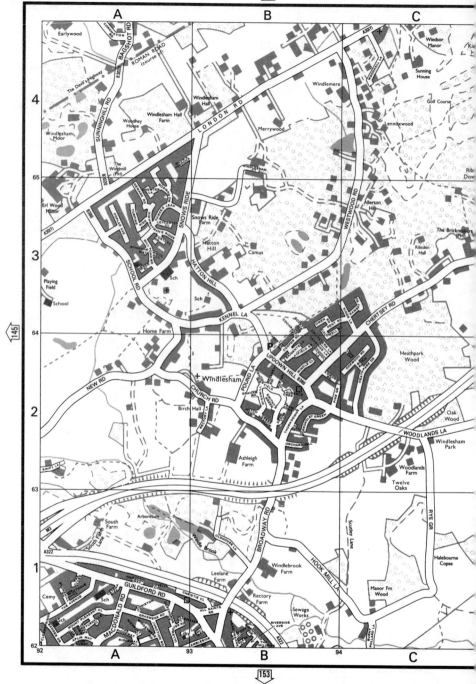

127

148

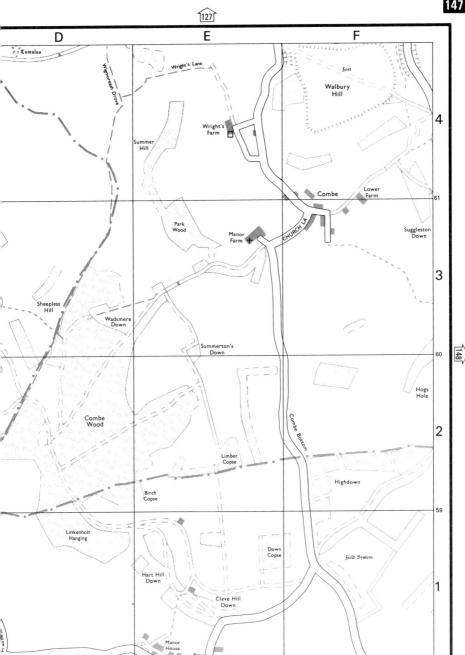

D   E   F

Tumulus

Wigmoreash Drove

Wright's Lane

Fort

Walbury
Hill

Wright's
Farm

Summer
Hill

4

Combe

Lower
Farm

61

Park
Wood

Manor
Farm

CHURCH LA

Suggleston
Down

3

Sheepless
Hill

Wadsmere
Down

Summerton's
Down

60

Combe Bottom

Hogs
Hole

Combe
Wood

2

Limber
Copse

Highdown

Birch
Copse

59

Linkenholt
Hanging

Down
Copse

Field System

Hart Hill
Down

Cleve Hill
Down

1

Manor
House

The Boot Inn (PH)

Linkenholt

D   36   E   37   F   58

not continued, see key diagram

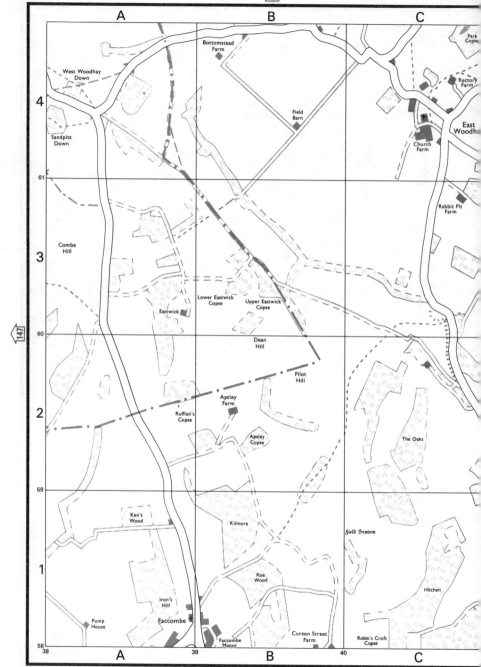

	A	B	C

147

West Woodhay Down

Bottomstead Farm

Park Copse

Rectory Farm

Field Barn

East Woodha

Sandpits Down

Church Farm

Rabbit Pit Farm

Combe Hill

Lower Eastwick Copse

Upper Eastwick Copse

Eastwick

Dean Hill

Pilot Hill

Ruffian's Copse

Apsley Farm

The Oaks

Apsley Copse

Ken's Wood

Kilmore

Field System

Roe Wood

Hitchen

Iron's Hill

Faccombe

Pump House

Faccombe Manor

Curzon Street Farm

Robin's Croft Copse

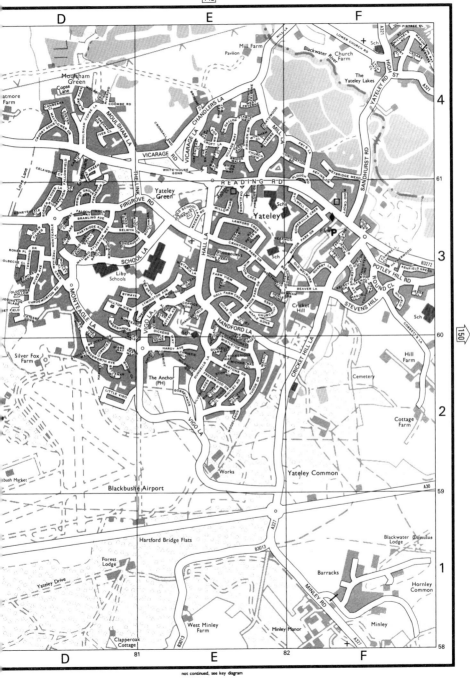

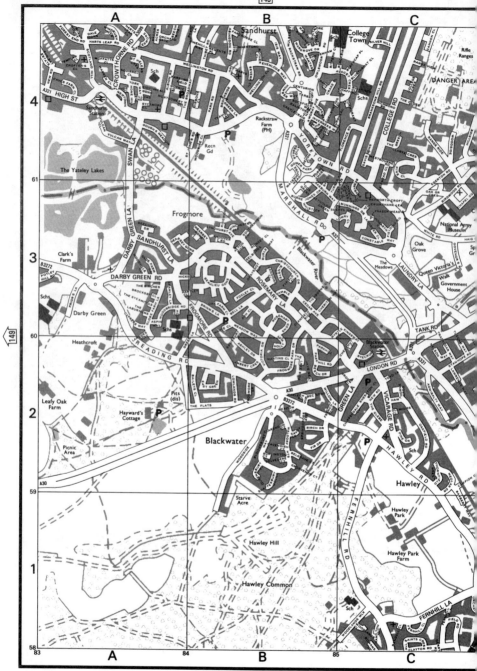

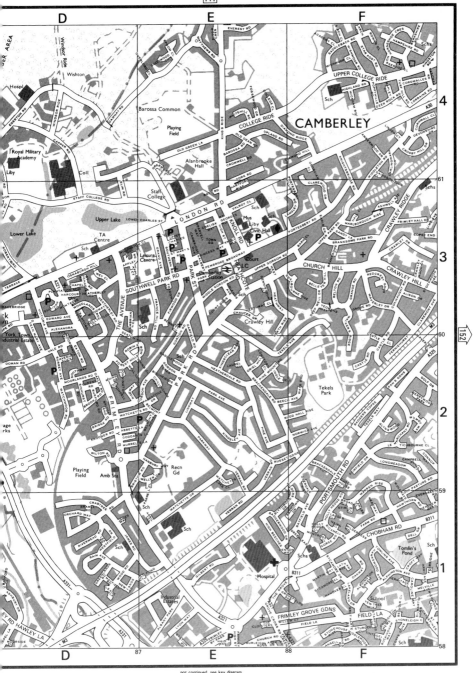

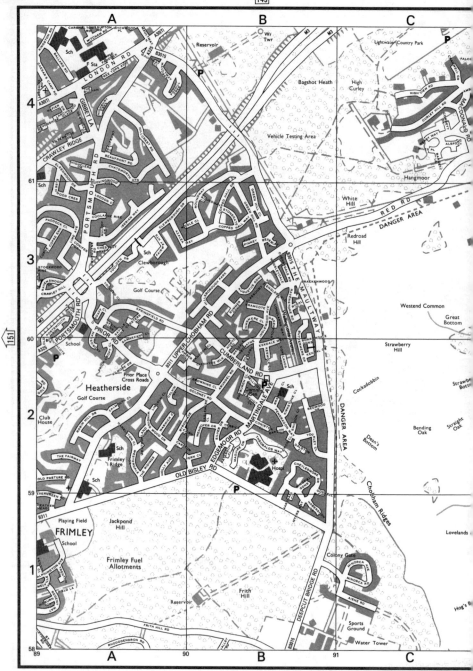

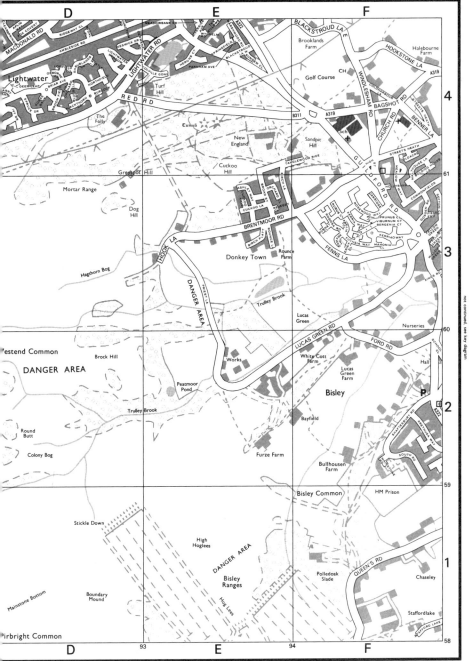

INDEX

EXPLANATION OF THE STREET INDEX REFERENCE SYSTEM

Street names are listed alphabetically and show the locality, the page number and a reference to the square in which the name falls on the map page.

Example: Rushey Way.   Read...87 E1

Rushey Way   This is the full street name, which may have been abbreviated on the map.

Read   This is the abbreviation for the town, village or locality in which the street falls.

87   This is the page number of the map on which the street name appears.

E1   The letter and figure indicate the square on the map in which the centre of the street falls. The square can be found at the junction of the vertical column carrying the appropriate letter and the horizontal row carrying the appropriate figure.

ABBREVIATIONS USED IN THE INDEX
Road Names

Approach	App	Lane	La
Avenue	Ave	North	N
Boulevard	Bvd	Orchard	Orch
Broadway	Bwy	Parade	Par
By-Pass	By-Ps	Passage	Pas
Causeway	Cswy	Place	Pl
Common	Comm	Pleasant	Plea
Corner	Cnr	Precinct	Prec
Cottages	Cotts	Promenade	Prom
Court	Ct	Road	Rd
Crescent	Cres	South	S
Drive	Dr	Square	Sq
Drove	Dro	Street,Saint	St
East	E	Terrace	Terr
Gardens	Gdns	Walk	Wlk
Grove	Gr	West	W
Heights	Hts	Yard	Yd

TOWNS, VILLAGES AND RURAL LOCALITIES

dermaston .... Alde	135 D4	Cold Ash .... Cold A	106 B4
dworth .... Aldw	32 C2	Combe .... Combe	147 F4
borfield .... Arbo	114 B2	Compton .... Comp	31 F2
scot .... Ascot	120 A3	Cookham .... Cook	20 A4
shampstead .... Asham	54 A4	Crowthorne .... Crow	143 D2
shford .... Ashf	97 F2	Datchet .... Datch	68 B3
ston Tirrold .... Ast T	12 C4	Dorney .... Dorn	41 D2
agshot .... Bags	145 E2	East Garston .... East G	47 E3
all Hill .... Ball H	129 E2	East Isley .... East I	30 C3
arkham .... Bark	115 E1	Englefield .... Eng G	95 E1
eech Hill .... Bee H	138 B3	Eton .... Eton	67 E4
eedon .... Beed	51 E4	Farnborough .... Farn	8 C1
eenham .... Been	108 C3	Farnham Common ...... Far C	22 B3
nfield .... Binf	90 B1	Fawley .... Fawl	27 E4
sham .... Bish	18 C4	Fawley (Bucks) ...... Faw (Bu)	15 E4
sley .... Bis	153 F2	Feltham .... Felt	98 C4
ackwater .... Black	150 B2	Finchampstead .... Finch	141 F1
ewbury .... Blew	12 A4	Flackwell Heath ...... Fla H	3 D4
ourne End .... Bou E	3 D1	Froxfield .... Frox	99 D3
xford .... Box	76 B2	Fulmer .... Fulm	23 E4
acknell .... Brac	118 C2	Goring .... Gori	34 B3
adfield .... Brad	82 B3	Great Shefford .... Gr She	48 A2
ightwalton .... Brig	28 C2	Greenham .... Gree	131 E4
impton .... Brim	133 F3	Ham .... Ham	126 B1
ucklebury .... Buck	80 C1	Hambledon .... Hamb	16 B4
urchett's Green .... Bur G	38 B4	Hampstead Norreys .. Hamp N	52 C3
urghfield Common ...... Bur C	110 C1	Hamstead Marshall ..... Ham M	129 D4
urleigh .... Burl	119 E4	Harlington .... Harl	71 E4
urnham .... Burn	21 E2	Harmonsworth .... Harm	70 B4
amberley .... Camb	151 F4	Headley .... Head	132 B1
aversham .... Caver	59 E2	Henley-on-Thames ... Hen-O-T	15 E1
haddleworth .... Chadd	49 D4	Hermitage .... Herm	79 D4
harvil .... Char	61 D3	Holyport .... Holy	65 D4
hertsey .... Chert	124 A1	Horton .... Hort	69 D2
hieveley .... Chiev	51 D1	Hungerford .... Hung	100 C3
hilton .... Chil	10 C4	Hurley .... Hurl	17 F2
hilton Foliat .... Chil F	72 C1	Hurst .... Hurst	88 C3
holsey .... Chol	14 A4	Inkpen .... Ink	127 E3

Iver .... Iver	44 C4	Stanwell .... Stan	70 B1
Iver Heath .... Iver H	23 F2	Stoke Poges .... Sto P	22 C2
Kintbury .... Kint	102 A1	Streatley .... Stre	34 A4
Knowle Hill .... Know H	37 F2	Sulham .... Sulh	56 C1
Lambourn .... Lamb	25 E1	Sulhamstead .... Sulhd	110 B3
Leckhampstead .... Leckh	50 A3	Swallowfield .... Swal	139 E3
Letcombe Bassett .... Let B	6 C4	Tadley .... Tad	134 C1
Lightwater .... Light	153 D4	Taplow .... Tapl	20 C1
Linkenholt .... Link	147 E1	Thatcham .... That	106 C2
Little Marlow .... Lit M	2 B3	Theale .... Thea	83 E2
Maidenhead .... Maid	39 F2	Tidmarsh .... Tidm	56 B1
Mapledurham .... Maple	57 F3	Twyford .... Twyf	61 E3
Marlow .... Mar	1 A1	Upper Basildon .... Upp B	55 E2
Marlow Bottom .... Mar B	1 B3	Virginia Water .... Vir W	122 B3
Medmenham .... Medm	17 D3	Waltham St Lawrence .. W St L	62 C3
Mortimer .... Mort	137 D3	Wargrave .... Warg	36 B1
Moulsford .... Moul	13 F2	Wentworth .... Went	121 F2
Newbury .... Newb	104 C2	West End .... West E	153 F3
Newell Green .... New G	91 E2	West Isley .... West I	10 A1
Newtown .... Newt	131 D2	West Woodhay .... West W	128 B2
Oakley Green .... Oak G	66 A3	Whitchurch-on-Thames Whi-O-T	56 B4
Old Windsor .... Old W	95 D4	White Waltham .... Whi Wa	63 F4
Padworth .... Padw	109 F1	Wickham .... Wick	75 E2
Pangbourne .... Pang	56 A3	Windlesham .... Windl	146 B2
Peasemore .... Pease	50 C4	Windsor .... Wind	67 F3
Purley on Thames ..... Pur O T	57 D3	Winkfield .... Wink	92 B3
Reading .... Read	85 D3	Winnersh .... Winn	88 A2
Remenham Hill .... Rem H	16 B1	Winterbourne .... Wint	77 E3
Sandhurst .... Sand	150 B4	Wokingham .... Woki	116 A4
Shepperton .... Shepp	125 F2	Woodburn Green ...... Woo G	3 F4
Shinfield .... Shin	113 F3	Woodley .... Wood	88 A4
Shiplake .... Shipl	35 F1	Woolhampton .... Wool	108 B1
Silchester .... Silc	136 B1	Wraysbury .... Wray	95 F4
Slough .... Slough	42 C3	Yateley .... Yate	149 E3
Sonning .... Sonn	60 C2	Yattendon .... Yatt	53 F1
South Stoke .... Sou S	14 B2		
Staines .... Stai	96 C1		
Stanford Dingley .... Stan D	81 E2		

INDEX OF STREET NAMES

Abattoirs Rd. Read ... 86 A4
Abbetts La. Camb ... 151 D2
Abbey Cl. Brac ... 118 B2
Abbey Cl. Newb ... 131 D4
Abbey Cl. Slough ... 41 F3
Abbey Cl. Woki ... 116 B4
Abbey Gdns. Chert ... 124 A2
Abbey Green. Chert ... 124 A2
Abbey Park. Bur C ... 110 C2
Abbey Rd. Bou E ... 2 C3
Abbey Rd. Chert ... 124 A1
Abbey Rd. Shepp ... 125 D1
Abbey Rd. Vir W ... 122 B3
Abbey Rd. Went ... 121 D1
Abbey Sq. Read ... 86 A4
Abbey St. Read ... 86 A4
Abbey Way. Bish ... 18 B3
Abbot Cl. Stai ... 97 E1
Abbot's Rd. Bur C ... 110 C1
Abbot's Wlk. Read ... 86 A4
Abbot's Wlk. Wind ... 66 C3
Abbots Dr. Vir W ... 122 B3
Abbots Rd. Newb ... 105 D1
Abbotsbury. Brac ... 117 F2
Abbotts Way. Slough ... 41 E3
Abelia Cl. Camb ... 153 F3
Aberford Cl. Read ... 85 E4
Abex Rd. Newb ... 105 E2
Abingdon Cl. Brac ... 118 C2
Abingdon Dr. Caver ... 59 E3
Abingdon Rd. East I ... 30 C4
Abingdon Rd. Sand ... 143 E1
Abingdon Wlk. Maid ... 19 F2
Abney Ct Dr. Bou E ... 3 D1
Aborfield Cl. Slough ... 42 C2
Abrahams Rd. Hen-O-T ... 15 E2
Acacia Ave. Crow ... 143 E1
Acacia Ave. Stai ... 125 D2
Acacia Ave. Wray ... 68 C2
Acacia Ct. Brac ... 118 A3
Acacia Mews. Harm ... 70 B4
Acacia Rd. Read ... 86 B3
Acacia Rd. Stai ... 97 D2
Academy Cl. Camb ... 151 F4
Accommodation La. Harm ... 70 A4
Ackrells Mead. Sand ... 142 C1
Acorn Dr. Woki ... 116 B4
Acorn Gr. Harl ... 71 F4
Acorn Rd. Black ... 150 A3
Acre Pas. Wind ... 67 E3
Acre Rd. Read ... 113 D4
Acre The. Mar ... 1 C1
Adam Cl. Slough ... 42 A3
Adam Cl. Tad ... 134 C1
Adam Ct. Hen-O-T ... 15 F1
Adams Way. Read ... 86 C1
Addington Cl. Wind ... 67 D2
Addington Rd. Read ... 86 B3
Addiscombe Chase. Sulh ... 57 D2
Addiscombe Rd. Crow ... 143 E2
Addison Cl. Iver ... 44 C4
Addison Ct. Maid ... 20 A1
Addison Rd. Read ... 59 D1
Adelaide Cl. Slough ... 42 A2
Adelaide Rd. Ashf ... 97 E2
Adelaide Rd. Read ... 86 C4
Adelaide Sq. Wind ... 67 E3
Adelphi Gdns. Slough ... 42 C2
Adkins Rd. W St L ... 62 C4
Admirals Ct. Read ... 86 A3
Admiralty Way. Sand ... 150 C2
Admoor La. Been ... 109 E4
Adwell Dr. Winn ... 87 E1
Adwell Sq. Hen-O-T ... 15 E1
Adwood Ct. That ... 106 C2
Agar Cres. Brac ... 91 D1
Agars Pl. Datch ... 68 A4
Agate Cl. Woki ... 115 F4
Aggisters La. Woki ... 115 E2
Agincourt Cl. Woki ... 115 F3
Agricola Way. That ... 106 C1
Ainsdale Cres. Read ... 85 D2
Aintree Cl. Newb ... 105 E1
Aintree Cl. Stan ... 69 F3
Aintree. Lamb ... 25 D1
Airport Way. Stan ... 70 A2
Aisne Rd. Camb ... 152 C1
Ajax Ave. Slough ... 42 A3
Alan Pl. Read ... 85 D3
Alan Way. Slough ... 43 E4
Alandale Cl. Read ... 113 E4
Albain Cres. Stan ... 70 A3
Albany Park Dr. Winn ... 88 A2
Albany Park. Camb ... 151 E1
Albany Park. Stan ... 69 E4
Albany Pl. Eng G ... 96 B2
Albany Rd. Old W ... 68 A1
Albany Rd. Read ... 85 E4
Albany Rd. Wind ... 67 E3
Alben Rd. Binf ... 90 B2
Albert Ave. Chert ... 124 A3
Albert Cl. Slough ... 42 C2
Albert Rd. Ashf ... 97 F3
Albert Rd. Bags ... 145 F1
Albert Rd. Brac ... 118 A4
Albert Rd. Camb ... 151 E3
Albert Rd. Caver ... 58 C2
Albert Rd. Crow ... 143 D3
Albert Rd. Eng G ... 95 E1

Albert Rd. Hen-O-T ... 15 F1
Albert Rd. Newb ... 105 D2
Albert Rd. Old W ... 68 A1
Albert Rd. Wind ... 67 F2
Albert Rd. Woki ... 116 A3
Albert St. Maid ... 39 F4
Albert St. Slough ... 42 C2
Albert St. Wind ... 67 D3
Albion Cl. Slough ... 43 D3
Albion Rd. Sand ... 150 A4
Albion Terr. Read ... 86 B4
Albury Cl. Read ... 58 B1
Albury Gdns. Read ... 84 C2
Alcot Cl. Crow ... 143 D2
Aldborough Spur. Slough ... 42 C4
Aldbourne Ave. Read ... 87 D2
Aldbourne Rd. Burn ... 41 A4
Aldeburgh Cl. Caver ... 59 E4
Aldebury Rd. Maid ... 19 F3
Alden View. Wind ... 66 B3
Aldenham Cl. Caver ... 59 E4
Aldenham Terr. Brac ... 118 B2
Alder Cl. Eng G ... 95 F2
Alder Cl. Slough ... 41 F3
Alder Dr. Read ... 84 B3
Alder Gr. Yate ... 149 E3
Alderbourne La. Fulm ... 23 F4
Alderbrook Cl. Finch ... 142 C3
Alderbury Rd W. Slough ... 43 F2
Alderbury Rd. Slough ... 43 F2
Alderfield Cl. Thea ... 83 F2
Alderley Cl. Wood ... 60 C1
Alderman Willey Cl. Woki ... 116 A3
Alders The. That ... 106 B2
Alderside Wlk. Eng G ... 95 F2
Aldin Ave S. Slough ... 43 D2
Aldridge Rd. Slough ... 22 A1
Aldwick Dr. Maid ... 39 E3
Aldworth Cl. Brac ... 118 A3
Aldworth Cl. Read ... 85 E3
Aldworth Gdns. Crow ... 143 D3
Aldworth Rd. Comp ... 31 F2
Aldworth Rd. Upp B ... 55 D3
Alexander Rd. Stai ... 96 B2
Alexander Rd. That ... 106 C1
Alexandra Ave. Camb ... 151 D3
Alexandra Cl. Ashf ... 98 B1
Alexandra Cl. Stai ... 97 E1
Alexandra Cl. Ashf ... 98 B1
Alexandra Cl. Ashf ... 98 C2
Alexandra Cl. Ashf ... 98 C1
Alexandra Rd. Eng G ... 95 E1
Alexandra Rd. Maid ... 39 E4
Alexandra Rd. Read ... 86 B4
Alexandra Rd. Slough ... 42 B2
Alexandra Rd. Wind ... 67 E3
Alford Cl. Read ... 84 B4
Alfred St. Read ... 85 F4
Alice La. Burn ... 21 D1
Alison Cl. Bur C ... 110 C1
Alison Dr. Camb ... 151 F3
All Hallows Rd. Caver ... 59 E2
All Saints Cl. Woki ... 116 B4
All Saints Cres. Black ... 150 C1
All Saints Rise. New G ... 91 F1
All Saints' Ave. Maid ... 39 E4
All Saints' Rd. Light ... 146 B1
All Souls' Rd. Ascot ... 120 A3
Allanson Rd. Mar ... 1 C2
Allcot Cl. Felt ... 98 C4
Allcroft Rd. Read ... 86 B3
Allenby Rd. Camb ... 151 D3
Allenby Rd. Maid ... 39 D4
Allendale Cl. Sand ... 143 D1
Allendale Rd. Read ... 87 D2
Allerds Rd. Burn ... 22 A3
Alleyns La. Cook ... 19 E4
Allhusen Gdns. Fulm ... 23 F4
Alliance Ct. Ashf ... 98 B2
Allison Gdns. Pur O T ... 57 E3
Allkins Ct. Wind ... 67 E3
Allnatt Ave. Winn ... 88 B1
Allonby Cl. Read ... 87 E1
Allsmoor La. Brac ... 118 C3
Allyn Cl. Stai ... 96 C1
Alma Rd. Eton ... 41 F1
Alma Rd. Wind ... 67 E3
Alma St. Read ... 85 E4
Almners Rd. Chert ... 123 D1
Almond Ave. Newb ... 105 D3
Almond Cl. Eng G ... 95 D1
Almond Cl. Wind ... 67 D3
Almond Cl. Woki ... 115 E2
Almond Dr. Caver ... 59 F2
Almond Rd. Burn ... 21 E1
Almonts Way. Slough ... 43 D4
Almswood Rd. Tad ... 135 D1
Alpha St N. Slough ... 42 C2
Alpha St S. Slough ... 42 C2
Alphington Ave. Camb ... 151 F1
Alphington Green. Camb ... 151 F1
Alpine St. Read ... 86 A3
Alsace Wlk. Camb ... 151 D1
Alsford Cl. Camb ... 152 C4
Alston Mews. That ... 106 B1
Alston Wlk. Caver ... 59 E1
Altmore. Bur G ... 38 C2
Alton Ct. Stai ... 123 F4

Alton Ride. Black ... 150 B3
Altona Way. Slough ... 42 A4
Altwood Bailey. Maid ... 39 D3
Altwood Cl. Burn ... 41 F4
Altwood Cl. Maid ... 39 D3
Altwood Dr. Maid ... 39 D3
Altwood Rd. Maid ... 39 D3
Alvista Ave. Burn ... 41 D4
Alwyn Rd. Maid ... 39 D4
Alwyns Cl. Chert ... 124 A2
Alwyns La. Chert ... 123 F2
Amanda Ct. Slough ... 43 E2
Ambarrow Cres. Sand ... 142 C1
Ambarrow La. Sand ... 142 C1
Ambassador. Brac ... 117 F2
Amber Hill. Camb ... 152 A2
Amberley Cl. Newb ... 104 C2
Amberley Ct. Maid ... 20 B2
Amberley Dr. Twyf ... 61 E3
Amberley Rd. Burn ... 41 F4
Amberwood Dr. Camb ... 151 F4
Amblecote Rd. Read ... 86 D4
Ambleside Cl. Wood ... 87 F4
Ambleside Dr. Felt ... 98 C4
Ambleside Dr. Felt ... 98 C4
Ambleside Rd. Light ... 153 D4
Ambleside Way. Stai ... 96 A1
Ambrook Road. Read ... 113 D4
Ambrose Pl. Read ... 85 F4
Ambury Rd. Comp ... 32 C2
Amen Corner Bsns Park. Brac ... 117 F4
Amerden Cl. Tapl ... 40 B4
Amerden La. Tapl ... 40 B4
Amerden La. Tapl ... 40 C2
Amerden Way. Slough ... 42 A2
Amersham Rd. Caver ... 59 E1
Amethyst Cl. Woki ... 115 E4
Amherst Rd. Read ... 87 D3
Amity Rd. Read ... 86 C4
Amity St. Read ... 86 C4
Amners Farm Rd. Bur C ... 112 A4
Ampere Rd. Newb ... 105 D2
Ancaster Dr. Ascot ... 119 F4
Ancastle Gr. Hen-O-T ... 15 E1
Andermans. Wind ... 66 B3
Anderson Ave. Read ... 87 D3
Anderson Cres. Arbo ... 114 C1
Anderson Dr. Ashf ... 98 B2
Andrew Pl. Bags ... 145 E4
Andover Cl. Read ... 57 E1
Andover Dro. Ham M ... 130 A2
Andover Rd. Ball H ... 130 B3
Andover Rd. Black ... 150 B3
Andover Rd. Newb ... 130 B3
Andrew Cl. Woki ... 116 C3
Andrews Cl. Thea ... 83 F2
Andrews Rd. Read ... 87 D2
Andrews Way. Mar B ... 1 B4
Angel Cl. Newb ... 105 D2
Angel Mead. Wool ... 108 B1
Angel Pl. Binf ... 90 B1
Angle Field Rd. Caver ... 59 E2
Anglers Way. Read ... 86 B4
Anglesey Cl. Ashf ... 98 A3
Angus Cl. Read ... 84 C2
Annadale. Cold A ... 79 E1
Anne Cl. Maid ... 19 F1
Anneforde Pl. Brac ... 91 D1
Anners Cl. Stai ... 123 E3
Annesley Gdns. Winn ... 88 B2
Annett Cl. Shepp ... 125 F3
Anscuff Rd. Slough ... 22 A1
Ansell Rd. Camb ... 151 F1
Anslow Pl. Slough ... 41 E4
Anson Cres. Read ... 113 E4
Anstey Pl. Bur C ... 111 D2
Anstey Rd. Read ... 86 A4
Anston Cl. Read ... 114 A4
Antares Cl. Woki ... 115 F3
Anthony Way. Slough ... 41 E3
Antrim Rd. Wood ... 87 E3
Apex Dr. Camb ... 151 E1
Aplin Way. Light ... 146 A1
Apple Cl. Pur O T ... 57 D2
Apple Cl. Woki ... 115 F3
Apple Tree Cl. Newb ... 130 C4
Apple Tree Way. Sand ... 143 E1
Appleby End. Read ... 85 D4
Appleby Gdns. Felt ... 98 C4
Applecroft. Maid ... 20 B3
Appleford Cl. That ... 106 B1
Appleford Rd. Read ... 85 D3
Appletree La. Shin ... 113 D1
Appletree La. Slough ... 43 E2
Appletree Pl. Brac ... 118 A4
Appley Cl. Camb ... 151 D3
Appley Dr. Camb ... 151 D3
Approach Rd. Ashf ... 98 B1
Approach Rd. Tapl ... 40 C4
April Cl. Camb ... 151 E1
Aquila Cl. Woki ... 115 F3
Aragon Cl. Ashf ... 98 C1
Arbor La. Winn ... 88 A2
Arbor Meadows. Winn ... 88 A2
Arborfield Rd. Shin ... 113 F2
Arbour Cl. Read ... 85 F3
Arcade The. Gori ... 34 B3
Arcade The. Newb ... 105 D2

Archangel Way. That ... 106 C2
Archer Cl. Maid ... 39 E4
Archway Rd. Caver ... 59 D1
Arden Cl. Brac ... 119 D4
Ardingly. Brac ... 118 A2
Ardler Rd. Caver ... 59 E1
Ardrossan Ave. Camb ... 152 A3
Ardwell Cl. Crow ... 142 C3
Arenal Dr. Crow ... 143 E2
Arethusa Way. Bis ... 153 F2
Argosy Gdns. Stai ... 96 C1
Argosy La. Stan ... 97 E4
Argyle Rd. Newb ... 104 C1
Argyle Rd. Read ... 85 F4
Argyle St. Read ... 85 F4
Arkle Ave. That ... 105 F2
Arkley Ct. Holy ... 40 B1
Arkwright Dr. Brac ... 117 E4
Arkwright Rd. Read ... 86 A2
Arkwright Rd. Stan ... 69 F3
Arlington Bsns Park. Read ... 84 A2
Arlington Cl. Brac ... 118 C4
Arlington Cl. Maid ... 38 C4
Arlington Rd. Ashf ... 97 F2
Arlington Square. Brac ... 118 A4
Armadale Ct. Read ... 85 E3
Armitage Ct. Ascot ... 120 B2
Armitage Dr. Camb ... 151 F1
Armour Hill. Read ... 57 E1
Armour Rd. Read ... 57 E1
Armstrong Rd. Eng G ... 95 E1
Armstrong Way. Wood ... 88 A4
Arncliffe. Brac ... 118 A2
Arndale Way. Eng G ... 96 A1
Arnett Ave. Woki ... 141 F4
Arnewood Ave. Tad ... 135 E1
Arnhem Rd. Newb ... 105 D2
Arnold Rd. Stai ... 97 E1
Arnside Cl. Twyf ... 61 E4
Arrowhead Rd. Thea ... 83 F1
Arrowsmith Way. That ... 106 C1
Arthur Cl. Bags ... 145 F1
Arthur Rd. Read ... 86 B4
Arthur Rd. Slough ... 42 B2
Arthur Rd. Wind ... 67 D3
Arthur Rd. Woki ... 116 A3
Arthurstone Birches. Binf ... 90 B2
Arun Cl. Winn ... 88 A1
Arundel Cl. Maid ... 39 D4
Arundel Ct. Slough ... 43 E1
Arundel Rd. Camb ... 152 B2
Arundel Rd. Wood ... 87 F4
Ascot Cl. Felt ... 98 A3
Ascot Rd. Holy ... 40 A1
Ascot Rd. Holy ... 64 C4
Ascot Rd. New G ... 91 F4
Ash Cl. Brig ... 28 B2
Ash Cl. Sand ... 150 B3
Ash Cl. Slough ... 44 A2
Ash Gr. Felt ... 98 C4
Ash Gr. Stai ... 97 E1
Ash Gr. Sto P ... 22 C3
Ash La. Bur C ... 111 D2
Ash La. Wind ... 66 B3
Ash Rd. Newt ... 131 F2
Ash Rd. Newt ... 132 A2
Ash Rd. Read ... 84 C4
Ash Rd. Stai ... 125 D3
Ash Tree Gr. Ham M ... 129 D4
Ash Way. Woki ... 115 E2
Ashampstead Rd. Brad ... 82 A4
Ashampstead Rd. Read ... 85 D2
Ashampstead Rd. Upp B ... 55 D3
Ashbourne Gr. Maid ... 39 E2
Ashbourne Way. That ... 106 A2
Ashbourne. Brac ... 117 F2
Ashbrook Rd. Old W ... 95 D4
Ashburton Rd. Read ... 86 B1
Ashbury Dr. Camb ... 151 D1
Ashbury Dr. Read ... 84 B4
Ashby Ct. Read ... 113 D4
Ashby Way. Harm ... 71 F4
Ashcroft Cl. Caver ... 58 C3
Ashcroft Ct. Burn ... 21 D2
Ashcroft Rd. Read ... 39 E4
Ashdale Cl. Stan ... 97 F3
Ashdale Park. Brac ... 142 B3
Ashdene Cl. Stai ... 98 B1
Ashdown Cl. Brac ... 119 D4
Ashdown. Maid ... 20 A2
Ashen Cross. Slough ... 44 A4
Ashenden Wlk. Far C ... 22 B4
Ashfield Green. Yate ... 149 F3
Ashford Ave. Ashf ... 98 A1
Ashford Cl. Ashf ... 97 F2
Ashford Cres. Ashf ... 97 F3
Ashford Hd. Read ... 132 C1
Ashford Ind Est. Felt ... 98 B2
Ashford La. Dorn ... 41 D2
Ashford Rd. Felt ... 98 C3
Ashford Rd. Stai ... 97 E1
Ashgrove Rd. Ashf ... 98 B2
Ashleigh Ave. Stan ... 96 C1
Ashley Cl. Read ... 87 D1

Ashley Cl. Shepp ... 125
Ashley Dr. Black ... 150
Ashley Hill Pl. Know H ... 38
Ashley Park Ave. Shepp ... 125
Ashley Park Cres. Shepp ... 125
Ashley Park. Maid ... 20
Ashley Rd. Read ... 85
Ashley Way. West E ... 153
Ashman Pl. Kint ... 102
Ashman Rd. That ... 106
Ashmere Cl. Bur C ... 84
Ashmere Terr. Read ... 85
Ashmore Green Rd. Cold A ... 106
Ashmore Rd. Read ... 86
Ashridge Green. Brac ... 118
Ashridge Rd. Woki ... 116
Ashton Cl. Read ... 85
Ashton Pl. Maid ... 39
Ashton Rd. Newb ... 105
Ashton Rd. Woki ... 116
Ashtrees Rd. Wood ... 87
Ashurst Dr. Stai ... 124
Ashview Cl. Ashf ... 97
Ashview Gdns. Ashf ... 97
Ashville Way. Woki ... 116
Ashwell Ave. Camb ... 151
Ashwood Cl. Read ... 84
Ashwood Dr. Newb ... 105
Ashwood Pt. Eng G ... 95
Ashwood. Wood ... 87
Ashworth Dr. That ... 106
Askew Dr. Shin ... 113
Aspen Cl. Slough ... 42
Aspen Cl. Stai ... 96
Aspin Way. Black ... 150
Astleham Way. Stai ... 124
Astley Cl. Woki ... 115
Aston Ave. Read ... 57
Aston Cl. Pangb ... 56
Aston Ferry La. Rem H ... 16
Aston La. Rem H ... 16
Aston Mead. Wind ... 66
Aston St. Ast T ... 12
Astor Cl. Winn ... 88
Astra Mead. Burl ... 92
Afield Gr. Windl ... 146
Atherton Cl. Read ... 84
Atherton Cl. Stan ... 70
Atherton Cres. Hung ... 100
Athrustone Cl. Read ... 85
Atherton Pt. Lamb ... 25
Atherton Rd. Hung ... 100
Athlone Cl. Maid ... 19
Atrebatti Rd. Sand ... 143
Auckland Cl. Maid ... 40
Auckland Rd. Read ... 87
Audley Cl. Newb ... 105
Audley Dr. Maid ... 39
Audley St. Read ... 85
Audley Way. Burl ... 119
Augur Cl. Stai ... 96
Augustine Cl. Stan ... 69
Augustine Wlk. New G ... 91
Augustus Gdns. Camb ... 152
Austen Gdns. Newb ... 131
Austin Rd. Wood ... 87
Australia Ave. Maid ... 39
Australia Rd. Slough ... 43
Autumn Cl. Caver ... 58
Autumn Cl. Slough ... 41
Autumn Wlk. Maid ... 38
Autumn Wlk. Warg ... 36
Avalon Rd. Bou E ... 3
Avalon Rd. Read ... 87
Avebury Sq. Read ... 86
Avebury. Brac ... 118
Avebury. Slough ... 42
Avenue Rd. Felt ... 98
Avenue Rd. Stai ... 96
Avenue Sucy. Camb ... 151
Avenue The. Ascot ... 92
Avenue The. Bou E ... 3
Avenue The. Camb ... 151
Avenue The. Crow ... 143
Avenue The. Eng G ... 96
Avenue The. Light ... 146
Avenue The. Mort ... 137
Avenue The. Old W ... 68
Avenue The. Wray ... 68
Averil Ct. Slough ... 43
Avington Cl. Read ... 85
Avocet Cres. Sand ... 150
Avon Cl. Read ... 84
Avon Cl. Slough ... 43
Avon Gr. Brac ... 91
Avon Pt. Read ... 86
Avon Rd. Ashf ... 98
Avon Way. Padw ... 109
Avondale Ave. Stai ... 124
Avondale Rd. Ashf ... 97
Avondale. Maid ...

157
ɤvonway. Newb
Birdhill Ave. Read

ɤnway. Newb 105 E2
ɤridge Rd. Read 86 B1
ɤridge. Brac 118 C2
ɤbridges Ave. Stai 96 B1
ɤsbury Cres. Slough 42 B3
ɤsham Way. Yate 149 D3
ɤsworth Ave. Slough 22 A1
ɤsworth Spur. Old W 95 D4
ɤsham Cl. Read 84 C4
ɤner Cl. Stai 123 F4
ɤner Dr. Stai 123 F4
ɤgarth Park. Holy 40 A1
ɤgarth. Brac 118 A2
ɤlea Way. Camb 152 A3
ɤlea Way. Slough 43 F4
ɤbington Rd. Read 113 E3
ɤchelors Acre. Wind 67 E3
ɤck La. Been 109 D4
ɤck La. Brad 81 F2
ɤck La. Brim 134 B2
ɤck La. Kint 127 F4
ɤck La. Shin 139 D4
ɤck La. Stan D 81 F2
ɤck St. East G 47 E3
ɤcksideans. Warg 36 B1
ɤcon Cl. Sand 150 B3
ɤd Godesberg Way. Maid 39 F4
ɤden Cl. Stai 97 D1
ɤder Gdns. Slough 42 A2
ɤder Way The. Wood 88 A3
ɤdgebury Rise. Mar B 1 B4
ɤdgemore La. Hen-O-T 15 E2
ɤdger Cl. Maid 39 E2
ɤdger Dr. Light 146 A1
ɤdger Dr. Twyf 61 E4
ɤdgers Copse. Camb 151 F2
ɤdgers Croft. Mort 137 D3
ɤdgers Hill. Vir W 122 B2
ɤdgers Holt. Yate 149 D3
ɤdgers Rise. Caver 59 D3
ɤdgers Sett. Crow 142 C3
ɤdgers Way. Brac 118 C4
ɤdgers Way. Mar B 1 B4
ɤdgers Wlk. Shipl 36 A2
ɤdgers Wood. Far C 22 B4
ɤdgerwood Dr. Camb 151 E1
ɤdminton Rd. Maid 39 D3
ɤgnols Way. Newb 104 C1
ɤgshot Green. Bags 145 F2
ɤgshot Rd. Ascot 120 A1
ɤgshot Rd. Brac 118 B2
ɤgshot Rd. Eng G 95 E1
ɤgshot Rd. Sunn 120 A1
ɤgshot Rd. West E 153 F4
ɤgents La. Windl 146 B2
ɤiley Cl. Maid 39 F4
ɤiley Cl. Wind 67 D3
ɤiley's La. Hurst 62 C2
ɤileys Cl. Black 150 B2
ɤily Ave. That 106 A2
ɤin Ave. Camb 151 D1
ɤinbridge Rd. Bur C 84 A2
ɤird Cl. Slough 42 A2
ɤird Rd. Arbo 140 C4
ɤird Rd. Bark 140 C4
ɤkeham La. Eng G 95 E1
ɤker St. Ast T 12 C4
ɤker St. Read 85 F4
ɤkers La. Maid 38 C4
ɤldwin Rd. Burn 21 E1
ɤldwin's Shore. Eton 67 E4
ɤlfour Cres. Brac 118 A2
ɤlfour Cres. Newb 130 B3
ɤlfour Dr. Bur C 84 A2
ɤlfour Rd. Mar 1 B2
ɤlintore Ct. Sand 150 B4
ɤll Pit Rd. Beed 30 A3
ɤll Pit Rd. East I 30 A3
ɤllamore Cl. Bur C 84 A2
ɤllard Green. Wind 66 C4
ɤllard Rd. Camb 152 A4
ɤllencrief Rd. Sunn 120 C1
ɤlliol Rd. Caver 58 B2
ɤlliol Way. Crow 143 F1
ɤlmoral Cl. Slough 41 F4
ɤlmoral Gdns. Wind 67 E2
ɤlmoral. Maid 19 D1
ɤlmore Dr. Caver 59 D2
ɤmburgh Cl. Read 86 B2
ɤmford Pl. Bur C 84 A2
ɤnbury Ave. Slough 41 F4
ɤnbury Gdns. Caver 59 E2
ɤnbury. Brac 118 C1
ɤncroft Cl. Ashf 98 A2
ɤncroft Pl. Bur C 84 A2
ɤnd La. Eng G 96 A2
ɤngors Cl. Iver 44 C4
ɤngors Rd S. Iver 44 C4
ɤnk Side. Woki 141 F3
ɤnks Spur. Slough 42 A2
ɤnkside Cl. Read 86 B1
ɤnnard Rd. Maid 39 D3
ɤnnister Cl. Slough 43 F2
ɤnnister Gdns. Yate 149 F3
ɤnnister Pl. Brim 133 F3
ɤnnister Rd. Bur C 110 C1
ɤrbara Cl. Shepp 125 D2
ɤrbara's Meadow. Sulh 57 D1
Barber Cl. Hurst 88 C4
Barberry Way. Black 150 C1
Barbon Cl. Camb 152 B2
Barbrook Cl. Read 57 E2
Barchester Rd. Slough 43 F2
Barclay Rd. Bur C 84 B2
Barclose Ave. Caver 59 E2
Bardney Cl. Maid 39 E2
Bardolph's Cl. Maple 58 B4
Bardown. Chiev 51 D1
Barfield Rd. That 106 A2
Barge La. Swal 139 D3
Bargeman Rd. Maid 39 F2
Bargeman Rd. Maid 39 F3
Barholm Cl. Winn 87 F1
Barkby. Read 87 E1
Barker Ct. Hurst 88 C4
Barker Green. Brac 118 A2
Barker Rd. Chert 123 F1
Barkham Rd. Bark 115 E2
Barkham Rd. Woki 115 E2
Barkham Ride. Bark 141 F4
Barkham Ride. Woki 141 F4
Barkham St. Bark 115 E1
Barkhart Dr. Woki 116 B4
Barkhart Gdns. Woki 116 B4
Barkwith Cl. Winn 87 F1
Barley Cl. That 106 C1
Barley Fields. Woo G 3 F4
Barley Mead. New G 91 F1
Barley Mow Rd. Eng G 95 E2
Barley Mow Way. Stai 125 D3
Barley Wlk. Read 84 A3
Barn Cl. Ashf 98 A2
Barn Cl. Brac 118 B4
Barn Cl. Camb 151 F3
Barn Cl. Far C 22 A4
Barn Cl. Kint 102 A1
Barn Cl. Maid 19 F1
Barn Cl. Read 85 E2
Barn Cres. Newb 130 B4
Barn Dr. Maid 39 D2
Barn La. Hen-O-T 15 E2
Barn Owl Way. Bur C 111 D2
Barnard Cl. Caver 59 E3
Barnards Hill. Mar 1 B1
Barnes Rd. Camb 151 F1
Barnes Way. Iver 44 C3
Barnett Green. Brac 118 A2
Barnett La. Camb 152 C4
Barnfield. Iver 44 C4
Barnfield. Slough 41 E3
Barnhill Cl. Mar 1 B2
Barnhill Gdns. Mar 1 B2
Barnhill Rd. Mar 1 B2
Barnsdale Rd. Read 86 B2
Barnway. Eng G 95 E2
Barnwood Cl. Read 85 F4
Baron Ct. Read 85 F4
Barons Mead. Hen-O-T 15 E1
Barons Way. Stai 96 B1
Barossa Rd. Camb 151 E4
Barr's Rd. Burn 41 D4
Barracane Dr. Crow 143 D3
Barrack La. Wind 67 E3
Barracks La. Shin 113 D1
Barrett Cres. Woki 116 C3
Barrington Cl. Read 87 D3
Barris Head. Crow 143 F1
Barry Ave. Wind 67 E4
Barry Pl. Read 86 A4
Bartelotts Rd. Slough 21 F1
Bartholemew Pl. New G 91 F1
Bartholemew St. Newb 104 C1
Bartlemy Cl. Newb 130 C4
Bartlemy Rd. Newb 130 C4
Barton Cl. Shepp 125 D2
Barton Rd. Read 84 A4
Barton Rd. Slough 43 F2
Bartons Dr. Yate 149 E2
Barwell Cl. Crow 142 C2
Basemoors. Brac 118 C4
Basford Way. Wind 66 B2
Basil Cl. Read 86 C1
Basingstoke Rd. Alde 109 D1
Basingstoke Rd. Read 86 A2
Basingstoke Rd. Shin 139 E3
Basingstoke Rd. Swal 139 E3
Baskerville La. Shipl 36 A2
Baslow Rd. Winn 88 A1
Basmore Ave. Shipl 36 A2
Bass Mead. Cook 19 F3
Bassett Cl. Winn 114 B4
Bassett Rd. Let B 6 C4
Bassett Way. Slough 21 F1
Batcombe Mead. Brac 118 C1
Bates Cl. Slough 43 F4
Bath Rd. Been 108 B1
Bath Rd. Brad 108 B1
Bath Rd. Bur G 38 B3
Bath Rd. Burn 41 E4
Bath Rd. Camb 151 E3
Bath Rd. Frox 99 D2
Bath Rd. Harl 71 E3
Bath Rd. Harm 70 B3
Bath Rd. Hung 100 C4
Bath Rd. Know H 38 B3
Bath Rd. Maid 38 B3
Bath Rd. Newb 104 B3
Bath Rd. Padw 108 B1
Bath Rd. Read 85 E3
Bath Rd. Slough 41 E4
Bath Rd. Sonn 60 C1
Bath Rd. That 108 B1
Bath Rd. Thea 108 B1
Bath Rd. Warg 62 A4
Bath Rd. Wool 108 B1
Bathurst Cl. Iver 44 C2
Bathurst Rd. Winn 88 A1
Bathurst Wlk. Iver 44 C2
Battery End. Newb 130 B3
Battle Cl. Newb 104 B2
Battle Rd. Gori 34 C4
Battle Rd. Newb 130 B3
Battle St. Read 85 F4
Battlemead Cl. Maid 20 B2
Batty's Barn Cl. Woki 116 B3
Baxendales The. Newb 105 E1
Bay Cl. Read 86 C1
Bay Dr. Brac 118 C4
Bay Rd. Brac 118 C4
Bay Tree Ct. Burn 21 E1
Bay Tree Rise. Read 84 B3
Baydon Dr. Read 85 F3
Baydon Rd. East G 46 B2
Baydon Rd. Gr She 46 B2
Baydon Rd. Lamb 46 B2
Bayfield Ave. Camb 151 F1
Bayford Cl. Camb 151 D1
Bayford Dr. Read 84 C2
Bayley Cres. Burn 41 D4
Bayley Ct. Winn 88 A1
Baylis Rd. Slough 42 C3
Bayliss Rd. Warg 36 B1
Baysfarm Ct. Harm 70 B3
Beacon Rd. Felt 71 D1
Beaconsfield Rd. Far C 22 B3
Beaconsfield Way. Read 87 D1
Beal's La. Sulh 84 A4
Beale Cl. Woki 116 A4
Bean Oak Rd. Woki 116 C3
Beancroft Rd. That 106 B1
Bear La. Newb 105 D2
Bear La. Warg 37 D2
Beard's Rd. Ashf 98 C1
Bearwood Path. Winn 88 A1
Bearwood Rd. Woki 115 E3
Beatty Dr. Read 84 C4
Beauchief Cl. Read 113 F4
Beaufield Cl. Wood 87 E4
Beaufort Cl. Mar 1 C1
Beaufort Gdns. Ascot 119 F4
Beaufort Gdns. Mar 1 C1
Beaufort Pl. Maid 40 B2
Beauforts. Eng G 95 E2
Beaufront Cl. Camb 152 A4
Beaufront Rd. Camb 152 A4
Beaulieu Cl. Brac 119 D3
Beaulieu Cl. Datch 68 A3
Beaulieu Gdns. Sand 150 B3
Beaumont Cl. Maid 39 D2
Beaumont Dr. Ashf 98 B2
Beaumont Gdns. Brac 118 C2
Beaumont Rd. Slough 42 B4
Beaumont Rd. Wind 67 E3
Beaumont Rise. Mar 1 C1
Beaver La. Yate 149 F3
Beaver Way. Wood 88 A4
Beavers Cl. Tad 135 D1
Becket Cl. Woki 116 C3
Beckford Ave. Brac 118 A2
Beckford Cl. Woki 88 C1
Beckfords. Upp B 55 D3
Beckings Way. Fla H 3 E4
Bede Wlk. Read 86 B2
Bedfont Cl. Felt 71 E1
Bedfont Ct. Stan 70 A2
Bedfont La. Felt 98 C4
Bedfont Rd. Felt 98 B3
Bedfont Rd. Stan 70 C1
Bedford Ave. Slough 42 A4
Bedford Cl. Maid 39 D2
Bedford Cl. Newb 130 B3
Bedford Dr. Far C 22 A3
Bedford Gdns. Woki 115 F4
Bedford La. Sunn 121 D2
Bedford Rd. Read 85 F4
Bedfordshire Way. Woki 115 F3
Bedwins La. Cook 19 D3
Beech Ave. Camb 151 E2
Beech Cl. Ashf 98 B2
Beech Cl. Bur C 111 D2
Beech Cl. Stan 97 E4
Beech Dr. Black 150 B2
Beech Glen. Brac 118 A3
Beech Hill Rd. Bee H 138 C3
Beech Hill Rd. Sunn 120 C2
Beech La. Gori 14 C1
Beech La. Read 87 D1
Beech Rd. Felt 98 C4
Beech Rd. Maple 58 B4
Beech Rd. Newt 132 A2
Beech Rd. Pur O T 57 D3
Beech Rd. Read 86 C1
Beech Rd. Slough 43 F2
Beech Ride. Sand 143 D1
Beech Tree La. Stai 124 A4
Beech Wlk. That 106 C1
Beecham Rd. Read 85 E4
Beechbrook Ave. Yate 149 F3
Beechcroft Cl. Ascot 120 B3
Beechcroft. Brac 118 A3
Beechcroft. Hamp N 53 D3
Beeches Dr. Far C 22 A4
Beeches Rd. Far C 22 A4
Beeches The. Gori 34 A3
Beeches The. Read 57 E2
Beechingstoke. Mar 1 C2
Beechmont Ave. Went 122 B2
Beechnut Cl. Woki 115 F3
Beechnut Dr. Black 150 A3
Beechtree Ave. Eng G 95 D1
Beechtree Ave. Mar B 1 B3
Beechwood Ave. Read 84 B4
Beechwood Ave. Stai 97 D1
Beechwood Ave. Wood 87 E4
Beechwood Cl. Burl 92 C1
Beechwood Dr. Maid 39 D3
Beechwood Dr. Mar 18 A4
Beechwood Gdns. Slough 42 C2
Beechwood Rd. Slough 42 B4
Beechwood Rd. Went 122 A1
Beedon Dr. Brac 117 F2
Beehive La. Brac 117 E4
Beehive Rd. Brac 117 E4
Beehive Rd. Stai 96 C2
Beeston Way. Read 114 A4
Beggars Hill Rd. Char 61 D1
Beighton Cl. Read 113 F4
Beir Path The. Sou S 14 A2
Belfast Ave. Slough 42 B4
Belgrave Ct. Black 150 B2
Belgrave Rd. Slough 42 C3
Bell Cl. Slough 43 D4
Bell Corner. Chert 123 F1
Bell Ct. Hurl 17 F2
Bell Foundary La. Woki 116 B4
Bell Foundry La. Woki 116 B4
Bell Hill. Ham M 130 A2
Bell Hill. Newb 130 A2
Bell Holt. Newb 130 B3
Bell La. Comp 32 C2
Bell La. Eton 41 F1
Bell La. Hen-O-T 15 F2
Bell La. Ink 127 E2
Bell La. Sand 150 B3
Bell Pl. Bags 145 F2
Bell St. Hen-O-T 15 F1
Bell St. Maid 39 F3
Bell View Cl. Wind 66 C3
Bell View. Wind 66 C3
Bell Weir Cl. Wray 96 A3
Belle Ave. Read 87 D3
Belle Vue Cl. Stai 124 A4
Belle Vue Rd. Hen-O-T 35 E4
Belle Vue Rd. Read 85 F4
Bellever Hill. Camb 151 F3
Bellingham Cl. Camb 152 B2
Bellingham Wlk. Caver 59 D3
Bells Hill Green. Sto P 23 D3
Bells Hill. Sto P 23 D2
Bells La. Hort 69 D2
Bellswood La. Iver 44 A4
Belmont Cres. Maid 39 E4
Belmont Dr. Maid 39 E4
Belmont Mews. Camb 151 E2
Belmont Park Ave. Maid 39 E4
Belmont Park Rd. Maid 39 E4
Belmont Rd. Camb 151 E2
Belmont Rd. Crow 143 D3
Belmont Rd. Maid 39 E4
Belmont Rd. Read 85 E4
Belmont Vale. Maid 39 E4
Belmont. Slough 42 A4
Belton Rd. Camb 151 F3
Belvedere Ct. Black 150 B2
Belvedere Dr. Newb 131 D4
Belvedere Wlk. Winn 88 A2
Belvoir Cl. Camb 151 F1
Bembridge Ct. Slough 42 C2
Bembridge Pl. Read 86 B4
Benbricke Green. Brac 91 D1
Bence The. Stai 123 D3
Bencombe Rd. Mar B 1 C3
Benedict Dr. Felt 98 B4
Benedict Green. New G 91 F1
Benen-stock Rd. Stan 70 A1
Benetfeld Rd. Binf 90 A1
Benham Hill. Newb 105 F2
Benham Hill. That 105 F2
Benham La. Swal 139 E2
Benhams La. Faw (Bu) 15 F4
Benner La. West E 153 F4
Bennet Rd. Read 86 A1
Bennett Cl. Newb 104 C3
Bennett Ct. Camb 151 E3
Bennett's Hill. Bur C 111 E4
Bennetts Cl. Slough 42 A3
Benning Cl. Wind 66 B2
Benning Way. Woki 116 B4
Bennings Cl. Brac 91 D1
Benson Cl. Read 86 B2
Benson Cl. Slough 43 D3
Benson Rd. Crow 142 C3
Bentley Park. Burn 21 E2
Bentley Rd. Slough 42 A3
Benyon Ct. Read 85 F3
Benyon Mews. Read 85 F3
Beomonds Row. Chert 124 A1
Bere Court Rd. Pangb 56 A2
Bere Rd. Brac 118 C2
Beresford Ave. Slough 43 E3
Beresford Rd. Read 85 F4
Bergenia Ct. Camb 153 F3
Berkeley Ave. Read 85 F3
Berkeley Cl. Stan 96 B3
Berkeley Gdns. Shepp 125 F1
Berkeley Mews. Mar 1 C1
Berkeley Rd. Newb 104 C1
Berkley Cl. Maid 39 D4
Berkshire Ave. Slough 42 A4
Berkshire Dr. Read 84 B4
Berkshire Rd. Camb 151 F4
Berkshire Rd. Hen-O-T 35 E4
Berkshire Way. Brac 117 E3
Berners Cl. Slough 41 F3
Bernersh Cl. Sand 143 E1
Berries Rd. Cook 20 A4
Berry Field. Slough 43 E4
Berry Hill. Tapl 40 B4
Berrybank. Sand 150 C3
Berrylands Rd. Caver 59 D2
Berrys La. Bur C 85 D1
Berrys Rd. Buck 107 E3
Berryscroft Rd. Stai 97 E1
Berstead Cl. Read 87 D1
Berwick Ave. Slough 42 A3
Berwick Cl. Mar 1 B2
Berwick La. Mar 1 B2
Berwick Rd. Mar 1 B2
Beryl Cl. Woki 115 F4
Bessel's Way. Blew 12 A4
Bestobell Rd. Slough 42 B4
Betam Rd. Read 86 B4
Betchworth Ave. Read 87 D2
Bethany Waye. Felt 98 C4
Bethesda Cl. Upp B 55 D3
Bethesda St. Upp B 55 D4
Betjeman Wlk. Yate 149 D2
Betteridge Rd. That 106 C1
Beverley Cl. Camb 152 B3
Beverley Cl. Mar 1 B1
Beverley Cl. That 106 B2
Beverley Ct. Slough 43 D2
Beverley Gdns. Maid 19 D1
Beverley Gdns. Warg 36 C1
Beverley Rd. Read 57 E1
Beverley Rd. Shepp 125 F4
Bevers The. Mort 137 D3
Bexley Ct. Read 85 E3
Bexley St. Wind 67 E3
Bibury Cl. Wood 87 E2
Bicknell Rd. Camb 151 F1
Bideford Cl. Wood 87 E3
Bideford Spur. Slough 22 A1
Big La. Lamb 25 D2
Bigbury Gdns. Read 86 B2
Bigfrith La. Cook 19 D3
Biggs La. Bark 141 D4
Billet Bridge. Stai 97 D2
Billet La. Slough 44 A4
Billet Rd. Stan 97 D3
Billing Ave. Woki 141 F3
Billingbear La. Binf 90 A3
Billington Way. Cold A 106 B3
Binbrook Cl. Winn 87 E1
Binfield Rd. Binf 116 C4
Binfield Rd. Brac 118 A4
Binfield Rd. Woki 116 C4
Bingham Dr. Stai 97 E1
Bingham Rd. Burn 41 D4
Binghams The. Maid 40 A2
Bingley Gr. Wood 60 C1
Binsted Dr. Black 150 B3
Birch Ave. Read 85 D4
Birch Cl. Camb 151 F4
Birch Dr. Black 150 B2
Birch Gr. Shepp 125 F4
Birch Gr. Slough 42 A4
Birch Gr. Wind 66 B3
Birch Hill Rd. Brac 118 A1
Birch La. Burl 119 D4
Birch La. Silc 136 C3
Birch La. West E 153 E3
Birch Platt. West E 153 E3
Birch Rd. Bur C 111 D2
Birch Rd. Tad 134 C1
Birch Rd. Windl 146 C2
Birch Rd. Woki 142 A4
Birch Side. Crow 142 C3
Birch Tree View. Light 146 A1
Birch View. Read 86 C1
Birches The. Black 150 A3
Birches The. Gori 34 A3
Birchetts Cl. Brac 118 A4
Birchfields. Camb 151 E2
Birchington Rd. Wind 67 D3
Birchland Cl. Silc 136 C3
Birchmead. Winn 88 B1
Birchview Cl. Yate 149 E2
Birchwood Cl. Caver 59 E3
Birchwood Dr. Light 146 B1
Birchwood Rd. Newb 105 E2
Birchwood The. Read 57 D3
Bird Mews. Woki 116 A3
Birdhill Ave. Read 86 B1

Birds La. Wool

Birds La. Wool 107 F2
Birdwood Rd. Maid 39 D4
Birdwood Rd. Sand 151 D4
Birkbeck Rd. Crow 143 F1
Birkdale. Brac 117 F1
Birkhall Cl. Read 84 B3
Birley Rd. Slough 42 B4
Bishop Ct. Maid 39 E3
Bishop Duppas Park. Shepp .125 F1
Bishop's La. New G 92 A4
Bishop's La. Wink 92 A4
Bishop's Rd. Read 87 D3
Bishopdale. Brac 118 A3
Bishops Cl. Tad 135 D1
Bishops Dr. Felt 71 E1
Bishops Dr. Woki 116 B4
Bishops Farm Cl. Oak G 66 A3
Bishops Gr. Windl 146 B2
Bishops Orch. Far C 22 A1
Bishops Rd. Brad 81 F2
Bishops Rd. Slough 43 D2
Bishops Way. Stai 96 B1
Bishops Wlk. Bou E 3 F3
Bishopsgate Rd. Eng G 95 D2
Bishopswood La. Tad 134 C1
Bishopswood Rd. Tad 134 C1
Bissley Dr. Maid 39 D2
Bitham La. Ham 126 B3
Bitham La. Ink 127 D2
Bitham Rd. Farm 8 B4
Bittern Cl. Sand 150 B4
Bitterne Ave. Read 84 A3
Bix Hill. Faw (Bu) 15 D3
Bix La. Maid 38 C4
Black Boy La. Hurl 17 E2
Black Butts Cotts. Cook 20 A4
Black Horse Cl. Wind 66 B3
Black Park Rd. Fulm 23 F2
Black Park Rd. Iver H 23 F2
Blackamoor La. Maid 40 A4
Blackberry Cl. Shepp 125 F3
Blackbird Cl. Bur C 111 D2
Blackbird Cl. Sand 150 B4
Blackcap Pl. Sand 150 C4
Blackdown Way. That 106 B1
Blackett Cl. Stai 123 F4
Blacklands Rd. Buck 107 E3
Blackley Cl. Winn 87 F2
Blackmeadows. Brac 118 B2
Blackmoor Cl. Burl 119 E4
Blackmoor Wood. Burl 119 E4
Blacknest Rd. Went 121 D2
Blackpond La. Far C 22 A2
Blacksmith Row. Slough 44 A1
Blacksmith's La. Stai 124 B3
Blacksmiths La. Twyf 124 B3
Blackstroud La E. Light 146 B1
Blackstroud La W. Light 153 E4
Blackthorn Dell. Slough 43 E2
Blackthorn Dr. Light 153 D4
Blackthorne Rd. Stan 69 F2
Blackwater Cl. Caver 59 F2
Blackwater Cl. Shin 113 D1
Blackwater Rise. Bur C 84 A2
Blagdon Rd. Read 86 B1
Blagrave La. Caver 58 B2
Blagrave St. Read 86 A4
Blagrove Rise. Read 84 B3
Blagrove La. Woki 115 F2
Blagrove La. Woki 115 F2
Blair Rd. Slough 42 C3
Blaire Park. Yate 149 D4
Blake Cl. Crow 143 E2
Blake Cl. Woki 116 C4
Blake's La. Tad 135 D3
Blakeney Fields. Gr She 48 A2
Blakes Cotts. Read 86 B4
Blakes La. Warg 37 D1
Blakes Rd. Warg 36 C2
Blakes Ride. Yate 149 D3
Blanchard Cl. Wood 88 A4
Bland's Cl. Bur C 110 C1
Blandford Cl. Slough 43 E2
Blandford Rd N. Slough 43 E2
Blandford Rd S. Slough 43 E2
Blandford Rd. Read 113 E4
Blandy Rd. Hen-O-T 35 E4
Blandy's La. Upp B 55 D3
Blandys Hill. Kint 128 A4
Blatch's Cl. Thea 83 E2
Blay's La. Eng G 95 D1
Blays Cl. Eng G 95 E1
Bledlow Cl. Newb 130 B3
Blenheim Cl. Slough 43 F3
Blenheim Cl. Woki 115 F3
Blenheim Gdns. Read 86 C3
Blenheim Rd. Caver 59 D2
Blenheim Rd. Maid 39 D4
Blenheim Rd. Newb 104 C1
Blenheim Rd. Read 86 C3
Blenheim Rd. Slough 43 E2
Bletchmore Cl. Harl 71 E4
Blewburton Wlk. Brac 118 C3
Blewbury Dr. Read 84 A4
Blewbury Hill. Blew 12 B4
Blinco La. Slough 43 F4
Blind La. Bou E 3 D3
Blind La. Fa H 3 D3
Blind La. Lamb 25 D1

Blomfield Dale. Brac 117 E4
Blomfield Dr. Brac 91 E1
Blondell Cl. Harm 70 B4
Bloomfield Rd. Maid 39 D3
Bloomfieldhatch La. Bee H .138 A4
Bloomfieldhatch La. Shin 112 C2
Bloomsbury Way. Black 150 B2
Blossom Ave. Thea 83 F2
Blossom La. Thea 83 F2
Bloxworth Cl. Brac 118 C3
Blue Ball La. Eng G 95 E2
Blue Coat Wlk. Brac 118 B2
Bluebell Dr. Bur C 110 C2
Bluebell Hill. Brac 118 C4
Bluebell Meadow. Winn 88 B2
Bluebell Rise. Light 153 D4
Bluecoats. That 106 B2
Bluethroat Cl. Sand 150 C4
Blumfield Cres. Burn 41 F4
Blumfield Ct. Slough 21 E1
Blundell's Rd. Read 84 C4
Blunts Ave. Harm 71 D4
Blyth Ave. That 106 C1
Blythe Cl. Iver 44 C4
Blythewood La. Ascot 119 F4
Blythwood Dr. Camb 151 E1
Boames La. Ham M 129 F3
Boarlands Cl. Slough 41 F3
Boathouse Reach. Hen-O-T ..15 F1
Bobgreen Ct. Read 113 E4
Bobmore La. Mar 1 C2
Bockhampton Rd. Lamb 25 E1
Bockmer La. Medm 17 D4
Bodens Ride. Brac 119 F1
Bodmin Ave. Slough 42 A4
Bodmin Cl. That 106 B1
Bodmin Rd. Wood 87 E3
Body Rd. Read 85 F4
Bog La. Brac 119 D3
Boham's Rd. Blew 11 E3
Bolding House La. West E ...153 F4
Boldrewood. Bur C 110 C1
Boleyn Cl. Stai 96 C2
Bolingbroke Way. That 106 C2
Bolney Rd. Shipl 36 A3
Bolton Ave. Wind 67 E2
Bolton Cres. Wind 67 E2
Bolton Rd. Wind 67 E2
Bolton's La. Harl 71 E4
Bolwell Cl. Twyf 61 F2
Bomer Cl. Harm 71 D4
Bomford Cl. Herm 78 C3
Bond St. Eng G 95 E2
Bone La. Newb 105 E2
Bones La. Shipl 35 D2
Booth Dr. Stai 97 E1
Borderside. Slough 43 D4
Borderside. Yate 149 D3
Borrowdale Cl. Stai 96 A1
Borrowdale Gdns. Camb 152 B2
Borrowdale Rd. Winn 88 A2
Boscombe Cl. Stai 123 E4
Boscowen Way. That 107 D1
Bosham Cl. Read 114 A4
Bosman Dr. Windl 146 A3
Bostock La. Thea 83 D1
Boston Ave. Read 85 F3
Boston Gr. Slough 42 B4
Boston Rd. Hen-O-T 35 F4
Bosworth Gdns. Wood 87 F2
Botany Cl. That 106 C2
Bothy The. Warg 36 B1
Botmoor Way. Chadd 48 C4
Bottisham Cl. Winn 114 B4
Bottle La. Binf 91 D3
Bottle La. Know H 38 A2
Bottle La. New G 91 D3
Bottom La. Sulhd 110 B4
Bouldish Farm Rd. Ascot 119 F3
Boult St. Read 86 B4
Boult's Wlk. Read 86 A3
Boulters Cl. Maid 20 B1
Boulters Cl. Slough 42 A2
Boulters Ct. Maid 20 B1
Boulters Ct. Wood 87 D3
Boulters Gdns. Maid 20 B1
Boulters La. Maid 20 B1
Boulton Rd. Read 86 A2
Boultons La. Binf 90 C1
Boundary Cl. Read 84 B3
Boundary La. Caver 58 C2
Boundary Pl. Woo G 3 E4
Boundary Rd. Newb 105 D1
Boundary Rd. Stai 97 E2
Boundary Rd. Tapl 40 C4
Boundary Rd. Woo G 3 E4
Bourn Cl. Winn 87 E1
Bourne Arch. That 106 A2
Bourne Ave. Chert 124 A3
Bourne Ave. Read 86 C4
Bourne Ave. Wind 67 E2
Bourne Cl. Bou E 3 D3
Bourne Cl. Bur C 84 A2
Bourne End Rd. Bou E 20 C4
Bourne End Rd. Tapl 20 C4
Bourne Meadow. Stai 123 D3
Bourne Rd. Pangb 56 C3
Bourne Rd. Slough 42 B2
Bourne Rd. That 106 A2

Bourne Rd. Went 122 B2
Bourne Vale. Hung 100 B3
Bourneside. Went 122 A1
Bourton Cl. Read 84 C4
Bouverie Way. Slough 43 F1
Boveney Cl. Slough 42 A2
Boveney New Rd. Eton 41 F1
Boveney Rd. Dorn 41 E1
Bovingdon Hts. Mar 1 C1
Bowden Cl. Felt 98 C4
Bowden Rd. Ascot 120 B2
Bower Way. Slough 41 F3
Bowes Rd. Stai 96 C1
Bowes Rd. That 106 B1
Bowfell Cl. Read 57 E1
Bowland Drive. Brac 118 A2
Bowling Ct. Hen-O-T 15 E2
Bowling Green La. Pur O T ...57 D3
Bowling Green Rd. That 106 A3
Bowman Ct. Woki 142 C2
Bowmans Cl. Burn 41 F1
Bowry Dr. Wray 68 C1
Bowyer Cres. Woki 116 B4
Bowyer Dr. Slough 41 F3
Bowyer's La. New G 91 E3
Boxford Ridge. Brac 118 A3
Boyd Ct. Brac 118 A4
Boyn Hill Ave. Maid 39 E3
Boyn Hill Cl. Maid 39 E3
Boyn Hill Rd. Maid 39 E3
Boyn Valley Rd. Maid 39 E3
Boyne Dene. Maid 39 E4
Bracebridge. Camb 151 D3
Bracken Bank. Burl 119 E4
Bracken Cl. Far C 22 B4
Bracken Cl. Read 57 E1
Bracken La. Yate 149 D3
Bracken Rd. Maid 39 E2
Bracken Way. Bur C 111 D1
Bracken Way. Fla H 3 D4
Brackendale Cl. Camb 151 F2
Brackendale Rd. Camb 151 E2
Brackenforde. Slough 43 E2
Brackens The. Brac 143 D4
Brackenwood Dr. Tad 135 D1
Brackenwood. Bur C 110 C1
Brackenwood. Camb 152 B3
Bracknell Beeches. Brac 118 A3
Bracknell Cl. Camb 144 C1
Bracknell Rd. Bags 145 F3
Bracknell Rd. Brac 143 F4
Bracknell Rd. Camb 145 D1
Bracknell Rd. New G 91 F2
Bracknell Rd. Warf 92 A3
Bracknell Rd. Wink 92 A3
Bradcutts La. Cook 19 F4
Bradenham La. Bish 18 B3
Bradfields. Brac 118 B2
Bradford Rd. Slough 42 A4
Brading Way. Pur O T 57 E3
Bradley Cl. Kint 102 A1
Bradley Rd. Slough 42 C3
Bradmore Way. Read 114 A4
Bradshaw Cl. Wind 66 C3
Bradwell Rd. Read 57 E2
Braemar Gdns. Slough 42 A2
Braemore Cl. That 106 B1
Brakendale Way. Read 87 D3
Bramber Cl. Slough 42 A3
Bramber Mews. Caver 59 F2
Bramble Cl. Shepp 125 E3
Bramble Cres. Read 84 C4
Bramble Dr. Maid 39 D1
Brambledown. Stai 124 A4
Bramblegate. Crow 143 D3
Brambles The. Brac 142 B3
Bramcote. Camb 152 B3
Bramley Cl. Chert 124 A1
Bramley Cl. Maid 39 E2
Bramley Cl. That 87 D2
Bramley Cl. Stai 97 E1
Bramley Gr. Brac 142 B3
Bramley Rd. Camb 151 A3
Bramley Rd. Silc 135 D1
Bramley Silc 136 A1
Bramling Ave. Yate 149 D3
Brammas Cl. Slough 42 B2
Brampton Chase. Shipl 36 A2
Bramshaw Rd. Read 58 A1
Bramshill Cl. Arbo 140 C4
Bramwell Cl. That 106 C1
Bran Cl. Read 84 C4
Brandon Ave. Wood 88 A4
Brandon Cl. Camb 152 B2
Brands Rd. Slough 69 D4
Branksome Cl. Camb 151 F3
Branksome Hill Rd. Sand 150 C4
Branksome Park Rd. Camb .151 F3
Brants Bridge. Brac 118 C3
Brants Wlk. Newb 104 C1
Bravington Cl. Stai 124 C2
Bray Cl. Maid 40 B2
Bray Cl. Holy 40 A3
Bray Rd. Maid 40 A3
Bray Rd. Read 57 D2
Braybank. Maid 40 B2
Braybrooke Gdns. Warg 36 B1
Braybrooke Rd. Brac 91 D1
Braybrooke Rd. Warg 36 B1

Braye Cl. Sand 143 E1
Brayfield Rd. Maid 40 B2
Brayford Rd. Read 113 E4
Braywick Rd. Maid 40 A3
Braywood Ave. Eng G 96 A1
Braziers La. Wink 92 B2
Breach Sq. Hung 100 B2
Breadcroft La. Bur G 38 C2
Breadcroft Rd. Whi Wa 38 C2
Bream Cl. Mar 18 B4
Brecon Rd. Wood 87 F4
Bredon Rd. Woki 88 C1
Bredward Cl. Burn 21 D1
Breech The. Sand 150 B4
Breedons Hill. Pangb 56 B3
Bremer Rd. Stan 97 D3
Brendon Cl. Harl 71 E4
Brendon Cl. Read 57 F1
Brent Cl. That 106 B1
Brent Gdns. Read 86 A2
Brent Rd. Bou E 3 D2
Brentmoor Rd. West E 153 E3
Brerewood. Read 86 C1
Bret Harte Rd. Camb 151 F1
Brendon Cl. Read 137 D4
Brewhouse Hill. Froxf 99 D2
Briant's Ave. Caver 59 E1
Briants Piece. Herm 79 D3
Briar Ave. Light 153 D4
Briar Cl. Burn 41 D4
Briar Cl. Caver 59 D3
Briar Dene. Maid 19 E1
Briar Glen. Cook 19 F3
Briar Rd. Stai 125 D2
Briar Way. Slough 42 A4
Briarlea Rd. Mort 136 C3
Briars Cl. Pangb 56 C3
Briars The. Slough 43 F1
Briars The. Stan 70 A1
Briarwood Cl. Felt 98 C3
Briarwood. Woki 141 F3
Brickfield La. Burn 21 D2
Brickfield La. Harl 71 E4
Bridge Ave. Cook 19 F3
Bridge Cl. Shepp 125 F1
Bridge Cl. Slough 41 F3
Bridge Cl. Stai 96 C2
Bridge End. Camb 151 D2
Bridge Gdns. Stai 98 B1
Bridge La. Went 122 C2
Bridge Rd. Ascot 120 B2
Bridge Rd. Bags 145 F2
Bridge Rd. Camb 151 D2
Bridge Rd. Chert 124 A1
Bridge Rd. Maid 40 A4
Bridge St. Caver 59 D1
Bridge St. Hung 100 B3
Bridge St. Iver 69 E4
Bridge St. Maid 40 A4
Bridge St. Newb 105 D2
Bridge St. Read 86 A4
Bridge St. Shepp 125 F1
Bridge St. Stai 96 C2
Bridge View. Went 121 D1
Bridge Wlk. Yate 149 E4
Bridgeman Dr. Wind 67 D3
Bridges Cl. Woki 115 F4
Bridges The. Silc 136 B3
Bridgestone Dr. Bou E 3 E2
Bridgewater Cl. Read 58 B1
Bridgewater Ct. Slough 44 A1
Bridgewater Terr. Wind 67 E3
Bridgewater Way. Wind 67 E3
Bridle Cl. Maid 19 F1
Bridle Rd. Maid 19 F1
Bridlepath Way. Felt 98 C4
Bridlington Spur. Slough 42 A2
Bridport Cl. Read 87 E1
Bridport Way. Slough 22 A1
Brierley Pl. Pur O T 57 E2
Briff La. Buck 107 E4
Brigham Rd. Read 59 D1
Brighton Rd. Read 87 D3
Brighton Spur. Slough 22 A1
Brightside Ave. Stai 97 E1
Brill Cl. Caver 59 D2
Brill Cl. Mar 1 B1
Brimblecombe Cl. Woki 89 D1
Brimpton Rd. Brim 133 F4
Brimpton Rd. Read 85 D2
Brimpton Rd. Tad 134 B1
Brind Cl. Wood 88 B4
Brinn's La. Sand 150 B3
Brisbane Rd. Read 85 D4
Bristol Cl. Stan 70 C1
Bristol Way. Slough 42 C3
Bristow Cres. Camb 151 E2
Bristow Ct. Mar 2 A2
Bristow Rd. Camb 151 E2
Britannia Way. Stan 97 E4
Britten Rd. Read 86 A3
Britwell Rd. Burn 21 D1
Brixham Rd. Read 86 A1
Broad Hinton. Twyf 61 F2
Broad La. Bou E 3 F3
Broad La. Brac 118 B3
Broad La. Buck 107 E3
Broad Oak Ct. Slough 22 B1

Broad Oak. Slough 22
Broad Platts. Slough 43
Broad St. East I 30
Broad St. Read 86
Broad St. West E 153
Broad St. Woki 116
Broad Street Mall The. Read ...86
Broadacre. Stai 97
Broadcommon Rd. Hurst 89
Broadhalfpenny La. Tad 135
Broadlands Ave. Shepp 125
Broadlands Cl. Read 84
Broadlands Dr. Sunn 120
Broadley Green. Windl 146
Broadmark Rd. Slough 43
Broadmeadow End. That 106
Broadmoor La. W St L 63
Broadmoor La. Whi Wa 63
Broadrich Heath. New G 91
Broadwater Cl. Wray 95
Broadwater La. Hurst 61
Broadwater Park. Holy 40
Broadwater Rd. Holy 40
Broadway The. Newb 105
Broadway The. Sand 150
Broadway The. Stai 124
Broadway. Brac 118
Broadway. That 106
Brocas Rd. Bur C 110
Brocas St. Eton 67
Brocas Terr. Eton 67
Brock Gdns. Read 85
Brock La. Maid 39
Brock Way. Vir W 122
Brockenhurst Dr. Yate 149
Brockenhurst Rd. Ascot 120
Brockenhurst Rd. Brac 119
Brocklands. Yate 149
Brockley Cl. Read 85
Brocks La. Buck 80
Brocks Way. Shipl 36
Brocksby Cl. Camb 152
Broken Furlong. Eton 67
Broken Way. Newt 131
Bromley Wlk. Read 85
Brompton Cl. Winn 87
Brompton Dr. Maid 39
Brompton Rd. Slough 22
Brook Cl. Sand 143
Brook Cl. Woki 116
Brook Cres. Slough 41
Brook Dr. Ashf 98
Brook Dr. Brac 118
Brook La. Hurst 61
Brook Path. Slough 41
Brook Path. Slough 41
Brook Rd. Bags 145
Brook Rd. Camb 151
Brook St W. Read 86
Brook St. Read 86
Brook St. Wind 67
Brookbank. Bou E 3
Brookdene Cl. Maid 19
Brooke Pl. Binf 90
Brookers Cnr. Crow 143
Brookers Hill. Read 113
Brookers Row. Crow 143
Brookfield Rd. Bou E 3
Brookhouse Dr. Bou E 3
Brooklands Cl. Stai 123
Brooklyn Dr. Caver 59
Brookmill The. Read 85
Brooks Rd. That 106
Brooksby Rd. Read 57
Brookside Ave. Wray 68
Brookside Cl. Read 87
Brookside. Chert 123
Brookside. Iver 44
Brookside. Read 84
Brookside. Sand 150
Brookside. Woki 115
Broom Acres. Sand 150
Broom Cl. Black 150
Broom Cl. Read 84
Broom Field. Light 153
Broom Gr. Woki 141
Broom Hill. Cook 19
Broom Hill. Sto P 23
Broome Cl. Yate 149
Broomfield Cl. Went 121
Broomfield Park. Went 121
Broomfield Rd. Read 84
Broomfield Rd. Stai 96
Broomhall La. Sunn 120
Broomsquire Rd. Bags 145
Broughton Cl. Read 58
Broughton Cl. Read 58
Brownfields Gdns. Maid 19
Browngraves Rd. Harl 71
Browning Cl. Camb 151
Browning Cl. That 106

wnlow Dr. Brac 91 E1
wnlow Rd. Read 85 F4
wnrig Cres. Brac 118 C4
wnrigg Rd. Ashf 98 A2
wnsfield Rd. That 106 B2
an Rd. Newb 130 C4
ce Ave. Shepp 125 E2
be Cl. Slough 42 A3
ce Rd. Wood 87 E4
ce Wlk. Wind 66 B3
denell. Wind 66 C2
Render Rd. Newb 104 C3
nel Cl. Maid 39 F3
nel Dr. Wood 60 C1
nel Rd. Maid 39 E3
nel Rd. Read 85 D2
nel Rd. Thea 83 F1
nel Way. Slough 42 C3
nswick Hill. Read 85 F4
nswick St. Read 85 F3
nswick. Brac 118 A1
on Way. Brac 118 C1
unt Ave. Slough 42 C4
ants La. Yatt 53 F1
our Cl. Read 113 E4
er Pl. Wind 66 B2
caneer Cl. Wood 88 A4
cleuch Rd. Datch 68 A4
han The. Camb 152 A4
hanan Dr. Woki 141 F4
hurst Cl. Maid 152 B4
hurst Hill. Brac 118 C3
hurst La. Ascot 121 D3
hurst Rd. Ascot 120 C4
hurst Way. Read 87 D2
kden Cl. Wood 88 A3
kham Hill. Chadd 48 B3
khurst Gr. Woki 116 C3
khurst Hill. Brac 118 C3
khurst La. Ascot 121 D3
khurst Rd. Ascot 120 C4
khurst Way. Read 87 D2

Burley Way. Black 150 B3
Burlingham Cl. Read 113 E3
Burlings The. Ascot 119 F4
Burlington Ave. Slough .. 42 C2
Burlington Cl. Felt 98 B4
Burlington Cl. Black 150 B2
Burlington Rd. Burn 41 D4
Burlington Rd. Read 84 B4
Burlington Rd. Slough 42 C2
Burlsdon Way. Woki 118 C4
Burn Moor Chase. Brac . 118 C1
Burn Wlk. Burn 21 D1
Burne-Jones Dr. Sand .. 150 B3
Burnet Cl. Camb 153 F3
Burnetts Rd. Wind 66 C3
Burney Bit. Silc 135 F1
Burnham Cl. Bou E 3 D2
Burnham Cl. Wind 66 B3
Burnham Gr. Brac 91 E1
Burnham La. Slough 41 F4
Burnham Rd. Tad 134 C1
Burnham Rise. Caver 59 E3
Burniston Cl. Winn 87 F1
Burns Cl. Wood 87 F2
Burns Wlk. That 106 B2
Burnt Oak. Cook 19 F4
Burnt Oak. Woki 141 F4
Burnt Pollard La. West E 146 C1
Burnthouse La. Bur C ... 112 A3
Burncroft Rd. Read 85 D3
Burrell Rd. Compe 31 F2
Burroughs Cres. Bou E ... 3 D2
Burroway Rd. Slough 44 A2
Burrows Hill Cl. Stan 70 B2
Burton Cl. Wind 146 B2
Burton Way. Wind 66 C2
Burtons Hill. Kint 102 A1
Burway Cres. Chert 124 A3
Burwell Cl. Winn 87 E1
Burys Bank Rd. Gree 132 A3
Burys Bank Rd. That 132 A3
Bush Rd. Stai 96 C2
Business Centre The. Woki 116 A2
Business Village The. Slough 43 D3
Butchers La. Whi Wa 63 E4
Bute St. Read 85 D3
Butler Cl. Mar 2 A2
Butler Rd. Bags 145 F1
Butler Rd. Crow 143 D3
Butlers Cl. Wind 66 B3
Butson Cl. Newb 104 C2
Buttenshaw Ave. Bark ... 141 D4
Buttenshaw Cl. Bark 141 D4
Butter Market. Read 86 A4
Buttercup Square. Stan ... 97 E4
Butterfield. Bou E 3 D2
Buttermere Ave. Slough .. 43 D4
Buttermere Cl. Felt 98 C4
Buttermere Dr. Camb ... 152 B3
Buttermere Gdns. Brac . 118 B3
Buttermere Way. Stai 96 A1
Buttersteep Rise. Brac . 119 E1
Butts Hill Rd. Wood 87 F4
Buxton Ave. Caver 59 D2
Buxton Rd. Ashf 97 E2
Bybend Cl. Far C 22 A2
Byefield Rd. Read 85 D2
Byeways Cl. Warg 37 F2
Byland Dr. Holy 40 A1
Byreton Cl. Read 87 D1
Byron Ave. Camb 152 A2
Byron Cl. Mar 1 C2
Byron Cl. Newb 130 C4
Byron Cl. Twyf 61 F2
Byron Cl. Yate 149 D2
Byron Dr. Crow 143 D2
Byron Rd. Read 87 D4
Byron Rd. Twyf 61 F2
Bythorn Cl. Winn 87 F1
Byways. Burn 41 D4
Byways. Yate 149 D3
Bywood. Brac 118 A1
Byworth Cl. Read 113 D4

Cabin Moss. Brac 118 C1
Cabrera Ave. Went 122 B3
Cabrera Cl. Went 122 B2
Cadbury Cl. Ashf 98 C1
Cadbury Rd. Ashf 98 C1
Caddy Cl. Eng G 96 B3
Cadogan Cl. Holy 65 D4
Cadogan Cl. Read 84 C4
Cadwell Dr. Maid 39 E2
Caesar's Camp Rd. Camb 152 A4
Caesar's Way. Shepp ... 125 E2
Cages Wood Dr. Far C 22 A4
Cain Rd. Binf 117 F4
Cain Rd. Brac 117 F4
Cain's La. Harm 71 F1
Cairn Cl. Camb 152 A2
Cairngorm Rd. That 106 B1
Caistor Cl. Bur C 84 A2
Calard Dr. That 106 A3
Calbourne Dr. Bur C 84 B2
Calbroke Rd. Slough 21 F1
Calcot Cl. Read 84 C3
Calcot Place Dr. Read 84 C2
Caldbeck Dr. Wood 87 F4
Calder Cl. Maid 19 F1

Calder Cl. Read 84 C4
Calder Ct. Maid 19 E1
Calder Ct. Slough 43 F1
Calder Way. Stan 69 F2
Caldwell Rd. Windl 146 B3
Caledonia Rd. Stan 97 F4
Caleta Cl. Caver 59 E1
Calfridus Way. Brac 118 C3
Calleva Park. Alde 134 C1
Callin's La. W St L 63 D2
Callington Rd. Read 86 B1
Callis Farm Cl. Stan 70 C1
Callow Hill. Vir W 122 B4
Calshot Pl. Bur C 84 B2
Calshot Rd. Harm 71 D3
Calshot Way. Harm 71 D3
Calvin Cl. Camb 152 A2
Camberley Rd. Harm 71 D2
Camborne Cl. Crow 143 D1
Camborne Cl. Harm 71 D2
Camborne Rd S. Harm 71 D2
Camborne Way. Harm 71 D2
Cambria Gdns. Stan 97 F4
Cambrian Cl. Camb 151 D3
Cambrian Way. Brac 142 A4
Cambrian Way. Bur C 84 B2
Cambridge Ave. Burn 21 D2
Cambridge Ave. Slough .. 42 A4
Cambridge Cl. Harm 70 B4
Cambridge Cl. Crow 143 E2
Cambridge Rd. Mar 1 B1
Cambridge Rd. Sand 143 F1
Cambridge Rd. Stai 96 B3
Cambridge Wlk. Camb .. 151 E3
Cambridgeshire Cl. Woki 115 F3
Camden Pl. Bou E 3 D2
Camden Pl. Bur C 84 A2
Camden Rd. Maid 19 E1
Camellia Way. Woki 115 E4
Camilla Cl. Ashf 98 C1
Camley Gdns. Maid 39 D4
Camley Park Dr. Maid 38 C4
Camm Ave. Wind 66 C3
Camp Rd. Padw 110 B1
Campbell Cl. Yate 149 F3
Campbell Pl. Camb 151 F2
Campbell Rd. Wood 87 E3
Campbeltown. Maid 20 A1
Campion Cl. Black 150 C2
Campion Way. Woki 116 C4
Canada Rd. Slough 43 D2
Canal Walk. Hung 100 B3
Canal Way. Read 86 B4
Canal Wharf. Slough 44 A2
Canberra Cl. Yate 149 D4
Canberra Rd. Harm 71 D2
Candleford Cl. Brac 91 E1
Candover Cl. Harm 70 B4
Canford Ct. Read 85 E4
Cannock Cl. Maid 40 A3
Cannock Way. Wood 87 E1
Cannon Cl. Sand 150 C4
Cannon Court Rd. Cook ... 19 E2
Cannon Court Rd. Maid ... 19 E2
Cannon Hill Cl. Maid 40 B1
Cannon Hill. Brac 118 B2
Cannon La. Maid 38 C2
Cannon La. Whi Wa 38 C2
Cannon St. Read 85 F4
Cannondown Rd. Cook ... 19 F3
Canon Hill Dr. Maid 40 B1
Canopus Way. Stan 97 F4
Cansfield End. Newb 104 C2
Canterbury Ave. Slough .. 22 B1
Canterbury Rd. Read 86 B2
Cantley Cres. Woki 116 A4
Capper Rd. Camb 151 D4
Captains Gorse. Upp B ... 54 C3
Caraway Rd. Read 87 D1
Carbery La. Ascot 120 A3
Carbinswood La. Buck .. 108 A3
Cardiff Rd. Read 58 C1
Cardigan Gdns. Read 86 C3
Cardigan Rd. Read 86 C3
Cardinal Cl. Caver 59 F1
Cardinal's Wlk. Ashf 98 C1
Cardinals The. Brac 118 A3
Cardinals Wlk. Slough 41 E4
Cardwell Cres. Ascot ... 120 B2
Carew Rd. Ashf 98 B1
Carey Cl. Wind 67 D2
Carey Rd. Woki 116 B3
Carey St. Read 85 F4
Cares Cl. Caver 34 A4
Carisbrooke Cl. Caver 59 E3
Carisbrooke Cl. Maid 39 E3
Carisbrooke Cl. Slough ... 42 C3
Carland Cl. Read 87 D1
Carlile Gdns. Twyf 61 E1
Carlingwark Dr. Camb .. 151 F4
Carlisle Rd. Read 57 F2
Carlisle Rd. Slough 42 A3
Carlton Cl. Camb 152 A2
Carlton Cl. Wood 87 F3
Carlton Rd. Ashf 98 C1
Carlton Rd. Caver 59 D2
Carlton Rd. Slough 43 D3

Carlyle Rd. Stai 97 D1
Carmarthen Rd. Slough .. 42 C3
Carnarvon Rd. Read 86 C3
Carnation Dr. Burl 92 A1
Carnegie Rd. Newb 105 D1
Carnoustie. Brac 117 F1
Carolina Pl. Woki 141 F4
Caroline Cl. Ashf 98 A1
Caroline Cl. Mar 1 C2
Caroline Dr. Woki 116 A4
Caroline Pl. Stan 71 F4
Caroline St. Read 85 F4
Caroline Way. Camb 151 F1
Carrick Gdns. Wood 87 E4
Carrick La. Yate 149 F3
Carrington Ave. Fla H 3 D4
Carrington Rd. Slough 42 C3
Carroll Cres. Ascot 119 F3
Carron Cl. Read 85 D4
Carsdale Cl. Read 85 F3
Carshalton Rd. Camb ... 145 D1
Carshalton Way. Wood ... 87 E1
Carston Gr. Read 84 C2
Carter Cl. Wind 67 D3
Carter's Hill. Binf 90 A2
Carters Rise. Read 84 C2
Cartmel Dr. Wood 87 E3
Cary Cl. Newb 130 B3
Casey Ct. Stan D 81 E2
Cassia Dr. Read 86 C1
Cassiobury Ave. Felt 98 C4
Castle Ave. Datch 68 A4
Castle Cl. Camb 151 F2
Castle Cl. Stai 96 C2
Castle Cres. Read 85 F3
Castle Ct. Maid 39 E4
Castle Dr. Maid 39 E4
Castle End Rd. W St L 62 A4
Castle Gr. Newb 104 C3
Castle Hill Rd. Eng G 95 D3
Castle Hill Rd. Eng G 95 E3
Castle Hill Terr. Maid 39 F4
Castle Hill. Maid 39 F4
Castle Hill. Read 85 F3
Castle Hill. Swal 140 B4
Castle La. Wint 104 C3
Castle Mews. Maid 39 F4
Castle Rd. Camb 151 F2
Castle St. Read 86 A4
Castle St. Slough 42 C2
Castlecraig Ct. Sand 150 B4
Castleton Ct. Mar 1 C1
Castleview Rd. Slough 43 E1
Castor Ct. Yate 149 D4
Caswall Cl. Binf 90 B1
Caswall Ride. Yate 149 F3
Catalina Cl. Wood 88 A4
Catcliffe Way. Read 113 F4
Catena Rise. Light 146 A1
Catesby Gdns. Yate 149 D3
Catherine Dr. Ashf 98 C1
Catherine Rd. Newb 105 D1
Catherine St. Read 85 F4
Catlin Cres. Shepp 125 E2
Catmore Rd. Farn 29 E4
Catmore Rd. West I 29 E1
Caunter Rd. Newb 104 B2
Causeway The. Maid 40 B2
Causeway The. Mar 1 C1
Causeway The. Stai 96 B2
Causmans Way. Read 57 E1
Cavalier Cl. Newb 105 E3
Cavalier Cl. Thea 83 E1
Cavalry Cres. Wind 67 E2
Cavendish Cl. Ashf 98 C1
Cavendish Cl. Burn 41 D4
Cavendish Cl. Ashf 98 C1
Cavendish Cl. Black 150 B2
Cavendish Gdns. Winn ... 88 A2
Cavendish Meads. Ascot 120 B2
Cavendish Rd. Ashf 98 C1
Cavendish Rd. Caver 59 F3
Caversham Park Rd. Caver 59 F3
Caversham Rd. Caver 59 D1
Caves Farm Cl. Sand ... 150 A4
Cawcott Dr. Wind 66 B3
Cawsham Gdns. Caver ... 59 E2
Caxton Cl. Read 58 B1
Cecil Aldin Dr. Pur O T 57 E2
Cecil Cl. Ashf 98 B1
Cecil Rd. Ashf 98 B1
Cecil Rd. Iver 44 C4
Cecil Way. Slough 21 F1
Cedar Ave. Black 150 B3
Cedar Chase. Tapl 20 B1
Cedar Cl. Bags 145 F2
Cedar Cl. Stai 124 B3
Cedar Cl. Woki 116 B3
Cedar Ct. Eng G 96 A2
Cedar Ct. Mar 1 C1
Cedar Dr. Brac 91 E1
Cedar Dr. Mar B 1 A2
Cedar Dr. Pangb 56 B2
Cedar Dr. Windl 121 D1
Cedar Mount. Newb 130 C4
Cedar Rd. Felt 98 B4
Cedar Rd. Read 86 C1
Cedar Way. Slough 43 F1
Cedar Way. Stai 98 C1

Cedar Wood Cres. Caver . 59 D2
Cedars Cl. Sand 149 F4
Cedars Rd. Maid 40 A4
Cedars The. Read 57 E1
Celandine Cl. Crow 143 E3
Celandine Cl. Yate 149 D4
Celandine Dr. That 106 C2
Celia Cres. Stai 97 E1
Cell Farm Ave. Old W 68 A1
Celsea Pl. Choi 14 A4
Cemetery La. Shepp 125 D1
Central Dr. Slough 41 F3
Centre The. Shepp 125 F1
Centurion Cl. Read 86 A3
Centurion Cl. Sand 150 B4
Century Rd. Stai 96 B2
Cerotus Pl. Chert 123 F1
Ceviot Rd. Sand 142 C1
Chaffinch Cl. Sand 150 B4
Chaffinch Cl. Woki 115 F3
Chagford Rd. Read 86 A1
Chain St. Read 86 A4
Chainhill Rd. Farn 8 A4
Chalcraft Cl. Hen-O-T 35 E4
Chalfont Cl. Read 87 D1
Chalfont Cl. Read 87 D1
Chalfont Way. Read 87 D1
Chalford Rd. Newb 104 C1
Chalfont. Woo G 3 F3
Chalgrove Cl. Maid 40 A3
Chalgrove Way. Caver 59 E3
Chalk Hill. Ast T 12 C4
Chalk Hill. Shipl 35 E3
Chalk Pit La. Burn 21 D2
Chalkhousegreen La. Maples 59 D4
Chalklands. Bou E 3 D2
Chalkpit La. Mar 1 A2
Challenge Rd. Felt 98 B2
Challenor Cl. Woki 141 F4
Challis Pl. Brac 117 E4
Challow Ct. Maid 19 E1
Chalmers Rd E. Ashf 98 B2
Chalmers Rd. Ashf 98 A2
Chalvey Gdns. Slough 42 C2
Chalvey Gr. Slough 42 A2
Chalvey Park. Slough 42 C2
Chalvey Rd E. Slough 42 C2
Chalvey Rd W. Slough 42 B2
Chamberlain's Gdns. Arbo 114 C1
Champion Rd. Caver 59 E1
Chancellor's Way The. Read 86 C2
Chanctonbury Dr. Sunn . 120 C1
Chandlers Cl. Felt 98 C4
Chandlers La. Yate 149 E4
Chandos Rd. Stai 96 B2
Chandos Rd. Newb 131 D4
Chantry Cl. Wind 67 D3
Chantry Mead. Hung 100 B3
Chantry Rd. Bags 145 E1
Chantry Rd. Chert 124 B1
Chapel Cl. Sou S 14 B2
Chapel Ct. That 106 C2
Chapel Hill. Read 84 B4
Chapel La. Asham 54 A4
Chapel La. Bags 145 E1
Chapel La. Binf 90 B1
Chapel La. Camb 151 D1
Chapel La. Herm 78 C2
Chapel La. Herm 79 E4
Chapel La. Lamb 25 D2
Chapel La. Shin 113 D1
Chapel La. Silc 135 D1
Chapel La. Sto P 23 D3
Chapel La. Swal 139 E2
Chapel La. Yatt 53 F1
Chapel Rd. Camb 151 D3
Chapel Rd. Fla H 3 D4
Chapel Row. Twyf 61 E2
Chapel Sq. Sand 150 C3
Chapel St. Maid 20 A2
Chapel St. Slough 42 C2
Chapel St. That 106 B2
Chaplain's Hill. Crow 143 E2
Chaplin Cres. Sunn 98 C1
Chapman La. Fla H 3 D3
Chapman La. Fla H 3 D3
Chapter Mews. Wind 67 E4
Charaston Cl. Read 86 A3
Chard Cl. Wood 87 F3
Chard Rd. Harm 71 D3
Charlbury Cl. Brac 118 C3
Charles Evans Way. Caver 59 E1
Charles Gdns. Slough 43 D4
Charles Rd. Stai 97 E1
Charles Sq. Brac 118 B4
Charles St. Chert 123 F1
Charles St. Newb 130 B3
Charles St. Read 85 F4
Charles St. Wind 67 D3
Charlotte Way. Mar 1 C1
Charlton Cl. Slough 42 A2
Charlton Cl. Woki 141 F4
Charlton La. Swal 143 E1
Charlton La. Shepp 125 E3
Charlton La. Swal 139 E3

160

Charlton Pl. Newb

Colnebridge Cl. S

Charlton Pl. Newb 105 D2
Charlton Rd. Stai 125 E4
Charlton Sq. Oak G 66 B3
Charlton Way. Oak G 66 B3
Charlton. Oak G 66 B3
Charlville Dr. Bur C 84 A2
Charmwood Cl. Newb 104 C3
Charnham La. Hung 100 B4
Charnham Park. Hello 100 B4
Charnham St. Hung 100 B3
Charnwood. Ascot 120 C2
Charrington Rd. Bur C 84 B2
Charta Rd (E). Stai 96 B1
Charta Rd (S). Stai 96 B1
Charta Rd (W). Stai 96 B2
Charter Cl. Slough 42 C2
Charter Rd. Newb 131 D4
Charter Rd. Slough 41 F3
Charterhouse Cl. Brac 118 C2
Charters La. Ascot 120 B2
Charters Rd. Sun 120 C1
Charters Rd. Windl 120 C1
Charters Way. Windl 120 C1
Charvil House Rd. Char 61 D3
Charvil La. Sonn 60 C2
Charwood Rd. Woki 116 C4
Chase Gdns. Binf 90 B2
Chase The. Bur C 84 B2
Chase The. Crow 143 D3
Chase The. Mar 2 A2
Chaseside Ave. Twyf 61 E4
Chaseside Gdns. Chert 124 A1
Chatfield. Slough 42 A4
Chatham St. Read 85 F4
Chatsworth Ave. Winn 88 A1
Chatsworth Cl. Caver 59 E3
Chatsworth Cl. Maid 39 E3
Chatsworth Hts. Camb 152 A4
Chatteris Way. Winn 114 B4
Chattern Hill. Ashf 98 A2
Chattern Rd. Ashf 98 B2
Chatton Cl. Read 114 A4
Chaucer Cl. Caver 59 D3
Chaucer Cl. Woki 116 C3
Chaucer Cres. Newb 104 C3
Chaucer Gr. Camb 151 E3
Chaucer Rd. Ashf 97 F2
Chaucer Rd. Crow 143 D2
Chaucer Way. Woki 115 F3
Chauntry Cl. Maid 40 B3
Chauntry Rd. Maid 40 A3
Chavey Down Rd. Burl 92 A1
Chawridge La. Wink 92 B4
Chazey Cl. Maple 58 B4
Chazey Rd. Caver 58 B2
Cheam Cl. Brac 118 B2
Cheap St. Comp 31 F3
Cheap St. Newb 105 D1
Cheapside Rd. Ascot 120 B4
Cheapside. Read 86 A4
Cheddar Rd. Harm 71 D3
Cheddington Cl. Read 84 C3
Cheeseman Cl. Woki 116 B4
Chelford Way. Caver 58 C2
Chelsea Cl. Read 57 F1
Chelwood Dr. Sand 142 C1
Chelwood Rd. Read 87 D1
Cheney Cl. Binf 90 B1
Cheniston Gr. Maid 38 C4
Chepstow Rd. Read 57 E1
Chequer La. Bee H 138 C1
Chequers Orch. Iver 44 C4
Chequers Way. Wood 87 E4
Cherbury Cl. Brac 118 C3
Cherington Gate. Maid 19 D1
Cherington Way. Ascot 119 F4
Cheriton Ave. Twyf 61 E3
Cheriton Cl. Newb 131 D4
Cheriton Way. Black 150 B3
Cherries The. Slough 43 D4
Cherry Ave. Slough 43 E2
Cherry Cl. Caver 59 E4
Cherry Cl. Fla H 3 D4
Cherry Cl. Newb 104 C2
Cherry Garden La. Bur G 38 C2
Cherry Orch. Gr She 48 A2
Cherry Orch. Stai 97 D2
Cherry Orch. Sto P 23 D3
Cherry Rise. Fla H 3 D4
Cherry Tree Ave. Stai 97 D1
Cherry Tree Cl. Sand 143 E1
Cherry Tree Dr. Brac 118 B3
Cherry Tree Gr. Woki 115 E2
Cherry Tree La. Fulm 23 F3
Cherry Tree Rd. Far C 22 B3
Cherry Way. Shepp 125 F3
Cherrydale Rd. Camb 152 B3
Cherrygarden La. Whi Wa 63 F4
Cherrywood Ave. Eng G 95 D1
Cherrywood Gdns. Fla H 3 D4
Chertsey Bridge Rd. Shepp 124 B1
Chertsey La. Stai 96 C1
Chertsey Rd. Felt 98 C2
Chertsey Rd. Shepp 124 B1
Chertsey Rd. Windl 146 C3
Chervil Way. Bur C 111 D1
Cherwell Cl. Maid 40 A4
Cherwell Cl. Slough 69 D4
Cherwell Rd. Bou E 3 D2
Cherwell Rd. Caver 59 D3
Cheseridge Rd. Comp 31 E2
Cheshire Ct. Slough 43 D2
Chessholme Ct. Ashf 98 C1
Chessholme Rd. Ashf 98 B1
Chester Cl. Ashf 98 B2
Chester Cl. Newb 105 E1
Chester Rd. Harm 71 D2
Chester Rd. Slough 42 B4
Chester St. Caver 59 D1
Chester St. Read 85 E4
Chesterblade La. Brac 118 C1
Chesterfield Rd. Ashf 97 F2
Chesterfield Rd. Newb 105 D1
Chesterman St. Read 86 A3
Chesters Rd. Camb 152 A3
Chesterton Dr. Stan 97 D1
Chesterton Rd. That 106 B3
Chestnut Ave. Camb 152 A3
Chestnut Ave. Caver 59 F2
Chestnut Ave. Slough 43 F2
Chestnut Ave. Went 121 F3
Chestnut Cl. Ashf 98 A2
Chestnut Cl. Ashf 98 C1
Chestnut Cl. Black 150 C3
Chestnut Cl. Eng G 95 E1
Chestnut Cl. Harl 71 D4
Chestnut Cl. Maid 20 A1
Chestnut Cl. Medm 17 E4
Chestnut Cl. Thea 83 F2
Chestnut Cres. Newb 105 D2
Chestnut Cres. Shin 113 F2
Chestnut Dr. Bur C 111 D2
Chestnut Dr. Eng G 95 E1
Chestnut Dr. Wind 66 C2
Chestnut Gr. Pur O T 57 E3
Chestnut Gr. Stai 97 E1
Chestnut La. Lamb 25 F2
Chestnut Manor Cl. Stai 97 D2
Chestnut Rd. Ashf 98 A2
Chestnut Wlk. Hung 100 B2
Chestnut Wlk. Shepp 125 F3
Chestnuts The. Shipl 36 A2
Chetwode Cl. Woki 116 C3
Cheveley Gdns. Burn 21 E2
Cheviot Cl. Camb 152 B2
Cheviot Cl. Hart 71 E4
Cheviot Cl. Maid 40 A3
Cheviot Cl. Newb 130 B3
Cheviot Dr. Char 61 D2
Cheviot Rd. Slough 44 A1
Chewter Cl. Bags 145 F2
Chewter La. Windl 146 A3
Cheylesmore Dr. Camb 152 B2
Cheyne Rd. Ashf 98 B1
Chichester Ct. Slough 43 D2
Chichester Rd. Read 84 C4
Chicory Cl. Read 86 C1
Chievley Cl. Read 84 B4
Chilcombe Way. Read 87 E1
Child St. Lamb 25 D1
Childrey Way. Read 84 B4
Chillingham Way. Camb 151 E2
Chilsey Green Rd. Chert 123 F1
Chiltern Cl. Hen-O-T 35 D4
Chiltern Cl. Newb 130 B3
Chiltern Cres. Read 87 D4
Chiltern Dr. Char 61 D2
Chiltern Green. Fla H 3 D4
Chiltern Rd. Burn 41 D4
Chiltern Rd. Caver 59 E2
Chiltern Rd. Maid 40 A3
Chiltern Rd. Mar 1 B1
Chiltern Rd. Sand 142 C1
Chiltern View. Pur O T 57 E3
Chiltern Wlk. Pangb 56 C3
Chilterns Cl. Fla H 3 D4
Chilterns Park. Bou E 3 D3
Chilton Way. Hung 100 B3
Chilwick Rd. Slough 21 F1
Chippendale Cl. Black 150 C2
Chippendale Cl. Tad 134 C1
Chippenham Cl. Read 113 F4
Chipstead Rd. Harm 71 D2
Chisbury Cl. Brac 118 C2
Chitterfield Gate. Harm 71 D4
Chittering Cl. Winn 87 E1
Chive Rd. Read 87 D1
Chivers Dr. Woki 141 F4
Chives Pl. New G 91 F1
Chobham La. Went 122 A1
Chobham Rd. Camb 151 F1
Chobham Rd. Went 121 D1
Choke La. Cook 19 D2
Cholmeley Pl. Read 86 C4
Cholmeley Rd. Read 86 C4
Cholmeley Terr. Read 86 C4
Cholsey Rd. That 106 C2
Choseley Cl. Know H 37 F2
Choseley Rd. Know H 37 F2
Chrislaine Cl. Stan 70 B1
Christchurch Dr. Black 150 B3
Christchurch Gdns. Read 86 B3
Christchurch Rd. Harm 71 D2
Christchurch Rd. Read 86 B3
Christchurch Rd. Vir W 122 B3
Christie Cl. Light 146 B1
Christie Hts. Newb 131 D4
Christie Wlk. Yate 149 E2
Christmas La. Far C 22 B4
Christopher Ct. Newb 105 D1
Chudleigh Gdns. Read 86 B1
Church App. Stai 123 E3
Church Cl. Eton 67 E4
Church Cl. Ham M 129 F3
Church Cl. Lamb 25 D2
Church Cl. Maid 39 E3
Church Cl. Stai 124 B3
Church Cl. Winn 88 B1
Church Croft. Hung 100 B3
Church Dr. Maid 40 B2
Church End La. Read 84 C4
Church Farmbarns. Mort 137 E3
Church Gate. That 106 B2
Church Gr. Slough 43 E4
Church Hams. Woki 141 E3
Church Hill. Binf 90 B3
Church Hill. Camb 151 F3
Church Hill. Chil 10 B4
Church Hill. East I 30 C3
Church Hill. Hurst 88 C3
Church La. Arbo 114 B2
Church La. Ascot 120 B3
Church La. Asham 54 A3
Church La. Bark 115 E1
Church La. Binf 90 B2
Church La. Brim 133 F3
Church La. Bur C 111 F3
Church La. Chiev 51 D1
Church La. Combe 147 F3
Church La. Finch 141 F2
Church La. Ham M 129 F4
Church La. Hung 100 B3
Church La. Maid 40 B2
Church La. New G 91 E3
Church La. Newb 104 B2
Church La. Padw 110 B2
Church La. Read 113 E3
Church La. Shipl 35 F1
Church La. Silc 136 C1
Church La. Slough 43 E4
Church La. Sto P 22 C1
Church La. Swal 140 B3
Church La. That 106 B2
Church La. Twyf 61 F3
Church La. Wind 67 E3
Church La. Yatt 53 F1
Church Mews. Pur O T 57 E3
Church Path. Maid 40 B2
Church Rd E. Crow 143 D3
Church Rd W. Crow 143 D2
Church Rd. Alde 135 D4
Church Rd. Ascot 120 A3
Church Rd. Ashf 97 F2
Church Rd. Bags 145 E2
Church Rd. Brac 118 B4
Church Rd. Burl 119 D4
Church Rd. Camb 151 E1
Church Rd. Caver 59 D1
Church Rd. Cook 19 D3
Church Rd. Eng G 96 A2
Church Rd. Far C 22 B1
Church Rd. Frox 99 D3
Church Rd. Ham 126 A1
Church Rd. Lit M 2 B3
Church Rd. Maid 40 A3
Church Rd. Newb 105 D3
Church Rd. Pangb 56 B3
Church Rd. Read 87 D3
Church Rd. Sand 143 F1
Church Rd. Sand 150 C4
Church Rd. Shepp 125 D1
Church Rd. Silc 135 F1
Church Rd. Sunn 121 D2
Church Rd. Swal 139 E3
Church Rd. West E 153 F4
Church Rd. Windl 146 B2
Church Rd. Wink 92 B3
Church Rd. Wood 87 F4
Church Side. East I 30 C3
Church Sq. Shepp 125 D1
Church St. Blew 12 A4
Church St. Burn 21 E1
Church St. Caver 59 D1
Church St. Crow 143 D3
Church St. Frox 99 D1
Church St. Gr She 48 A2
Church St. Hamp N 52 C3
Church St. Hen-O-T 15 E1
Church St. Hung 100 B3
Church St. Kint 102 A1
Church St. Read 86 A3
Church St. Slough 42 B2
Church St. Slough 42 C2
Church St. Stai 96 C2
Church St. Thea 83 F2
Church St. Twyf 61 E2
Church St. Warg 36 B1
Church St. Wind 67 E3
Church View. Been 109 D3
Church View. Whi Wa 63 F4
Church View. Yate 149 E3
Church Views. Maid 39 F4
Church Way. Hung 100 B3
Church Wlk. Chert 124 A2
Churchfield Mews. Slough 43 D4
Churchill Cl. Fla H 3 D4
Churchill Cl. Fla H 3 E4
Churchill Cres. Yate 149 E3
Churchill Dr. Mar 1 C2
Churchill Dr. Winn 88 A1
Churchill Rd. Slough 43 F1
Churchward Wlk. Read 84 C2
Churchway. West I 10 A1
Churn Rd. Comp 31 E3
Cinnamon Cl. Read 86 C1
Cintra Ave. Read 86 B3
Cippenham Cl. Slough 41 F3
Cippenham La. Slough 42 A3
Circle Hill Rd. Crow 143 E3
Circuit La. Read 85 E3
City Rd. Read 84 A4
Clacy Green. Brac 91 D1
Clandon Ave. Stai 96 B1
Clanfield Cres. Read 57 E1
Clanfield Ride. Black 150 B3
Clappers Meadow. Maid 20 B1
Clapps Gate Rd. Silc 135 F1
Clapton App. Woo G 3 E4
Clare Ave. Woki 116 B4
Clare Dr. Far C 22 A4
Clare Gdns. Eng G 96 A2
Clare Rd. Maid 39 E3
Clare Rd. Slough 41 E4
Clare Rd. Stan 70 C1
Clare Rd. Stan 97 F4
Clare Wlk. Newb 130 B3
Claredon Cl. Winn 88 B1
Clarefield Cl. Maid 19 D1
Clarefield Dr. Maid 19 D1
Clarefield Rd. Maid 19 D1
Claremont Ave. Camb 151 F3
Claremont Dr. Shepp 125 D2
Claremont Gdns. Mar 1 C1
Claremont Rd. Mar 1 C1
Claremont Rd. Stai 96 B2
Claremont Rd. Wind 67 E3
Clarence Cres. Wind 67 E3
Clarence Dr. Eng G 95 E2
Clarence Rd. Hen-O-T 15 E1
Clarence Rd. Wind 67 D3
Clarence St. Eng G 95 F1
Clarence St. Stai 96 C2
Clarence Way. Read 84 A2
Clarendon Ct. Black 150 B2
Clarendon Ct. Slough 43 D3
Clarendon Gdns. Newb 105 D2
Clarendon Rd. Ashf 97 F2
Clarendon Rd. Read 87 D3
Clares Green Rd. Shin 113 D2
Clarewood Dr. Camb 151 F3
Clark's Gdns. Hung 100 B3
Clarke Cres. Sand 150 C4
Classics The. Lamb 25 D1
Claverdon. Brac 118 A1
Clay Cl. Fla H 3 D4
Clay Cl. Pur O T 57 D1
Clay Hill Cres. Newb 105 E3
Clay La. Been 108 C3
Claydon Gdns. Camb 151 D1
Clayhall La. Old Wind 67 F1
Clayhill Cl. Brac 119 D3
Clayton Gr. Brac 118 C4
Clayton Rd. Black 150 C1
Clayton Wlk. Read 86 B2
Claytons Meadow. Bou E 3 D2
Clearsprings. Camb 153 D4
Clearsprings. Light 146 A1
Cleaves Way. Ashf 98 C1
Cleeve Ct. Felt 98 C4
Cleeve Down. Gori 34 B4
Cleeve Rd. Gori 34 A4
Clements Cl. Shin 113 D1
Clements Cl. Slough 43 D2
Clements Mead. Sulh 57 D1
Clements Rd. Hen-O-T 15 E2
Clent Rd. Read 86 A2
Cleopatra Pl. New G 91 F1
Cleve Ct. Wind 66 C2
Clevedon Dr. Read 87 D1
Clevedon Rd. Read 57 F2
Clevehurst Cl. Sto P 23 D3
Cleveland Cl. Maid 40 A3
Cleveland Cl. Woo G 3 F4
Cleveland Dr. Stai 124 A4
Cleveland Gr. Newb 104 C2
Cleveland. Char 61 D2
Clevemede. Gori 34 B4
Clewborough Dr. Camb 152 A3
Clewer Ave. Wind 67 D3
Clewer Ct Rd. Wind 67 D4
Clewer Fields. Wind 67 D3
Clewer Hill Rd. Wind 66 C2
Clewer New Town. Wind 67 D3
Clewer Park. Wind 67 D4
Clifford Gr. Ashf 98 A2
Clifford Way. Bou E 3 D3
Clifton Cl. Maid 40 A2
Clifton Rd. Harm 71 D2
Clifton Rd. Newb 104 C1
Clifton Rd. Slough 43 D2
Clifton Rd. Woki 116 A4
Clifton Rise. Warg 36 C1
Clifton Rise. Wind 66 B3
Clifton St. Read 85 F4
Clintons Green. Brac 118 A4
Clive Ct. Slough 42 B2
Clive Green. Brac 118
Clivedale Rd. Wood 87
Cliveden Mead. Maid 20
Cliveden Pl. Shepp 125
Cliveden Rd. Tapl 20
Clivemont Rd. Maid 39
Clockhouse La E. Stai 96
Clockhouse La W. Eng G 96
Clockhouse La. Ashf 98
Clockhouse La. Felt 98
Cloister Mews. Thea 83
Cloisters The. Camb 151
Cloisters The. Caver 59
Clonmel Way. Burn 21
Close End. Lamb 25
Close The. Bou E 3
Close The. Bur C 111
Close The. Burl 119
Close The. Gr She 48
Close The. Hamp N 52
Close The. Hen-O-T 35
Close The. Light 146
Close The. Sand 150
Close The. Slough 41
Close The. That 106
Close The. Vir W 122
Close The. Wood 87
Clough Dr. Herm 78
Clove Cl. Read 86
Clover Cl. Woki 116
Clover La. Yate 149
Club La. Crow 143
Clumps The. Felt 98
Clyde Rd. Stan 97
Clyve Way. Stai 123
Coach House Cl. Camb 151
Coach Ride. Mar 1
Coalport Way. Read 57
Cobb Cl. Datch 68
Cobbett's La. Yate 149
Cobblers Cl. Far C 22
Cobham Rd. Wood 87
Cochrane Cl. That 106
Cochrane Pl. Windl 146
Cock La. Brad 82
Cock's La. New G 92
Cock's La. Wink 92
Cock-a-Dobby. Sand 143
Cockett Rd. Slough 43
Cockney Hill. Read 84
Cody Cl. Read 88
Coe Spur. Slough 42
Coftards. Slough 43
Cold Ash Hill. Cold A 106
Coldharbour Cl. Hen-O-T 35
Coldharbour Cl. Stai 123
Coldharbour La. Stai 123
Coldharbour La. West E 153
Coldharbour Rd. Hung 100
Coldicutt St. Caver 59
Coldmoorholme La. Bou E 2
Colemans Moor La. Wood 87
Colemans Moor Rd. Wood 88
Colenorton Cres. Eton 41
Coleridge Ave. Yate 149
Coleridge Cl. Crow 143
Coleridge Cl. Twyf 61
Coleridge Cres. Stan 69
Coleridge Rd. Ashf 97
Coley Ave. Read 85
Coley Hill. Read 85
Coley Park Rd. Read 85
Coley Pl. Read 86
Colin Way. Slough 42
Collaroy Rd. Cold A 106
College Ave. Maid 39
College Ave. Slough 42
College Ave. Stai 96
College Cl. Camb 151
College Cres. Sand 150
College Cres. Wind 67
College Glen. Maid 39
College Piece. Mort 136
College Rd. Maid 39
College Rd. Read 86
College Rd. Slough 41
College Ride. Bags 145
College Ride. Camb 151
College Rise. Maid 39
College Way. Ashf 97
Colleton Dr. Twyf 61
Collier Cl. Maid 19
Colliers Way. Read 85
Collingwood Rise. Camb 152
Collingwood Wlk. Read 84
Collins Cl. Newb 105
Collins Dr. Herm 78
Collinswood Rd. Far C 22
Collis St. Read 86
Colliston Wlk. Read 84
Collum Green Rd. Sto P 23
Coln Cl. Maid 39
Colnbrook By-Pass. Iver 69
Colnbrook By-Pass. Slough 69
Colndale Rd. Stan 69
Colne Bank. Hort 69
Colne Orchard. Iver 44
Colne Way. Wray 96
Colnebridge Cl. Stai 96

th Cl. Read 114 A4
s La. Chert 124 A2
Rd. Felt 98 C4
Rd. Slough 43 D2
Cl. Bur C 84 B2
a La. That 107 D1
a Ct. Woki 42 A1
Gdns. Light 153 E4
Cl. Yate 149 E3
Cl. Herm 79 E4
Way. Pur O T 57 E3
Cl. Yate 149 E3
View. Hung 100 B2
mere Cl. Wind 67 D3
Rd. Stan 97 E4
Way. Wood 88 A4
Cl. Woki 116 C4
rcial Rd. Read 86 A1
rcial Rd. Stai 97 D1
n Hill. Brad 82 C2
n La. Brig 28 B3
n La. Eton 42 B1
n Rd. Dorn 41 A1
n Rd. Eton 42 A1
n Rd. Fla H 3 D4
n Rd. Head 132 C1
n Rd. Slough 44 A1
n The. Fla H 3 D4
n Wood. Far C 22 B4
nfield La. Bark 141 D4
nfields. West E 153 F3
ins Rd. Woki 88 C1
n Ave. Read 57 D3
n Cl. Brac 117 F2
n Cl. Read 87 E2
n Cl. Sand 143 E1
n Cl. Slough 41 F4
n Dr. Maid 39 D4
ne Wlk. Brac 118 B2
de Way. Slough 42 B2
de Way. Wood 88 A4
Cl. Sulh 57 F2
Rd. Stai 124 B3
r Ct. Slough 42 C3
ere Cl. Read 87 E2
ve Cl. Alde 135 D4
Cl. Tad 134 C1
Crest. Newb 130 B2
Dr. Camb 152 A3
Dr. Sulh 57 D1
La. Stai 96 B2
s The. Brac 143 D4
nam Rd. Read 113 E3
sby Cl. Mad 39 E2
sby La. Holy 65 E3
sby. Brac 118 B3
ro Ave. Caver 58 C3
ro Way. Caver 58 C2
n Cl. Camb 152 B2
n Cl. That 106 A2
n Cl. Wood 87 F3
n Cres. Slough 41 E4
n Ct. Light 146 A1
n Dr. Read 57 F1
n Way. Stai 96 A1
e Way. Ashf 97 F2
ght Cl. Crow 142 C2
ght Cl. Mad 19 F1
ght Cl. Read 85 E4
ght Cl. Yate 149 D3
ght Rd. Bags 145 E2
ght Rd. Camb 151 F3
ght Rd. Newb 105 D2
ght Rd. Read 85 E4
ght Rd. Slough 43 D2
on Cl. Mar 1 A1
e Way. Camb 151 F2
le Way. Sand 150 C3
ution Rd. Read 85 E4
Cl. Wood 88 A3
Tower Rd. Harm 71 D2
rt Lodge. Ashf 98 A2
rt Rd. Ashf 98 A2
rt Rd. Wind 67 D3
y Dr. Ashf 98 B1
y Rd. Brac 118 B4
y Rd. Harm 71 D2
y Rd. Read 84 B3
y Rd. Slough 41 D4
am Cl. Sand 143 E1
am Dean Bottom La. Cook 19 E4
am Rd. Brac 117 F4
am Rd. Maid 19 F1
am Rd. Maid 19 F2
ne Rise. Camb 152 A3
rdie Rd. Ashf 98 B2
Ct. That 106 C2
e Hill. Farn 28 A4
e Pine. Brac 118 B2
e Rd. Comp 31 F2
e Rd. Yate 149 D4
e Sq. That 106 C2
e. The. Stre 33 F3
es La. Woki 115 E3
estury La. Box 76 B1
Cl. Read 113 E4
Rd. Hen-O-T 15 E2

Cooper Rd. Windl 146 B2
Cooper Way. Slough 42 A2
Cooper's Hill La. Eng G 95 C2
Coopers Cl. Stai 96 C2
Coopers Cres. That 106 B2
Cope Hall La. Ham M 130 B4
Copelands Cl. Camb 152 B2
Copenhagen Cl. Read 113 E4
Copped Hall Dr. Camb 152 B3
Copped Hall Way. Camb 152 B3
Copper Beech Cl. Wind 66 B3
Copperage Rd. Farn 9 D1
Copperdale Cl. Read 86 C2
Coppermill Rd. Hort 69 D1
Coppermill Rd. Wray 69 D1
Coppice Cl. Newb 131 D4
Coppice Dr. Wray 95 E4
Coppice Gdns. Crow 142 C3
Coppice Gdns. Yate 149 E3
Coppice Green. Brac 90 C1
Coppice Rd. Wood 87 F2
Coppice The. Ashf 98 A1
Coppins La. Iver 44 C4
Copse Ave. Caver 59 F2
Copse Cl. Camb 152 A3
Copse Cl. Mar 1 B1
Copse Cl. Read 57 E2
Copse Dr. Woki 116 A4
Copse End. Camb 152 A3
Copse Mead. Wood 60 C1
Copse The. Warg 36 C2
Copse Way. Woki 141 F4
Copthorn Cl. Maid 39 D2
Copthorne Cl. Shepp 125 E2
Copthorne Dr. Light 146 A1
Corbett Dr. Camb 152 C4
Corbett Gdns. Wood 87 F4
Corbridge Rd. Read 86 B2
Corby Cl. Wood 61 D1
Corby Dr. Eng G 95 E1
Cordelia Gdns. Stan 97 F4
Cordelia Rd. Stan 97 F4
Corderoy Cl. That 106 C1
Corderoy Pl. Chert 123 F2
Cordwalles Rd. Camb 151 F4
Cordwalles Rd. Maid 39 F4
Cordwallis St. Maid 39 F4
Cores End Rd. Bou E 3 D2
Corfe Gdns. Camb 151 F1
Corfe Gdns. Slough 42 A3
Corfe Mews. Caver 59 F2
Corfe Pl. Maid 39 E4
Corfield Cl. Finch 141 F2
Coriander Way. Read 86 C1
Cormorant Pl. Sand 150 C4
Cornbunting Cl. Sand 150 B4
Cornerside. Ashf 98 B1
Cornfield Green. Woki 115 F4
Cornfield Rd. Wood 88 A4
Cornfields. Yate 149 D2
Cornflower Cl. Woki 115 E4
Cornwall Ave. Slough 22 B1
Cornwall Cl. Camb 151 F4
Cornwall Cl. Eton 41 F1
Cornwall Cl. Maid 19 F1
Cornwall Cl. Pur O T 57 D2
Cornwall Cl. Woki 115 E3
Cornwall Way. Stai 96 C1
Cornwall Rd. Old W 68 A1
Cornwood Gdns. Read 86 B2
Coronation Ave. Slough 43 F4
Coronation Rd. Ascot 120 A4
Coronation Rd. Bish 38 A3
Coronation Rd. Brac 120 A1
Coronation Rd. Stai 149 F4
Coronation Sq. Read 85 D2
Coronation Sq. Woki 116 B4
Corrie Gdns. Went 122 B1
Corrine Cl. Read 84 C2
Corsair Cl. Stan 97 F4
Corsair Rd. Stan 97 F4
Corsham Rd. Read 84 C2
Corsham Way. Crow 143 D3
Corwen Rd. Read 84 C2
Coster Cl. Newb 104 B3
Cotswold Cl. Maid 40 A3
Cotswold Cl. Slough 42 B2
Cotswold Cl. Stai 97 D2
Cotswold Rd. Sand 142 C1
Cotswold Way. Read 57 E1
Cottage Farm Way. Stai 123 E3
Cottage La. Bur C 85 E1
Cotterell Cl. Brac 91 D1
Cottesbrooke Cl. Stan 69 E3
Cottesmore Rd. Wood 87 E3
Cottesmore. Brac 118 A1
Coulson Way. Burn 41 D4
County La. New G 91 F1
Course Rd. Ascot 120 B1
Court Cl. Holy 40 B1
Court Cres. Slough 42 B4
Court Dr. Maid 20 B2
Court Gdns. Camb 151 E3
Court Hill Rd. Farn 7 D1
Court Hill Let B 7 D1
Court La. Burn 22 C1
Court La. Iver 44 C3
Court La. Slough 41 D2
Court Rd. Maid 20 B2

Courtenay Dr. Caver 59 D4
Courtfield Rd. Ashf 98 A1
Courtfields Dr. Maid 39 E3
Courthouse Rd. Maid 39 E4
Courtlands Ave. Slough 43 E1
Courtlands Hill. Pangb 56 B2
Courtlands Rd. Newb 105 D1
Courtlands. Maid 39 F3
Courtney Rd. Harm 71 D2
Courts Rd. Read 87 D2
Courtyard The. Thea 83 F2
Coventry Rd. Read 86 C4
Coverdale Way. Slough 21 F1
Covert The. Sunn 120 A1
Cow La. East I 30 C4
Cow La. Mool 13 F2
Cow La. Read 58 C1
Cowley Ave. Chert 123 F1
Cowley La. Chert 123 F1
Coworth Cl. Sunn 121 D2
Coworth Rd. Sunn 121 D2
Cowper Cl. Chert 123 F2
Cowper Rd. Slough 22 A1
Cowper Way. Read 85 E2
Cowslade. Newb 104 B3
Cowslip Cl. Read 84 A3
Cox Green La. Maid 39 E2
Cox Green Rd. Maid 39 E2
Cox Green. Sand 150 B4
Cox's La. Mool 107 E2
Coxborrow Cl. Cook 19 F4
Coxeter Rd. Newb 104 C2
Crabtree Cl. Herm 78 C3
Crabtree Rd. Camb 151 D1
Crabtree Rd. Stai 123 E4
Craddock Rd. Read 86 A2
Crafts End. Chil 10 C4
Craig Ave. Read 85 D4
Craigwell Cl. Stai 123 F4
Crail Cl. Woki 116 A2
Crake Pl. Sand 150 B4
Cramond Ct. Felt 98 C4
Cranborne Gdns. Read 58 A1
Cranborne Ave. Bur C 84 B2
Cranbourne Ave. Wind 66 C3
Cranbourne Cl. Slough 42 B3
Cranbourne Hall Caravan Site. Wink 93 B2
Cranbourne Rd. Slough 42 B3
Cranbrook Dr. Maid 19 E1
Cranbury Rd. Read 85 E4
Crane Cl. Sand 150 B4
Crane Wharf. Read 86 A4
Cranewater. Harl 71 F4
Cranford Cl. Hurst 88 C3
Cranford Cl. Stan 97 F4
Cranford Cl. Harl 71 F4
Cranford La. Harm 71 F3
Cranford La. Harm 71 F3
Cranford Park Dr. Yate 149 E3
Cranleigh Rd. Felt 98 C2
Cranmer Cl. Sulh 57 D2
Cranwell Gr. Light 152 C4
Cranwell Gr. Stai 124 C3
Craufurd Rise. Maid 39 F4
Craven Cl. Kint 102 A1
Craven Dene. Newb 105 D2
Craven Rd. Ink 127 D3
Craven Rd. Newb 104 C1
Craven Rd. Read 86 B3
Craven Way. Kint 102 A1
Crawford Cl. Read 87 D2
Crawford Pl. Newb 104 C2
Crawley Chase. Burl 92 A1
Crawley Dr. Camb 151 F3
Crawley Hill. Camb 151 F3
Crawley Ridge. Camb 151 F3
Crawley Wood Cl. Camb 151 F3
Crawshay Dr. Caver 59 D4
Crayle St. Slough 22 A1
Crayonne Cl. Stai 125 F4
Crecy Cl. Woki 115 F3
Creden Cl. Maid 39 E4
Crediton Cl. Wood 88 A3
Crees Meadow. Windl 146 B2
Cremyll Rd. Read 58 C1
Crescent Ave. Read 86 C3
Crescent Dr. Maid 39 F4
Crescent Rd. Read 57 E1
Crescent Rd. Shepp 125 E2
Crescent Rd. Woki 116 B3
Crescent The. Ashf 97 F2
Crescent The. Chert 124 A3
Crescent The. Eng G 95 F1
Crescent The. Harl 71 E4
Crescent The. Kint 102 A1
Crescent The. Maid 39 F4
Crescent The. Mort 137 D2
Crescent The. Padw 109 E2
Crescent The. Read 87 E2
Crescent The. Shepp 125 F1
Crescent The. Shipl 36 A2
Crescent The. Slough 42 C2
Crescent The. Thea 83 F2
Cress Rd. Slough 42 A2

Cressex Cl. Binf 90 B1
Cressingham Rd. Read 86 B1
Cressington Pl. Bou E 3 D2
Cresswell Rd. Newb 105 E2
Cresswells Mead. Holy 40 B1
Crest Cl. Twyf 61 F3
Crest The. Caver 59 E3
Creswell Dr. Read 113 E3
Cricket Field Gr. Crow 143 E2
Cricket Hill La. Yate 149 F2
Cricket Hill. Finch 141 F1
Cricketers La. Burl 92 A2
Cricketers La. Windl 146 B2
Cricketers. Box 103 F3
Crimp Hill Rd. Eng G 95 D3
Crimp Hill. Old W 95 D3
Crisp Gdns. Binf 90 C1
Crisp Rd. Hen-O-T 15 E2
Crispin Cl. Caver 58 B3
Crispin Way. Far C 22 B4
Crocker Cl. Ascot 119 F4
Crockhamwell Rd. Wood 87 F3
Crocus Way. Woki 115 E4
Croft Cl. Harl 71 E4
Croft Cl. Woki 116 A1
Croft La. Newb 104 C2
Croft La. Yate 149 E4
Croft Rd. Gori 34 B3
Croft Rd. Hung 100 B3
Croft Rd. Mort 136 C3
Croft Rd. Newb 130 C4
Croft Rd. Woki 116 A1
Croft Road. Shin 113 E1
Croft The. Brac 91 D1
Croft The. Kint 102 A1
Croft The. Maid 39 E3
Croft The. Yate 2 A2
Croft Way. Camb 151 F1
Crofter's Cl. Sand 150 A4
Crofters. Old W 68 A1
Crofthill Rd. Slough 22 A1
Crofton Cl. Brac 118 C2
Crofts The. Shepp 125 F3
Cromer Cl. Camb 152 A4
Cromer Rd W. Harn 71 D2
Cromer Rd. Harm 71 D3
Cromwell Dr. Slough 42 C4
Cromwell Gdns. Mar 1 C1
Cromwell Rd. Ascot 120 A3
Cromwell Rd. Camb 151 D3
Cromwell Rd. Caver 59 D1
Cromwell Rd. Hen-O-T 35 F4
Cromwell Rd. Maid 39 E4
Cromwell Rd. Mar 1 C1
Cromwell Rd. Newb 105 E3
Cromwell. Embl. Yate 149 E4
Crondell Ct. Camb 151 D2
Cropper Cl. That 107 D2
Crosby Gdns. Yate 149 D4
Crosby Hill Dr. Camb 151 F4
Cross Fell. Brac 118 A3
Cross Gates Cl. Brac 118 C3
Cross Keys Rd. Sou S 14 B2
Cross La. Bee H 138 B4
Cross Oak. Wind 67 D3
Cross Rd. Windl 121 D1
Cross St. Read 86 A4
Cross St. Woki 116 B3
Crossfields Cl. Read 113 F4
Crossland Rd. Read 86 A4
Crossways. Stai 96 B1
Crossways. Stai 98 C1
Crossways. Wood 87 F3
Crosswell Cl. Stai 125 E4
Crosthwaite Way. Slough 41 E4
Crouch La. Wink 92 C4
Crow Piece La. Burn 21 F2
Crowfield Dr. That 106 A2
Crowle Rd. Lamb 25 D1
Crown Acre Cl. That 106 B2
Crown La. Burn 22 A2
Crown La. Maid 40 A4
Crown La. Mar 1 B1
Crown La. Thea 83 F2
Crown La. Went 122 B2
Crown Meadow. Iver 69 D4
Crown Pl. Read 86 B3
Crown Rd. Mar 1 B1
Crown Rd. Mar 122 B2
Crown Row. Brac 118 B2
Crown St. Eng G 96 A2
Crown St. Read 86 A4
Crowsley Rd. Shipl 36 A2
Crowthorne Rd N. Brac 118 A3
Crowthorne Rd. Brac 117 F1
Crowthorne Rd. Brac 118 A4
Crowthorne Rd. Sand 143 D1
Croxley Rise. Maid 39 E3
Croydon Rd. Harm 71 E3
Cruikshank Lea. Sand 150 C3
Crummock Cl. Slough 41 E4
Crutchley Rd. Woki 116 B4
Cuckoo La. Brac 90 C4
Cuckoo Pound. Shepp 125 F3
Cuckoo Vale. West E 153 E3
Culford Cl. Winn 87 E1
Culham Dr. Maid 19 F1

Cullen Cl. Yate 149 E3
Cullern's Pas. Maid 39 F3
Culley Way. Maid 39 D2
Culloden Way. Woki 115 F3
Culver Croft. Binf 90 C1
Culver La. Read 87 D4
Culver Rd. Newb 130 C4
Culver Rd. Read 86 C3
Culver Rd. Sand 143 E1
Cumberland Ave. Slough 22 B1
Cumberland Dr. Brac 118 B4
Cumberland Rd. Ashf 97 D3
Cumberland Rd. Camb 152 B2
Cumberland Rd. Read 86 C4
Cumberland St. Stai 96 B2
Cumberland Way. Woki 115 E3
Cumbernauld Gdns. Ashf 98 C2
Cumbria Cl. Maid 39 E2
Cumnor Way. Brac 118 C3
Curl Way. Woki 116 A3
Curlew Cl. That 106 B2
Curlew Dr. Read 84 B3
Curley Hill Rd. Light 152 C4
Curling Way. Newb 105 E2
Curls Rd. Maid 39 E2
Curridge Green. Herm 78 C2
Curridge Piece. Herm 78 C3
Curridge Rd. Herm 78 B2
Curriers La. Burn 21 F4
Curtis Rd. Read 84 B2
Curzon St. Read 85 F4
Cutbush Cl. Read 114 A4
Cutbush La. Read 114 A4
Cutting Hill. Ham 126 A2
Cygnet Cl. That 106 A2
Cypress Cl. Brac 142 A4
Cypress Rd. Stai 125 F4
Cypress Rd. Wood 88 A3
Cypress Way. Black 150 A3
Cypress Wlk. Eng G 95 D1
Cyril Vokins Rd. Gree 105 F1

Dacre Ave. Caver 59 F2
Dagmar Rd. Wind 67 E3
Dairy La. Hamb 16 A4
Dalby Cres. Newb 131 D4
Dalby Cres. Newb 131 E4
Dalcross. Brac 118 C2
Dale Cl. Sunn 121 D2
Dale Cl. Slough 42 B2
Dale Gdns. Sand 150 A4
Dale Lodge Rd. Sunn 121 D2
Dale Rd. Ashf 98 C1
Dale Rd. Read 86 A3
Dale Rd. Shepp 125 F1
Daleham Ave. Eng G 96 A1
Dalston Cl. Camb 152 B2
Dalton Cl. Read 84 C4
Damar Gdns. Hen-O-T 35 F4
Damask Cl. Camb 153 F3
Dandridge Cl. Slough 43 E1
Dandridge Dr. Bou E 3 E2
Dane Rd. Ashf 98 B1
Danehill. Read 114 A4
Danvers Cl. That 106 B1
Danywern Dr. Winn 88 B1
Darby Green La. Black 150 A3
Darby Green Rd. Black 150 A3
Darby La. Upp B 55 D3
Darell Rd. Caver 58 C3
Dark La. Brad 82 B4
Dark La. Read 57 D1
Dark La. Warg 36 B1
Dark La. Wick 101 D4
Darleydale Cl. Crow 143 E1
Darling's La. Bish 18 C1
Darrell Cl. Slough 43 F1
Dart Cl. Slough 69 D4
Dart Cl. That 106 A3
Dart Cl. Woki 141 F3
Dartington Ave. Wood 87 E2
Dartmouth Cl. Brac 118 C3
Darvill's La. Slough 42 B2
Darvills La. W St L 62 C1
Darwall Dr. Burl 119 E4
Darwin Cl. Read 86 A1
Darwin Rd. Slough 42 A3
Dashwood Cl. Brac 118 B4
Dashwood Cl. Slough 43 E1
Datchet Pl. Slough 68 A3
Datchet Rd. Hort 68 C3
Datchet Rd. Hort 68 C2
Datchet Rd. Old W 68 A2
Datchet Rd. Wind 67 E4
Dauntless Rd. Bur C 111 D2
Davenport Rd. Brac 118 C4
Daventry Cl. Stan 69 F3
Daventry Ct. Brac 118 A2
David Cl. Harl 71 E4
David Rd. Stan 69 F3
David Smith Ct. Read 84 C3
Davis Cl. Mar 1 C1
Davis Cl. Winn 88 A1
Davis Gdns. Sand 150 C4
Davis St. Hurst 88 B3
Davis Way. Hurst 88 B3
Dawes East Rd. Burn 21 E1
Dawes Moor Cl. Slough 43 E4

Dawley Ride. Stan

Elmhurst Rd. F

Dawley Ride. Stan 69 F3
Dawlish Rd. Read 86 B1
Dawn Redwood Cl. Hort ... 69 D2
Dawnay Cl. Ascot 119 F4
Dawnay Rd. Sand 151 D4
Dawsmere Cl. Camb 152 B3
Dawson Cl. Wind 67 D3
De Beauvoir Rd. Read ... 86 C3
De Bohun Rd. Read 86 A4
De Havilland Way. Stan ... 70 C1
De Montfort Gr. Hung 100 B2
De Montfort Rd. Newb 104 C3
De Montfort Rd. Read 59 D1
De Vitre Green. Woki 116 C4
Deacon Cl. Woki 116 B4
Deacon Way. Read 58 A1
Deaconfield. Sou S 14 B2
Deacons La. Herm 79 E4
Deadman's La. Thea 83 E2
Deadmans La. Gree 131 D4
Deadmoor La. Newt 130 C1
Deadmoor La. Newt 130 C1
Deal Ave. Slough 41 F4
Dean Cl. Wind 66 B2
Dean La. Cook 19 E4
Dean St. Mar 1 B1
Deanfield Ave. Hen-O-T ... 15 E1
Deanfield Cl. Mar 1 B2
Deanfield Rd. Hen-O-T ... 15 E1
Deans Cl. Sto P 23 D2
Deans Cl. Wind 146 B2
Deansgate Rd. Read 86 A3
Deansgate. Brac 118 A1
Decies Way. Sto P 23 D2
Dedmere Cl. Mar 1 C1
Dedmere Rd. Mar 1 C1
Dedmere Rise. Mar 1 C1
Dedworth Dr. Wind 66 C3
Dedworth Rd. Wind 66 B3
Dee Rd. Read 85 D4
Deena Cl. Slough 41 F3
Deep Field. Datch 68 A4
Deep Well Dr. Camb 151 F3
Deepcut Bridge Rd. Camb ... 152 B1
Deepdene Cl. Read 85 F4
Deepfield Rd. Brac 118 B4
Deer Leap. Camb 153 D4
Deer Rock Hill. Brac 118 B2
Deer Rock Rd. Camb 151 F4
Deerhurst Ave. Winn 88 B1
Deerhurst Cl. Read 84 C2
Deerswood. Maid 20 A1
Defford Cl. Woki 88 C1
Delafield Dr. Bur C 84 B2
Delaford Cl. Iver 44 C4
Delamere Rd. Read 87 D4
Delane Dr. Winn 88 A1
Delaney Cl. Read 84 C4
Delft Cl. Read 84 C4
Dell Cl. Far C 22 B4
Dell Gr. Camb 151 F1
Dell Rd. Finch 142 A2
Dell Rd. Read 57 E1
Dell The. Wra 38 C2
Dell The. Yate 149 E3
Dellars Hill. Hurl 38 A4
Delph The. Winn 87 E1
Delta Way. Stai 123 E4
Denbury Gdns. Read 113 E4
Denby Way. Read 57 F1
Dene Cl. Brac 118 B4
Dene Cl. Read 87 D2
Dene Hollow. Chil 10 C4
Dene Way. Newb 105 D3
Denford La. Hung 101 D4
Denford La. Wick 101 D4
Denham Cl. Maid 39 E3
Denham Dr. Yate 149 F3
Denham Rd. Brac 118 B2
Denham Rd. Eng G 96 A2
Denhose Cl. Read 87 D1
Denison Rd. Felt 98 C2
Denly Way. Light 146 B1
Denman Dr. Ashf 98 A1
Denmark Ave. Wood 61 D1
Denmark Rd. Newb 105 D2
Denmark Rd. Read 86 B3
Denmark St. Maid 39 F4
Denmark St. Woki 116 B3
Denmead Ct. Brac 118 C2
Dennis Cl. Ashf 98 B1
Dennis Way. Slough 41 E3
Dennistord Rd. East I ... 31 D3
Dennistoun Cl. Camb ... 151 E3
Denny Rd. Slough 43 F1
Denton Cl. That 106 B1
Denton Rd. Woki 116 B3
Denton Way. Camb 151 E1
Depot Rd. Maid 40 A3
Deppdale. Brac 118 A3
Derby Cl. Lamb 25 D1
Derby Rd. Caver 59 D2
Derby Rd. Newb 104 C1
Derby St. Read 85 F4
Derek Rd. Maid 40 B4
Deri Dene Cl. Stan 70 C1
Derrick Cl. Bur C 84 B2
Derry Rd. Black 150 C1
Derwent Ave. Read 57 F1

Derwent Cl. Felt 98 C4
Derwent Cl. Woki 115 F3
Derwent Dr. Maid 39 E4
Derwent Dr. Slough 41 E4
Derwent Rd. Light 153 D4
Derwent Rd. Stai 96 A1
Derwent Rd. That 106 A2
Desborough Cl. Shepp ... 125 D1
Desborough Cres. Maid ... 39 E3
Deseronto Wharf. Slough ... 43 F2
Desford Way. Ashf 97 F3
Devenish La. Sunn 120 B1
Devenish Rd. Ascot 120 B1
Devenish Rd. Sunn 120 B1
Devereux Rd. Wind 67 E3
Deveron Dr. Read 85 D4
Devil's Highway The. Brac ... 142 C3
Devil's Highway The. Finch ... 142 C3
Devil's La. Stai 96 B1
Devitt Cl. Read 86 C1
Devon Ave. Slough 42 B4
Devon Cl. Sand 150 B4
Devon Cl. Woki 115 F3
Devon Dr. Caver 59 F2
Devonshire Cl. Slough ... 22 A2
Devonshire Dr. Camb ... 151 F4
Devonshire Gdns. Sulh ... 57 D2
Devonshire Green. Far C ... 22 A2
Devonshire Park. Read ... 86 C1
Dhoon Rise. Maid 39 F3
Diamedes Ave. Stan 97 E4
Diamond Hill. Camb 151 F4
Diamond Rd. Slough ... 43 D2
Diamond Ridge. Camb .. 151 F4
Diamond Way. Woki 115 F4
Diana Cl. Slough 43 F4
Dianthus Cl. Chert 123 F1
Dick Turpin Way. Harm ... 71 F2
Dickens Way. Yate 149 E3
Dickens Wlk. Newb 131 D4
Dido Rd. Chil 9 F4
Dieppe Cl. Woki 115 F3
Digby Rd. Newb 104 C2
Dines Way. Herm 79 E4
Dingle Rd. Ashf 98 A2
Disraeli Cl. Slough 69 D4
Ditchfield La. Woki 141 F4
Ditchling. Brac 118 A1
Ditton Park Rd. Datch ... 68 C4
Ditton Rd. Datch 68 C4
Ditton Rd. Slough 68 C4
Dobson's La. Faw (Bu) ... 15 E4
Dockett Eddy La. Shepp ... 124 C1
Doctors La. Herm 79 D3
Doddington Cl. Winn ... 87 E1
Doddsfield Rd. Slough ... 22 A1
Dodsells Well. Woki 41 F4
Dog La. Asham 54 A3
Doghurst Ave. Harl 71 D4
Doghurst Dr. Harl 71 D4
Dogkennel La. Fawl 27 E2
Doles Hill. Woki 115 E2
Doles La. Woki 115 E2
Dolman Rd. Newb 105 D2
Dolphin Ct N. Stai 97 D3
Dolphin Ct. Slough 43 D2
Dolphin Ct. Stan 97 D3
Dolphin Rd N. Stai 125 F4
Dolphin Rd S. Stai 125 F4
Dolphin Rd W. Stai 125 F4
Dolphin Rd. Slough 43 D2
Dolphin Rd. Stai 125 F4
Doman Rd. Camb 151 D2
Domoney Cl. That 106 C2
Don Cl. Read 85 D4
Donaldson Way. Read ... 88 A4
Doncastle Rd. Brac 117 F3
Donegal Cl. Caver 59 E2
Donkin Hill. Caver 59 E2
Donnington Cl. Buck ... 108 B4
Donnington Cl. Camb ... 151 D2
Donnington Gdns. Read ... 86 C3
Donnington Pl. Winn ... 88 B1
Donnington Rd. Read ... 86 B3
Donnington Sq. Newb ... 104 C3
Donnybrook. Brac 118 A1
Dorchester Cl. Maid ... 19 D1
Dorchester Ct. Read ... 85 E3
Dorchester Dr. Felt 71 F1
Dorian Dr. Ascot 120 C4
Doris Rd. Ashf 98 B1
Dorking Way. Bur C ... 84 A2
Dorly Cl. Shepp 125 F2
Dormer Cl. Crow 143 D3
Dormer Cl. Newb 130 C3
Dornels. Slough 43 E4
Dorney Reach Rd. Dorn ... 40 C2
Dorney Wood Rd. Burn ... 21 E3
Dorothy St. Read 86 A3
Dorset Rd. Ashf 97 E3
Dorset Rd. Wind 67 E3
Dorset St. Read 85 E4
Dorset Vale. New G ... 91 F1
Dorset Way. Woki 115 F3
Doublet Cl. That 106 A2
Douglas Cl. Mar 2 A2
Douglas Grange. Hurst ... 88 A2
Douglas La. Wray 68 C1
Douglas Rd. Caver 59 E1

Douglas Rd. Slough 42 B4
Douglas Rd. Stan 70 B1
Doultons The. Stan 97 D1
Douro Cl. Tad 134 B1
Dove Cl. Read 113 F4
Dove House Cres. Slough ... 21 F1
Dovecote Rd. Read 113 D4
Dovedale Cl. Caver 58 C2
Dovedale Cl. Crow 143 E1
Dover Rd. Slough 41 D4
Dover St. Read 86 A3
Doveton Way. Newb ... 105 D2
Dowding Cl. Wood 88 A4
Dower Park. Wind 66 C2
Down Pl. Oak G 66 A4
Downend La. Chiev 51 D1
Downfield La. W St L ... 63 D3
Downfield Rd. W St L ... 63 D2
Downing Path. Slough ... 21 F1
Downing Rd. Read 84 B4
Downlands. East G 47 E3
Downmill Rd. Brac 117 F4
Downs Cl. Lamb 46 C4
Downs Rd. Comp 32 A2
Downs Rd. Slough 43 E2
Downs Way. Chil 9 F4
Downs Way. Read 57 E1
Downshire Cl. Gr She ... 48 A2
Downshire Sq. Read .. 85 F3
Downshire Way. Brac ... 118 A3
Downside. Chert 123 F1
Downside. Chil 10 B4
Doyle Gdns. Yate 149 E2
Drake Ave. Slough 43 E1
Drake Ave. Stai 96 C2
Drake Cl. Brac 118 A2
Drake Cl. Woki 141 F4
Draper Cl. That 106 B1
Drawback Hill. Shipl ... 35 E3
Draycott. Brac 118 C2
Drayhorse Dr. Bags ... 145 F1
Drayton Cl. Brac 118 B4
Drayton Rd. Read 85 D4
Dresden Way. Read ... 57 F1
Drew Meadow. Far C ... 22 B4
Drewett Cl. Read 113 E3
Drift Rd. Holy 65 E2
Drift Rd. Wink 93 D4
Driftway Cl. Winn 87 E1
Drill Hall Rd. Chert ... 124 A1
Drive The. Ashf 98 B1
Drive The. Bou E 2 C2
Drive The. Newb 130 C4
Drive The. Read 87 D4
Drive The. Slough 43 F2
Drive The. Slough 68 A3
Drive The. Vir W 122 C2
Drive The. Wray 68 B1
Droitwich Cl. Brac 118 C3
Dromepath. Winn 88 A2
Dropmore Rd. Burn ... 21 E3
Droughtan La. Herm ... 79 D4
Drovers Way. Brac 118 C3
Drovers Way. Wood ... 87 F3
Druce Way. That 106 B2
Drummond Cl. Brac ... 118 C4
Drury La. Mort 137 D2
Dry Arch Rd. Sunn ... 120 C2
Dryden Cl. That 106 B3
Dryden. Brac 118 A1
Du Pre Wlk. Bou E ... 3 E2
Dudley Cl. Read 57 F1
Dudley Mews. Read ... 57 F1
Dudley Rd. Ashf 97 F2
Dudley Rd. Felt 98 B4
Duffield La. Sto P 22 C3
Duffield Park. Sto P ... 23 D1
Duffield Rd. Wood 60 C1
Duke Of Cornwall Ave. Camb ... 144 B1
Duke St. Hen-O-T 15 F1
Duke St. Read 86 A4
Duke St. Wind 67 E4
Duke's Ride. Crow 143 D3
Duke's Ride. Finch 143 D3
Dukes Cl. Ashf 98 B2
Dukes Covert. Bags ... 145 F3
Dukes Pl. Mar 1 B1
Dukes Ride. Silc 136 A1
Dukes Wood. Crow ... 143 D3
Dukeshill Rd. Brac 118 A4
Dulman Cl. Read 84 C4
Dulverton Gdns. Read ... 86 B1
Dumas Cl. Yate 149 E3
Dumbarton Way. Caver ... 59 F3
Dunally Park. Shepp ... 125 E1
Dunaways Cl. Read ... 87 E2
Dunbar Dr. Wood 88 A3
Dunboe Pl. Shepp 125 E1
Duncan Dr. Wind 116 C3
Duncan Gdns. Pur O T ... 57 E2
Duncan Rd. Wood 87 F3
Duncannon Cres. Wind ... 66 B2
Dundaff Cl. Camb 152 A3
Dundas Cl. Brac 118 A3
Dundee Rd. Slough ... 42 A4
Dundela Cl. Wood 87 F3
Dunford Pl. Binf 90 C1

Dungells Farm Cl. Yate ... 149 E2
Dungells La. Yate 149 E2
Dungrovehill La. Bish ... 18 B2
Dunholme Cl. Winn ... 87 F1
Dunholme End. Maid ... 39 E2
Dunkirk Cl. Woki 115 F3
Dunluce Gdns. Pangb ... 56 C3
Dunn Cres. Kint 102 A1
Dunnock Way. Warg ... 36 C2
Dunoon Cl. Read 84 C2
Dunsfold Rd. Read ... 84 C4
Dunsmore Gdns. Yate ... 149 D3
Dunstall Cl. Read 84 B4
Dunstan Rd. That 106 C2
Dunster Cl. Caver 59 E3
Dunster Gdns. Slough ... 42 A3
Dunt Ave. Hurst 88 C2
Dunt La. Hurst 88 C2
Duppas Cl. Shepp 125 E2
Durand Rd. Read 87 D1
Durham Ave. Slough ... 42 A4
Durham Cl. Read 113 E4
Durham Cl. Woki 115 F3
Durham Rd. Sand 143 F1
Durley Mead. Brac ... 118 C2
Durrell Way. Shepp ... 125 E2
Dutch Barn Cl. Stan ... 70 B1
Dutton Way. Iver 44 C4
Duval Pl. Bags 145 F2
Dwyer Rd. Read 85 D2
Dyer Straits. Chil 9 F4
Dyson Cl. Wind 67 D2
Dysonswood La. Maple ... 58 C4

Eagle Cl. Brac 143 D4
Eagle Cl. Woki 115 F3
Eagles Nest. Crow 143 D1
Earley Hill Rd. Read ... 87 D3
Earley Pl. Read 86 A4
Earleydene. Sunn 120 A1
Earls Gr. Camb 151 F3
Earlsfield Cl. Caver ... 59 F2
Earlsfield. Holy 40 B1
Earlswood. Brac 118 A1
Easby La. Winn 87 F1
Easington Dr. Winn ... 87 F1
East Burnham La. Burn ... 22 A2
East Cres. Wind 66 C3
East Dr. Read 84 C3
East Dr. Sto P 22 C1
East Dr. Vir W 122 A2
East Green. Black 150 B2
East La. Chiev 51 D1
East Paddock. Sun ... 18 C3
East Ramp. Harm 71 D3
East Rd. Felt 98 B4
East Rd. Maid 39 F3
East Rd. Maid 39 F4
East Ridge. Bou E 3 D2
East St. Read 86 A4
East Stratton Cl. Brac ... 118 C2
East View Cl. Warg ... 36 C1
East View Rd. Warg ... 36 C1
Eastbourne Rd. Slough ... 42 A4
Eastbridge. Slough ... 43 D3
Eastbury Ave. Read ... 57 D3
Eastbury Park. Winn ... 88 B1
Eastbury Shute. Lamb ... 46 C1
Eastchurch Rd. Harm ... 71 F2
Eastcourt Ave. Read ... 87 D3
Eastcroft. Slough 22 A1
Easterfield La. Whi-O-T ... 56 B4
Eastern Ave. Chert ... 124 A3
Eastern Ave. Read ... 86 C3
Eastern Dr. Bou E 3 E2
Eastern La. Crow 143 F2
Eastern Perimeter Rd. Harm ... 71 F3
Eastern Rd. Brac 118 B4
Eastfield Cl. Slough ... 43 D2
Eastfield La. White ... 56 B4
Eastfield Rd. Burn ... 41 D4
Eastfield. Blew 12 A4
Easthampstead Rd. Brac ... 116 C2
Easthampstead Rd. Brac ... 118 A4
Eastheath Ave. Woki ... 116 A2
Eastheath Gdns. Woki ... 116 A2
Eastleigh Rd. Harm ... 71 F2
Eastlyn Rd. Silc 135 F1
Easton Hill. Wick 76 A3
Eastwood Rd. Wood ... 87 F2
Eastworth Rd. Chert ... 124 A1
Eaton Pl. Read 85 F4
Eaton Rd. Camb 151 D2
Ebborn Sq. Winn 114 B4
Ebsworth Cl. Maid ... 20 B2
Eccles Cl. Caver 59 E1
Echelforde Dr. Ashf ... 98 A2
Eddington Hill. Hung ... 100 C4
Eddington Rd. Brac ... 117 F2
Eddystone Wlk. Stan ... 97 F4
Eden Cl. Slough 44 A1
Eden Way. Winn 88 A1
Edenhall Cl. Read ... 57 E2
Edenham Cl. Read ... 57 E1
Edenham Cres. Read ... 85 F3
Edgar Milward Cl. Read ... 58 A1
Edgbarrow Rise. Sand ... 143 D1
Edgcumbe Park Dr. Crow ... 143 D3
Edgecombe La. Newb ... 105 E3

Edgedale Cl. Crow ...
Edgehill St. Read ...
Edgell Cl. Vir W ...
Edgell Rd. Stai ...
Edgemoor Rd. Camb ...
Edgewood Cl. Brac ...
Edinburgh Ave. Slough ...
Edinburgh Dr. Stai ...
Edinburgh Gdns. Wind ...
Edinburgh Rd. Maid ...
Edinburgh Rd. Mar ...
Edinburgh Rd. Read ...
Edith Rd. Maid ...
Edmunds Way. Slough ...
Edney's Hill. Woki ...
Edward Ave. Camb ...
Edward Cl. Stai ...
Edward Rd. Harm ...
Edward Rd. Twyf ...
Edward Rd. Windl ...
Edward Way. Ashf ...
Edwards Cl. Slough ...
Edwards Hill. Lamb ...
Edwin Cl. That ...
Eeklo Pl. Newb ...
Egerton Rd. Read ...
Egerton Rd. Sand ...
Egerton Rd. Slough ...
Egham By-Pass. Eng G ...
Egham Ave. Camb ...
Egmont Dr. Read ...
Egremont Gdns. Slough ...
Egypt La. Far C ...
Eight Acres. Burn ...
Elan Cl. Read ...
Elbow Meadow. Stan ...
Eldart Cl. Read ...
Elder Cl. Read ...
Elderfield Cres. Chil ...
Elderfield Rd. Sto P ...
Eldon Pl. Read ...
Eldon Rd. Read ...
Eldon Sq. Read ...
Eldon St. Read ...
Eldon Terr. Read ...
Eldrick Ct. Felt ...
Elford Cl. Wood ...
Elgar Ave. Crow ...
Elgar Rd. Read ...
Elgarth Dr. Woki ...
Elgin Ave. Ashf ...
Elgin Cres. Harm ...
Eliot Cl. Caver ...
Eliot Cl. That ...
Eliot Dr. Mar ...
Elizabeth Ave. Bags ...
Elizabeth Ave. Newb ...
Elizabeth Ave. Stai ...
Elizabeth Cl. Brac ...
Elizabeth Cl. Hen-O-T ...
Elizabeth Ct. Read ...
Elizabeth Gdns. Ascot ...
Elizabeth Rd. Hen-O-T ...
Elizabeth Rd. Mar ...
Elizabeth Rd. Woki ...
Elizabeth Rout Cl. Shin ...
Elizabeth Way. Sto P ...
Elizabethan Cl. Stan ...
Elizabethan Way. Stan ...
Ellesfield Ave. Brac ...
Ellesmere Cl. Caver ...
Elliman Ave. Slough ...
Ellington Ct. Tapl ...
Ellington Gdns. Tapl ...
Ellington Park. Maid ...
Ellington Rd. Felt ...
Ellington Rd. Tapl ...
Elliot Rise. Burf ...
Ellis Ave. Slough ...
Ellis Rd. Crow ...
Ellison Cl. Wind ...
Ellison Way. Woki ...
Elm Bank. Yate ...
Elm Cl. Far C ...
Elm Cl. Stan ...
Elm Cotts. Ball H ...
Elm Croft. Datch ...
Elm Dr. Bur C ...
Elm Gr. Maid ...
Elm La. Bou E ...
Elm La. Read ...
Elm Lodge Ave. Read ...
Elm Park Rd. Read ...
Elm Park. Windl ...
Elm Rd. Felt ...
Elm Rd. Maple ...
Elm Rd. Read ...
Elm Rd. Wind ...
Elm Tree Cl. Ashf ...
Elmar Green. Slough ...
Elmbank Ave. Eng G ...
Elmcroft Cl. Felt ...
Elmcroft Cl. Read ...
Elmcroft. Gori ...
Elmdon Rd. Harm ...
Elmhurst Rd. Gori ...
Elmhurst Rd. Read ...

163
hurst Rd. Slough
Forndon Cl. Winn

'st Rd. Slough 44 A2
'st Rd. That 106 A3
gh Ct. Caver 59 E2
Cl. Woki 88 C1
ve. That 106 C2
r. Bou E 3 E2
d. Woki 116 A3
ott La. Slough 41 F3
igh Rd. Stai 96 C2
ne Dr. Read 57 E1
ay. Ashf 98 A2
od Rd. Slough 43 D3
od. Maid 20 A2
ood Cres. Camb 152 A3
ood Dr. Camb 152 A4
e Ave. Stan 97 F4
Rd. Read 57 F2
Ave. Caver 59 E3
Cl. Read 57 E1
th Cl. Felt 98 C4
Ave. Caver 59 F3
Dr. Maid 39 E4
on Way. Read 85 D4
n Cl. Winn 87 F1
on Rd. Gori 34 B4
Cl. Eng G 96 A1
e. Slough 42 B4
. Harm 71 F3
. Thea 83 F2
kment The. Wray 95 E4
Rd. Slough 44 A2
n Cres. Arbo 114 C1
ok Way. Read 84 A2
ld Cl. Woki 115 F4
ld Ct. Slough 42 C2
Acres. Upp B 55 D3
Down Cl. Brac 119 D3
s Bldgs. Eton 67 E4
Cl. Woki 115 F4
The. Warg 36 C1
rook Gate. Woki 115 F4
rook Rd. Woki 115 F4
rook Vale. Woki 89 D1
r Green Ct. Caver 59 E3
ts Nest. Binf 90 B1
ts Park. Binf 90 B1
iew Cl. Woki 115 F4
ss Rd. Read 84 B3
ne Cl. Read 84 B4
ne Gr. Newb 104 C1
ne Pl. Newb 104 C1
ne Rd. Ham M 104 C1
ne Rd. Newb 104 C1
ne St. Ham M 130 B3
ne St. Newb 130 B3
ne Way. Brim 133 F3
Rd. Harm 71 F3
ield Cl. Eng G 95 E1
ield Rd. Thea 83 E2
eart Dr. Felt 71 F1
urst. Eng G 95 E1
nere Park. Burl 119 F3
nere Rd. Brac 90 C1
field. Camb 152 B3
n Gdns. Wray 68 B1
dale Cl. Felt 98 C4
dale Cres. Slough 41 E4
dale Rd. Read 86 B2
dale Way. That 106 A2
dale. Brac 118 A3
Cl. Stan 97 E4
Way. Stan 97 E4
ne Rd. Wood 88 A4
rise Way. That 107 D1
g Cl. Read 85 F4
g Way. Brac 118 C3
n Cl. Camb 151 E4
n Cres. Newb 105 D1
n Ct. Read 85 F3
Sq. Harm 71 F3
ve. Caver 59 D3
Cl. Camb 153 F3
Cl. Slough 41 F3
ll Cl. Winn 87 F1
wald Cl. Chert 123 F1
n Court Dr. Read 87 D4
n Court Gdns. Read 87 D4
n Dene. Newb 104 C1
n Rd. Read 86 B3
Wlk. That 106 A2
ton Dr. Wind 67 D3
e Cl. Silc 135 F1
Cres. Harm 71 F3
Rd. Camb 145 D1
le Gdns. Holy 40 A1
le Rd. Winn 88 A2
le Way. Camb 152 B2
Cl. Read 85 D4
Ave. Slough 42 A4
Pl. Lamb 25 D2
St. Newb 130 B4
St. Read 86 A3
Rd. Ashf 97 F2
Cl. Datch 68 A4
Ct. Eton 67 E4
Pl. Mar 1 B1
Rd. Datch 68 A4
Rd. Harl 71 F4
Sq. Eton 67 E4
Eton Wick Rd. Eton 42 A1
Eustace Cres. Woki 116 B4
Evedon. Brac 118 A1
Evelyn Cres. Shepp 125 F4
Evelyn Ct. Wood 87 F3
Evelyn Way. Shepp 125 F4
Evendon's La. Bark 115 F1
Evendons Cl. Woki 116 A2
Evenlode Rd. Bou E 3 D2
Evenlode Way. Sand 150 B4
Evenlode. Maid 39 F4
Everard Ave. Slough 42 C2
Everest Rd. Camb 151 E4
Everest Rd. Crow 143 D3
Everest Rd. Stan 97 F4
Evergreen Dr. Read 84 C2
Evergreen Rd. Camb 152 A1
Evergreen Way. Stan 97 E4
Evergreen Way. Woki 115 F3
Everington La. Yatt 53 D1
Everland Rd. Hung 100 B3
Eversley Rd. Arbo 114 C1
Eversley St. Finch 141 D1
Eversley Way. Stai 123 E4
Evesham Rd. Caver 59 D3
Evesham Wlk. Crow 143 E1
Evreham Rd. Iver 44 C4
Evreux Cl. That 106 C1
Ewing Way. Newb 131 D4
Exbourne Rd. Read 113 E4
Exchange Rd. Ascot 120 B2
Exeforde Ave. Ashf 98 A2
Exeter Ct. Read 113 D4
Exeter Gdns. Yate 149 D4
Exeter Rd. Stan 71 F2
Exeter Rd. Thea 83 F2
Exeter Way. Stan 71 F3
Exmoor Rd. That 106 B2
Explorer Ave. Stan 97 F4
Exwick Sq. Read 113 E4
Eylham. Pur O T 57 D3
Eynsford Cl. Caver 59 F3
Eynsham Rd. Wood 87 F4

Fagg's Rd. Harm 71 F2
Fair Lawn Green. Read 86 C1
Fair Mile. Hen-O-T 15 E2
Fairacre. Maid 39 E3
Fairacres Ind Est. Wind 66 B3
Faircroft. Slough 22 A1
Faircross Quarters. Herm 78 C3
Faircross Rd. Read 85 E3
Faircross. Brac 118 A3
Fairfax. Brac 118 A4
Fairfield App. Wray 68 B1
Fairfield Ave. Datch 68 B4
Fairfield Ave. Stai 96 C2
Fairfield Cl. Datch 68 B4
Fairfield Dr. Camb 151 F2
Fairfield La. Far C 22 A2
Fairfield Rd. Burn 21 E1
Fairfield Rd. Gori 34 B4
Fairfield Rd. Wray 68 B1
Fairfield. Comp 31 E2
Fairfields. Hung 100 B3
Fairford Rd. Maid 39 F4
Fairford Rd. Read 57 E1
Fairhaven. Eng G 95 F2
Fairholme Rd. Ashf 97 F2
Fairholme. Felt 98 C4
Fairlawn Park. Wind 66 C2
Fairlawns Cl. Stai 97 D1
Fairlea. Maid 39 D2
Fairlie Rd. Slough 42 A4
Fairlight Ave. Wind 67 E3
Fairlop Cl. Bur C 84 B2
Fairmead Cl. Sand 150 C4
Fairmead Rd. Shin 113 F3
Fairoak Way. Tad 134 B1
Fairsted Cl. Read 85 D4
Fairview Ave. Read 87 D3
Fairview Ct. Stai 97 D1
Fairview Dr. Stai 124 C2
Fairview Estate. Hen-O-T 35 F4
Fairview Rd. Burn 41 D4
Fairview Rd. Hung 100 B3
Fairview Rd. Slough 21 F1
Fairview Rd. Woki 116 B3
Fairwater Dr. Wood 87 E3
Fairway Ave. Read 84 B3
Fairway Dr. Char 61 D3
Fairway Hts. Camb 152 A3
Fairway The. Burn 21 E2
Fairway The. Camb 152 A2
Fairway The. Fla H 3 E4
Fairway The. Maid 39 D2
Fairway. Chert 124 A1
Fairways. Ashf 98 A1
Fakenham Cl. Read 114 A4
Fakenham Way. Crow 143 E1
Falaise. Eng G 95 F2
Falcon Ave. Read 86 C1
Falcon Cl. Camb 152 C4
Falcon Dr. Stan 70 C1
Falcon Fields. Tad 135 D1
Falcon House Gdns. Ball H 129 F1
Falcon Way. Shepp 125 F4
Falcon Way. Woki 115 F3
Falcon Way. Yate 149 D3
Falcons Croft. Woo G 3 F4
Falconwood. Eng G 95 F2
Falkland Dr. Newb 130 C4
Falkland Garth. Newb 130 B4
Falkland Rd. Caver 59 D1
Falkland Rd. Newb 130 B3
Fallowfield Cl. Caver 59 D2
Fallowfield. Yate 149 D4
Falmouth Cl. Camb 152 A2
Falmouth Rd. Read 113 E4
Falmouth Rd. Slough 42 A4
Falmouth Way. That 106 C2
Falstaff Ave. Read 86 C1
Fane Way. Maid 39 E3
Fanes Cl. Brac 117 F4
Faraday Cl. Arbo 140 C4
Faraday Cl. Slough 42 A4
Faraday Rd. Bark 141 D4
Faraday Rd. Newb 105 D2
Faraday Rd. Slough 42 A4
Farcrosse Cl. Sand 150 B4
Fareham Dr. Yate 149 D4
Faringdon Cl. Sand 143 E1
Faringdon Dr. Brac 118 B2
Faringdon Wlk. Read 85 D2
Farleigh Mews. Caver 59 F3
Farley Copse. Brac 117 F4
Farm Cl. Ascot 120 B2
Farm Cl. Brac 117 F4
Farm Cl. Brac 143 E4
Farm Cl. Chert 123 D2
Farm Cl. Gori 34 B3
Farm Cl. Holy 40 B1
Farm Cl. Maid 39 D4
Farm Cl. Pur O T 57 E3
Farm Cl. Shepp 125 D1
Farm Cl. Stai 96 C2
Farm Cl. Yate 149 E3
Farm Cres. Slough 43 E4
Farm Dr. Read 84 A3
Farm Lea. Woo G 3 F4
Farm Rd. Bou E 2 C2
Farm Rd. Burn 41 D3
Farm Rd. Camb 151 F1
Farm Rd. Hen-O-T 35 F4
Farm Rd. Maid 39 D4
Farm Rd. Stai 97 D1
Farm View. Yate 149 E3
Farm Way. Stan 69 F1
Farm Yd. Wind 67 E4
Farman Cl. Wood 88 A4
Farmer's Rd. Stai 96 C2
Farmers Cl. Maid 39 D2
Farmers Cl. Read 113 E3
Farmers Way. Maid 39 D2
Farmiloe Cl. Pur O T 57 E2
Farnburn Ave. Slough 42 A4
Farnell Rd. Stan 97 D3
Farnham Cl. Brac 118 B4
Farnham Dr. Caver 59 F2
Farnham La. Slough 22 A2
Farnham Park La. Far C 22 B2
Farnham Rd. Slough 42 B4
Farningham. Brac 118 C2
Farnsfield Cl. Read 114 A4
Farrell Cl. Camb 151 E2
Farriers Cl. Wood 87 F4
Farrowdene Rd. Read 113 E4
Farthing Green La. Sto P 23 D2
Farthingales The. Maid 40 A4
Fatherson Rd. Read 86 B4
Faulkner Pl. Bags 145 F2
Faversham Rd. Crow 143 E1
Fawcett Cres. Wood 87 E3
Fawcett Rd. Wind 67 D3
Fawler Mead. Brac 118 C3
Fawley Bottom La. Faw (Bu) 15 E4
Fawley Cl. Maid 19 E1
Fawley Rd. Read 85 E3
Fawns Manor Cl. Felt 98 B4
Fawns Manor Rd. Felt 98 B4
Fawsley Cl. Stan 69 F4
Faygate Way. Read 87 D1
Feathers La. Wray 96 A3
Felbridge Cl. Camb 151 F1
Felix La. Shepp 125 F2
Felixstowe Cl. Winn 87 E1
Fellow Green Rd. West E 153 F3
Fellow Green. West E 153 F3
Fells The. Read 84 A3
Felstead Cl. Read 86 C2
Feltham Hill Rd. Ashf 98 A2
Feltham Rd. Ashf 98 A2
Felthorpe Cl. Read 114 A4
Felton Way. Read 84 B4
Fencote. Brac 118 B2
Fennel Cl. Newb 105 E3
Fennel Cl. Read 86 C1
Fenns La. West E 153 F3
Fenton Ave. Stai 97 E2
Fern Cl. Camb 152 B2
Fern Cl. Read 84 B3
Fern Dr. Burn 41 D4
Fern Glen. Read 57 E1
Fern La. Lit M 2 C3
Fern Wlk. Ashf 97 E2
Fernbank Cres. Burl 119 E4
Fernbank Pl. Burl 119 E4
Fernbank Rd. Burl 119 E4
Fernbank. Woki 141 E4
Fernbrook Rd. Caver 58 C3
Ferndale Ave. Read 85 D2
Ferndale Cl. Read 57 E2
Ferndale Rd. Ashf 97 F2
Ferne Cl. Gori 34 B4
Fernery The. Stai 96 C2
Fernhill Cl. Black 150 C1
Fernhill Cl. Brac 90 C1
Fernhill La. Black 150 C1
Fernhill Rd. Black 150 C1
Fernhill Wlk. Black 150 C1
Fernhurst Rd. Ashf 98 B2
Fernhurst Rd. Bur C 84 B2
Ferniehurst. Camb 151 F2
Fernley Ct. Maid 19 E1
Ferrard Cl. Burl 119 E4
Ferrier Gr. Newb 131 D4
Ferry Ave. Stai 96 C1
Ferry La. Bou E 3 D1
Ferry La. Gori 34 A3
Ferry La. Hamb 16 B3
Ferry La. Medm 17 D3
Ferry La. Shepp 125 D1
Ferry La. Sou S 14 A2
Ferry La. Stai 124 B3
Ferry La. Warg 36 B1
Ferry La. Wray 96 A3
Ferry Rd. Maid 40 B2
Ferry Rd. Sou S 14 B2
Fettiplace. Gr She 48 A2
Fetty Pl. Maid 39 E2
Fidler's La. East I 30 C4
Fidlers Wlk. Warg 36 C1
Field Cl. Bur C 111 D1
Field Cl. Harl 71 E4
Field End. Warg 36 C1
Field End. West E 153 F3
Field Farm Rd. Bur C 84 C1
Field House Cl. Brac 120 A1
Field Hurst. Slough 43 F1
Field La. Camb 151 F1
Field Park. Brac 118 B4
Field Rd. Black 150 C1
Field Rd. Pease 29 E1
Field Rd. Read 86 A3
Field View. Caver 59 D2
Field View. Felt 98 B2
Field View. Stai 96 B2
Fielden Pl. Brac 118 B4
Fieldfare Ave. Yate 149 D3
Fieldhead Gdns. Bou E 3 D2
Fieldhouse Ind Est. Mar 1 C1
Fieldhouse La. Mar 1 C1
Fieldhouse Way. Mar 1 C1
Fielding Gdns. Crow 143 D2
Fielding Rd. Maid 39 D4
Fielding Rd. Sand 150 C3
Fieldings The. Holy 65 D4
Fieldridge. Newb 105 E3
Fields The. Slough 42 B2
Fieldway. Winn 88 B1
Fifehead Cl. Ashf 97 F1
Fifield La. Holy 65 E2
Fifield Rd. Holy 65 E4
Fifth Rd. Newb 104 C1
Filbert Dr. Read 84 B4
Filey Rd. Read 86 C4
Filey Spur. Slough 42 A2
Filmer Rd. Wind 66 B3
Finbeck Way. Read 113 F4
Finch Ct. Maid 39 E3
Finch Rd. Read 87 E2
Finch Way. Bur C 111 D2
Fincham End Dr. Crow 142 C2
Finchampstead Rd. Finch 142 A4
Finchampstead Rd. Woki 142 A4
Findhorn Cl. Sand 150 B4
Finmere. Brac 118 B1
Finney Dr. Windl 146 B2
Finstock Cl. Winn 87 E1
Finstock Green. Brac 118 C3
Fir Cottage Rd. Bark 141 F4
Fir Cottage Rd. Woki 141 F4
Fir Dr. Black 150 B2
Fir Tree Ave. Sto P 22 C1
Fir Tree Cl. Ascot 120 A1
Fir Tree La. Newb 105 F2
Fir Tree Paddock. West I 10 A1
Fir's End. Bur C 111 D1
Firbank Pl. Eng G 95 D1
Fircroft Cl. Read 57 E1
Fircroft Cl. Sto P 23 D3
Fireball Hill. Sunn 120 B1
Firglen Dr. Yate 149 E4
Firgrove Rd. Yate 149 D3
Firlands Ave. Camb 151 E3
Firlands. Brac 118 B2
Firmstone Cl. Winn 87 E1
Firs Ave. Wind 66 C2
Firs Cl. Woki 141 F4
Firs Dr. Slough 43 F3
Firs La. Maid 38 C2
Firs Rd. Read 84 B3
Firs The. That 106 A2
First Ave. Mar 2 A1
First Cres. Slough 42 B4
Firtree Cl. Sand 142 C1
Firview Cl. Mar 1 C1
Firwood Dr. Camb 151 E3
Firwood Rd. Went 121 F2
Fisher Green. Binf 90 A1
Fisher's La. Cold A 79 D1
Fisherman's La. Alde 135 D4
Fisherman's Way. Bou E 3 D2
Fishermans Retreat. Mar 1 C1
Fishers Ct. Caver 59 E3
Fishers Wood. Went 121 E1
Fishery Rd. Maid 40 B3
Fishponds Cl. Woki 116 A2
Fishponds Rd. Woki 116 A2
Fitzrobert Pl. Eng G 96 A1
Fitzroy Cres. Wood 88 A3
Five Acre. Read 57 E1
Five Acres. Woo G 3 F4
Flag Staff Sq. That 106 C1
Flambards. Caver 59 E1
Flamborough Cl. Winn 87 F1
Flamborough Spur. Slough 42 A2
Flamingo Cl. Woki 115 F3
Flanders Ct. Stai 96 B2
Flats The. Black 150 B2
Flaxman Cl. Read 86 C1
Flecker Cl. That 106 B3
Fleet Cl. Woki 115 F3
Fleet Hill. Finch 141 E1
Fleet St. Finch 141 D1
Fleetham Gdns. Wood 87 E1
Fleetway. Stai 123 E3
Fleetwood Rd. Slough 42 C3
Fleming Cl. Arbo 140 C4
Fleming Rd. Newb 105 D2
Flemish Fields. Chert 124 A1
Fletcher Gdns. Brac 117 E4
Flexford Green. Brac 117 F2
Flintgrove. Brac 118 B4
Flintlock Cl. Stan 70 A2
Flodden Dr. Bur C 84 B2
Floral Way. That 106 C2
Florence Ave. Maid 39 F4
Florence Ave. Maid 40 A4
Florence Cl. Yate 149 E3
Florence Gdns. Stai 97 D1
Florence Rd. Sand 150 C4
Florence Wlk. Read 86 B4
Florian Gdns. Read 85 D3
Flower's Hill. Pangb 56 B2
Flowers Piece. Asham 54 A3
Fobney St. Read 86 A4
Fokerham Rd. That 106 C1
Folder's La. Brac 91 E1
Foliejohn Way. Whi Wa 38 C1
Folkestone Ct. Slough 44 A1
Follet Cl. Old W 68 A1
Folly La. Bur 110 C3
Folly La. Sulhd 110 C3
Folly Rd. Ink 127 F3
Folly Rd. Lamb 25 D2
Folly The. Newb 105 D1
Fontmell Cl. Ashf 98 A2
Fontmell Park. Ashf 98 A2
Fontwell Cl. Maid 39 D4
Fontwell Dr. Read 84 C3
Fontwell Rd. Newb 105 D1
Forbes Chase. Sand 150 B4
Forbury La. Kint 128 B4
Forbury Rd. Read 86 B4
Forbury The. Read 86 A4
Ford Cl. Ashf 97 F1
Ford Cl. Stai 125 D2
Ford La. Swal 140 A2
Ford Rd. Ashf 97 F2
Ford Rd. Bis 153 F2
Ford Rd. Chert 124 A1
Ford Rd. West E 153 F2
Fordbridge Cl. Chert 124 A1
Fordbridge Rd. Ashf 97 F2
Fordbridge Rd. Shepp 125 F2
Fordham Way. Winn 87 E1
Fordwater Rd. Chert 124 A1
Fordwells Dr. Brac 118 C3
Forehead The. Bee H 137 F2
Forest Cl. Brac 119 E3
Forest Cl. Tad 134 C1
Forest Dr. Stai 98 C1
Forest End Rd. Sand 150 A4
Forest Green Rd. Holy 65 D3
Forest Green. Brac 118 B4
Forest Hill. Read 57 F1
Forest Hills. Camb 151 D2
Forest Rd. Ascot 92 C1
Forest Rd. Binf 90 B2
Forest Rd. Burl 92 C1
Forest Rd. Crow 143 E3
Forest Rd. New G 92 C1
Forest Rd. Wind 66 C3
Foresters Sq. Brac 118 C3
Foresters Way. Crow 143 F2
Forge Cl. Caver 59 E1
Forge Cl. Kint 102 A1
Forge Dr. Far C 22 B3
Forge Hill. Hamp N 53 D3
Forge The. Hung 100 B3
Forlease Cl. Maid 40 A3
Forlease Dr. Maid 40 A3
Forlease Rd. Maid 40 A3
Formby Cl. Winn 87 F2
Forndon Cl. Winn 87 F1

Fortrose Cl. Sand 150 B4
Fortrose Wlk. Read 84 C2
Forty Green Dr. Mar 1 A1
Fosseway. Crow 143 D3
Fossewood Dr. Camb 151 E4
Foster Ave. Wind 66 C2
Fosters Gr. Windl 146 A3
Fosters La. Wood 87 F3
Fosters Path. Slough 21 F1
Fotherby Ct. Maid 40 A3
Fotheringay Gdns. Slough .. 42 A3
Foundary Ct. Chert 124 A1
Foundation Park. Maid 38 C2
Foundry La. Hort 69 D2
Fountain Gdns. Wind 67 E2
Fountains Garth. Brac 118 A3
Fourth Ave. Mar 2 A1
Fowler Cl. Read 87 D2
Fowlers La. Brac 118 A4
Fox Cl. Bur C 111 D2
Fox Covert Cl. Ascot 120 B2
Fox Covert. Light 153 D4
Fox Dr. Yate 149 E4
Fox La. Yate 149 D4
Fox Lane N. Chert 123 F1
Fox Lane S. Chert 123 F1
Fox Rd. Slough 43 E1
Foxborough Cl. Slough 44 A1
Foxborough. Swal 139 E3
Foxbury. Lamb 25 D1
Foxcombe Dr. Read 84 B4
Foxcote. Woki 142 A4
Foxdown Cl. Camb 151 E3
Foxes Piece. Mar 1 C2
Foxes Wlk. Char 61 D2
Foxglove Cl. Stan 97 E4
Foxglove Cl. Woki 115 E4
Foxglove Gdns. Read 85 F4
Foxhays Rd. Read 113 E4
Foxherne. Slough 43 E2
Foxhill Cl. Caver 60 A3
Foxhill Cres. Camb 152 A4
Foxhill La. Caver 59 F3
Foxhill Rd. Read 86 C3
Foxhollow Dr. Far C 22 B4
Foxhunt Gr. Read 84 C2
Foxhunter Way. That 105 F2
Foxley Cl. Sand 150 B3
Foxley La. Binf 90 B1
Framewood Rd. Sto P 23 E3
Framlingham Dr. Caver 59 F3
Frampton Cl. Wood 60 C1
France Hill Dr. Camb 151 E3
Frances Ave. Maid 20 B1
Frances Rd. Wind 67 E3
Frances The. That 106 B2
Francis Chichester Cl. Ascot .120 A2
Francis Cl. Stai 125 D3
Francis Gdns. New G 91 F1
Francis St. Read 86 A3
Francis Way. Slough 41 E3
Frank London Cl. Bou E 3 E2
Franklin Ave. Slough 42 A4
Franklin Ave. Tad 135 D1
Franklin St. Read 85 F4
Franklyn Cres. Wind 66 B2
Frascati Way. Maid 39 F4
Fraser Ave. Caver 59 E3
Fraser Mead. Sand 150 A2
Fraser Rd. Brac 118 A4
Frederick Pl. Woki 116 A3
Free Prae Rd. Chert 124 A1
Freeborn Way. Brac 118 C4
Freeman Cl. Shepp 125 F3
Freemans Cl. Hung 100 B3
Freemans Cl. Sto P 23 D3
Freemantle Rd. Bags 145 F2
Freesia Cl. Woki 115 E4
French Gdns. Black 150 B2
Frenchum Gdns. Slough 41 F3
Frensham Cl. Yate 149 D3
Frensham Green. Read 86 C1
Frensham Rd. Crow 143 D4
Frensham Wlk. Far C 22 B3
Frensham. Brac 118 B2
Freshfield Cl. Winn 87 F2
Freshwater Rd. Read 86 C4
Freshwood Dr. Yate 149 E2
Friar St. Read 86 A4
Friars Keep. Brac 118 A3
Friars Rd. Newb 131 D4
Friars Rd. Vir W 122 B3
Friars Way. Chert 124 A2
Friary Rd. Ascot 120 A2
Friary Rd. Wray 68 B1
Friary Rd. Wray 95 E4
Friary The. Old W 68 B1
Friday St. Hen-O-T 15 F1
Frieth Cl. Read 87 D2
Frilsham Rd. Read 85 D2
Frimley By-Pass. Camb 151 E1
Frimley Cl. Wood 87 E4
Frimley Green Rd. Camb 151 E1
Frimley Grove Gdns. Camb .. 151 F1
Frimley Hall Dr. Camb 151 F3
Frimley High St. Camb 151 E1
Frimley Rd. Camb 151 D2
Fringford Cl. Winn 87 E1
Frith Hill Rd. Camb 152 A1

Frithe The. Slough 43 D4
Frithwald Rd. Chert 123 F1
Frobisher Cres. Stan 97 F4
Frobisher Gdns. Stan 97 F4
Frobisher. Brac 118 B1
Frodsham Way. Sand 143 F1
Frog Hall Dr. Woki 116 C3
Frog La. Brac 118 A3
Frogmill. Hurl 17 E2
Frogmore Cl. Slough 42 A2
Frogmore Gr. Black 150 B2
Frogmore Park Dr. Black ... 150 B2
Frogmore Rd. Sand 150 B3
Frogmore Way. Read 85 D3
Fromer Rd. Bou E 3 E2
Fromont Dr. That 106 B2
Fromow Gdns. Windl 146 B2
Front St. East G 47 E3
Froxfield Ave. Read 85 F3
Froxfield Down. Brac 118 C2
Fruen Rd. Felt 98 C4
Fry Rd. Ashf 97 E2
Fry's La. Bags 145 E1
Fry's La. Yate 149 F4
Frymley View. Wind 66 B3
Fuchia Way. Camb 153 F3
Fuchsia Cl. Read 84 B3
Fullbrook Cl. Maid 40 A4
Fullbrook Cl. Woki 89 D1
Fullbrook Cres. Read 57 E2
Fuller Cl. That 106 C1
Fuller's La. Bur C 112 A2
Fullers La. Ball H 129 E1
Fulmead Rd. Read 85 E4
Fulmer Cl. Read 87 D1
Fulmer Common Rd. Fulm 23 F3
Fulmer Rd. Fulm 23 F4
Furlong Cl. Bou E 3 D2
Furlong Rd. Bou E 3 D2
Furness Way. Oak G 66 B3
Furness Way. Oak G 66 B3
Furness. Oak G 66 B3
Furnival Ave. Slough 42 A4
Furnival Cl. Went 122 B2
Furrow Way. Maid 39 D2
Furze Hill Cres. Crow 143 E2
Furze Platt Rd. Maid 19 D1
Furze Platt Rd. Maid 19 E1
Furze Rd. Maid 19 E1
Furze Rd. Tad 134 C1
Furzebank. Ascot 120 B3
Furzemoors. Brac 118 A2
Furzen Cl. Slough 22 A1
Fuzzens Wlk. Wind 66 C3
Fydlers Cl. Ascot 93 D1
Fyfield Cl. Black 150 B3
Fyfield Rd. That 106 B1
Fylingdales. That 106 B2

Gables Ave. Ashf 97 F2
Gables Cl. Datch 68 A4
Gables Cl. Maid 40 A4
Gabriels The. Newb 130 B3
Gage Cl. Maid 39 F2
Gainsborough Ave. Kint 102 A1
Gainsborough Cl. Camb 151 F4
Gainsborough Cl. Wood 88 A3
Gainsborough Cres. Hen-O-T . 35 E4
Gainsborough Dr. Ascot 119 E4
Gainsborough Dr. Maid 39 E2
Gainsborough Hill. Hen-O-T ... 35 E4
Gainsborough Rd. Hen-O-T ... 35 E4
Gainsborough Rd. Read 85 D3
Gainsborough. Brac 118 B2
Gainsborough. Cook 19 F3
Gairn Cl. Read 85 D4
Galahad Cl. Slough 42 A2
Gale Dr. Light 146 A1
Galley La. Head 132 B1
Galleymead Rd. Stan 69 F3
Gallop The. Yate 149 E4
Gallys Rd. Wind 66 B3
Galsworthy Dr. Caver 59 F3
Galsworthy Rd. Chert 124 A1
Galton Rd. Sunn 120 C2
Galvin Rd. Slough 42 B3
Garde Rd. Sonn 60 C2
Garden Cl. Ashf 98 B1
Garden Cl. Maid 39 D3
Garden Close La. Newb 130 B2
Gardeners La. Brad 55 E2
Gardens The. Harm 71 E1
Gardens The. Sou S 14 B2
Gardens The. Vir W 122 C2
Gardner Rd. Maid 19 F1
Garfield Rd. Camb 151 E3
Garford Cres. Newb 130 B4
Garlands Cl. Bur C 111 D1
Garnet Cl. Mar 1 B1
Garnet Field. Yate 149 D3
Garnet Hill. Read 86 A3
Garnet St. Read 86 A3
Garrard Rd. Slough 21 F1
Garrard St. Read 86 A4
Garrett Rd. Woki 141 F4
Garrick Cl. Stai 97 D1
Garson La. Wray 95 E4
Garson's La. New G 92 A4

Garston Cl. Read 85 D2
Garston Cres. Read 84 A3
Garston Gr. Woki 115 F1
Garswood. Brac 118 B2
Garth Cl. Winn 88 B1
Garth Rd. Mort 137 D3
Garth Sq. Brac 91 D1
Garthlands. Maid 19 E1
Gas Works Rd. Read 86 B4
Gascon's Gr. Slough 22 A1
Gaskell Mews. Newb 131 D4
Gaskells End. Maple 58 B4
Gaston Bridge Rd. Shepp .. 125 E2
Gaston Way. Shepp 125 E2
Gatcombe Cl. Read 84 B2
Gatehampton Rd. Gori 34 B3
Gatewick Cl. Slough 42 C3
Gatward Ave. Maid 39 D2
Gaveston Rd. Slough 21 F1
Gayhurst Cl. Caver 59 E3
Geffers Ride. Ascot 119 F4
Geneva Cl. Shepp 125 F3
Geoffreyson Rd. Caver 58 C3
George Cl. Mar 1 C2
George Green Rd. Slough .. 43 F4
George St. Caver 59 D1
George St. Read 85 F4
George St. Stai 96 C2
Georgeham Rd. Crow 143 E1
Georgian Cl. Camb 151 F4
Georgian Cl. Stai 97 D2
Gerrards Cross Rd. Sto P ... 23 D4
Gibbel La. Camb 152 A4
Gibbons Cl. Sand 150 B4
Gibbs Cl. Woki 141 F3
Gibson Cl. Slough 43 F1
Gibson Pl. Stan 70 B1
Gifford Cl. Caver 60 B1
Gilbert Rd. Camb 151 E1
Gilbey Wlk. Bou E 3 E2
Gilchrist Way. Bish 38 A3
Giles Travers Cl. Stai 123 E3
Gillette Way. Read 86 A1
Gilliat Rd. Slough 42 C3
Gilliatt Cl. Iver 44 C4
Gillott's La. Shipl 35 E4
Gillotts Cl. Hen-O-T 35 D4
Gilman Cres. Wind 66 B2
Gilmore Cl. Slough 43 E2
Gilmore Cres. Ashf 98 A2
Gilpin Way. Harl 71 F4
Gilroy Cl. Newb 130 B3
Gingells Farm Rd. Char 61 D3
Gipsy La. Brac 118 B4
Gipsy La. Hung 100 C4
Gipsy La. Read 57 F1
Gipsy La. Read 87 E2
Gipsy La. Woki 114 B4
Gipsy La. Woki 116 B2
Girton Cl. Crow 143 F1
Glade Rd. Mar 1 C1
Glade The. Ascot 120 B2
Glade The. Newb 130 C4
Glade The. Pur O T 57 E2
Glade The. Stai 97 D1
Gladridge Cl. Read 87 E2
Gladstone Cl. Kint 102 A1
Gladstone Ind Est. Maid 39 F4
Gladstone La. Cold A 106 B4
Gladstone Way. Slough 42 A3
Glaisdale. That 106 B1
Glamis Way. Read 84 A2
Glanmor Rd. Slough 43 D3
Glanty The. Stai 96 A2
Glasgow Rd. Slough 42 A4
Glassonby Wlk. Camb 152 B3
Glebe Cl. Dorn 40 C2
Glebe Cl. Light 146 B1
Glebe Cl. Moul 13 F3
Glebe Gdns. Sonn 60 C2
Glebe La. Sonn 60 C2
Glebe Rd. Maid 40 A3
Glebe Rd. Old W 68 A1
Glebe Rd. Pur O T 57 E2
Glebe Rd. Read 86 B3
Glebe Rd. Stai 96 B1
Glebe Rd. Stai 97 D2
Glebe Ride. Gori 34 A3
Glebe The. Aldw 32 C2
Glebe The. Black 150 C2
Glebefields. Newb 105 D3
Glebeland Gdns. Shepp 125 E2
Glebeland Rd. Camb 150 C2
Glebelands Rd. Woki 116 B4
Glebewood. Brac 118 B2
Glen Ave. Ashf 98 A2
Glen Cl. Stai 125 D3
Glen Innes. Sand 143 F1
Glen The. Stai 135 F1
Glen The. Slough 43 E1
Glenapp Grange. Mort 136 C3
Glenavon Gdns. Slough 43 E2
Glenavon Gdns. Yate 149 E2
Glenbeigh Terr. Read 85 F3
Glendale Ave. Newb 130 B3
Glendale Rd. Tad 135 D1

Glendevon Rd. Wood 87 F4
Gleneagles Cl. Stan 70 B1
Glenfield Rd. Ashf 98 B1
Glenhaven Dr. Stan 70 B1
Glenhurst Cl. Black 150 C2
Glenmore Cl. That 106 B1
Glennon Cl. Read 85 E2
Glenrosa Rd. Read 85 D4
Glentworth Pl. Slough 42 B3
Glenwood Dr. Read 84 B4
Glenwood. Brac 118 B3
Globe Farm La. Black 150 A3
Gloucester Ave. Slough 42 B4
Gloucester Cres. Stai 97 E1
Gloucester Ct. Read 85 E4
Gloucester Dr. Stai 96 B3
Gloucester Gdns. Bags .. 145 F2
Gloucester Pl. Wind 67 E3
Gloucester Rd. Bags 145 F2
Gloucester Rd. Maid 19 F1
Gloucester Rd. Newb 104 C1
Gloucester Rd. Read 85 E4
Glyme Wlk. Read 84 C2
Glynswood. Camb 151 F2
Goaters Rd. Burl 119 E4
Goddard Cl. Shin 113 F3
Goddard Cl. Stai 124 C3
Goddard Ct. Winn 88 A1
Goddards La. Camb 151 D2
Goddington Rd. Bou E 3 D3
Godolphin Rd. Slough 42 B3
Godstow Cl. Wood 87 F4
Goffs Rd. Ashf 98 B3
Gogmore Farm Cl. Chert .. 123 F1
Gogmore La. Chert 124 A1
Gold Cup La. Burl 119 E4
Goldcrest Cl. Yate 149 D3
Goldcrest Way. Read 84 A3
Golden Ball La. Cook 19 D2
Golden Oak. Far C 22 B3
Golden Orb Wood. Brac 117 E4
Goldfinch La. Newt 131 F2
Golding Cl. That 106 C2
Goldney Rd. Camb 152 B2
Goldsmid Rd. Read 85 F4
Goldsmith Cl. That 106 B3
Goldsmith Way. Crow 143 D2
Goldsworthy Way. Slough ... 41 E4
Goldthorpe Gdns. Read .. 113 F4
Goldwell Dr. Newb 104 C2
Golf Dr. Camb 152 A2
Goodboy's La. Bur C 112 A1
Goodboy's La. Mort 112 A1
Goodchild Rd. Woki 116 B3
Goodings Green. Woki 116 C3
Goodliffe Gdns. Pur O T ... 57 E2
Goodman Park. Slough 43 E3
Goodman Pl. Stai 96 C2
Goodrich Cl. Caver 59 F3
Goodways Dr. Brac 118 B4
Goodwin Cl. Bur C 84 C2
Goodwin Meadows. Woo G ... 3 F3
Goodwin Rd. Slough 21 F1
Goodwin Wlk. Newb 130 B3
Goodwood Cl. Bur C 111 D1
Goodwood Cl. Camb 151 D1
Goodwood Rise. Mar B 1 B4
Goodwood Way. Newb 105 E1
Goose Cnr. New G 91 F2
Goose Green Way. That .. 106 C2
Goose Green. Far C 22 A2
Goose Green. Lamb 25 D2
Goose La. Leck 49 F3
Goose Pool. Chert 123 F1
Gordon Ave. Camb 151 E2
Gordon Cl. Stai 97 D1
Gordon Cres. Camb 151 E2
Gordon Cres. Comp 31 F2
Gordon Dr. Shepp 125 E1
Gordon Pl. Read 85 E4
Gordon Rd. Ashf 97 F3
Gordon Rd. Camb 151 E3
Gordon Rd. Maid 39 E4
Gordon Rd. Newb 105 D1
Gordon Rd. Shepp 125 E2
Gordon Rd. Stai 96 B2
Gordon Rd. That 106 A3
Gordon Rd. Wind 66 C3
Gordon Wlk. Yate 149 F3
Gore End Rd. Ball H 129 D2
Gore Rd. Burn 21 D1
Goring La. Bur C 111 F2
Goring Rd. Stai 96 C2
Gorrick Sq. Brac 116 A2
Gorse Bank. Light 153 D4
Gorse Dr. Wood 88 A4
Gorse Hill La. Vir W 122 B3
Gorse Hill Rd. Vir W 122 B3
Gorse Meade. Slough 42 A3
Gorse Rd. Camb 151 F1
Gorse Rd. Cook 19 F3
Gorse Ride N. Woki 141 F4
Gorse Ride S. Woki 141 F3
Gorselands. Caver 59 D3
Gorselands. Newb 130 B3
Gorselands. Tad 135 E1

Gorselands. Yate
Gosbrook Rd. Caver
Gosden Rd. West E
Gosforth Cl. Read
Goslar Way. Wind
Gosling Green. Slough
Gosling Rd. Slough
Gosnell Cl. Camb
Gossmore Cl. Mar
Gossmore La. Mar
Goswell Hill. Wind
Goswells Rd. Wind
Gothic Ct. Harl
Gothic Ct. Sand
Gough's Barn La. New G
Gough's La. New G
Gough's Meadow. Sand
Gould Rd. Felt
Govenor's Rd. Sand
Govett Ave. Shepp
Govett Gr. Windl
Gower Park. Sand
Gower St. Read
Gower The. Stai
Graces La. Chiev
Graffham Cl. Read
Grafton Cl. Maid
Grafton Cl. Slough
Grafton Cl. Felt
Grafton Rd. Read
Graham Cl. Blew
Graham Cl. Maid
Graham Cl. Read
Graham Rd. Cook
Graham Rd. Wind
Grahame Ave. Pangb
Gramp's Hill. Let B
Grampian Cl. Harl
Grampian Rd. Sand
Grampian Way. Slough
Granby Ct. Read
Granby End. Bur C
Granby Gdns. Read
Grand Ave. Camb
Grange Ave. Crow
Grange Ave. Read
Grange Cl. Gori
Grange Ct. Way
Grange Dr. Bou E
Grange Gdns. Far C
Grange La. Cook
Grange Pl. Stai
Grange Rd. Brac
Grange Rd. Camb
Grange Rd. Cook
Grange Rd. Eng G
Grange Rd. Hen-O-T
Grange The. Burn
Grange The. Old W
Grange Way. Iver
Grangely Cl. Bur C
Grangewood. Slough
Grant Ave. Slough
Grant Cl. Shepp
Grant Rd. Crow
Grant Wlk. Sunn
Grantham Cl. Sand
Grantham Rd. Read
Granthams The. Lamb
Granville Ave. Slough
Granville Rd. Read
Grasmere Ave. Read
Grasmere Ave. Slough
Grasmere Cl. Felt
Grasmere Cl. Stai
Grasmere Par. Slough
Grasmere Rd. Light
Grass Hill. Caver
Grassington Pl. That
Grassmead. That
Grassmere Cl. Winn
Grassy La. Maid
Grattan Ct. Mar
Gratton Dr. Wind
Gratton Rd. Read
Gratwicke Rd. Read
Gravel Hill. Box
Gravel Hill. Caver
Gravel Hill. Hen-O-T
Gravel Rd. Caver
Gravelly Cl. Ball H
Graveney Dr. Caver
Gravett Cl. Hen-O-T
Gray's Pl. Slough
Gray's Rd. Slough
Grayling Cl. Mar
Grays Cres. Wood
Grays La. Ashf
Grays Park Rd. Sto P
Grayshot Dr. Sand
Grazeley Rd. Shin
Great Hollands Rd. Brac
Great Hollands Rd. Brac
Great Hollands Sq. Brac
Great Knollys St. Read
Great Severals. Kint
Great South West Rd. Felt
Great South West Rd. Harm
Green Acre Mount. R

...Burn D4
Maid 19 F1
s. Fla H 3 E4
t. Woki 116 C4
Woki 116 B4
gon La. Fla H 3 D4
Cl. Shin 113 D1
Yate 149 E4
n Rd. Bags 145 F2
sh Cl. Brac 142 C3
Cl. Camb 152 B3
Rd. Camb 152 B3
Aschf 98 C1
Bags 145 F1
Black 150 C2
Bur C 85 D1
Bur G 38 A3
Burn 21 E2
Caver 35 D1
Far C 22 A3
Hen-O-T 35 E4
Holy 64 A3
Hurst 88 C2
Maid 40 A3
Maid 40 A3
Newb 104 C1
Padw 110 B1
Pangb 56 B2
Sand 150 B3
Sand 150 B4
Shepp 125 E2
Slough 68 A3
Stai 96 A2
Stai 123 F4
That 106 B2
Wind 67 D3
Woki 88 B1
Yate 149 D4
e Cl. Camb 151 D4
s Ct. Burn 21 E1
s Cl. Ashf 98 C1
s. Ashf 98 C1
t. Stai 96 C3
Read 87 D3
Vir W 123 F4
Brac 118 A3
s. Burn 21 D1
n. Chil 10 C4
s. Datch 68 A4
t. Slough 42 B2
h Thea 83 E1
s. Woki 115 F4
s Wray 68 C1
ges. Mar 2 D2
y. Burn 21 D2
od. Burl 119 E4
n Cl. Eng G 95 E1
s Wind 66 C3
es Ave. Winn 88 A2
es La. Winn 88 A2
es. Ball H 129 F1
t Gdns. Read 84 C3
n Mews. Slough 42 B3
elde End. Stai 97 E1
Ave. Maid 39 F3
s Ave. Slough 42 A4
ll Way. Brac 143 D4
n Rd. Read 113 D4
ts. Maid 40 A3
n Cl. Read 84 A3
h Cl. Wood 88 B3
n Maid. Newb 105 D2
s Rd. Newb 105 D1
n Wood. Brac 118 B2
en. Yate 149 D3
me. Camb 152 B3
y. Brac 118 A3
ds Rd. Camb 151 D1
ds Rd. Newb 105 D1
ds Rd. Stai 97 D1
ts. Ball H 129 F1
ds. Fla H 3 E4
s Ave. Caver 59 D4
s Cl. Yate 149 E4
s. Camb 151 F1
ss. Stai 125 D2
Rd. Slough 42 A4
t. Bou E 3 D3
e. Crow 142 C3
e. Slough 42 A4
ard La. Arbo 114 B4
y Dr. Stai 124 A4
h. The. Fawl 27 E4
y Dr. The. Slough 41 E3
ys Dr. Maid 39 D4
ys Dr. Sunn 120 C1
ys. Ball H 129 F1
s. Eng G 95 F2
ys. Lamb 25 D1
s. Sand 143 D1
od Gr. Winn 88 B3
od Rd. Crow 143 D3
od Rd. Read 84 C3
Cl. Winn 114 B4
l. Maid 39 F3
Pl. Maid 39 F3
.... 39 F3

Grenville Cl. Burn 21 D2
Gresham Rd. Slough 42 A4
Gresham Rd. Stai 96 C3
Gresham Rd. Stai 97 D2
Gresham Way. Read 58 A1
Grey's Rd. Hen-O-T 35 E4
Greyberry Copse Rd. Gree 131 E4
Greyfriars Dr. Ascot 120 A2
Greyfriars Rd. Read 86 A4
Greys Ct. Read 86 B4
Greys Hill. Hen-O-T 15 E1
Greystoke Ct. Crow 143 D2
Greystoke Rd. Caver 59 E2
Greystoke Rd. Slough 41 F4
Griffin Cl. Maid 39 F3
Griffin Cl. Slough 42 B2
Griffiths Cl. That 106 C1
Grindle Cl. Cold A 106 B3
Gringer Hill. Maid 39 F4
Grosvenor Ct. Black 150 B2
Grosvenor Dr. Maid 40 C4
Grosvenor Rd. Caver 59 E2
Grosvenor Rd. Stai 97 D1
Grove Cl. Brac 142 C4
Grove Cl. Old W 95 D4
Grove Cl. Slough 43 D2
Grove Cotts. Caver 59 D3
Grove Cross Rd. Camb 151 E1
Grove Ct. Eng G 96 A2
Grove End. Windl 145 F3
Grove Hill. Caver 59 D2
Grove La. Wink 92 A2
Grove Rd. Burn 21 F2
Grove Rd. Camb 151 F3
Grove Rd. Caver 59 D3
Grove Rd. Chert 123 F2
Grove Rd. Hen-O-T 15 F1
Grove Rd. Maid 39 F4
Grove Rd. Newb 104 C3
Grove Rd. Shepp 125 E2
Grove Rd. Wind 67 E3
Grove The. Burl 119 E4
Grove The. Camb 151 E1
Grove The. Eng G 96 A2
Grove The. Read 86 B4
Grove The. Slough 43 D2
Grove The. That 106 B2
Grove The. Twyf 61 E3
Grovefields Ave. Camb 151 E1
Groveland Pl. Read 85 D4
Groveland Rd. Newb 104 C3
Grovelands Ave. Winn 88 B1
Grovelands Cl. Maid 39 F2
Grovelands Rd. Read 85 D4
Grovelands Rd. Shin 113 E1
Groveley Rd. Ashf 98 A3
Groves Lea. Mort 136 C3
Groves Way. Cook 19 F3
Grovestile Waye. Felt 98 B4
Grubwood La. Cook 19 D4
Guards Club Rd. Maid 40 B4
Guards Rd. Oak G 66 B3
Guildford Ave. Felt 98 C4
Guildford Rd. Bags 145 F2
Guildford Rd. Bis 153 F4
Guildford Rd. Light 153 F4
Guildford Rd. West E 153 F4
Guildford St. Chert 124 A1
Guildford St. Stai 97 D1
Gun St. Read 86 A4
Gunthorpe Rd. Mar 2 A2
Gurney Cl. Caver 58 B3
Gurney Dr. Caver 58 B3
Gwendale. Maid 19 E1
Gweneth Ct. Mar 1 B2
Gwent Cl. Maid 39 D2
Gwyn Cl. Newb 130 C4
Gwynne Cl. Read 57 E2
Gwynne Cl. Wind 66 B3
Gwyns Piece. Lamb 25 D2
Gypsy La. Mar 1 C2
Gypsy La. Sto P 22 C4

Halfpenny La. Chol 13 F3
Halfpenny La. Went 121 D1
Halifax Cl. Maid 39 D4
Halifax Rd. Maid 39 D4
Halifax Way. Maid 39 D4
Halkingcroft. Slough 43 E2
Hall Cl. Camb 151 F3
Hall Ct. Datch 68 A4
Hall Farm Cres. Yate 149 E3
Hall La. Harl 71 E4
Hall La. Yate 149 E3
Hall Meadow. Burn 21 E2
Hall Place La. Bur G 38 A4
Hallbrook Gdns. Binf 90 C1
Halldore Hill. Cook 19 F4
Halley Dr. Ascot 119 E4
Hallgrove Bottom. Windl 145 F3
Hallmead Cl. Shepp 125 F3
Hallford Rd. Shepp 125 F3
Halls La. Read 86 C1
Halls La. W St L 63 D3
Halls Rd. Read 84 B3
Halpin Cl. Read 84 B2
Halstead Cl. Wood 87 F4
Ham La. Eng G 95 D2
Ham La. Old W 68 B2
Ham Rd. Ham 126 A2
Hamble Ave. Black 150 B2
Hambleden Wlk. Maid 19 F2
Hambledon Cl. Winn 87 F1
Hambleton Cl. Camb 152 A2
Hambridge La. Gree 105 F1
Hambridge Rd. Newb 105 E1
Hamilton Ave. Hen-O-T 15 F1
Hamilton Cl. Chert 123 F1
Hamilton Cl. Felt 98 C2
Hamilton Cl. Black 150 C1
Hamilton Cl. Newb 131 D4
Hamilton Dr. Sunn 120 C1
Hamilton Gdns. Burn 21 D1
Hamilton Rd. Felt 98 C2
Hamilton Rd. Read 85 F3
Hamilton Rd. Slough 42 A4
Hamilton Rd. Warg 36 C1
Hamlet St. Brac 118 C4
Hammond Cl. That 106 C1
Hammond End. Far C 22 B4
Hammond Way. Light 146 A1
Hammonds Heath. Mort 137 D3
Hampden Cl. Sto P 23 D1
Hampden Rd. Caver 59 D1
Hampden Rd. Maid 39 D4
Hampden Rd. Slough 43 F2
Hampdens The. Newb 130 B3
Hampshire Ave. Slough 42 B4
Hampshire Rd. Camb 151 F4
Hampshire Rise. New G 91 F1
Hampshire Way. Woki 115 E3
Hampstead Hill. Caver 60 B4
Hampstead Norreys Rd. Herm 79 D4
Hampton Rd. Newb 104 C1
Hanbury Cl. Burn 41 D4
Hanbury Dr. Bur C 84 B4
Hanbury Way. Camb 151 E2
Hancocks Mount. Ascot 120 B2
Hancombe Rd. Sand 143 D1
Handford La. Yate 149 E3
Hanger Rd. Tad 134 C1
Hangerfield Cl. Yate 149 E3
Hangman's Stone La. Chadd 49 D3
Hanley Cl. Wind 66 B3
Hannibal Rd. Stan 97 F4
Hanover Cl. Camb 151 F1
Hanover Cl. Eng G 95 D1
Hanover Cl. Slough 43 D3
Hanover Cl. Wind 66 C3
Hanover Gdns. Brac 117 F1
Hanover Way. Wind 66 C3
Hanwood Cl. Wood 87 E4
Hanworth Cl. Brac 118 B2
Hanworth La. Chert 123 F1
Hanworth Rd. Brac 118 A1
Harcourt Cl. Dorn 40 C2
Harcourt Cl. Hen-O-T 15 E1
Harcourt Cl. Stai 96 B1
Harcourt Dr. Read 86 C2
Harcourt Rd. Brac 118 A2
Harcourt Rd. Camb 151 D3
Harcourt Rd. Dorn 40 C2
Harcourt Rd. Wind 66 C3
Hardell Cl. Eng G 96 A2
Harding Rd. Wood 87 F4
Hardwell Way. Brac 118 C3
Hardwick Cl. Maid 39 D4
Hardwick La. Chert 123 E1
Hardwick Rd. Read 84 C4
Hardwick Rd. Whi-O-T 56 B4
Hardy Ave. Yate 149 E2
Hardy Cl. Caver 59 D3
Hardy Cl. Slough 42 A3
Hardy Cl. That 106 B3
Hardy Green. Crow 143 D2
Hare Shoots. Maid 39 F3
Harefield Cl. Winn 88 B1
Harefield Rd. Maid 39 F3
Harewood Dr. Cold A 106 B4
Harewood Pl. Slough 43 D2
Hargrave Rd. Maid 39 E4
Hargreaves Way. Read 84 C2

Harkness Rd. Burn 41 D4
Harlech Ave. Caver 59 E3
Harlech Rd. Black 150 B2
Harley Rd. Caver 59 D1
Harlington Cl. Harl 71 E4
Harlton Cl. Winn 114 B4
Harmans Water Rd. Brac 118 B2
Harmar Cl. Woki 116 C3
Harmondsworth La. Harm 70 C4
Harness Cl. Read 113 D3
Harold Rd. Kint 102 A1
Harpesford Ave. Went 122 B2
Harpton Cl. Yate 149 E4
Harrier Cl. Wood 88 A3
Harrington Cl. Newb 105 F3
Harrington Cl. Read 87 E1
Harrington Cl. Wind 66 C2
Harris Cl. Lamb 25 D2
Harris Cl. Read 88 A4
Harris Way. Stai 125 F4
Harrison Cl. Twyf 61 E2
Harrison Ct. Stai 125 D2
Harrison Way. Slough 41 E3
Harrogate Ct. Slough 44 A1
Harrogate Rd. Caver 58 C2
Harrow Bottom Rd. Went 122 C2
Harrow Cl. Maid 19 F1
Harrow Ct. Read 85 F3
Harrow La. Maid 19 F1
Harrow Rd. Ashf 98 A3
Harrow Rd. Slough 43 F2
Harrow Way. Stai 125 E4
Hart Cl. Brac 91 D1
Hart Dyke Cl. Brac 116 A1
Hart St. Hen-O-T 15 F1
Hart St. Read 85 F4
Hart's La. Sulhd 110 B3
Hartford Rise. Camb 151 E3
Hartigan Pl. Read 88 A4
Hartland Cl. Slough 42 B3
Hartland Rd. Read 86 B1
Hartley Cl. Black 150 A3
Hartley Cl. Sto P 23 E2
Hartley Court Rd. Shin 112 C3
Hartley Way. That 106 C2
Hartmead Rd. That 106 C2
Harts Cl. Arbo 114 C1
Harts Hill Rd. That 106 B2
Harts Leap Cl. Sand 143 E1
Harts Leap Rd. Sand 150 A4
Hartsbourne Rd. Read 87 D2
Hartshill Rd. Tad 134 C1
Hartslock Dr. Pangb 56 A3
Hartslock View. Upp B 34 C1
Harvard Cl. Wood 88 A4
Harvard Rd. Crow 143 F1
Harvest Cl. Read 84 A3
Harvest Cl. Yate 149 D2
Harvest Ct. Stai 125 D3
Harvest Green. Newb 104 C1
Harvest Hill Rd. Maid 39 F2
Harvest Rd. Bou E 3 E1
Harvest Rd. Eng G 95 E1
Harvest Ride. New G 91 F1
Harvey Rd. Shepp 125 F1
Harvey Rd. Slough 44 A2
Harwich Cl. Winn 87 E1
Harwich Rd. Slough 42 A4
Harwood Gdns. Old W 95 D4
Harwood Rd. Mar 1 B1
Harwoods Rise. Ball H 129 F1
Haslemere Cl. Camb 152 B2
Haslemere Rd. Wind 67 D3
Haslett Rd. Shepp 125 F4
Hasting Cl. Maid 40 B1
Hatch Cl. Buck 108 B4
Hatch End. Windl 146 B2
Hatch Gate La. Know H 37 D3
Hatch La. Buck 108 B4
Hatch La. Bur C 111 E3
Hatch La. Harm 70 B4
Hatch La. Wind 67 D3
Hatch Ride. Brac 142 C4
Hatch Ride. Brac 143 D4
Hatch The. Oak G 66 C4
Hatchet La. Ascot 93 D2
Hatchet La. Old W 93 D2
Hatchet La. Wink 93 D2
Hatchets La. Buck 80 B4
Hatchett Rd. Felt 98 B4
Hatchgate Cl. Cold A 106 B4
Hatchgate Copse. Brac 117 F2
Hatchgate Gdns. Burn 21 E1
Hatfield Cl. Maid 39 E3
Hatfield Ct. Bur C 84 A2
Hatfield Rd. Slough 43 D2
Hatford Rd. Read 86 C3
Hatherley Rd. Read 86 C3
Hatherwood. Yate 149 F3
Hatton Ave. Far C 22 B1
Hatton Cl. Wind 67 E3
Hatton Hill. Asham 54 A4
Hatton Hill. Windl 146 B3
Hatton Rd. Felt 98 A4
Hatton Rd. Harm 71 F1
Haughurst Hill. Tad 134 B1
Havelock Cres. Maid 39 D4
Havelock Rd. Maid 39 D4

Havelock Rd. Woki 116 A3
Havelock St. Woki 116 A3
Haven Rd. Ashf 98 A3
Haven The. Kint 102 A1
Haversham Dr. Brac 118 A2
Haw La. Asham 53 F4
Hawkchurch Rd. Read 113 E4
Hawkedon Way. Winn 87 F1
Hawker Way. Wood 88 A4
Hawkes Cl. Woki 116 A4
Hawkes Leap. Windl 146 A3
Hawkesbury Dr. Bur C 84 C2
Hawkesworth Dr. Bags 145 F1
Hawkins Cl. Brac 119 D4
Hawkins Way. Woki 116 C3
Hawks Hill. Bou E 3 E1
Hawkshill Rd. Slough 22 A1
Hawksway. Stai 96 C3
Hawkswood Ave. Camb 151 F1
Hawkswood La. Fulm 23 F4
Hawksworth Rd. Bur C 111 D2
Hawley Cl. Bur C 84 B2
Hawley La. Camb 151 D1
Hawley Rd. Black 150 C2
Hawley Way. Ashf 98 A2
Haws La. Stan 70 A1
Hawthorn Cl. Brac 118 A4
Hawthorn Cl. Mar 1 C2
Hawthorn Gdns. Read 86 C1
Hawthorn La. Far C 22 B4
Hawthorn La. New G 91 F4
Hawthorn Rd. Camb 151 F1
Hawthorn Rd. Newb 105 D2
Hawthorn Way. Sonn 60 C1
Hawthorne Cres. Black 150 C2
Hawthorne Cres. Slough 44 C4
Hawthorne Rd. Caver 59 F2
Hawthorne Rd. Stai 96 B2
Hawthorne Way. Gr She 48 A2
Hawthorne Way. Stan 97 E4
Hawthornes. Sulh 57 D2
Hawthorns The. Char 61 D2
Hawthorns The. Stan 69 F3
Hawtrey Cl. Slough 43 D2
Hawtrey Rd. Wind 67 E3
Hay La. Fulm 23 E4
Hay Rd. Read 85 F3
Hayes La. Bark 115 E2
Hayes Pl. Mar 1 B1
Hayfield Cl. Read 84 B4
Hayley Green. New G 91 F2
Haymill Rd. Slough 21 E1
Haynes Cl. Slough 43 F1
Hayse Hill. Wind 66 B3
Haywards Cl. Hen-O-T 15 E1
Haywards Mead. Eton 41 F1
Haywards The. That 106 B2
Haywood Ct. Read 86 C4
Haywood Way. Read 84 C3
Haywood. Brac 118 B1
Hazel Cl. Bur C 111 D3
Hazel Cl. Eng G 95 D1
Hazel Cl. Mar B 1 B3
Hazel Cl. Woki 115 F3
Hazel Cres. Read 86 C1
Hazel Dr. Wood 87 E3
Hazel Gr. Stai 97 E1
Hazel Gr. That 106 B3
Hazel Green. Tad 134 B1
Hazel Rd. Pur O T 57 E2
Hazelbank Rd. Chert 124 B1
Hazelbank. Woki 141 F3
Hazeldene. Chiev 51 D1
Hazelhurst Rd. Burn 21 E2
Hazell Cl. Maid 39 F4
Hazell Hill. Brac 118 B3
Hazell Way. Sto P 22 C3
Hazlemere Ct. Harm 71 F1
Hazlewood Cl. Read 57 E1
Hazlewood Cl. Binf 90 C2
Hazlemere Rd. Slough 43 D3
Heacham Cl. Read 114 A4
Headington Cl. Maid 39 D4
Headington Cl. Woki 116 B4
Headington Dr. Woki 116 B4
Headington Rd. Maid 39 D4
Headley Cl. Wood 88 A4
Headley Park Ind Est. Wood 87 F4
Headley Rd E. Wood 88 A4
Headley Rd. Wood 88 A4
Heads La. Ink 128 A3
Heads La. West W 128 A3
Hearmon Cl. Yate 149 F3
Hearn Rd. Wood 87 F3
Hearn Wlk. Brac 118 C4
Hearne Dr. Holy 40 A1
Hearsey Gdns. Black 150 A3
Heath Cl. Harl 71 E4
Heath Cl. Stan 70 B1
Heath Cl. Vir W 122 B3
Heath Cl. Woki 116 A2
Heath Dr. Caver 35 D1
Heath End Rd. Tad 134 C1
Heath End. Tad 98 C1
Heath Hill Rd N. Crow 143 D3
Heath Hill Rd S. Crow 143 D3
Heath La. That 106 B3

Heath Rd. Bags

Heath Rd. Bags 145 F2
Heath Rd. Beac 3 F4
Heath Rd. Brad 82 A1
Heath Rd. Read 87 D3
Heath Rd. Silc 135 F1
Heath Ride. Finch 142 B3
Heath Ride. Woki 142 B3
Heath Rise. Camb 151 E3
Heath Rise. W W 122 B3
Heathacre. Stan 69 F3
Heathcote Rd. Camb 151 E3
Heathcroft Ave. Ashf 98 C1
Heather Cl. Woki 141 F4
Heather Dr. Tad 134 C1
Heather Dr. Went 121 D1
Heather Mead. Camb 151 F1
Heatherdale Rd. Camb 151 E2
Heatherden Cl. Read 113 E4
Heatherdene Ave. Finch ... 142 C2
Heatherley Cl. Camb 151 D3
Heatherley Rd. Camb 151 D3
Heathermount Dr. Crow 143 D3
Heathermount. Brac 118 C3
Heathers The. Stan 97 F4
Heatherside Dr. Vir W 122 A2
Heatherway. Crow 143 D3
Heathfield Ave. Ascot 120 C2
Heathfield Ave. Read 84 B3
Heathfield Ave. Shipl 35 D1
Heathfield Cl. Shipl 35 D1
Heathfield Rd. Bou E 20 C4
Heathfield Rd. Tapl 20 C4
Heathlands Dr. Maid 39 D3
Heathlands Rd. Woki 116 C1
Heathlands. Tad 134 C1
Heathmoors. Brac 118 B2
Heathpark Dr. Windl 146 C2
Heathrow Cl. Harm 70 A3
Heathway Cl. Camb 151 E3
Heathway. Burl 119 F4
Heathway. Camb 151 E3
Heathway. Read 84 B4
Heathwood Cl. Yate 149 E4
Heavens Lea. Bou E 3 E1
Hebden Cl. That 106 B1
Hedge Lea. Woo G 3 E4
Hedgeway. Newb 105 E2
Hedingham Mews. Maid 39 E4
Hedley Rd. Fla H 3 D4
Hedsor Hill. Bou E 3 E1
Hedsor La. Bou E 3 F1
Hedsor Rd. Bou E 3 D1
Heelas Rd. Woki 116 A3
Helena Rd. Wind 67 E3
Helgiford Gdns. Ashf 98 C1
Hellyer Way. Bou E 3 E2
Helmsdale Cl. Read 85 D4
Helmsdale. Brac 118 C2
Helston Gdns. Read 86 A1
Helston La. Wind 67 D3
Helvellyn Cl. Stan 96 B1
Hemdean Hill. Caver 59 D2
Hemdean Rd. Caver 59 D2
Hemdean Rise. Caver 59 D2
Hempson Ave. Slough 43 E2
Hemsdale. Maid 19 D1
Hemwood Rd. Wind 66 B2
Hencroft St N. Slough 42 C2
Hencroft St S. Slough 42 C2
Henden Way. Stan 70 B1
Hendons Way. Holy 40 A1
Hengrave Cl. Winn 87 F1
Hengrove Cres. Ashf 97 E3
Henley Gdns. Yate 149 E3
Henley Rd. Bur G 18 A1
Henley Rd. Caver 60 B4
Henley Rd. Hurl 18 A1
Henley Rd. Maid 18 A4
Henley Rd. Mar 18 A4
Henley Rd. Shipl 60 B4
Henley Rd. Slough 41 F4
Henley Wood Rd. Read 87 E2
Henry Rd. Slough 42 B2
Henry St. Read 86 A3
Henrys The. That 106 B2
Henshaw Cres. Newb 130 B4
Hensworth Rd. Stan 97 E2
Henwick Cl. That 106 A3
Henwick La. That 106 A2
Henwood Copse. Upp B 55 D3
Hepplewhite Cl. Tad 134 C1
Hepworth Croft. Sand 150 B3
Hepworth Way. Shepp 125 F1
Herald Way. Wood 88 A3
Herbert Cl. Brac 118 A2
Hereford Cl. Stai 124 A4
Herewood Cl. Newb 104 C2
Heriot Rd. Chert 124 A1
Hermit's Hill. Bur C 111 E2
Hermitage Cl. Camb 151 F1
Hermitage Cl. Slough 43 E2
Hermitage Cl. Stai 125 D3
Hermitage Dr. Ascot 119 F4
Hermitage Dr. Twyf 61 E3
Hermitage La. Wind 67 D2
Hermitage Rd. Cold A 79 D1
Hermitage Rd. Herm 79 D1
Hermitage The. Lamb 46 C4
Hermits Cl. Bur C 111 D2

Herndon Cl. Eng G 96 A2
Heroes Wlk. Read 113 D4
Heron Cl. Burl 119 E4
Heron Dr. Twyf 61 F3
Heron Island. Caver 59 E1
Heron Rd. Woki 115 F3
Heron Shaw. Gori 34 B4
Heron Way. Bur C 85 F2
Heron Way. That 106 A2
Heron's Way. Woki 116 C4
Herondale. Brac 118 B1
Heronfield. Eng G 95 D1
Herongate. Hung 100 B4
Herons Ct. Light 153 E4
Herons Pl. Mar 1 C2
Herrick Cl. Camb 152 B2
Herrings La. Chert 124 A2
Herrings La. Windl 146 B2
Herriot Cl. Yate 149 E2
Herschel Park Dr. Slough .. 42 C2
Herschel St. Slough 42 C2
Hertford Cl. Caver 59 E3
Hertford Cl. Woki 115 F3
Hetherington Cl. Slough 21 F1
Hetherington Rd. Stai 125 E4
Hever Cl. Maid 39 E3
Hewett Ave. Caver 58 B2
Hewett Cl. Caver 58 B2
Hewlett Pl. Bags 145 F2
Hexham Cl. Crow 143 E1
Hexham Rd. Read 86 B2
Heywood Ave. Whi Wa 39 D1
Heywood Court Cl. Whi Wa . 39 D1
Heywood Gdns. Whi Wa 39 D1
Hibbert Rd. Maid 40 A2
Hibbert's Alley. Wind 67 E3
Hicks La. Black 150 A3
Higgs La. Bags 145 E2
High Beech. Brac 118 C3
High Beeches. Camb 151 E1
High Fields. Sunn 120 C2
High Heavens Wood. Mar B .. 1 B4
High Meadow. Caver 58 B2
High Rd. Cook 19 F3
High St Harlington. Harl 71 E4
High St. Ascot 120 A3
High St. Ascot 120 B2
High St. Bags 145 F2
High St. Box 76 A2
High St. Brac 118 A4
High St. Brac 118 B4
High St. Burn 21 E1
High St. Camb 151 E3
High St. Chiev 51 F1
High St. Comp 31 E2
High St. Cook 20 A4
High St. Crow 143 E2
High St. Datch 68 A3
High St. East I 30 C4
High St. Eng G 96 A2
High St. Eton 67 E4
High St. Gori 34 B3
High St. Harl 71 E4
High St. Harm 70 B4
High St. Hung 100 B3
High St. Iver 44 C4
High St. Iver 69 E4
High St. Kint 102 A1
High St. Lamb 24 C3
High St. Lamb 25 D1
High St. Maid 39 F4
High St. Maid 40 A2
High St. Maid 40 B2
High St. Mar 1 C1
High St. Pangb 56 B3
High St. Read 86 A4
High St. Sand 143 D1
High St. Sand 149 F3
High St. Shepp 125 E2
High St. Slough 42 B2
High St. Slough 42 B2
High St. Slough 44 A1
High St. Stai 96 C2
High St. Stan 70 B1
High St. Stre 9 D2
High St. Sunn 121 D2
High St. Tapl 20 C1
High St. That 106 B2
High St. Thea 83 F2
High St. Twyf 61 E2
High St. Warg 36 B1
High St. West E 153 F4
High St. Whi-O-T 56 B4
High St. Wick 73 D1
High St. Wind 67 E3
High St. Wray 68 C1
High Town Rd. Maid 39 F3
High Tree Dr. Read 87 D3
High View Cl. Mar B 1 B4
High View Rd. Light 152 C4
Highbeeches Cl. Mar B 1 B3
Highbridge Cl. Caver 59 F2
Highbridge Wharf. Read 86 A4
Highbury Cres. Camb 152 A4
Highbury Rd. Read 84 A4
Highclere Cl. Brac 118 C4
Highclere Dr. Camb 152 A4

Highclere. Ascot 120 B2
Highdown Ave. Caver 59 F4
Highdown Hill Rd. Caver ... 59 D4
Highdown Hill Rd. Maple ... 59 D4
Higher Alham. Brac 118 C1
Highfield Cl. Eng G 95 E1
Highfield Ave. Newb 105 D1
Highfield Cl. Woki 116 A3
Highfield Cl. Bur C 111 D2
Highfield La. Maid 39 D2
Highfield Park. Mar 18 A4
Highfield Park. Warg 36 C1
Highfield Rd. Bou E 3 D2
Highfield Rd. Chert 124 A1
Highfield Rd. Fla H 3 D4
Highfield Rd. Maid 39 D4
Highfield Rd. Newb 104 C1
Highfield Rd. Pur O T 57 E2
Highfield Rd. Shepp 125 F2
Highfield Rd. Wind 66 C2
Highfield. Brac 117 F2
Highfield. Read 87 D1
Highgate Rd. Wood 87 E3
Highgrove Park. Maid 39 F4
Highgrove St. Read 86 B3
Highgrove Terr. Read 86 A3
Highland Ave. Woki 115 F4
Highland Park. Felt 98 C2
Highland Rd. Camb 151 F4
Highlands La. Shipl 35 D4
Highlands. Fla H 3 D4
Highlea Ave. Fla H 3 D4
Highmead Cl. Read 86 C1
Highmoor Rd. Caver 58 C2
Highview Cres. Camb 144 C1
Highview. Read 84 A3
Highway Ave. Maid 39 D3
Highway Rd. Maid 39 D3
Highway. Crow 143 D3
Highwayman's Ridge. Windl .146 A3
Highwood Cl. Newb 105 E3
Highwood Cl. Yate 149 E2
Highwoods Cl. Mar B 1 B4
Highwoods Dr. Mar B 1 B4
Highworth Way. Sulh 57 D1
Hilary Cl. Read 113 E4
Hilborne Way. Bark 115 D1
Hilbury Rd. Read 87 D2
Hilcot Rd. Read 85 F3
Hildens Dr. Read 84 B4
Hilfield. Yate 149 F3
Hill Cl. Newb 130 B4
Hill Cl. Woo G 3 F4
Hill Copse View. Brac 118 C4
Hill Farm App. Woo G 3 F4
Hill Farm Rd. Mar B 1 C3
Hill Farm Rd. Tapl 20 C2
Hill Gdns. Stre 9 A3
Hill Lands. Warg 36 B1
Hill Piece. Chil 10 C4
Hill Rd. Bark 114 C1
Hill Rd. Newb 104 C2
Hill Rd. Read 86 A3
Hill Top Dr. Mar 1 A1
Hill View Rd. Wray 68 B1
Hillary Dr. Crow 143 D3
Hillary Rd. Slough 43 F2
Hillberry. Brac 118 B1
Hillborn Rd. Bark 140 C4
Hillbrow. Read 86 C1
Hillcrest Ave. Cook 19 F3
Hillcrest Rd. Camb 152 A4
Hillcrest. Tad 135 D1
Hillersdon. Slough 43 D4
Hillgreen La. Pease 50 B4
Hillhouse La. Head 133 E1
Hillingdon Ave. Stan 97 F4
Hillmead Cl. Tapl 40 C2
Hillrise. Slough 69 D4
Hills La. Cook 19 E3
Hillsborough Park. Camb .. 152 B3
Hillside Dr. Binf 90 B1
Hillside Park. Read 86 C1
Hillside Park. Windl 120 C4
Hillside Rd. Hung 100 B2
Hillside Rd. Mar 1 C2
Hillside Rd. Read 84 A2
Hillside. Bur C 111 E2
Hillside. East G 47 E3
Hillside. Maid 39 E3
Hillside. Sand 150 C4
Hillside. Slough 42 C2
Hillside. Went 122 B2
Hillside. Whi-O-T 56 B4
Hilltop Cl. Ascot 120 C4
Hilltop Rd. Caver 58 B3
Hilltop Rd. Read 87 D4
Hilltop Rd. Twyf 61 F4
Hilltop View. Yate 149 D3
Hillview Cl. Read 57 D1
Hilmanton. Read 113 F4
Hilperton Rd. Slough 42 C2
Hindhead Rd. Read 84 A4
Hinksey Cl. Slough 44 A2
Hinton Cl. Crow 143 D4
Hinton Dr. Crow 143 D4
Hinton Rd. Slough 44 A2
Hinton Rd. Hurst 88 C4
Hinton Rd. Slough 41 F3

Hintonhatch Cnr. Hurst 62 A1
Hirstwood. Pur O T 57 F1
Hirtes Ave. Shin 113 F3
Hitcham La. Tapl 20 C1
Hitcham Rd. Burn 41 D4
Hitchcock Cl. Stai 124 C3
Hitherhooks Hill. Binf 90 C1
Hitherhooks Hill. Brac 117 F4
Hithermoor Rd. Stan 70 A1
Hobart Cl. Mar 2 A2
Hobbis Dr. Maid 39 D3
Hockett La. Bish 19 D3
Hockett La. Cook 19 D3
Hockford La. Head 134 A2
Hockham Rd. Comp 31 F3
Hockley La. Sto P 23 D3
Hodgedale La. Warg 37 E3
Hodges Cl. Bags 145 F1
Hodsoll Rd. Read 85 F4
Hoe Benham La. Wick 102 C3
Hogarth Ave. Ashf 98 B1
Hogarth Ave. Read 84 C3
Hogarth Cl. Sand 150 C3
Hogarth Cl. Slough 43 F3
Holberton Rd. Read 113 F4
Holborn Hill. Let B 6 B4
Holborne Cl. Newb 130 B3
Holford Cl. Read 84 B4
Holkam Cl. Read 57 F1
Holland Gdns. Stai 123 F4
Holland Pines. Brac 117 F1
Hollands The. That 106 C2
Hollicombe Cl. Read 84 C4
Hollies The. Newb 130 B3
Hollins Wlk. Read 85 E3
Hollow Hill La. Iver 44 B3
Hollow La. Shin 113 F3
Hollow La. Vir W 122 B3
Holloway La. Harm 70 C4
Holly Ave. Camb 152 A2
Holly Cl. Eng G 95 D1
Holly Cl. Far C 22 B4
Holly Cres. Wind 66 C3
Holly Dr. Maid 39 F4
Holly Dr. Old Wind 67 F1
Holly Hedge Cl. Camb 151 F1
Holly Hedge Rd. Camb 151 F1
Holly La. Asham 54 B3
Holly Rd. Wood 88 A3
Holly Spring La. Brac 118 B4
Holly Way. Black 150 B2
Hollybank. West E 153 F3
Hollybush Hill. Sto P 23 D3
Hollybush La. Cook 19 D3
Hollybush La. Iver 44 A3
Hollybush La. Sulhd 110 C2
Hollybush Ride. Brac 142 B3
Hollybush Ride. Finch 142 B3
Hollycombe. Eng G 95 E2
Hollycroft Cl. Harm 71 D4
Hollycroft Gdns. Harm 71 D4
Hollydale Cl. Read 86 C1
Hollyfields Cl. Camb 151 D3
Hollyhook Cl. Brac 143 D3
Hollyn Cl. Winn 87 F1
Holmanleaze. Maid 40 A4
Holmbank Dr. Shepp 125 F3
Holmbury Ave. Brac 143 D4
Holmdale. Slough 43 E3
Holmdene. Bur C 111 D2
Holme Cl. Brac 142 B4
Holmemoor Dr. Sonn 60 C1
Holmes Cl. Ascot 120 B2
Holmes Cl. Woki 116 A2
Holmes Cres. Woki 116 A2
Holmes Rd. Read 87 D3
Holmewood Cl. Woki 116 A1
Holmlea Rd. Datch 68 B3
Holmlea Rd. Gori 34 B3
Holmlea Wlk. Datch 68 B3
Holmsdale Cl. Iver 44 C4
Holmwood Ave. Read 84 C2
Holmwood Cl. Maid 39 D3
Holsworthy Cl. Winn 87 F2
Holt Cl. Brig 49 F4
Holt La. Woki 116 A4
Holt Rd. Kint 102 A1
Holt The. Pur O T 57 E2
Holton Heath. Brac 118 C3
Holtspur Ave. Woo G 3 F4
Holtwood Rd. Ham M 129 D3
Holybrook Cres. Read 85 D2
Holybrook Rd. Read 85 E3
Holyport Cl. Holy 65 D4
Holyport Rd. Holy 65 D4
Holyrood Cl. Caver 59 E3
Holywell Cl. Stan 97 F4
Holywell Cl. Stan 97 F4
Home Cl. Brac 117 F4
Home Croft. Sulh 57 D1
Home Farm Cl. Read 86 B2
Home Farm Cl. Shepp 125 F3

Home Farm Way. Sto P ....
Home Mead Cl. Newb ....
Home Meadow Dr. Fla H ....
Home Meadow Fr ....
Home Park Farm La. Sonn
Home Park Rd. Yate ....
Homefield Way. Hung ....
Homers Rd. Wind ....
Homestead Rd. Maid ....
Homestead Rd. Stai ....
Homewaters Ave. Shepp ..
Homewood. Slough ....
Hone Hill. Sand ....
Honesty Bottom. Brig ......
Honey End La. Read ....
Honey Hill. Brac ....
Honey Hill. Lamb ....
Honey La. Hurl ....
Honeybottom Rd. Tad ......
Honeyfields. Hung ....
Honeyhill Rd. Brac ....
Honeysuckle Cl. Brac ......
Honeysuckle Cl. Yate ......
Honiton Rd. Read ....
Honnor Rd. Stai ....
Hook End La. Upp B ....
Hook La. West E ....
Hook Mill La. Light ....
Hookstone La. West E .....
Hopeful Cl. Chert ....
Hope Ave. Brac ....
Hopeman Cl. Sand ....
Hopwood Cl. Newb ....
Horewood Rd. Brac ....
Hormer Cl. Sand ....
Horn St. Comp ....
Hornbeam Cl. Pur O T .....
Hornbeam Cl. Sand ....
Hornbeam Cl. Woki ....
Hornbeam Gdns. Slough ..
Hornbeams. Swal ....
Horncastle Dr. Read ....
Horndean Rd. Brac ....
Horne La. Stoke ....
Hornes La. Vir W ....
Horne Rd. That ....
Hornsea Cl. Read ....
Horse Cl The. Caver ....
Horse Gate Ride. Ascot ...
Horsebrass Dr. Bags ....
Horseguards Dr. Maid .....
Horsell Ct. Chert ....
Horsemoor Cl. Slough .....
Horseshoe Cl. Camb ....
Horseshoe Cres. Bur C ...
Horseshoe Cres. Camb ...
Horseshoe Hill. Burn ......
Horseshoe Park. Pangb ...
Horseshoe Rd. Pangb .....
Horsham Rd. Crow ....
Horsham Rd. Felt ....
Horsnape Gdns. Binf ......
Horsneile La. Brac ....
Horton Cl. Maid ....
Horton Rd. Datch ....
Horton Rd. Hort ....
Horton Rd. Stan ....
Horton Rd. Maid ....
Horton Rd. Poyle ....
Hose Hill. Bur C ....
Hosier St. Read ....
Houlton Ct. Bags ....
Houston Way. Finch ....
Howard Ave. Slough ....
Howard Ct. Ashf ....
Howard Rd. Ashf ....
Howard Rd. Newb ....
Howard Rd. Woki ....
Howe La. Holy ....
Howgate Dr. Gori ....
Howth Dr. Wood ....
Hubberholme. Brac ....
Hubert Rd. Slough ....
Huckleberry Cl. Pur O T ..
Huddington Glade. Yate ..
Hudson Rd. Harl ....
Hudson Rd. Wood ....
Hugh Fraser Dr. Read .....
Hughenden Cl. Maid ....
Hughenden Rd. Slough ...
Hughes Rd. Ashf ....
Hughes Rd. Woki ....
Hull Cl. Slough ....
Humber Cl. That ....
Humber Cl. Woki ....
Humber Way. Sand ....
Humber Way. Slough ......
Hummer Rd. Eng G ....
Humphrey's La. East G ...
Hungerford Ave. Slough ..
Hungerford Cl. Sand ....
Hungerford Dr. Maid ....
Hungerford Dr. Read ......
Hungerford Hill. East G ...
Hungerford Hill. Lamb ....
Hungerford La. Hurst ......
Hungerford La. W St L ....
Hungerford Rd. Kint ....
Hunt's La. Tapl ....

Hill. Bur C 110 C2
mbe Cl. Burn 41 E4
mbe Cl. Slough 41 E4
mbe La N. Slough 41 E4
mbe La S. Burn 41 E3
mbe La S. Slough 41 E3
Meadow. Gr She 48 A2
Mews. Wind 67 E3
Way. Shin 113 D1
onshire Cl. Woki 115 E3
eld Way. Stai 96 B1
an Cl. Winn 87 F1
Ct. Read 86 C3
ns Meadow. Ascot ..119 F4
or Rd. Tad 135 D1
od La. Burn 20 C2
od La. Tapl 20 C2
gh St. Hurl 17 F2
a. Bish 18 A2
a. Hurl 18 A2
a Way. Read 88 A4
a Way. Wood 88 A4
Cl. Read 84 C4
Shepp 125 F1
Vir W 123 D4
rk Rd. Twyf 61 F1
........41 E4
. Twyf 1 C2
e Ave. Stai 97 D1
Way. Pur O T 57 E2
Cl. Woki 116 B4
l. Newb 105 D2
l. Read 87 D1
l. Windl 146 B2
d La. Brim 133 E3
d La. Shin 113 E2
d Rd. Shin 113 E1
en. Mar 1 C1
Newt 132 A1
r. Ashf 98 C1
he. Pur O T 57 E2
Wind 96 B2
Way. Read 86 A2
Brac 118 C2
d Rd. Wray 96 A3
eld Ave. Stai 96 B1
rk Rd. Stai 96 B2
d. Stai 96 B2
e. Stai 96 B2

Isis Way. Bou E 3 D2
Isis Way. Sand 150 B4
Island Cl. Stai 96 C2
Island Farm Rd. Bur C ..110 B1
Island Farm Rd. Bur C ..136 C4
Island Farm Rd. Sulhd ..110 B1
Island Rd. Bur C 85 F1
Island Rd. Read 85 F1
Island The. Eng G 96 A3
Islandstone La. Hurst 89 D3
Islet Park Dr. Maid 20 B2
Islet Park. Maid 20 B2
Islet Rd. Maid 20 B2
Ivanhoe Rd. Bark 141 C4
Iver La. Iver 44 C4
Iverdale Cl. Iver 44 C4
Iverna Gdns. Harm 71 E1
Ives Cl. Yate 149 D4
Ives Rd. Slough 44 A2
Ivy Cl. Holy 65 D4
Ivy Cres. Slough 41 F3
Ivy Dr. Light 153 D4
Ivybank. Read 57 E1
Ivydene Rd. Read 58 B1

Jack St. Newb 105 D2
Jackson Cl. Brac 118 A2
Jacob Cl. Brac 117 E4
Jacob Cl. Wind 66 C3
Jacob Rd. Sand 151 D4
James Butcher Dr. Thea ..83 F2
James Cl. Mar 1 C2
James Rd. Camb 151 D1
James St. Read 85 F4
James St. Wind 67 E4
James Watt Rd. Bark ..140 C4
James Way. Camb 151 D1
James's La. Bur C 111 F2
Jameston. Brac 118 B1
Jamnagar Cl. Stai 96 C1
Janson Ct. Read 85 F3
Japonica Cl. Woki 115 E2
Jaques's La. Sulhd 110 C3
Jarry Ct. Mar 1 C2
Jasmine Cl. Woki 115 E4
Jays Nest Cl. Black 150 B2
Jedburgh Cl. That 106 C2
Jefferson Cl. Slough 44 A1
Jeffries Ct. Bou E 3 D1
Jellicoe Cl. Slough 42 A2
Jenkins Hill. Bags 145 E1
Jennery La. Burn 21 E1
Jennetts Cl. Brad 81 F2
Jennings Field. Fla H 3 E4
Jennings Wharf. Wind 67 E4
Jenny's Wlk. Yate 149 F3
Jerome Cl. Mar 1 C2
Jerome Rd. Wood 87 F3
Jerrymoor Hill. Woki ..141 F4
Jesmond Dene. Newb 104 C2
Jesse Cl. Yate 149 F3
Jesse Terr. Read 85 F4
Jessiman Terr. Stai 125 D2
Jevington. Brac 118 B1
Jig's La. New G 91 E1
Job's La. Cook 19 D4
Jock's La. Binf 90 C1
Joel Cl. Read 87 D2
John Childs Cl. Newb 105 D1
John Hunt Cl. That 106 C1
John Nike Way. Binf 117 E4
John Taylor Ct. Slough 42 B3
John's Cl. Ashf 98 B2
Johnson's La. Cold A 106 B4
Jonathan Hill. Newt 131 D2
Jordan Cl. Caver 59 F3
Jordan Cl. Shin 113 E1
Jordan's La. Bur C 110 C1
Jordans Cl. Stan 97 E4
Joseph Cl. New G 91 F1
Josephine Cl. Read 85 F3
Jouldings La. Swal 140 B2
Jourdelay's Pas. Eton 67 E4
Journeys End. Slough 42 C4
Jubilee Ave. Burl 119 F4
Jubilee Ave. Woki 116 A4
Jubilee Cl. Burl 119 F4
Jubilee Cl. Silc 135 F1
Jubilee Cl. Stai 97 E4
Jubilee Rd. Bish 38 A3
Jubilee Rd. Finch 141 F2
Jubilee Rd. Read 87 D3
Jubilee Sq. Read 86 A3
Judy's Pas. Eton 67 E4
Julkes La. Arbo 114 B4
Junction Rd. Ashf 98 B2
Junction Rd. Light 146 A1
Junction Rd. Read 86 C3
Juniper Dr. Maid 40 A4
Juniper Gdns. Ashf 98 C1
Juniper La. Fla H 3 E4
Juniper La. Woo G 3 E4
Juniper Rd. Mar B 1 B3
Juniper Way. Read 57 E1
Juniper. Brac 118 B1
Junnipers The. Woki 115 E2
Jupiter Way. Woki 115 E2
Justice Cl. That 106 C1
Jutland Cl. Woki 115 F3

Jutland Pl. Stai 96 B2

Katesgrove La. Read 86 A3
Kathleen Saunders Ct. Thea ..83 F2
Kaywood Cl. Slough 43 E2
Keane Cl. Wood 87 F4
Kearsley Rd. Read 85 E3
Keates Green. Brac 118 A4
Keats Cl. Wood 87 F2
Keats La. Eton 67 E4
Keats Rd. Wood 143 D3
Keats Way. Crow 143 D2
Keble Rd. Maid 39 F4
Keble Way. Crow 143 F1
Keel Dr. Slough 42 B2
Keeler Cl. Wind 66 C2
Keepers Combe. Brac 118 B2
Keepers Farm Cl. Wind 66 C2
Keepers Farm Cl. Wind 66 C3
Keepers Wlk. Vir W 122 B2
Keephatch Rd. Woki 116 C4
Keighley Cl. That 106 B1
Kelburne Cl. Winn 88 B2
Keldholme. Brac 118 A1
Kelly Cl. Shepp 125 F4
Kelmscott Cl. Caver 58 C2
Kelpatrick Rd. Slough 41 E4
Kelsey Ave. Woki 141 F3
Kelsey Cl. Maid 39 E2
Kelsey Gr. Yate 149 F4
Kelso Mews. Caver 59 F3
Kelton Cl. Winn 87 F1
Kelvedon Way. Caver 58 C3
Kelvin Cl. Arbo 140 C4
Kelvin Rd. Newb 105 D2
Kemble Ct. Read 84 B2
Kemerton Cl. Bur C 84 B2
Kemp Ct. Bags 145 F1
Kempton Cl. Newb 105 E1
Kenavon Dr. Read 86 B4
Kendal Ave. Caver 59 F3
Kendal Ave. Shin 113 F3
Kendal Cl. Felt 98 C4
Kendal Cl. Slough 43 D3
Kendal Cl. That 106 B2
Kendal Dr. Slough 43 D3
Kendal Gr. Camb 152 B2
Kendrick Cl. Woki 116 B3
Kendrick Rd. Newb 130 B3
Kendrick Rd. Read 86 B3
Kendrick Rd. Slough 43 D2
Kenilworth Ave. Brac 118 B4
Kenilworth Ave. Read 85 E3
Kenilworth Cl. Slough 42 C2
Kenilworth Gdns. Stai 97 E2
Kenilworth Rd. Ashf 97 D3
Kenneally. Oak G 66 B3
Kennedy Cl. Far C 22 B2
Kennedy Cl. Maid 39 E3
Kennedy Cl. Mar 1 C2
Kennedy Cl. Newb 130 B3
Kennedy Dr. Pangb 56 C3
Kennedy Gdns. Read 87 D2
Kennel Ave. Ascot 119 F4
Kennel Cl. Ascot 92 C1
Kennel Green. Ascot 119 F4
Kennel La. Brac 91 D1
Kennel La. Cook 19 E4
Kennel La. Windl 146 B3
Kennel Ride. Ascot 92 C1
Kennel Wood. Ascot 119 F4
Kennet Cl. That 106 C2
Kennet Cl. Woki 115 F3
Kennet Pl. Bur C 111 D2
Kennet Rd. Kint 102 A1
Kennet Rd. Maid 39 F4
Kennet Rd. Newb 104 C2
Kennet Side. Newb 105 E2
Kennet St. Read 86 B4
Kennet Way. Hung 100 C4
Kennett Rd. Bou E 3 D2
Kennett Rd. Slough 44 A2
Kensington Rd. Read 85 E4
Kent Ave. Slough 42 C3
Kent Cl. Stai 97 E1
Kent Cl. Woki 115 E3
Kent Rd. Read 85 E4
Kent Rd. Windl 146 B3
Kent Way. Maid 19 F1
Kentigern Dr. Brac 143 F3
Kenton Cl. Brac 118 B3
Kenton Cl. Camb 152 A1
Kenton Cl. Mar 1 C1
Kenton Rd. Read 87 E2
Kenton's La. Warg 36 B4
Kenton's La. Wind 66 C3
Kentwood Cl. Read 57 F1
Kentwood Hill. Read 57 F1
Kenwood Cl. Harm 71 D4
Kenwood Cl. Maid 39 D4
Keppel Spur. Old W 95 D4
Keppel St. Wind 67 E3
Kepple Pl. Bags 145 F2
Kernham Dr. Pur O T 57 E2
Kerria Way. Camb 153 F3
Kerris Way. Read 87 D1
Kersey Cres. Newb 104 C3

Kesteven Way. Woki 115 F3
Keston Cl. Caver 59 E1
Kestrel Ave. Stai 96 C3
Kestrel Cl. That 106 A2
Kestrel Path. Slough 21 F1
Kestrel Way. Read 85 D2
Kestrel Way. Woki 115 F3
Keswick Cl. Camb 152 B2
Keswick Cl. Read 84 B4
Keswick Ct. Slough 42 C3
Keswick Dr. Light 153 D4
Keswick Gdns. Wood 87 F3
Keswick Rd. Stai 96 A1
Ketcher Green. Binf 90 B2
Kettering Cl. Bur C 84 C2
Kevins Dr. Yate 149 F4
Keynsham Way. Crow 143 E1
Keys La. Maid 39 F3
Kibble Green. Brac 118 B2
Kibblewhite Cres. Twyf 61 E3
Kidderminster Rd. Slough ..22 A1
Kidmore End Rd. Caver 59 D4
Kidmore End Rd. Maple 59 D4
Kidmore Rd. Caver 58 C3
Kidwells Cl. Maid 39 F4
Kidwells Park Dr. Maid 39 F4
Kier Park. Ascot 120 B3
Kilburn Cl. Bur C 84 B2
Kildare Gdns. Caver 59 E2
Killarney Dr. Maid 39 F4
Kilmartin Gdns. Camb 151 F1
Kilmington Cl. Brac 118 C1
Kilmiston Ave. Shepp 125 E2
Kilmore Dr. Camb 152 A2
Kilmuir Cl. Sand 150 B4
Kiln Cl. Harl 71 E4
Kiln Cl. Herm 79 E4
Kiln Cl. Herm 78 C3
Kiln La. Ascot 93 D1
Kiln La. Bou E 3 E2
Kiln La. Brac 118 A4
Kiln La. Mort 137 E3
Kiln La. Shipl 35 E1
Kiln La. Suln 85 E4
Kiln La. Sunn 121 D2
Kiln Pl. Maid 19 D2
Kiln Rd. Caver 59 E4
Kiln Rd. Newb 105 E3
Kiln Ride Extension. Woki ..142 A3
Kiln Ride. Upp B 54 C3
Kiln Ride. Woki 142 A4
Kiln View Rd. Read 86 B1
Kilnsea Dr. Read 87 E1
Kilnsea Dr. Winn 87 E1
Kilowna Cl. Char 61 D2
Kilross Rd. Felt 98 C4
Kimber Cl. Wind 67 D2
Kimbers Cl. Newb 104 C2
Kimber's La. Maid 39 F2
Kimberley Cl. Read 85 F3
Kimberley Cl. Slough 43 F1
Kimberley. Brac 118 B1
Kimbers Dr. Burn 21 E1
Kimbers Dr. Newb 104 B3
Kimmeridge. Brac 118 C2
Kimpton Cl. Read 113 F4
King Edward St. Slough 42 B2
King Edward VII Ave. Wind ..67 F4
King Edwards Rd. Burl 119 F4
King Edwards Rise. Burl 92 C1
King Edwards Rd. Burl 119 F4
King George Cl. Ashf 98 C2
King James Way. Hen-O-T ..35 E4
King John's Cl. Wray 68 B1
King St. Chert 124 A1
King St. Maid 39 F3
King St. Mort 137 D3
King St. Read 86 A4
King Stable St. Eton 67 E4
King Street La. Winn 88 B1
King's Ashf 98 C1
King's Cl. Stai 97 E1
King's Gr. Maid 39 F3
King's Keep. Sand 143 D1
King's Meadow Rd. Read 86 A4
King's Rd. Ascot 120 B2
King's Rd. Caver 59 E1
King's Rd. Crow 143 E3
King's Rd. Eng G 96 A2
King's Rd. Hen-O-T 15 E1
King's Rd. Read 86 B4
King's Rd. Slough 42 C2
King's Rd. Wind 67 E2
King's Ride. Ascot 119 E3
King's Ride. Brac 119 E3
King's Ride. Camb 151 E4
King's Ride Park. Brac 119 E2
King's Wlk. Sand 150 C3
Kingfisher Cl. Twyf 61 F2
Kingfisher Dr. Stai 96 C2
Kingfisher Dr. Wood 87 E3
Kingfisher Dr. Yate 149 D3
Kingfisher Pl. Read 86 A4
Kingham Cl. Maid 19 E2
Kingham Park. Maid 19 E2
Kings Cl. Hen-O-T 15 E1
Kings La. Cook 19 D4

Kings La. Eng G 95 D1
Kings La. Windl 146 C3
Kings Mead. Newb 130 B3
Kings Rd W. Newb 105 D1
Kings Rd. Newb 105 D1
Kings Rd. Silc 136 A1
Kings Rd. West E 153 F3
Kings Wlk. Read 86 A4
Kings Wood. Medm 17 E4
Kingsbridge Cotts. Brac ..142 C4
Kingsbridge Hill. Swal 139 D3
Kingsbridge Rd. Newb 104 C1
Kingsbridge Rd. Read 86 B1
Kingsbury Cres. Stai 96 B2
Kingsbury Dr. Old W 68 A1
Kingsclear Park. Camb 151 E2
Kingsdown Cl. Read 87 D1
Kingsfield. Wind 66 B3
Kingsford Cl. Wood 88 A3
Kingsgate St. Read 86 B4
Kingsland Grange. Newb ..132 C4
Kingsley Ave. Camb 151 E2
Kingsley Ave. Eng G 95 D1
Kingsley Cl. Char 61 D3
Kingsley Cl. Crow 143 D2
Kingsley Cl. Newb 105 D3
Kingsley Ct. Read 113 D4
Kingsley Dr. Mar B 1 B3
Kingsmere Rd. Brac 117 F4
Kingston Ave. Felt 71 F1
Kingston Cl. Read 87 E2
Kingston Gdns. Read 86 B1
Kingston La. Sulhd 110 B3
Kingston Rd. Camb 152 A4
Kingston Rd. Stai 97 E1
Kingsway. Black 150 B3
Kingsway. Caver 59 F3
Kingsway. Far C 22 B3
Kingsway. Iver 44 C4
Kingsway. Stan 97 E4
Kingsway. That 106 C1
Kingswick Cl. Ascot 120 B3
Kingswick Dr. Ascot 120 B3
Kingswood Cl. Eng G 95 E2
Kingswood Creek. Wray 68 B1
Kingswood Ct. Maid 39 F3
Kingswood Rise. Eng G 95 E2
Kinross Ave. Ascot 119 F2
Kinross Cl. Ashf 98 C2
Kinross Ct. Ascot 119 F2
Kinson Rd. Read 58 A1
Kintbury Rd. Kint 127 E3
Kipling Cl. That 106 B3
Kipling Cl. Yate 149 E2
Kirkfell Cl. Read 57 E1
Kirkham Cl. Caver 59 F3
Kirkham Cl. Crow 143 E1
Kirkstall Ct. Bur C 84 B2
Kirkstone Cl. Camb 152 B2
Kirkwall Spur. Slough 42 C4
Kirkwood Cres. Bur C 110 C2
Kirton Cl. Read 85 D4
Kirtons Farm Rd. Bur C 85 E1
Kitsmead La. Went 122 B1
Kittiwake Cl. Wood 88 A4
Kitwood Dr. Winn 87 F1
Klondyke. Mar 1 B1
Knapp Rd. Ashf 97 F2
Knapp The. Read 87 D2
Knappe Cl. Hen-O-T 35 E4
Knighton Cl. Caver 59 D2
Knights Cl. Stai 96 B1
Knights Cl. Wind 66 B3
Knights La. Ball H 129 E2
Knights Way. Caver 59 D3
Knightsbridge Cres. Stai 97 E1
Knightsbridge Dr. Head 132 A2
Knightsbridge Rd. Camb ..151 F1
Knightswood. Brac 118 A1
Knoll Cl. Let B 6 C4
Knoll Rd. Camb 151 E3
Knoll The. Pur O T 57 D1
Knoll Wlk. Camb 151 E3
Knollmead. Bur C 84 B2
Knollys Rd. Silc 135 F1
Knowle Cl. Caver 58 B2
Knowle Gr. Went 122 B1
Knowle Grove Cl. Went ..122 B1
Knowle Hill. Went 122 B1
Knowle Park Ave. Stai 97 D2
Knowle Rd. Wood 87 E2
Knowles Ave. Finch 142 C3
Knowsley Cl. Maid 19 D1
Knowsley Rd. Sulh 87 D2
Knox Green. Binf 90 B2
Korda Cl. Stai 124 C3
Kraemer Ct. Read 151 D2
Kybes La. Shin 112 B3
Kyle Cl. Brac 118 A3

La Roche Cl. Slough 43 E2
Laburnam Pl. Eng G 95 D1
Laburnham Rd. Maid 39 F3

Laburnham Rd. Read 87 D1
Laburnum Cl. Mar 1 C2
Laburnham Gdns. Read 86 C1
Laburnham Gr. Newb 105 D2
Laburnham Gr. Slough 69 D4
Laburnum Rd. Chert 124 A1
Laburnum Way. Stai 97 F4
Laburnums The. Black 150 A3
Lacey Cl. Stai 96 B1
Ladbroke Cl. Wood 87 F3
Ladbrooke Rd. Slough 42 B2
Ladwell Cl. Newb 130 B3
Lady Jane Ct. Caver 59 E2
Lady Margaret Rd. Sunn 120 C1
Ladybank. Brac 118 A1
Ladymask Cl. Read 84 C2
Laffords The. Brad 82 A1
Laggan Rd. Maid 19 F1
Laggan Sq. Maid 19 F1
Laird Cl. Bags 145 F1
Lake Ave. Slough 42 B3
Lake End Rd. Burn 41 D3
Lake End Rd. Burn 41 D2
Lake End Way. Crow 143 D2
Lake Rd. Vir W 122 A3
Lake Side The. Black 150 B2
Lakeland Dr. Camb 151 F1
Lakeside Dr. Sto P 22 C2
Lakeside Rd. Iver 69 F4
Lakeside. Brac 91 E1
Lakeside. Maid 20 A1
Lakeside. Read 87 D2
Lalande Cl. Woki 115 F3
Laleham Rd. Shepp 125 D2
Laleham Rd. Stai 96 C1
Laleham Rd. Stai 125 D2
Laleys Green. Herm 78 C2
Lamb Cl. That 106 B3
Lambert Ave. Slough 43 F2
Lambert Cres. Black 150 B2
Lambfields. Thea 83 E2
Lambly Hill. Vir W 122 B2
Lambourn Pl. Lamb 25 D2
Lambourn Rd. Newb 104 B3
Lambourne Cl. Read 84 B4
Lambourne Dr. Bags 145 E1
Lambourne Gdns. Read 39 E2
Lambourne Gdns. Read 87 E2
Lambourne Gr. Brac 118 C4
Lambs La. Shin 139 D4
Lambwood Hill. Shin 112 B1
Lamerton Rd. Read 86 B1
Lammas Ave. Wind 67 E3
Lammas Ct. Wind 67 E3
Lammas Dr. Wray 96 B2
Lammas Mead. Binf 90 C1
Lammas Rd. Slough 41 E4
Lamorna Cres. Read 57 E1
Lamp Acres. Newb 105 D3
Lamplighters Wlk. Read 84 C2
Lamsden Way. Bur C 111 D2
Lanark Cl. Camb 151 F1
Lanark Cl. Woki 88 A3
Lancashire Hill. New G 91 F1
Lancaster Ave. Slough 22 B1
Lancaster Cl. Hung 100 B2
Lancaster Cl. Read 86 B3
Lancaster Cl. That 106 B2
Lancaster Gdns. Read 87 D2
Lancaster Rd. Maid 39 D4
Lancaster Sq. Hung 100 B2
Lancastria Mews. Maid 39 E4
Lancelot Cl. Slough 42 A2
Lancing Cl. Read 85 E4
Lancing Rd. Felt 98 C3
Landen Cl. Woki 116 A2
Landon Way. Ashf 98 A1
Landrake Cres. Read 86 B1
Landseer Cl. Sand 150 C3
Landsend La. Char 61 D1
Lane End Cl. Shin 113 F3
Lane The. Chert 124 A3
Lane The. Cook 10 C4
Lane The. Silc 136 B1
Lane The. Vir W 122 C3
Lanes Wood. Mort 136 C3
Langborough Rd. Woki 116 B3
Langdale Cl. Maid 40 A3
Langdale Dr. Ascot 119 F4
Langdale Gdns. Read 86 C1
Langdon Cl. Camb 152 B2
Langford Cl. Caver 59 E3
Langham Pl. Eng G 95 F2
Langhams Way. Warg 36 C1
Langley Broom. Slough 43 F1
Langley Common Rd. Arbo ... 114 C1
Langley Common Rd. Bark ... 114 C1
Langley Cres. Harl 71 F4
Langley Dr. Camb 151 E3
Langley Hill Cl. Read 84 B3
Langley Hill. Read 84 B3
Langley Park Rd. Iver 44 B3
Langley Park Rd. Slough 44 B3
Langley Rd. Slough 43 D2
Langley Rd. Stai 96 C1
Langley Way. Mar 1 B1

Langton Cl. Maid 39 E4
Langton Way. Stai 96 B1
Langton's Meadow. Far C 22 B3
Langworthy End. Holy 65 D4
Langworthy La. Holy 65 E4
Lanriver Ct. Read 87 D1
Lansdowne Ave. Slough 42 C3
Lansdowne Ct. Slough 42 C3
Lansdowne Rd. Read 84 B4
Lansdowne Rd. Stai 97 D1
Lapwing Cl. Read 84 B3
Larch Ave. Ascot 120 C2
Larch Ave. Sunn 120 C2
Larch Ave. Woki 116 A4
Larch Cl. Bur C 111 D2
Larch Cl. Camb 151 F4
Larch Cl. Slough 42 A4
Larch Dr. Wood 87 F3
Larches Way. Black 150 A3
Larchfield Rd. Maid 39 F3
Larchside Cl. Shin 113 D1
Larchwood Dr. Eng G 95 D1
Larchwood Glade. Camb 152 A4
Larges Bridge Dr. Brac 118 B4
Larges La. Brac 118 B4
Larissa Ct. Read 57 F1
Lark Ave. Stai 96 C3
Larkham Cl. Felt 98 C3
Larkings La. Sto P 23 D2
Larks-Meade. Read 87 D1
Larksfield. Eng G 95 E1
Larkspur Cl. Woki 115 E4
Larkswood Cl. Read 57 E2
Larkswood Cl. Sand 143 D1
Larkswood Dr. Crow 143 D3
Lascelles Rd. Slough 43 D2
Lashbrook Mead. Shipl 36 A2
Lashbrook Rd. Shipl 36 A2
Lassell Gdns. Maid 40 A4
Lasswade Rd. Chert 123 F1
Latham Ave. Camb 151 F1
Latimer Dr. Bur C 84 B2
Latimer Rd. Woki 116 A3
Latimer. Brac 118 A1
Latton Cl. Chil 10 C4
Laud Way. Woki 116 C3
Laud's Cl. Hen-O-T 15 E1
Launceston Ave. Caver 59 F3
Launcestone Cl. Read 87 D1
Launder Ct. Camb 151 F1
Laundry La. Sand 150 C3
Lauradale. Brac 118 A3
Laurel Ave. Eng G 95 D2
Laurel Ave. Slough 43 F2
Laurel Cl. Camb 151 E2
Laurel Cl. Stan 69 F4
Laurel Cl. Woki 115 F3
Laurel Dr. Read 57 D3
Laurence Cres. Wind 146 B2
Lauser Rd. Stan 97 E4
Lavenham Dr. Wood 87 F4
Lawford Cres. Yate 149 E3
Lawkland. Far C 22 A1
Lawn Cl. Datch 68 B4
Lawrence Cl. Woki 116 B3
Lawrence Ct. Wind 67 E3
Lawrence Gr. Binf 117 E4
Lawrence Mead. Kint 102 A1
Lawrence Rd. Read 85 D4
Lawrence Way. Sand 150 C2
Lawrence Way. Slough 41 E4
Lawrences La. Cold A 106 B3
Lawson La. Chil 10 B4
Lawson Way. Windf 121 D2
Laxton Green. Maid 39 E2
Layburn Cres. Slough 69 D4
Layland's Green. Kint 102 A1
Laytm Rise. Sulh 57 E2
Layton's La. Shepp 125 F4
Le Marchant Rd. Camb 151 F2
Lea Cl. Mar B 1 B3
Lea Cl. Read 85 D2
Lea Croft. Crow 143 D3
Lea Rd. Camb 151 D1
Lea The. Stai 96 B1
Lea The. Woki 141 F4
Leacroft Cl. Stai 97 D2
Leacroft Rd. Iver 44 C4
Leacroft. Stai 121 D2
Leafield Copse. Brac 118 C3
Leaholme Gdns. Slough 41 E4
Leas Dr. Iver 44 C4
Leaver Rd. Hen-O-T 15 E1
Leaves Green. Brac 118 B2
Ledbury Cl. Read 58 A1
Ledbury Dr. Bur C 84 B2
Ledger La. Holy 65 E3
Ledger's Rd. Slough 42 B2
Ledran Cl. Winn 87 E1
Lee La. Bish 18 C1
Lee La. Maid 18 C1
Leeds Rd. Slough 42 C3
Lees Cl. Maid 39 D3
Lees Gdns. Maid 39 D3
Lees Wlk. Mar 1 B1
Leeson Gdns. Eton 41 F1
Leicester Cl. Hen-O-T 15 E2
Leicester. Brac 118 C1

Leigh Field. Mort 136 C3
Leigh Park. Datch 68 B4
Leigh Rd. Slough 42 A3
Leigh Sq. Wind 66 B3
Leighton Gdns. Maid 20 A1
Leiston Cl. Winn 87 E1
Leiston Spur. Slough 42 C1
Leith Cl. Brac 143 D4
Lemart Cl. Read 84 C4
Lemington Gr. Brac 118 A2
Leney Cl. Woki 116 B4
Lenham Cl. Woki 88 C1
Lennox Cl. Bur C 84 A2
Lennox Rd. Read 87 D3
Lent Green La. Burn 21 D1
Lent Rise Rd. Burn 41 D4
Leopold Wlk. Read 86 B4
Leppington. Brac 118 A1
Lerwick Dr. Slough 42 C4
Lesford Rd. Read 85 F3
Leslie Southern Ct. Newb 105 D2
Lesters Rd. Cook 19 D3
Letchworth Ave. Felt 98 C4
Letcombe Sq. Brac 118 C3
Letcombe St. Read 86 A4
Leverton La. Hung 73 D1
Lewendon Rd. Newb 104 C3
Lewins Way. Slough 41 F3
Lewis Wlk. Newb 130 B3
Lewisham Way. Crow 143 E1
Lexington Ave. Maid 39 E3
Lexington Gr. Read 113 E3
Leybum Cl. Wood 88 A4
Leycester Cl. Windl 146 A3
Leyland Gdns. Shin 113 F3
Leylands La. Stan 69 F2
Leys Gdns. Newb 104 C2
Leyside. Crow 143 D3
Lichfield Cl. Wood 87 E1
Lichfields. Brac 118 C4
Liddel Way. Ascot 119 F2
Liddell Cl. Finch 141 F2
Liddell Sq. Oak G 66 B3
Liddell. Oak G 66 B3
Lido Rd. Chil 10 B4
Lidstone Cl. Winn 114 B4
Liebenrood Rd. Read 85 E3
Lightlands La. Cook 19 F3
Lightwater Meadow. Light 153 D4
Lightwater Rd. Light 153 E4
Lightwood. Brac 118 B2
Lilac Cl. Pur O T 57 E3
Lilacs The. Woki 115 E2
Lillibrooke Cres. Maid 39 D2
Lily Hill Dr. Brac 118 C4
Lily Hill Rd. Brac 118 C4
Lima Ct. Read 85 F3
Lime Ave. Camb 152 A3
Lime Cl. Newb 105 E2
Lime Cl. Woki 115 F3
Lime Tree Rd. Gori 34 A3
Lime Wlk. Brac 118 B3
Lime Wlk. Maid 39 D4
Limecroft. Yate 149 E3
Limefield Cl. Winn 87 E2
Limerick Cl. Brac 118 A4
Limes Cl. Ashf 98 A2
Limes Rd. Eng G 95 F2
Limmer Cl. Woki 115 E2
Limmerhill Rd. Woki 115 F3
Linchfield Rd. Datch 68 B3
Lincoln Cl. Camb 152 A2
Lincoln Cl. Winn 88 A2
Lincoln Gdns. Twyf 61 E3
Lincoln Hatch La. Burn 21 F1
Lincoln Rd. Maid 39 D4
Lincoln Rd. Read 86 B2
Lincoln Way. Slough 41 E3
Lindale Cl. Vir W 122 A3
Lindale Rd. Crow 143 E3
Linden Ave. Maid 19 E1
Linden Cl. Holy 65 D4
Linden Cl. Newb 104 C2
Linden Cl. Woki 115 F2
Linden Ct. Camb 151 F4
Linden Dr. Far C 22 B2
Linden Hill La. Warg 37 E1
Linden Rd. Newt 131 E4
Linden Rd. Read 86 C1
Linden Way. Shepp 125 E2
Lindenhill Rd. Brac 117 F4
Lindores Rd. Holy 65 D3
Lindsay Cl. Stan 70 B1
Lindsay Dr. Shepp 125 E2
Lindsey Cl. Woki 115 F3
Lingfield Gdns. Felt 98 B4
Lingfield Rd. Newb 131 E4
Lingholm Cl. Maid 39 E3
Lingholm Cl. Read 84 C3
Lingwood. Brac 118 B2
Link Rd. Datch 68 B3
Link Rd. Felt 98 C4
Link Rd. Newb 105 D1

Link The. Slough 43 D4
Link The. Yate 149 E4
Link Way. Arbo 114 C1
Link Way. Stai 97 D1
Link Way. That 106 A2
Links App. Fla H 3 D4
Links Dr. Read 85 D4
Links Rd. Ashf 97 F2
Links Rd. Fla H 3 E4
Links The. Burl 119 F4
Links Way. Fla H 3 D4
Linkscroft Ave. Ashf 98 A1
Linkswood Rd. Burn 21 E2
Linkway. Camb 151 E2
Linkway. Crow 142 C3
Linnet Ave. Newt 131 F2
Linnet Cl. Read 84 A3
Lintott Ct. Stan 70 B1
Lion Cl. Stai 124 C3
Lip La. Wick 75 F2
Lipscomb Cl. Herm 79 D3
Lipscombe Cl. Newb 104 C2
Liscombe. Brac 118 A1
Lisle Cl. Newb 104 C3
Lismore Cl. Wood 87 F2
Lisset Rd. Maid 40 A3
Lister Cl. Pur O T 57 E3
Liston Rd. Mar 1 B1
Litcham Spur. Slough 42 B4
Lithgow's Rd. Harm 71 F2
Littington Cl. Winn 114 B4
Little Bowden La. Pangb 55 F2
Little Buntings. Wind 66 C2
Little Cl. Fla H 3 D3
Little Croft Rd. Gori 34 B3
Little Croft. Yate 149 E3
Little Elms. Harl 71 E4
Little Fryth. Woki 142 B3
Little Glebe. Sonn 60 C2
Little Heath Rd. Read 84 A4
Little Hill Rd. Hurst 88 A2
Little John's La. Read 85 E4
Little La. Buck 107 E3
Little London Rd. Silc 136 A1
Little Marlow Rd. Mar 1 C2
Little Moor. Sand 143 E1
Little Oak Dr. Read 84 B3
Little Paddock. Camb 152 A4
Little Ringdale. Brac 118 C3
Little St. Read 85 F4
Little Sutton La. Iver 44 B1
Little Sutton La. Slough 69 D4
Little Vigo. Yate 149 D2
Little Woodlands. Wind 66 C2
Littlebrook Ave. Slough 21 F1
Littlebrook Ave. Slough 41 F4
Littlecote Dr. Read 85 F3
Littlecote Rd. Frox 99 D3
Littlecroft Rd. Eng G 95 F2
Littledale Cl. Brac 118 C3
Littledown Rd. Slough 42 C3
Littlefield Green. Whi Wa 63 F3
Littlejohn's La. Read 58 B1
Littleport Spur. Slough 42 C4
Littlestead Cl. Caver 59 F3
Littleton La. Stai 124 C2
Littleton Rd. Stai 98 B1
Liverpool Rd. Read 86 C4
Liverpool Rd. Slough 42 A4
Livery Cl. Read 86 B4
Livingstone Gdns. Wood 87 F3
Livingstone Rd. Newb 105 D1
Llangar Gr. Crow 143 D3
Llanvair Cl. Ascot 120 A2
Llanvair Dr. Ascot 119 F2
Lochbridge Ct. Maid 40 B4
Lochinvar Cl. Slough 42 A2
Lochinver. Brac 118 A1
Lock Ave. Maid 20 B1
Lock La. Maid 39 E2
Lock Mead. Maid 20 B1
Lock Path. Dorn 66 B4
Lock Rd. Read 86 B4
Lock Rd. Mar 1 C1
Lockbridge Rd. Bou E 3 D2
Locke Gdns. Slough 43 E2
Lockets Cl. Wind 66 B3
Lockram Rd. Bur C 111 E1
Lockram Rd. Mort 111 E1
Locks Ride. Burl 92 B1
Lockstile Mead. Gori 34 B3
Lockstile Way. Gori 34 B3
Lockton Chase. Ascot 119 E3
Loddon Bridge Rd. Wo Wa 87 F3
Loddon Bridge Rd. Wood 87 F3
Loddon Cl. Camb 152 A3
Loddon Dr. Char 61 D4
Loddon Hall Rd. Twyf 61 F3
Loddon Rd. Bou E 3 D2
Loddon Spur. Slough 42 C4
Lodge Cl. Eng G 95 E2
Lodge Cl. Mar 1 A1
Lodge Gr. Yate 149 F3
Lodge Rd. Hurst 88 C4
Lodge Way. Ashf 98 A1
Lodge Way. Stai 125 E4
Lodge Way. Wind 66 C2
Logan Cl. Read 84 C4

Lois Dr. Shepp ....
Lomond Ave. Caver ....
London Rd. Ascot ....
London Rd. Ashf ....
London Rd. Bags ....
London Rd. Binf ....
London Rd. Black ....
London Rd. Blew ....
London Rd. Brac ....
London Rd. Camb ....
London Rd. Datch ....
London Rd. Eng G ....
London Rd. Newb ....
London Rd. Read ....
London Rd. Slough ....
London Rd. Stan ....
London Rd. That ....
London Rd. Twyf ....
London Rd. Went ....
London Rd. Windl ....
London St. Chert ....
London St. Read ....
Long Barn La. Read ....
Long Cl. Far C ....
Long Cl. Kint ....
Long Dr. Burn ....
Long Furlong Dr. Slough .....
Long Gr. Tad ....
Long Grove. Buck ....
Long Half Acre. Bish ....
Long Hedge. Lamb ....
Long Hill Rd. Burl ....
Long La. Brig ....
Long La. Cold A ....
Long La. Cook ....
Long La. Herm ....
Long La. Holy ....
Long La. Holy ....
Long La. Pur O T ....
Long La. Stan ....
Long La. Sulh ....
Long La. Winn ....
Long Mickle. Sand ....
Long Readings La. Slough ....
Long's Way. Woki ....
Longacre. Newb ....
Longbourne Way. Chert ....
Longbridge Rd. That ....
Longcroft Rd. That ....
Longdown Rd. Sand ....
Longfield Rd. Twyf ....
Longford Ave. Felt ....
Longford Ave. Stan ....
Longford Cl. Camb ....
Longford Way. Stan ....
Longhurst Cl. Caver ....
Longlands Way. Camb ....
Longleat Dr. Sulh ....
Longleat Gdns. Maid ....
Longleat Way. Felt ....
Longmead La. Burn ....
Longmead. Ball H ....
Longmead. Wind ....
Longmeadow. Camb ....
Longmoor La. Mort ....
Longmoors. Brac ....
Longmoors. Brac ....
Longridge Cl. Read ....
Longshot Ind Est. Brac ....
Longshot La. Brac ....
Longside Cl. Stai ....
Longview. Beac ....
Longwater La. Finch ....
Longwater Rd. Brac ....
Longwater Rd. Finch ....
Longworth Ave. Read ....
Longworth Dr. Maid ....
Lonsdale Cl. Maid ....
Lonsdale Way. Holy ....
Loosen Dr. Maid ....
Lord Knyvett Cl. Stan ....
Loring Rd. Wind ....
Lorne Cl. Slough ....
Lorne Pl. Read ....
Lorne St. Read ....
Lorraine Rd. Camb ....
Iory Hill La. Beac ....
Losfield Rd. Wind ....
Lossie Dr. Iver ....
Loughborough. Brac ....
Loundyes Cl. That ....
Lovatt Cl. Read ....
Love Green La. Iver ....
Love Hill La. Slough ....
Love La. Iver ....
Love La. Yate ....
Love's Cl. Bur C ....
Lovedean Ct. Brac ....
Lovejoy La. Wind ....
Lovel La. Wink ....
Lovel Rd. Wink ....
Lovelace Cl. Hurl ....
Lovelace Rd. Brac ....

169
vell Cl. Hen-O-T
Merton Cl. Maid

l Cl. Hen-O-T 35 E4
ls Cl. Light 146 A1
ock Rd. Read 58 B1
ock Rd. Read 58 B1
s Wood. Mort 136 C3
t Gdns. Maid 20 B2
t Rd. Stai 96 B2
rook Dr. Maid 39 D2
ury. Brac 118 C3
r Armour Rd. Read 57 E1
r Boyndon Rd. Maid 39 F3
r Britwell Rd. Slough 21 E1
r Broadmoor Rd. Crow 143 E2
r Brook St. Read 86 A3
r Bungalows. Gori 34 B4
r Canes. Yate 149 D3
r Charles St. Camb 151 E3
r Church Rd. Sand 149 F4
r Cippenham La. Slough 41 F3
r Common. Finch 140 C1
r Cookham Rd. Maid 20 B1
r Earley Way (W). Read 113 F4
r Earley Way. Read 114 B4
r Earley Way. Winn 114 B4
r Early Way (N). Winn 87 F1
r Elmstone Dr. Read 57 E1
r Field Rd. Read 86 A3
r Henley Rd. Caver 59 E2
r Lees Rd. Slough 22 A1
r Meadow Rd. Read 86 B1
r Mill Field. Bags 145 E1
r Nursery. Sunn 121 D2
r Pound La. Mar 18 B4
r Rd. Chil 10 B4
r Rd. Cook 19 F4
r Ridge. Bou E 3 D2
r Sandhurst Rd. Finch 142 B1
r Sandhurst Rd. Sand 142 B1
r Village Rd. Ascot 120 B2
r Way. That 105 F2
r Way. That 106 A2
r Wokingham Rd. Brac 142 B3
r Wokingham Rd. Finch 142 B3
s Cl. Shipl 36 A2
s Comm. Finch 140 C1
stoft Cl. Winn 87 E1
ield Cl. Light 153 D4
ield Green. Caver 59 F2
ield Rd. Caver 59 E3
ands Rd. Black 150 B2
ands Rd. Stan 70 B1
y Cl. Sand 150 B3
her Cl. Woki 115 F4
her Rd. Woki 115 F4
ood Cl. Felt 98 B4
ood. Read 87 E1
n Dr. Stai 97 E1
s Cl. Yate 149 E3
s Green Rd. West E 153 F2
y Cl. Sulh 57 D2
e Ave. Ashf 98 A1
ley Rd. Brac 116 A2
ley Wood. Brac 116 A2
more Dr. Read 87 D2
ington Ave. Vir W 122 C4
ow Cl. Newb 105 F3
ow Rd. Felt 98 C3
ow Rd. Maid 39 F3
ow. Brac 118 A1
Cl. Wind 66 C2
r Ave. Hen-O-T 15 E2
orth Rd. Read 113 E4
s Farm Rd. Wood 88 A4
y La. Read 85 E4
n Cl. Bags 145 E1
ombe Cl. Caver 59 E2
an's Haven. Know H 37 F3
rworth Cl. Brac 91 E1
n Cl. Read 113 F4
Gate Cl. Sand 149 F4
oft Cl. Gori 34 B4
ury. Brac 118 C3
ord Ave. Slough 42 B4
ord Rd. Read 86 C3
ey. Brac 118 A1
ey Cl. Slough 22 A1
ield Ct. Caver 59 D3
. Oak G 66 B2
e Gr. Read 57 E1
ington Ave. Yate 149 E3
ington Gate. Caver 58 C3
h Hill La. Slough 21 F1
h La. Lamb 25 D1
len Mews. Read 86 A2
hurst Ave. Black 150 B3
hurst Ave. Cook 19 F3
hurst Cl. Brac 119 D3
hurst Rd. Ascot 120 A3
hurst Rd. Gori 34 B3
hurst Rd. Read 58 A1
wood Dr. Old W 68 A1
e Cl. Went 122 C2
e Crossing Rd. Chert 123 D2
e La. Chert 123 D1
e Rd. Went 122 C2
grove Ave. Ashf 98 B2
ham Gdns. Maid 19 D1
ham Rd. Crow 143 D3
nouth Rd. Read 59 D1
Lynn Cl. Ashf 98 B2
Lynton Cl. Wood 87 E3
Lynton Ct. Newb 105 D2
Lynton Green. Maid 39 F4
Lynwood Ave. Eng G 95 F1
Lynwood Ave. Slough 43 E2
Lynwood Chase. Brac 91 E1
Lynwood Cres. Sunn 120 C2
Lyon Cl. That 106 C1
Lyon Rd. Crow 143 E3
Lyon Sq. Read 85 D4
Lyon Way. Camb 151 E1
Lysander Cl. Wood 88 A4
Lytham Cl. Read 85 E2
Lytham End. Sulh 57 D2
Lytham Rd. Wood 87 F4
Lytham. Brac 117 F2
Macbeth Ct. Brac 118 C4
Macdonald Rd. Light 153 D4
Mace Cl. Read 87 D1
Mackay Cl. Read 84 C2
Mackenzie St. Slough 42 C2
Macklin Cl. Hung 100 B3
Macphail Cl. Woki 116 C4
Macrae Rd. Yate 149 E3
Maddle Rd. Lamb 24 B4
Madeira Wlk. Wind 67 E3
Madingley. Brac 118 A1
Mafeking Rd. Wray 96 A3
Magdalen Rd. Stai 124 C3
Magdalene Rd. Crow 143 F1
Magill Cl. Shin 113 D1
Magna Carta La. Wray 95 F4
Magna Rd. Eng G 95 D1
Magnolia Cl. Sand 143 E1
Magnolia Gdns. Slough 43 E2
Magnolia Way. Woki 115 F3
Magpie Cl. That 106 A2
Magpie Way. Read 84 A3
Magpie Way. Slough 21 F1
Maguire Dr. Camb 152 B2
Mahonia Cl. Camb 153 F3
Maiden Erlegh Dr. Read 87 D2
Maiden Lane Centre. Read 87 E1
Maiden Pl. Read 87 E1
Maidenhead Bsns Cps. Whi Wa 38 C1
Maidenhead Court Park. Maid 20 A2
Maidenhead Rd. Binf 89 E2
Maidenhead Rd. Cook 19 F3
Maidenhead Rd. New G 91 D3
Maidenhead Rd. Oak G 66 C4
Maidenhead Rd. Wind 66 C4
Maidens Green. Burl 92 A3
Maidensfield. Winn 88 B1
Main Dr. Burl 119 D4
Main St. Chil 10 B4
Main St. Yate 149 E4
Mainprize Rd. Brac 118 C4
Mainstone Rd. Bis 153 F2
Maise Webster Cl. Stan 97 E4
Maitland Rd. Read 85 F4
Majendie Cl. Newb 104 B3
Major's Farm Rd. Datch 68 C4
Makepiece Rd. Brac 91 D1
Maker Cl. Read 85 D2
Makins Rd. Hen-O-T 35 E4
Malders La. Cook 19 E2
Malders La. Maid 19 E2
Maldon Cl. Read 85 E3
Malet Cl. Stai 96 B1
Malham Fell. Brac 118 A3
Malham Rd. That 106 B2
Mallard Cl. Read 87 D2
Mallard Cl. Twyf 61 F2
Mallard Dr. Slough 41 F3
Mallard Row. Read 86 A4
Mallard Way. Yate 149 D3
Mallards The. Stai 124 A4
Mallards Way. Light 153 D4
Mallory Ave. Caver 59 E3
Mallow Park. Maid 19 E1
Mallowdale Rd. Brac 118 C1
Malone Rd. Wood 87 E3
Malpas Rd. Slough 43 D3
Malt Hill. Eng G 95 F2
Malt Hill. New G 91 F3
Malt House. Old W 95 D4
Malt Shovel La. Lamb 24 C2
Maltby Way. Read 114 A4
Malthouse Cl. That 106 C1
Malthouse La. Read 85 F4
Malthouse La. West E 153 F4
Maltings Pl. Read 86 A4
Maltings The. West I 10 A1
Malton Ave. Slough 42 A3
Malvern Cl. Wood 87 F3
Malvern Ct. Newb 104 C1
Malvern Rd. Harl 71 F4
Malvern Rd. Maid 19 E1
Malvern Way. Twyf 61 E4
Malyons The. Shepp 125 E2
Man's Hill. Bur C 111 E1
Manchester Rd. Read 86 C4
Mandeville Cl. Read 84 C3
Mandeville Ct. Eng G 96 A2
Mandeville Rd. Stai 125 D2
Manea Cl. Winn 114 B4
Manfield Cl. Slough 22 A1
Manners Rd. Wood 87 E4
Mannock Way. Read 88 A4
Manor Cl. Brac 91 D1
Manor Cres. Comp 31 E2
Manor Ct. Mar 1 B2
Manor Farm Ave. Shepp 125 D2
Manor Farm Cl. Wind 66 C2
Manor Farm Cotts. Old W 68 A1
Manor Farm La. Eng G 96 A2
Manor Farm La. Tidm 56 B1
Manor Farm Rd. Read 86 A1
Manor Gr. Holy 65 E3
Manor House Ct. Shepp 125 D1
Manor House Dr. Ascot 93 D1
Manor House La. Slough 68 A3
Manor La. Chiev 51 D1
Manor La. Harl 71 E4
Manor La. Herm 79 D4
Manor La. Leckh 49 F3
Manor La. Maid 39 F2
Manor La. Newb 105 F3
Manor La. That 105 F3
Manor Leaze. Stai 96 A2
Manor Park Cl. Read 84 B3
Manor Park Dr. Woki 141 F3
Manor Park Dr. Yate 149 E3
Manor Park. Frox 99 D2
Manor Pl. Newb 104 B3
Manor Pl. Stai 97 D2
Manor Rd. Ashf 98 A2
Manor Rd. Farn 7 D4
Manor Rd. Gori 34 A3
Manor Rd. Hen-O-T 35 E4
Manor Rd. Maid 39 F2
Manor Rd. Shepp 125 F1
Manor Rd. Whi-O-T 56 B4
Manor Rd. Wind 66 C3
Manor Rd. Woki 116 A1
Manor Way. Bags 145 F2
Manor Way. Eng G 95 F1
Manor Way. Holy 65 D4
Manor Wood Gate. Shipl 36 A2
Manorcrofts Rd. Eng G 96 A1
Manse Cl. Harl 71 E4
Mansel Cl. Slough 43 D4
Mansell Cl. Wind 66 C3
Mansell Dr. Newb 130 B3
Mansfield Cl. Burl 119 E4
Mansfield Cres. Brac 118 A2
Mansfield Pl. Burl 119 E4
Mansfield Rd. Read 85 F3
Mansfield Rd. Woki 115 F3
Mansion House St. Newb 105 D2
Mansion La. Iver 44 B3
Manston Dr. Brac 118 B2
Mant Cl. Wick 75 E3
Manygate La. Shepp 125 E2
Maple Cl. Maid 39 E3
Maple Cl. Sand 142 C1
Maple Cl. Sand 150 B3
Maple Cl. Winn 88 B2
Maple Cres. Newb 105 D2
Maple Cres. Slough 43 D3
Maple Ct. Eng G 95 D1
Maple Ct. Gori 34 A3
Maple Dr. Brac 143 E4
Maple Dr. Camb 152 C4
Maple Gdns. Read 86 C1
Maple Gdns. Stan 97 F3
Maple Gdns. Yate 149 E3
Maple La. Upp B 55 D3
Maple Rise. Mar 1 C2
Mapledene. Caver 58 C2
Mapledurham Dr. Pur O T 57 E3
Mapledurham View. Read 57 E1
Mapledurham Wlk. Maid 19 F2
Maplin Park. Slough 44 B2
Marathon Cl. Read 88 A4
Marbeck Cl. Wind 66 B3
Marchant Ct. Mar 2 A2
Marchwood Ave. Caver 59 E4
Marconi Rd. Newb 105 D2
Marcus Cl. Read 85 D4
Mardale. Camb 152 B2
Mare La. Whi Wa 63 F2
Marefield Rd. Mar 1 B1
Marefield. Read 87 E1
Marescroft Rd. Slough 41 F4
Marfleet Cl. Winn 87 F1
Margaret Cl. Read 113 E4
Margaret Cl. Stai 97 E1
Marigold Cl. Brac 142 C3
Marina Way. Iver 44 C3
Marina Way. Slough 41 E3
Mariners La. Brad 82 A2
Marion Ave. Shepp 125 D2
Marish Wharf. Slough 43 F2
Markby Way. Winn 87 F1
Market La. Slough 44 B2
Market Pl. Brac 118 A4
Market Pl. Hen-O-T 15 E1
Market Pl. Newb 105 D2
Market Pl. Read 86 A4
Market Pl. Woki 116 B3
Market Sa. Mar 1 B1
Market Sq. Stai 96 C2
Market St. Brac 118 A4
Market St. Gree 105 F1
Market St. Maid 39 F4
Market St. Newb 105 D1
Market St. Wind 67 E3
Markham Centre The. Thea 83 F1
Marks Rd. Woki 116 A4
Marlborough Ave. Read 86 B3
Marlborough Cl. Maid 39 D3
Marlborough Ct. Read 85 F3
Marlborough Rd. Ashf 97 F2
Marlborough Rd. Maid 39 D3
Marlborough Rd. Slough 43 F1
Marlborough Rise. Camb 151 F3
Marlborough Way. Read 84 A2
Marlin Ct. Mar 1 B1
Marling Cl. Read 57 E1
Marlow Bottom. Mar B 18 B2
Marlow Bridge La. Bish 18 C4
Marlow Mill. Mar 1 C1
Marlow Rd. Bish 18 C2
Marlow Rd. Bou E 2 B3
Marlow Rd. Hen-O-T 15 F2
Marlow Rd. Lit M 2 B3
Marlow Rd. Maid 39 F4
Marlow Rd. Mar B 1 A3
Marlowes The. Newb 130 C4
Marlston Rd. Herm 79 E3
Marmion Rd. Hen-O-T 35 F4
Marriott Cl. Harm 71 E1
Mars Cl. Woki 115 F3
Marsack St. Caver 59 E1
Marsh La. Herm 78 B2
Marsh La. Hung 100 A3
Marsh La. Newb 105 D2
Marsh La. Tapl 40 C3
Marsh Rd. That 106 C2
Marshall Cl. Camb 152 B2
Marshall Cl. Read 57 E2
Marshall Rd. Sand 150 B3
Marshalls Ct. Newb 104 B3
Marshfield. Old W 68 B3
Marshland Sq. Caver 59 D3
Marshwood Rd. Light 153 E4
Marston Way. Ascot 119 F4
Marten Pl. Sulh 57 D2
Martin Cl. Wind 66 B3
Martin Cl. Wood 87 F3
Martin Rd. Maid 39 F4
Martin Rd. Slough 42 C2
Martin Way. Camb 151 F1
Martin's Plain. Sto P 22 C2
Martindale Ave. Camb 152 B2
Martineaux La. Hurst 88 C4
Martins Cl. Black 150 B2
Martins Dr. Woki 116 A4
Martins La. Brac 118 C3
Martins The. That 106 C1
Marunden Green. Slough 21 F1
Maryland. Woki 141 F4
Mary Mead. New G 91 F1
Maryside. Slough 43 F2
Mascoll Path. Slough 21 F1
Masefield Rd. That 106 B2
Masefield Way. Stan 97 F4
Mason Cl. Yate 149 F3
Mason Pl. Sand 149 F4
Mason St. Read 85 F4
Masonic Hall Rd. Chert 123 F2
Masons Rd. Slough 41 F3
Mathisen Way. Stan 69 F3
Matlock Rd. Caver 58 C2
Matson Dr. Rem H 15 F1
Mattewsgreen Rd. Woki 116 A4
Matthews La. Stai 96 C2
Matthews Rd. Camb 144 B1
Maultway Cl. Camb 152 A4
Maultway Cres. Camb 152 A4
Maultway N. Camb 145 D1
Maultway The. Camb 152 B3
Mawbray Cl. Read 87 E1
Maxine Cl. Sand 143 D1
Maxwell Cl. Wood 87 F4
Maxwell Rd. Ashf 98 B1
May Cl. Sand 143 E1
May Fields. Woki 115 D4
May Tree Cl. Mar B 1 B3
May's La. Padw 136 A4
Maybrick Cl. Sand 142 C1
Maybury Cl. Slough 41 E4
Mayfair Dr. Newb 104 C1
Mayfair. Read 84 B4
Mayfield Ave. Read 84 A2
Mayfield Cl. Ashf 98 A1
Mayfield Dr. Caver 59 E2
Mayfield Gdns. Stai 96 C1
Mayfield Rd. Camb 151 D1
Mayfield Rd. Woo G 3 F3
Mayflower Dr. Yate 149 D4
Mayflower Way. Far C 22 B4
Maynard Cl. Cold A 106 B3
Mayo Rd. Shepp 125 F1
Mayow Cl. That 106 C1
Maypole Rd. Burn 41 D4
Mays Cl. Read 87 D3
Mays La. Read 87 D3
Mays Rd. Woki 116 C3
Mc Carthy Way. Woki 141 F4
McCrae's Wlk. Warg 36 B1
Mead Ave. Slough 44 A2
Mead Cl. Eng G 95 F4
Mead Cl. Mar 1 C2
Mead Cl. Pease 50 B4
Mead Cl. Read 84 A3
Mead Cl. Slough 44 A2
Mead Cl. Stai 96 A1
Mead La. Chert 124 A1
Mead La. Upp B 55 F4
Mead The. Gr She 48 A2
Mead Way. Slough 41 E4
Mead Wlk. Slough 44 A2
Meadfield Ave. Slough 44 A2
Meadfield Rd. Slough 44 A2
Meadhurst Rd. Chert 124 A1
Meadow Cl. Black 150 B2
Meadow Cl. Gori 34 B3
Meadow Cl. Mar 1 C1
Meadow Cl. Moul 13 F2
Meadow Cl. Old W 68 A1
Meadow Cl. That 106 B2
Meadow Cres. Comp 31 F3
Meadow Ct. Stai 96 C3
Meadow Gdns. Stai 96 B2
Meadow La. Eton 67 E4
Meadow Rd. Ashf 98 B2
Meadow Rd. Hen-O-T 15 F1
Meadow Rd. Newb 130 C4
Meadow Rd. Read 58 C1
Meadow Rd. Read 87 E2
Meadow Rd. Slough 43 F2
Meadow Rd. Went 121 F2
Meadow Rd. Woki 116 A3
Meadow View La. Holy 64 C4
Meadow View. Mar B 1 C3
Meadow View. Stan 69 F1
Meadow View. Winn 88 B2
Meadow Walk. Woki 116 A3
Meadow Way. Bou E 3 D3
Meadow Way. Brac 91 D1
Meadow Way. Dorn 40 C2
Meadow Way. Holy 65 E3
Meadow Way. Old W 68 A1
Meadow Way. Sand 150 B3
Meadow Way. Thea 83 F2
Meadow Way. West E 153 F3
Meadow Way. Woki 116 A3
Meadowbank Rd. Light 146 B1
Meadowbrook Cl. Stan 69 F3
Meadowcroft Rd. Read 113 E4
Meadows The. Fla H 3 D4
Meadowside Rd. Pangb 56 B3
Meadway Cl. Stai 97 D1
Meadway The. Read 84 C4
Meadway. Ashf 98 A2
Meadway. Camb 151 F1
Meadway. Stai 97 D1
Meare Estate. Woo G 3 F4
Mearings The. Bur C 111 F3
Measham Way. Read 87 E1
Meashill Way. Chil 9 F4
Meavy Gdns. Read 86 A1
Medallion Pl. Maid 40 A4
Medina Cl. Woki 115 F4
Medlake Rd. Stai 96 B1
Medlar Dr. Black 150 C2
Medway Cl. That 106 A3
Medway Cl. Woki 115 F4
Melbourne Ave. Slough 42 B4
Melbourne Ave. Winn 88 B1
Melbury Cl. Chert 124 A1
Meldreth Way. Winn 87 E1
Meldrum Cl. Newb 130 B3
Melford Green. Caver 59 F3
Melksham Cl. Read 113 F4
Melling Cl. Winn 87 F2
Melody Cl. Winn 88 B2
Melrose Ave. Read 87 D3
Melrose Gdns. Arbo 114 C1
Melrose. Brac 118 A1
Melton Ct. Maid 39 F3
Melville Ave. Camb 151 F1
Membury Wlk. Brac 118 C3
Memorial Ave. Shipl 35 F1
Menair Cl. Read 87 D1
Mendip Cl. Char 61 D2
Mendip Cl. Harl 71 E4
Mendip Cl. Slough 44 A1
Mendip Rd. Brac 118 C2
Menpes Rd. Purl 57 E2
Meon Cl. Tad 135 D1
Merchants Pl. Read 86 A4
Mercia Rd. Maid 39 E2
Mercian Way. Slough 41 E3
Mercury Ave. Woki 115 F3
Mere Cl. Mar 1 C1
Mere Rd. Shepp 125 D2
Mere Rd. Slough 42 C2
Mereoak La. Shin 112 C2
Merlewood. Brac 118 B2
Merlin Cl. Slough 69 D4
Merlin Mead. Burl 92 A1
Merrifield Cl. Winn 114 B4
Merrivale Gdns. Read 86 A1
Merron Cl. Yate 149 E3
Merryhill Green Hill. Winn 88 B2
Merryhill Rd. Brac 118 A4
Merryman Dr. Brac 143 D3
Merryweather Cl. Woki 115 F1
Merrywood Park. Camb 151 F2
Mersey Way. That 106 A3
Merton Cl. Maid 39 E2

170

Merton Rd. Crow

Normanhurst. As

Merton Rd. Crow 143 F1
Merton Rd. Read 86 A1
Merton Rd. Slough 43 D2
Merton Rd. Slough 43 D2
Mervyn Rd. Shepp 125 E1
Merwin Way. Wind 66 B2
Metcalf Rd. Ashf 98 A2
Meteor Cl. Wood 88 A4
Mews The. Read 86 C3
Mey Cl. Read 84 B3
Meyrick Dr. Newb 130 B3
Michael Cl. Maid 39 E3
Michaelmas Cl. Yate 149 E2
Micheldever Way. Brac 118 C2
Michelet Cl. Light 146 A1
Micklands Rd. Caver 59 F2
Mickle Hill. Sand 143 D1
Midcroft. Slough 22 A1
Middle Cl. Camb 152 B3
Middle Cl. Newb 130 B4
Middle Gordon Rd. Camb 151 E3
Middle Green. Slough 43 F3
Middle Hill. Eng G 95 E2
Middle Wlk. Burn 21 E1
Middlefields. Twyf 61 F3
Middlegreen Rd. Slough 43 E3
Middlemoor Rd. Camb 151 F1
Middleton Rd. Camb 151 F4
Midway Ave. Chert 124 A3
Midway Ave. Stai 123 D3
Midwinter Cl. Read 84 C4
Milbanke Ct. Brac 117 F4
Milbanke Way. Brac 117 F4
Mildenhall Cl. Winn 87 E1
Mildenhall Rd. Slough 42 C4
Mile Elm. Mar 2 A2
Miles Pl. Camb 152 C4
Miles Way. Wood 88 A4
Milestone Ave. Char 61 D3
Milestone Cres. Char 61 D2
Milestone Way. Caver 59 E3
Milford Rd. Read 58 C1
Milkhouse Rd. Box 103 E2
Mill Bank. Kint 102 A2
Mill Cl. Woki 115 F4
Mill Farm Ave. Stai 98 C1
Mill Field. Bags 145 E2
Mill Green. Binf 90 C1
Mill Green. Caver 59 E1
Mill House La. Stai 123 D3
Mill La. Ascot 121 D4
Mill La. Brac 117 F3
Mill La. Bur C 84 C2
Mill La. Cook 20 B4
Mill La. Hen-O-T 35 F4
Mill La. Hort 69 D2
Mill La. Hurl 17 F2
Mill La. Lamb 25 E2
Mill La. Newb 105 D2
Mill La. Padw 109 E1
Mill La. Read 86 A4
Mill La. Read 87 F2
Mill La. Sand 149 E4
Mill La. Shipl 36 A1
Mill La. Stai 123 E3
Mill La. Tapl 40 B4
Mill La. Wind 67 D4
Mill La. Winn 87 F1
Mill La. Winn 87 F1
Mill La. Yate 149 E4
Mill Mead. Stai 96 C2
Mill Pl. Datch 68 B3
Mill Pond Rise. Windl 146 A3
Mill Rd. Bur C 84 C1
Mill Rd. Caver 59 E1
Mill Rd. Gori 34 B4
Mill Rd. Mar 1 C1
Mill Rd. Shipl 36 A2
Mill Reef Cl. That 105 F2
Mill Ride. Burl 119 E4
Mill St. Iver 69 E4
Mill St. Slough 42 C3
Millbank Cres. Wood 87 F3
Millbank. Mar 1 C1
Millboard Rd. Bou E 3 D2
Millbridge Rd. Yate 149 D4
Millbrook Way. Stan 69 F3
Milldown Ave. Gori 34 B4
Milldown Rd. Gori 34 B4
Miller's Field. Gr She 48 A2
Millers Cl. Gori 34 A4
Millers Cl. Stai 97 D2
Millers Gr. Read 84 C2
Millers La. Old W 68 A1
Milley La. Warg 62 A4
Milley Rd. W St L 62 C3
Millfield. Lamb 25 D1
Millfield. Stai 125 E4
Millgreen La. Head 132 C2
Millins Cl. Sand 143 F1
Millmead. Woki 116 A4
Millmere. Yate 149 E4
Mills Spur. Old W 95 D4
Millside. Bou E 3 E2
Millstream La. Slough 41 F3
Millstream Way. Woo G 3 F4
Millworth La. Shin 113 F2
Milman Cl. Brac 119 D4
Milman Rd. Read 86 A3
Milner Rd. Burn 41 D4
Milsom Cl. Shin 113 F3
Milton Cl. Brac 118 A2
Milton Cl. Hen-O-T 15 E1
Milton Cl. Hort 69 D2
Milton Dr. Stai 124 C3
Milton Dr. Woki 116 A3
Milton Gdns. Stan 97 F4
Milton Gdns. Woki 116 A3
Milton Rd. Eng G 95 F2
Milton Rd. Far C 22 B1
Milton Rd. Read 87 D4
Milton Rd. Woki 116 A4
Milton Way. Twyf 61 F3
Milverton Cl. Maid 39 D2
Milward Gdns. Brac 117 E4
Mina Ave. Slough 43 E2
Minchin Green. Binf 90 B2
Minden Cl. Woki 115 F3
Minley Rd. Yate 149 F1
Minniecroft Rd. Burn 21 D1
Minorca Ave. Camb 152 C1
Minorca Rd. Camb 152 C1
Minstead Cl. Brac 118 C3
Minstead Dr. Yate 149 E3
Minster St. Read 86 A4
Minster Way. Slough 43 F2
Minsterley Ave. Shepp 125 F3
Mint Cl. Read 86 C1
Minton Cl. Read 84 C4
Minton Rise. Burn 41 D4
Mirador Cres. Slough 43 E3
Mire La. W St L 62 B2
Misborne Ct. Slough 44 A1
Mistletoe Rd. Yate 149 E2
Mitcham Cl. Read 86 A3
Mitcham Rd. Camb 145 D1
Mitcham Rd. Camb 145 D1
Mitchell Cl. Slough 42 A2
Mitchell Way. Wood 88 A4
Mitford Cl. Read 113 E4
Mitre Cl. Shepp 125 E2
Mixnams La. Chert 124 A3
Moat Dr. Slough 43 E4
Modbury Gdns. Read 86 B1
Moffatts Cl. Sand 150 A4
Moffy Hill. Maid 19 F1
Mohawk Way. Wood 88 A4
Mole Rd. Arbo 114 C3
Moles Cl. Woki 116 B3
Mollison Cl. Wood 88 A4
Molly Millar Bridge. Woki 116 A2
Molly Millar's La. Woki 116 A2
Molyneux Rd. Windl 146 B2
Monarch Cl. Felt 98 C4
Mondial Way. Stan 71 E4
Moneyrow Green. Holy 65 D4
Monk's La. Newb 130 C4
Monkey Island La. Holy 40 C1
Monks Cl. Ascot 120 A2
Monks Dr. Ascot 120 A2
Monks Hollow. Mar B 1 C3
Monks Rd. Vir W 122 B3
Monks Rd. Wind 66 B3
Monks Way. Harm 70 C4
Monks Way. Read 85 E3
Monks Way. Stai 97 E1
Monks Wlk. Ascot 120 A2
Monksfield Way. Slough 22 A1
Monkshood Cl. Woki 116 C4
Monkswood Cl. Newb 130 C4
Mons Cl. Woki 115 F3
Mons Wlk. Stai 96 B2
Monsell Gdns. Stai 96 C2
Montacute Dr. That 106 C1
Montagu Rd. Slough 68 A3
Montague Cl. Camb 151 D3
Montague Cl. Light 146 A1
Montague Rd. Slough 42 C3
Montague St. Caver 59 E1
Montague St. Read 86 B4
Montague Terr. Newb 131 D4
Monteagle La. Yate 149 D3
Monteagle La. Yate 149 E3
Montem La. Slough 42 B2
Montgomery Cl. Sand 150 A4
Montgomery Dr. Shin 113 D1
Montgomery Pl. Slough 43 E4
Montgomery Rd. Newb 130 C4
Montpelier Ct. Wind 67 E3
Montpelier Dr. Caver 59 E3
Montrose Ave. Datch 68 B4
Montrose Ave. Slough 42 A4
Montrose Cl. Ashf 98 B2
Montrose Cl. Camb 151 F1
Montrose Dr. Maid 39 D3
Montrose Rd. Felt 71 E1
Montrose Way. Datch 68 B4
Montrose Wlk. Read 84 C2
Monument Cl. Newb 130 B4
Monycrower Dr. Maid 39 F4
Moor Cl. Sand 143 F1
Moor Cl. Woki 141 F4
Moor Copse Cl. Read 87 D2
Moor End. Holy 40 B1
Moor La. Harm 70 B4
Moor La. Maid 19 F1
Moor La. Newb 104 C2
Moor La. Stan 96 B3
Moor Pl. Windl 146 A3
Moorbridge Rd. Maid 40 A4
Moordale Ave. Brac 90 C1
Moore Cl. Slough 42 A2
Moore Grove Cres. Eng G 95 F1
Moores Green. Woki 116 C4
Moores La. Eton 41 F1
Moores Pl. Hung 100 B3
Moorfield Terr. Maid 40 A4
Moorfields Cl. Stai 123 F4
Moorhayes Dr. Stai 124 B3
Moorland Rd. Harm 70 B4
Moorlands Dr. Maid 38 C4
Moorlands Pl. Camb 151 D2
Moorlands Rd. Camb 151 D2
Moormede Cres. Stai 96 C2
Moors The. Pangb 56 B3
Moors The. That 106 B1
Moorside Cl. Camb 151 D1
Moorside Cl. Maid 19 F1
Moorside. Woo G 3 F4
Moorstown Ct. Slough 42 C2
Moray Ave. Sand 150 B4
Mordaunt Dr. Crow 143 D2
Morden Cl. Brac 118 C3
Moreau Wlk. Slough 43 F4
Morecambe Ave. Caver 58 C3
Moreland Ave. Iver 69 E4
Moreleigh Cl. Read 113 E4
Morella Cl. Vir W 122 B3
Morello Dr. Slough 43 F3
Moretaine Rd. Ashf 97 E3
Moreton Way. Slough 41 E3
Morgan Rd. Read 86 B3
Moriston Cl. Read 85 D4
Morlands Ave. Read 85 D3
Morley Cl. Slough 43 F2
Morley Cl. Yate 149 D3
Morley Pl. Hung 100 B3
Mornington Ave. Woki 141 F4
Mornington Cl. Tad 134 C1
Mornington Rd. Ashf 98 B2
Morpeth Cl. Read 86 B2
Morrice Cl. Slough 44 A1
Mortimer Cl. Read 113 E4
Mortimer La. Mort 137 E3
Mortimer Rd. Slough 43 E2
Morton Rd. Hort 69 D3
Moss Cl. Caver 59 E2
Mossy Vale. Maid 19 E1
Moulsham Copse La. Yate 149 D4
Moulsham La. Yate 149 D4
Mount Cl The. Went 122 B2
Mount Cl. Far C 22 B4
Mount Cl. Newb 105 D1
Mount Felix. Shepp 125 F1
Mount La. Brac 118 B4
Mount La. Chadd 49 D4
Mount Lee. Eng G 95 F2
Mount Pleasant Cl. Light 146 A1
Mount Pleasant Gr. Read 86 A3
Mount Pleasant. Brac 118 B3
Mount Pleasant. Read 86 A3
Mount Pleasant. Sand 143 D1
Mount Pleasant. Tad 135 D1
Mount Pleasant. Woki 116 A3
Mount Rd. That 106 C2
Mount St. Read 86 A3
Mount The. Caver 58 C2
Mount The. Caver 59 D2
Mount The. Read 86 B3
Mount The. Went 122 B2
Mount View. Hen-O-T 15 E1
Mountain Ash. Mar B 1 B3
Mountbatten Cl. Newb 105 E3
Mountbatten Cl. Slough 43 D2
Mountbatten Rise. Sand 142 C1
Mountfield. Gori 34 B4
Mounts Hill. Old W 93 E3
Mounts Hill. Wink 93 E3
Mountsfield Cl. Stan 70 A1
Mowbray Cres. Eng G 96 A2
Mowbray Dr. Read 85 D4
Mower Cl. Woki 116 C4
Moyleen Rise. Mar 1 B1
Muckhatch La. Stai 123 D4
Mud La. Finch 140 C1
Mud La. Pease 50 B3
Muirfield Cl. Read 86 B4
Mulberry Ave. Stan 97 F4
Mulberry Cl. Crow 143 E2
Mulberry Cl. Sand 143 E1
Mulberry Cl. Wood 87 F3
Mulberry Dr. Slough 43 F1
Mulberry Trees. Shepp 125 E1
Mulberry Way. Thea 83 F2
Mulfords Hill. Tad 135 D1
Mullins Rd. Stai 96 B2
Mulroy Dr. Camb 152 A3
Mumbery Hill. Warg 36 C1
Muncaster Cl. Ashf 98 A2
Muncaster Rd. Ashf 98 A2
Munces Rd. Mar B 1 B3
Mundaydean La. Mar 1 A2
Mundesley Spur. Slough 42 C4
Mundesley St. Read 86 A3
Munkle Marsh. That 107 D2
Munnings Dr. Sand 150 C3
Munro Ave. Wood 87 F2
Murdoch Cl. Stai 97 D2
Murdoch Rd. Woki 116 B3
Murray Ct. Ascot 120 B2
Murray Rd. Woki 116 A3
Murrellhill La. Binf 117 E4
Murrells La. Camb 151 D2
Murrin Rd. Maid 39 E4
Mushroom Castle La. Burl 92 A1
Mustard La. Sonn 60 C1
Mustard Mill Rd. Stai 96 C2
Muswell Cl. Thea 83 F2
Mutton Oaks. Brac 117 E4
Myers Way. Camb 152 B1
Myline Sq. Woki 116 B3
Myrke The. Datch 42 C1
Myrke The. Slough 42 C1
Myrtle Ave. Harm 71 F1
Myrtle Cl. Bur C 111 D2
Myrtle Cl. Light 153 D4
Myrtle Cl. Stan 69 F3
Myrtle Cl. Sulh 57 E2
Myrtle Cres. Slough 42 C3
Myrtle Dr. Black 150 B3
Myton Wlk. Thea 83 F2

Nabbs Hill Cl. Read 84 B3
Nairn Cl. Camb 151 F1
Nalderhill Rd. Box 103 D3
Napier Cl. Crow 143 E3
Napier Dr. Camb 152 A4
Napier Rd. Ashf 98 B1
Napier Rd. Crow 143 E2
Napier Rd. Harm 70 B3
Napier Rd. Maid 39 D3
Napier Rd. Read 86 B4
Napier Wlk. Ashf 98 B1
Napper Cl. Burl 119 E4
Narromine Dr. Read 84 C2
Naseby. Brac 118 A1
Nash Cl. Read 87 D2
Nash Gdns. Ascot 119 F4
Nash Grove La. Woki 115 F1
Nash Park. Binf 90 A1
Nash Rd. Slough 44 A1
Nashdom La. Burn 21 D3
Natalie Cl. Felt 98 B4
Neath Gdns. Read 84 C4
Needham Cl. Wind 66 C3
Neil Cl. Ashf 98 B2
Nell Gwynn Ave. Shepp 125 E2
Nell Gwynne Ave. Ascot 120 B3
Nell Gwynne Cl. Ascot 120 B3
Nelson Cl. Brac 118 C4
Nelson Cl. Slough 43 E1
Nelson Rd. Ashf 97 F2
Nelson Rd. Caver 59 E1
Nelson Rd. Harm 70 C3
Nelson Rd. Wind 66 C2
Nelson Way. Sand 150 C2
Nelson's La. Hurst 89 D3
Nene Rd. Harm 71 D3
Neptune Cl. Woki 115 F3
Neptune Rd. Harm 71 E3
Netherton. Brac 118 A3
Netley Cl. Caver 59 F3
Netley Rd (N). Harm 71 E3
Netley Rd. Stan 71 E3
Nettlecombe. Brac 118 C2
Nettleton Rd. Harm 71 D3
Nevelle Cl. Binf 117 E4
Neville Cl. Sto P 22 C3
Neville Cl. W St L 62 C3
Neville Dr. That 106 C2
Nevis Rd. Read 57 E2
New Bath Rd. Char 61 E3
New Bath Rd. Twyf 61 E3
New Bath Rd. Warg 61 E3
New Bright St. Read 86 A3
New Ct. Mar 1 B1
New Forest Ride. Brac 118 C2
New Forest Ride. Burl 119 D3
New Ham Rd. Harm 71 E3
New Hill. Pur O T 57 E3
New Lane Hill. Read 84 C3
New Meadow. Burl 119 E4
New Mile Rd. Ascot 120 B4
New Mill La. Finch 140 C1
New Mill Rd. Bark 140 C2
New Park Rd. Ashf 98 B2
New Rd. Black 150 C2
New Rd. Bou E 3 D2
New Rd. Brac 118 B4
New Rd. Bur C 111 F1
New Rd. Burl 92 C1
New Rd. Cook 19 F4
New Rd. Crow 143 E3
New Rd. Datch 68 B3
New Rd. Felt 71 E1
New Rd. Harl 71 E4
New Rd. Holy 65 D4
New Rd. Hurl 17 F2
New Rd. Mar B 1 B3
New Rd. Mort 111 F1
New Rd. Newb 105 E1
New Rd. Read 86 B3
New Rd. Sand 150 A4
New Rd. Shipl 36 A2
New Rd. Slough 44 A2
New Rd. Stai 96 B2
New Rd. Stai 12
New Rd. Twyf 6
New Rd. Twyf 6
New Rd. Windl 14
New Rd. Woki 11
New Square. Felt 9
New St. Bee H 13
New St. Hen-O-T 1
New St. Stai 9
New Way. Brad 8
New Wickham La. Eng G 9
New Wickham La. Stai 9
New Wokingham Rd. Crow ... 14
New Zealand Ave. Shepp 12
Newall Rd. Harm 7
Newalls Rise. Warg 3
Newark Rd. Windl 14
Newark St. Read 8
Newber Way. Slough 42
Newbery Cl. Read 57
Newbewrry Cres. Wind 6
Newbold Rd. Newb 10
Newbolt Cl. That 10
Newbury Dr. Maid 40
Newbury Hill. Hamp N 52
Newbury La. Comp 31
Newbury Rd. Gr She 48
Newbury Rd. Harm 70
Newbury Rd. Herm 79
Newbury Rd. Lamb 25
Newbury Rd. Stan 71
Newbury St. Kint 102
Newbury St. Lamb 25
Newcastle Rd. Read 86
Newchurch Rd. Slough 41
Newchurch Rd. Tad 135
Newfield Gdns. Mar 1
Newfield Rd. Mar 1
Newfield Way. Mar 1
Newhaven Cres. Ashf 98
Newhaven Spur. Slough 22
Newhurst Gdns. New G 91
Newlands Ave. Caver 59
Newlands Cl. Yate 149
Newlands Dr. Maid 39
Newlands Dr. Stan 69
Newlyn Gdns. Read 86
Newlyn Rd. Harm 71
Newman Rd. Harm 71
Newmarket Cl. Winn 87
Newport Cl. Newb 105
Newport Rd. Harm 71
Newport Rd. Newb 105
Newport Rd. Read 59
Newport Rd. Slough 21
Newquay Dr. Read 87
Newton Ave. Caver 59
Newton Cl. Slough 43
Newton Ct. Old W 68
Newton La. Old W 68
Newton Rd. Harm 70
Newton Rd. Hen-O-T 35
Newton Rd. Mar 1
Newtonside Orch. Old W 68
Newtown Gdns. Hen-O-T 35
Newtown Rd. Hen-O-T 35
Newtown Rd. Newb 131
Newtown Rd. Sand 150
Newtown. Tad 135
Niagara Rd. Hen-O-T 35
Nicholas Rd. Hen-O-T 35
Nicholls. Oak G 66
Nicholson Wlk. Eng G 96
Nicholsons La. Maid 39
Nideggen Cl. That 106
Nightingale Cres. Brac 118
Nightingale Gdns. Sand 150
Nightingale La. Mort 137
Nightingale Park. Burn 21
Nightingale Rd. Wood 87
Nightingales The. Newb 131
Nightingales The. Stan 97
Nimrod Cl. Wood 88
Nimrod Rd. Harm 71
Nimrod Way. Harm 71
Nimrod Way. Read 86
Nine Mile Ride. Bark 142
Nine Mile Ride. Brac 142
Nine Mile Ride. Woki 142
Nixey Cl. Slough 43
Noakes Hill. Asham 54
Nobel Dr. Stan 71
Nobles Way. Eng G 95
Norcot Rd. Read 84
Norden Cl. Maid 39
Norden Rd. Maid 39
Norelands Dr. Burn 21
Nores Rd. Read 113
Norfolk Ave. Slough 42
Norfolk Cl. Woki 115
Norfolk Park Cotts. Maid 39
Norfolk Rd. Maid 39
Norlands La. Stai 123
Norlands. That 106
Norman Ave. Hen-O-T 15
Norman Rd. Ashf 98
Norman Rd. Caver 59
Normandy Wlk. Stai 96
Normanhurst. Ashf 98

171

rmans The. Slough

Parsons Cl. Bark

ans The. Slough 43 D4
anstead Rd. Read 84 B4
ay Rise. Newb 130 B3
oor Rd. Bur C 110 C1
ys Ave. Woki 116 B4
ys Dr. Maid 39 E2
s Field. Chadd 49 D4
s La. Chadd 49 D4
s Rd. Read 87 D3
s Rd. Stai 96 C2
Burnham Cl. Burn 21 D2
Cl. Felt 71 E1
Cl. Medm 17 E4
Cl. Wind 66 C3
Croft. Woo G 3 F3
Dr. Sulhd 110 B4
Dr. Went 121 F2
End La. Went 121 D1
Fryerne. Yate 149 E4
Gr. Chert 123 F2
Green. Brac 118 B4
Green. Maid 19 F1
Green. Slough 42 C3
Hatton Rd. Harm 71 E3
Links Rd. Fla H 3 D4
Lodge Dr. Burl 119 E4
Park. Iver 44 B2
Rd. Burl 119 D4
Rd. Felt 71 E1
Rd. Maid 39 F4
Rd. Moul 13 F2
St. Caver 59 D1
St. Eng G 95 F1
St. Read 85 F4
St. Wink 93 D3
Standen Rd. Hung 100 A2
Star La. Maid 39 E3
Town Cl. Maid 19 F1
Town Mead. Maid 19 F1
Town Moor. Maid 19 F1
Town Rd. Maid 19 F1
Wlk. Thea 83 F2
am Cl. Winn 87 F2
ampton Ave. Slough 42 B4
ampton Cl. Brac 118 C3
borough Rd. Slough 22 A1
bourne Cl. Read 87 D1
brook Copse. Brac 118 C2
brook Rd. Caver 59 E3
brook St. Newb 105 D2
bury Ave. Twyf 61 F3
bury La. Twyf 61 F3
cott. Brac 118 A1
court Ave. Read 86 B2
croft Cl. Eng G 95 D2
croft Gdns. Eng G 95 D2
croft La. Newb 104 C2
croft Rd. Eng G 95 D2
croft Villas. Eng G 95 D2
croft. Slough 22 A1
dean. Maid 19 F1
end Cl. Fla H 3 E4
ern Ave. Newb 105 D3
ern Hts. Bou E 3 D3
ern Perimeter Rd W. Harm 70 C3
ern Perimeter Rd. Harm 71 E3
ern Rd. Slough 22 B1
ern Woods. Fla H 3 E4
field Ave. Shipl 36 A2
field Ct. Chert 124 A4
field Ct. Hen-O-T 15 E2
field End. Hen-O-T 15 E2
field Rd. Eton 41 F1
field Rd. Maid 19 F1
field Rd. Read 59 D1
field Rd. Shipl 36 A2
field Rd. Stai 124 A4
field Rd. That 106 A2
field. Light 153 D4
fields. Chiev 51 D2
fields. Lamb 25 D2
gate Dr. Camb 152 A4
ington Cl. Brac 118 C2
mead Rd. Slough 41 F4
olt Rd. Harm 70 C3
rop Rd. Harm 71 F3
umberland Ave. Read 86 B2
umberland Cl. Stan 70 C1
umberland Cres. Felt 71 F1
umbria Rd. Maid 39 D2
view. Hung 100 B3
way. Newb 105 D1
way. That 106 B3
way. Woki 115 F4
wood Dr. Newb 105 E2
wood Rd. Harm 70 B3
on Cl. Newb 130 B3
on Park. Ascot 120 B2
on Rd. Camb 152 B3
on Rd. Read 86 C4
on Rd. Swal 139 E2
on Rd. Woki 116 B3
on Rd. Wood 87 F3
way Dr. Slough 43 D4
wich Ave. Camb 151 F2
wich Dr. Wood 87 E4
wood Cres. Harm 71 E3
wood Rd. Read 86 C4
ey End. Eng G 95 E1

Notton Way. Read 113 F4
Nuffield Dr. Crow 143 F1
Nuffield Rd. Bark 140 C4
Nugee Ct. Crow 143 D3
Nugent Ct. Mar 1 C2
Nun's Acre. Gori 34 A4
Nuneaton. Brac 118 C2
Nunhide La. Sulh 83 F3
Nuns Wlk. Vir W 122 B2
Nuptown La. Burl 91 F4
Nursery Gdns. Purl 57 D3
Nursery Gdns. Shepp 125 F4
Nursery Gdns. Stai 97 D1
Nursery La. Burl 119 F4
Nursery La. Slough 43 E3
Nursery Rd. Burn 41 D4
Nursery Rd. Shepp 125 F4
Nursery Way. Wray 68 B1
Nursery Wlk. Mar 1 A1
Nut La. W St L 62 C3
Nutbean La. Swal 139 F3
Nuthatch Dr. Read 87 D2
Nuthurst. Brac 118 C2
Nutley Cl. Yate 149 E3
Nutley. Brac 118 A1
Nutmatch Cl. Stan 97 F4
Nutmeg Cl. Read 86 C1
Nutter's Hill. Swal 140 A4
Nutty La. Stai 125 E3

Oak Ave. Sand 143 E1
Oak Ave. Stai 96 B1
Oak Dr. Bur C 110 C1
Oak Dr. Wood 88 A3
Oak End Way. Padw 109 E2
Oak Farm Cl. Sand 150 B3
Oak Grove Cres. Sand 150 C3
Oak Hill. Frox 99 E2
Oak La. Eng G 95 F4
Oak La. Wind 67 D3
Oak Stubbs La. Dorn 40 C2
Oak Tree Ave. Mar 1 C2
Oak Tree Cl. Mar 1 B2
Oak Tree Cl. Tad 135 D1
Oak Tree Cl. Went 122 B2
Oak Tree Copse. Read 57 F2
Oak Tree Dr. Eng G 95 E2
Oak Tree Mews. Brac 118 B3
Oak Tree Rd. Mar 1 B2
Oak Tree Rd. Read 57 E1
Oak Tree Rd. That 106 C1
Oak Tree Wlk. Pur O T 57 E3
Oak View. Read 84 B4
Oak Way. Felt 98 C4
Oak Way. Wood 87 E2
Oakdale Cl. Read 84 B4
Oakdale Wlk. Wood 88 A4
Oakdale. Brac 118 B2
Oakdene. Bur C 111 D1
Oakdene. Sunn 120 C2
Oaken Gr. Maid 19 E1
Oaken Gr. Newb 130 B4
Oakengates. Brac 118 A1
Oakfield Ave. Slough 42 A3
Oakfield Rd. Ashf 98 A2
Oakfield Rd. Black 150 C2
Oakfield Rd. Bou E 3 D2
Oakfield Rd. Silc 135 F1
Oakhall Dr. Ashf 98 C2
Oakham Cl. Read 57 E1
Oakhurst. Maid 20 A2
Oaklands Cl. Ascot 92 C1
Oaklands Dr. Ascot 92 C1
Oaklands Dr. Woki 116 A3
Oaklands La. Crow 143 D4
Oaklands Park. Woki 116 A2
Oaklands. Yate 149 E3
Oaklea Dr. Finch 140 C1
Oakley Cres. Slough 42 C3
Oakley Green Rd. Holy 66 A3
Oakley Green Rd. Oak G 66 A3
Oakley Rd. Camb 151 D2
Oakley Rd. Caver 58 C2
Oakley Rd. Newb 105 E2
Oakridge. West E 153 F3
Oaks Rd. Shipl 36 A2
Oaks Rd. Stan 70 B1
Oaks The. Brac 118 B4
Oaks The. Yate 149 E3
Oakside Way. Read 113 F4
Oaktree Way. Sand 143 D1
Oakway Dr. Camb 151 F1
Oakwood Rd. Brac 118 C4
Oakwood Rd. Vir W 122 B2
Oakwood Rd. Windl 146 C2
Oareborough. Brac 118 C3
Oast House Cl. Wray 95 F4
Oatlands Dr. Shepp 125 F1
Oatlands Dr. Slough 42 B4
Oatlands Rd. Shin 113 F3
Oban Ct. Slough 42 B2
Oban Gdns. Wood 87 F2
Obelisk Way. Camb 151 E3
Oberon Way. Stai 124 C3
Ockwells Rd. Maid 39 E2
Octavia Way. Stai 97 D1
Octavia. Brac 118 A1
Oddfellows Rd. Newb 104 C1
Odell Cl. Read 114 A4

Odencroft Rd. Slough 22 A1
Odiham Ave. Caver 59 F3
Odiham Rd. Swal 139 E1
Odney La. Cook 20 A4
Ogmore Cl. Read 84 C4
Okingham Cl. Sand 143 E1
Old Barn Cl. Caver 59 D3
Old Bath Rd. Char 61 D3
Old Bath Rd. Newb 104 C2
Old Bath Rd. Sonn 60 B1
Old Bisley Rd. Camb 152 B2
Old Bracknell Cl. Brac 118 A3
Old Bracknell La E. Brac 118 A3
Old Bracknell La W. Brac 118 A3
Old Charlton Rd. Shepp 125 E2
Old Court Cl. Maid 39 D2
Old Dean Rd. Camb 151 E4
Old Elm Dr. Read 84 B4
Old Farm Cres. Read 57 E1
Old Farm Dr. Brac 91 E1
Old Ferry Dr. Wray 68 B1
Old Fives Ct. Burn 21 D1
Old Forest Rd. Read 88 C1
Old Forge Cl. Maid 40 A2
Old Forge Cres. Shepp 125 D2
Old Green La. Camb 151 E4
Old Hayward La. Hung 73 E2
Old Kiln Rd. Fla H 3 D4
Old La The. Read 85 F3
Old La. Ham M 102 C1
Old La. Head 133 F1
Old Lands Hill. Brac 118 B4
Old Marsh La. Dorn 40 C2
Old Mill La. Maid 40 B2
Old Newtown Rd. Newb 104 C1
Old Orchard The. Bur C 84 C2
Old Pasture Rd. Camb 151 F2
Old Pond Cl. Camb 151 E1
Old Portsmouth Rd. Camb 152 A3
Old Post Office La. Maid 39 F4
Old Sawmill La. Crow 143 E3
Old School Ct. Wray 95 F4
Old School La. Yate 149 E3
Old Slade La. Iver 44 C1
Old St. Chiev 51 E3
Old St. Chiev 51 F1
Old St. Herm 78 C4
Old Station La. Wray 69 D1
Old Station Way. Bou E 3 F3
Old Vicarage Way. Bou E 3 E2
Old Watery La. Woo G 3 F4
Old Welmore. Yate 149 F3
Old Whitley Wood. Read 113 E3
Old Wokingham Rd. Brac 143 E3
Oldacre. West E 153 F4
Oldacres. Maid 40 A4
Oldbury Rd. Chert 123 F1
Oldbury. Brac 117 F3
Oldcorne Hollow. Yate 149 D3
Olde Farm Dr. Black 150 A3
Oldershaw Mews. Maid 39 D4
Oldfield Cl. Read 87 D4
Oldfield Rd. Maid 40 A4
Oldhouse La. Light 146 B1
Oldmoor La. Woo G 3 F4
Oldstead. Brac 118 B2
Oldway La. Slough 41 E3
Oleander Cl. Brac 143 D4
Oliver Dr. Read 84 B3
Oliver Rd. Ascot 120 A3
Oliver's Paddock. Mar B 1 B3
Ollerton. Brac 118 A1
Omega Way. Stai 123 E4
Omer's Rise. Bur C 110 C2
One Pin La. Far C 22 B4
Onslow Dr. Ascot 93 D1
Onslow Gdns. Caver 59 E2
Onslow Mews. Chert 124 A2
Onslow Rd. Went 121 D1
Opal Way. Woki 115 F4
Opendale Rd. Burn 41 D4
Opladen Way. Brac 118 C2
Orbit Cl. Woki 141 F3
Orchard Ave. Ashf 98 B1
Orchard Ave. Harm 71 E1
Orchard Ave. Slough 41 E4
Orchard Ave. Wind 67 D3
Orchard Chase. Hurst 88 C4
Orchard Cl. Ashf 98 B1
Orchard Cl. Black 150 C1
Orchard Cl. Hen-O-T 15 F1
Orchard Cl. Herm 79 E4
Orchard Cl. Maid 40 A2
Orchard Cl. Newb 105 E3
Orchard Cl. Pur O T 57 E2
Orchard Cl. Shin 113 D1
Orchard Cl. Shipl 35 F1
Orchard Cl. West E 153 E3
Orchard Cl. Woki 116 B3
Orchard Cl. Wool 108 B1
Orchard Ct. Harm 70 B4
Orchard Ct. Read 113 E4
Orchard Dr. Bou E 3 E2
Orchard Estate. Twyf 61 F3
Orchard Gate. Far C 22 B4
Orchard Gate. Sand 150 A4
Orchard Gr. Fla H 3 D4
Orchard Gr. Maid 39 E4
Orchard Hill. Windl 146 B2

Orchard Park Cl. Hung 100 B2
Orchard Pl. Woki 116 B3
Orchard Rd. Hurst 88 C4
Orchard Rd. Mort 137 D3
Orchard Rd. Old W 68 A1
Orchard St. Read 86 A3
Orchard The. Eng G 96 A2
Orchard The. Fla H 3 D4
Orchard The. Light 153 D4
Orchard The. Mar 1 C2
Orchard The. Thea 83 F2
Orchard The. Vir W 122 C2
Orchard Way. Ashf 97 F3
Orchard Way. Camb 151 D1
Orchard Way. Slough 43 F3
Orchardene. Newb 105 D2
Orchardville. Burn 21 D1
Orchids The. Chil 10 B4
Oregon Ave. Read 57 E2
Oregon Wlk. Woki 141 F4
Oriel Hill. Camb 151 E2
Oriental Rd. Ascot 120 B3
Orion. Brac 118 A1
Orkney Cl. Bur C 84 C2
Ormonde Rd. Woki 116 A3
Ormsby St. Read 85 F4
Orrin Cl. Read 85 D4
Orts Rd. Newb 105 D1
Orts Rd. Read 86 B4
Orville Cl. Wood 88 A4
Orwell Cl. Caver 58 C2
Orwell Cl. Wind 67 E2
Osborne Ave. Stan 97 F4
Osborne Dr. Light 153 D4
Osborne La. New G 91 E2
Osborne Mews. Wind 67 E3
Osborne Rd. Eng G 95 F1
Osborne Rd. Read 85 D4
Osborne Rd. Wind 67 E2
Osborne Rd. Woki 116 B3
Osborne St. Slough 42 C2
Osbourne Ct. Wind 67 E3
Osman's Cl. Burl 92 A1
Osnaburgh Hill. Camb 151 D3
Osney Rd. Maid 19 F1
Osterley Cl. Woki 116 C3
Osterley Dr. Caver 59 F3
Ostler Gate. Maid 19 E1
Oswald Cl. New G 91 F1
Otter Cl. Brac 143 D4
Ouseley Rd. Old W 95 E4
Overbury Ave. Woki 88 C1
Overdale Rise. Camb 151 F2
Overdown Rd. Read 57 E1
Overlanders End. Read 57 F2
Overlord Cl. Camb 151 E4
Owen Rd. Newb 105 D3
Owen Rd. Windl 146 B3
Owl Cl. Woki 115 F3
Owlsmoor Rd. Sand 143 E1
Owston. Read 87 E1
Oxenhope. Brac 118 A3
Oxford Ave. Burn 21 D2
Oxford Ave. Harl 71 F4
Oxford Ave. Slough 41 F4
Oxford Cl. Stai 98 B1
Oxford Rd E. Wind 67 E3
Oxford Rd. Mar 1 B1
Oxford Rd. Newb 104 B3
Oxford Rd. Read 58 A1
Oxford Rd. Sand 143 F1
Oxford Rd. Wind 67 D3
Oxford Rd. Woki 116 A3
Oxford St. Caver 59 D1
Oxford St. Hung 100 C4
Oxford St. Lamb 25 D2
Oxford St. Newb 104 C2

Pack and Prime La. Hen-O-T 15 E1
Padbury Cl. Felt 98 C4
Paddick Cl. Sonn 60 C2
Paddock Cl. Camb 152 A3
Paddock Cl. Whi Wa 39 D1
Paddock Hts. Twyf 61 F2
Paddock Rd. Caver 59 E1
Paddock Rd. Newb 130 C4
Paddock The. Crow 143 D3
Paddock The. Maid 19 E1
Paddock The. Newb 105 E1
Paddock The. Slough 68 A3
Paddocks The. Fla H 3 D4
Paddocks Way. Chert 124 A1
Padstow Cl. Slough 43 F2
Padstow Gdns. Read 86 A1
Padworth Rd. Mort 136 B4
Padworth Rd. Silc 136 B4
Page Rd. Felt 98 B4
Page's Croft. Woki 116 B3
Paget Cl. Mar 1 C2
Paget Dr. Maid 39 D2
Paget Rd. Slough 43 F1
Pagoda The. Maid 20 A1
Paice Green. Woki 116 B4
Paices Hill. Alde 135 D3
Paley St. Holy 64 A3
Palmer Cl. Brac 143 D4
Palmer Park Ave. Read 87 D3
Palmer School Rd. Woki 116 B3
Palmer's Hill. Asham 54 B3

Palmer's La. Bur C 111 D1
Palmer's La. Bur C 112 A2
Palmera Ave. Bur C 84 B2
Palmers Cl. Maid 39 D2
Palmerston Ave. Slough 43 D2
Palmerstone Rd. Read 87 D3
Pamber Heath Rd. Silc 135 F1
Pamela Row. Holy 65 D4
Pan's Gdns. Camb 151 F2
Panbourne Hill. Pangb 56 B3
Pangbourne Rd. Upp B 55 E2
Pangbourne St. Read 58 A1
Pankhurst Dr. Brac 118 B2
Pantile Row. Slough 44 A1
Papist Way. Chol 14 A4
Paprika Cl. Read 86 C1
Parade The. Ashf 98 C1
Parade The. Bou E 3 D2
Parade The. Wood 87 F4
Paradise Rd. Hen-O-T 15 E1
Paradise Way. Buck 108 B4
Park Ave. Camb 151 E2
Park Ave. Stai 96 B1
Park Ave. Stai 97 D1
Park Ave. That 106 B2
Park Ave. Woki 116 A3
Park Ave. Wray 68 B2
Park Cl. Wind 67 E3
Park Cres. Read 85 D3
Park Cres. Sunn 120 C2
Park Crnr. Wind 66 C2
Park Dr. Sunn 120 C2
Park End. Newb 105 D2
Park Gr. Read 85 D3
Park La. Bark 141 D3
Park La. Bee H 137 E1
Park La. Box 103 D1
Park La. Burn 21 F4
Park La. Camb 151 E3
Park La. Char 61 D2
Park La. Hort 69 D2
Park La. Newb 105 D2
Park La. Read 84 B4
Park La. Slough 43 D2
Park La. That 106 B2
Park Rd. Ashf 98 A2
Park Rd. Brac 118 B4
Park Rd. Camb 151 E2
Park Rd. Eng G 96 A2
Park Rd. Far C 22 B2
Park Rd. Hen-O-T 15 F1
Park Rd. Sand 150 B4
Park Rd. Shepp 125 D1
Park Rd. Stan 70 B1
Park Rd. Sto P 22 B2
Park Rd. Woki 116 A3
Park St. Bags 145 F2
Park St. Camb 151 E3
Park St. Hung 100 B3
Park St. Maid 39 F4
Park St. Newb 105 D2
Park St. Slough 42 C2
Park St. Stan 69 E3
Park St. Wind 67 E3
Park The. Lamb 25 D2
Park View Dr N. Char 61 D3
Park View Dr S. Char 61 D2
Park View. Bags 145 F2
Park Wall La. Upp B 34 B1
Park Way. Hung 100 C2
Park Way. Newb 105 D2
Park Wlk. Pur O T 57 E3
Parkcorner La. Arbo 114 C3
Parkgate. Burn 21 E1
Parkhill Cl. Black 150 B2
Parkhill Dr. Read 57 E1
Parkhill Rd. Black 150 B2
Parkhouse La. Read 85 E3
Parkland Ave. Slough 43 E1
Parkland Dr. Brac 118 C4
Parkland Gr. Ashf 98 A2
Parkland Rd. Ashf 98 A2
Parkside Rd. Read 85 E3
Parkside Rd. Sunn 121 D2
Parkside Rd. That 106 B3
Parkside. Hen-O-T 15 E1
Parkside. Maid 19 E1
Parkstone Dr. Camb 151 E2
Parkview Chase. Slough 41 F4
Parkview. Fla H 3 D4
Parkway Dr. Sonn 60 C2
Parkway. Camb 151 E2
Parkway. Crow 143 D3
Parkway. Mar 2 A2
Parlaunt Rd. Slough 44 A1
Parliament La. Burn 20 C3
Parnham Ave. Light 153 E4
Parry Green N. Slough 43 F1
Parry Green S. Slough 44 A1
Parsley Cl. Read 86 C1
Parson's Wood La. Far C 22 B3
Parsonage Gdns. Mar 1 C1
Parsonage La. Far C 22 B2
Parsonage La. Hung 100 B3
Parsonage La. Lamb 25 D1
Parsonage La. Wind 67 D3
Parsonage Pl. Lamb 25 D2
Parsonage Rd. Eng G 95 E2
Parsons Cl. Bark 141 D4

Parsons Cl. Newb 104 C1
Parsons Field. Sand 150 A4
Part La. Swal 139 F2
Parthia Cl. Read 86 A3
Partridge Ave. Yate 149 D3
Partridge Dr. Read 84 B3
Partridge Mead. Maid 19 F1
Paschal Rd. Camb 151 F4
Pasture Cl. Read 114 A4
Patches Field. Mar B 1 C3
Paterson Cl. Camb 152 B2
Paterson Rd. Ashf 97 E2
Pates Manor Dr. Felt 98 B4
Patricia Cl. Slough 41 F3
Patrick Rd. Caver 59 D3
Patriot Pl. Read 86 B4
Patten Ash Dr. Woki 116 C4
Patten Ave. Yate 149 E3
Pavenham Cl. Read 114 A4
Pavilion Gdns. Stai 97 D1
Pavy Cl. That 106 C1
Paxton Ave. Slough 42 B2
Payley Dr. Woki 116 C4
Paynesdown Rd. That 106 A2
Peace La. Cook 19 F3
Peach St. Woki 116 B3
Peachy Dr. That 106 C1
Peacock Ave. Felt 98 B4
Peacock La. Brac 117 E3
Peacock Rd. Mar 2 A2
Pear Tree La. Newb 105 E3
Pear Tree Rd. Ashf 98 B2
Pearce Cl. Maid 19 F1
Pearce Rd. Maid 19 F1
Pearces Orch. Hen-O-T 15 E2
Pearl Gdns. Slough 42 A3
Pearmain Cl. Shepp 125 D2
Pearman's Glade. Read 113 F4
Pearson Rd. Sonn 60 B2
Pearson Way. Wood 87 F3
Peascod Pl. Wind 67 E3
Peascod St. Wind 67 E3
Pease Hill. Buck 107 F4
Peasemore Hill. Pease 50 A4
Pebble Hill. Kint 128 A3
Peddlars Gr. Yate 149 F3
Peel Cl. Caver 59 E1
Peel Cl. Wind 67 D2
Peel Cl. Slough 42 A4
Peg's Green Cl. Read 85 D3
Pegasus Cl. That 106 A2
Pegasus Ct. Read 84 B4
Peggotty Pl. Crow 143 F1
Peket Cl. Stai 123 F4
Pelican La. Newb 105 D2
Pelican Rd. Ade 135 F1
Pell St. Read 86 A3
Pelling Hill. Old W 95 D4
Pemberton Gdns. Bur C 84 B2
Pemberton Rd. Slough 21 F1
Pembroke Broadway. Camb .. 151 E3
Pembroke Cl. Ascot 120 B2
Pembroke Cl. Bur C 111 E2
Pembroke Pl. Caver 59 E2
Pembroke Rd. Newb 105 D2
Pembroke. Brac 118 A1
Pembury Ct. Harl 71 E4
Pendals Cl. Hamp N 52 C3
Pendell Ave. Harl 71 F4
Pendennis Ave. Caver 59 F3
Pendine Pl. Brac 118 A2
Pendlebury. Brac 118 A1
Pendragon Way. Camb 152 B2
Pendred Rd. Read 113 E3
Peninsular Cl. Felt 71 F1
Penling Cl. Cook 19 F3
Penn Cl. Caver 59 D3
Penn Meadow. Sto P 22 C2
Penn Rd. Datch 68 B3
Penn Rd. Farc 22 B1
Penn Rd. Newb 104 B3
Pennfields. Twyf 61 F3
Pennine Cl. Read 84 A3
Pennine Way. Char 61 D2
Pennine Way. Harl 71 E4
Pennylets Green. Sto P 23 D3
Pennypiece. Gori 34 B4
Penroath Ave. Read 86 A3
Penroath Ave. Read 85 E3
Penrose Ave. Wood 87 F3
Penrose Cl. Newb 104 C2
Penrose Ct. Eng G 95 E1
Penry La. Shepp 125 F1
Pensford Cl. Crow 143 D4
Penshurst Rd. Maid 39 E3
Pentland Ave. Stai 125 D2
Pentland Cl. Read 84 C3
Pentland Pl. That 106 B1
Pentland Rd. Slough 42 A4
Pentlands The. Kint 102 B2
Penton Ave. Stai 123 F4
Penton Hall Dr. Stai 124 A4
Penton Hook Rd. Stai 124 A4
Penton Rd. Stai 96 C1
Penwood Cl. Maid 39 D4
Penwood Gdns. Brac 117 E2
Penwood La. Mar 1 B1
Penwood Rd. Ball H 130 B2

Penyston Rd. Maid 39 E4
Penzance Spur. Slough 22 A1
Peppard La. Hen-O-T 35 F4
Peppard Rd. Caver 59 E3
Pepper La. Read 86 B2
Pepys Cl. Slough 69 D4
Perch Cl. Mar 18 B4
Percival Rd. Felt 98 C3
Percy Ave. Ashf 98 A2
Percy Bryant Rd. Stai 98 C1
Percy Pl. Slough 68 A3
Peregrine Cl. Brac 118 A2
Peregrine Cl. Woki 115 F3
Peregrine Rd. Shepp 125 F4
Periam Cl. Hen-O-T 35 E4
Perkins Way. Woki 116 A3
Perrin Cl. Ashf 97 F2
Perry Oaks Dr. Harm 70 B3
Perry Oaks. Brac 118 C4
Perry Way. Brac 118 C4
Perry Way. Camb 152 C4
Perrycott. Wind 66 C2
Perryhill Dr. Sand 142 C1
Perryman Way. Slough 21 F1
Perserverance Hill. Hen-O-T .. 35 D3
Perth Ave. Slough 42 A4
Perth Cl. Wood 61 D1
Perth Trad Est. Slough 42 A4
Peterhouse Cl. Crow 143 F1
Petersfield Ave. Slough 43 D3
Petersfield Rd. Stai 97 E1
Petersfield Rd. Stai 97 E2
Petrel Cl. Woki 115 F3
Petts La. Stai 125 D3
Petworth Ave. Read 84 C2
Petworth Ct. Wind 67 D3
Pevensey Ave. Caver 59 F3
Pevensey Rd. Slough 42 A4
Pewsey Vale. Brac 118 C2
Pheasant Cl. Winn 88 B1
Pheasants Croft. Maid 39 D3
Philip Dr. Fla H 3 E4
Philip Rd. Stai 97 E1
Phillimore Rd. Caver 59 E4
Phipps Cl. Whi Wa 39 D1
Phipps Rd. Burn 41 F4
Phoebe Ct. Read 86 A3
Phoenix Cl. Woki 115 F3
Phoenix Wlk. Newb 130 B3
Phyllis Court Dr. Faw (Bu) 15 F2
Pickering. Brac 118 A3
Picket Post Cl. Brac 118 C3
Picketts La. Pangb 55 F2
Pickford Dr. Slough 43 F3
Pickins Piece. Hort 69 D3
Pickwell Cl. Wood 87 E1
Picton Way. Caver 59 D2
Pierce's Hill. Read 57 E1
Piercefield. Bur C 84 B2
Pierson Rd. Wind 66 B3
Pigeonhouse La. Wink 92 C2
Pigeons Farm Rd. Gree 131 E4
Piggott's Rd. Caver 59 E1
Pigott Rd. Woki 116 C4
Pike Cl. Mar 18 B4
Pike St. Newb 105 D2
Pikeshaw Way. Read 57 E1
Pimento Dr. Read 86 A3
Pincents La. Sulh 84 A3
Pinchurst. Bur C 111 D2
Pinchington La. Gree 131 D4
Pine Ave. Camb 151 E2
Pine Cl. Maid 39 D4
Pine Cl. Sand 150 C4
Pine Croft Rd. Woki 116 A1
Pine Dr. Black 150 C2
Pine Dr. Mort 136 C3
Pine Dr. Woki 142 A4
Pine Gr. Twyf 61 E3
Pine Gr. Windl 146 B2
Pine Mount Rd. Camb 151 E2
Pine Ridge Rd. Bur C 111 D2
Pine Ridge. Newb 105 E3
Pine Way. Eng G 95 D1
Pinecote Dr. Sunn 120 C1
Pinecroft. Mar 1 B2
Pinefields Cl. Crow 143 D2
Pinehill Rd. Crow 143 E2
Pinehill Rise. Sand 150 B4
Pinehurst. Ascot 120 B2
Pinetree Ct. Caver 59 D3
Pinewood Ave. Crow 143 E3
Pinewood Cl. Tad 134 B1
Pinewood Dr. Stai 97 D2
Pinewood Gdns. Bags 145 E2
Pinewood Rd. Vir W 122 A3
Pinewood Rd. Went 122 A3
Pingewood Rd S. Bur C 112 B4
Pingewood Rd S. Shin 112 B4
Pingewood Rd. Bur C 85 D1
Pinglestone Cl. Harm 70 C4
Pink La. Burn 21 D2
Pinkneys Dr. Maid 38 C4
Pinkneys Rd. Maid 39 D4
Pinks La. Tad 134 C1
Pipers Cl. Burn 21 E1
Pipers Ct. That 107 D1
Pipers End. Vir W 122 B3
Pipers Way. That 107 D1

Pipit Cl. That 106 A2
Pippins Ct. Ashf 98 A1
Pippins The. Slough 43 F3
Pipsons Cl. Yate 149 E3
Pitch Pl. Binf 90 B2
Pitcroft Ave. Read 87 D3
Pitfield La. Mort 137 E2
Pitfield La. Silc 137 E2
Pitford Rd. Wood 88 A4
Pitt's La. Read 87 D4
Pitts La. Binf 90 B1
Pitts Rd. Slough 42 B3
Plackett Way. Slough 41 E3
Plaitinson Rd. Read 113 E3
Planes The. Chert 124 B1
Plantation Cl. Herm 78 C3
Plantation Rd. Camb 151 D3
Plantation Rd. Chil 9 F4
Plantation Rd. Tad 134 C1
Plantation Row. Camb 151 D3
Platt La. Lamb 25 E3
Play Platt. That 83 F2
Players Green. Wood 87 F3
Playhatch Rd. Caver 60 A3
Plough La. Sto P 23 D2
Plough La. Woki 116 C3
Plough Rd. Yate 149 F4
Ploughlands. Brac 117 F4
Ploughlands. Brac 117 F4
Ploughlees La. Slough 42 C3
Plover Cl. Stai 96 C3
Plover Cl. Woki 115 F3
Plowden Way. Shipl 35 F1
Plumpton Rd. Newb 105 E1
Plumtrees. Read 87 D1
Pluto Rd. Chil 9 F4
Plymouth Ave. Wood 87 E3
Plymouth Rd. Slough 41 F4
Plympton Cl. Winn 87 F2
Pococks La. Eton 42 C1
Poffley Pl. That 107 D2
Pointers Cl. Chiev 51 D1
Points The. Maid 39 D2
Polehampton Cl. Twyf 61 E2
Pollard Cl. Old W 68 A1
Pollard Gr. Camb 152 B2
Pollardrow Ave. Brac 117 F4
Polsted Rd. Read 57 E1
Pond Cl. Newb 130 B4
Pond Croft. Yate 149 F3
Pond Head La. Read 87 E2
Pond La. Herm 79 E4
Pond La. Maple 57 F4
Pond Moor Rd. Brac 118 A2
Pond Rd. Stai 96 B1
Pondside Cl. Harl 71 E4
Pool La. Slough 42 C4
Pool La. W St L 63 D3
Poole Cl. Read 85 D4
Pooley Ave. Stai 96 A2
Pooley Green Cl. Stai 96 B2
Pooley Green Rd. Stai 96 B2
Poolmans Rd. Wind 66 B2
Pope Cl. Felt 98 C3
Popes Cl. Iver 69 E4
Popes La. Cook 19 E4
Popeswood Rd. Binf 117 E4
Popham Cl. Brac 118 C2
Poplar Ave. Read 84 C3
Poplar Ave. Windl 146 A3
Poplar Cl. Stan 69 F3
Poplar Gdns. Read 86 C1
Poplar La. Hurst 62 A1
Poplar La. Winn 88 B2
Poplar Rd. Ashf 98 B2
Poplars Gr. Maid 20 A1
Poplars The. Ascot 120 A2
Poppy Dr. That 106 C2
Poppy Way. Read 84 B3
Poppyhills Rd. Camb 151 F4
Porchester Rd. Newb 105 D1
Porchester. Ascot 120 A3
Porchfield Cl. Read 113 F3
Porlock Cl. That 106 B1
Porlock Pl. Bur C 84 B2
Porter Cl. Winn 114 B4
Porter End. Newb 131 D4
Portesbery Hill Dr. Camb 151 F3
Portesbury Rd. Camb 151 F3
Portland Cl. Slough 21 E1
Portland Cres. Felt 98 B2
Portland Gdns. Read 84 B4
Portland Rd. Ashf 97 F3
Portlands. Mar 1 B1
Portlock Rd. Maid 39 E4
Portman Cl. Brac 118 A4
Portman Rd. Read 58 B1
Portnall Dr. Went 121 F2
Portnall Rd. Went 121 F2
Portnall Rise. Went 121 F2
Portrush Rd. Wood 87 E3
Portsmouth Rd. Camb 152 A4
Portway Cl. Read 85 F3
Portway. Swal 139 F2
Portway. Tad 134 C1
Post Horn Pl. Read 84 C2
Post Office La. Slough 43 E4
Post Office Rd. Ink 127 F3
Posting House Mews. Newb . 104 C2

Potley Hill Rd. Yate 149 F3
Pottery La. Ink 127 F3
Pottery Rd. Read 57 F1
Potts Pl. Mar 1 B1
Poulcott. Wray 68 C1
Pound Cres. Mar 1 B1
Pound La. Hurst 89 D3
Pound La. Lit M 2 B2
Pound La. Mar 1 B1
Pound La. Newb 104 B2
Pound La. Sonn 60 C1
Pound La. That 106 A2
Pound Piece. Hung 100 B3
Pound Rd. Chert 124 A1
Pound St. Newb 104 C1
Pound The. Cook 19 F4
Poundfield La. Cook 19 F4
Powis Cl. Maid 39 D2
Powney Rd. Maid 39 E4
Poyle La. Burn 21 D2
Poyle Rd. Stan 69 F3
Poynings. Iver 44 C1
Precincts The. Burn 21 E1
Prescott Rd. Stan 69 F3
Prescott. Brac 117 F1
Preston Rd. Read 86 A3
Preston Rd. Slough 43 E3
Preston Rd. Stai 125 D2
Prestwood. Slough 43 D4
Pretoria Rd. Chert 123 F1
Priest Ave. Woki 116 C3
Priest Hill. Caver 59 D2
Priest Hill. Eng G 95 E3
Priest La. West E 153 E4
Priestwood Ave. Brac 117 F4
Priestwood Court Rd. Brac .. 118 A4
Primrose Cl. Pur O T 57 E3
Primrose La. Winn 88 B2
Primrose Lea. Mar 1 B1
Primrose Way. Sand 143 D1
Prince Albert Dr. Brac 118 B2
Prince Andrew Cl. Maid 20 A1
Prince Andrew Rd. Maid 20 A1
Prince Andrew Way. Burl 119 E4
Prince Consort Gdns. Wind 67 E3
Prince Consort Dr. Brac 119 E3
Prince Dr. Sand 143 D1
Prince Hold Rd. That 106 A2
Prince of Wales Ave. Read 85 E4
Prince William Dr. Read 57 E1
Prince's La. Pease 50 B3
Prince's St. Read 86 B4
Princes Cl. Eton 41 F1
Princes Ct. Old W 68 A1
Princes Rd. Asnf 97 F2
Princes Rd. Eng G 95 F1
Princes Rd. Felt 98 C3
Princes St. Slough 43 D2
Princes Way. Bags 145 F1
Princes Ave. Wind 67 D2
Princess Marina Dr. Bark 115 D1
Princess Marina Dr. Bark 140 C4
Princess St. Maid 39 F3
Princess Way. Camb 151 E3
Prior Croft Cl. Camb 152 A2
Prior End. Camb 152 A3
Prior Rd. Camb 152 A3
Priors La. Black 150 A3
Priors Cl. Maid 40 A1
Priors Cl. Slough 43 D2
Priors Rd. Tad 135 D1
Priors Rd. Wind 66 B2
Priors Way. Maid 40 A1
Priors Wood. Woki 142 B3
Priory Ave. Caver 59 D1
Priory Ave. Hung 100 B3
Priory Cl. Hung 100 B3
Priory Cl. Went 121 D1
Priory Cl. Winn 88 B2
Priory Green. Stai 97 D2
Priory La. New G 91 E1
Priory Mews. Stai 97 D2
Priory Rd. Burl 119 D4
Priory Rd. Hung 100 B2
Priory Rd. Newb 105 D1
Priory Rd. Slough 41 E4
Priory The. Winn 88 B2
Priory Way. Datch 68 A4
Priory Way. Harm 70 C4
Priory Wlk. Brac 118 C3
Proctors Rd. Woki 116 C3
Promenade Rd. Caver 59 D1
Prospect Ave. Read 84 C4
Prospect Ct. Read 85 D3
Prospect La. Eng G 95 D2
Prospect Pl. Hurl 17 F2
Prospect Pl. Newb 105 D1
Prospect Pl. Stai 96 C2
Prospect Rd. Hung 100 B3
Prospect Rd. Maid 40 A1
Prospect St. Caver 59 D1
Prospect St. Read 85 F4
Providence La. Harl 71 E4
Providence Pl. Maid 39 F4
Prune Hill. Eng G 95 E1

Prunus Cl. Camb 15
Pudding Hill. Know H 3
Pudding La. Brig ....
Puffers Way. Newb 10
Pump La N. Lit M ....
Pump La. Shin 11
Pump La. Wink 12
Pumpkin Hill. Burn ....
Pundles La. Whi Wa ....
Purbrook Ct. Brac ....
Purcell Rd. Crow 14
Purfield Dr. Warg ....
Purley La. Pur O T ....
Purley Rise. Pur O T ....
Purley Village. Pur O T ....
Purley Way. Pangb ....
Pursell Cl. Maid ....
Purton Ct. Farc ....
Purton La. Farc ....
Putman Pl. Hen-O-T ....
Pyegrove Chase. Brac 11
Pyke Hill. Asham ....
Pyke Hill. Newb 10
Pyrcroft Rd. Chert 12

Quadrant Ct. Brac 11
Quadrant The. Maid ....
Qualitas. Brac ....
Quantock Ave. Caver ....
Quantock Cl. Char ....
Quantock Cl. Harl ....
Quantock Cl. Slough ....
Quantocks The. That 10
Quarrington Cl. That 10
Quarry Bank. Light ....
Quartz La. Yate 14
Quarrydale Dr. Mar ....
Quartz Cl. Woki ....
Quaves Rd. Slough ....
Quebec Gdns. Black 15
Quebec Rd. Hen-O-T 3
Queen Anne's Cl. Old W ....
Queen Anne's Rd. Wind ....
Queen Annes Gate. Caver ......
Queen Charlotte St. Wind 6
Queen Cl. Hen-O-T ....
Queen Elizabeth Rd. Camb .. 14
Queen Mary Ave. Camb 15
Queen Mary Rd. Stai 12
Queen St. Caver ....
Queen St. Chert 12
Queen St. Hen-O-T ....
Queen St. Maid ....
Queen Victoria St. Read ....
Queen's Cl. Old W ....
Queen's Cotts. Read 8
Queen's Cl. Slough 4
Queen's Dr The. Read 8
Queen's La. Maid 3
Queen's Mead. Datch 6
Queen's Pl. Ascot 12
Queen's Rd. Ascot 15
Queen's Rd. Bis 15
Queen's Rd. Caver 5
Queen's Rd. Datch 6
Queen's Rd. Eng G 9
Queen's Rd. Mar ....
Queen's Rd. Newb 10
Queen's Rd. Read 8
Queen's Rd. Slough ....
Queen's Rd. Wind ....
Queens Acre. Wind 6
Queens Cl. Burl 11
Queens Gate. Wind ....
Queens Hill Rise. Ascot 12
Queens Park Gdns. Felt ....
Queens Park Gdns. Felt ....
Queens Pine. Brac 11
Queens Rd. Eton 4
Queens Way. Kint 10
Queens Wlk. Ashf 9
Queensborough Dr. Caver 5
Queensbury Pl. Black 15
Queenshill Lodge. Ascot 12
Queensmere Rd. Slough 4
Queensway. Caver ....
Queensway. Maid ....
Quentin Rd. Wood ....
Quentin Rd. Wood ....
Quinbrookes. Slough 4
Quince Cl. Ascot 12
Quincy Rd. Eng G 9
Quintills. Brac ....
Quoiting Sq. Mar ....
Quoitings Dr. Mar ....

Rackstraw Rd. Crow 14
Radbourne Rd. Bur C 8
Radcliffe Way. Brac 11
Radcot Ave. Slough 4
Radcot Cl. Maid ....
Radcot Cl. Winn 8
Radical Ride. Woki 14
Radley Bottom. Woki 10
Radnor Cl. Hen-O-T ....
Radnor Rd. Brac 11
Radnor Rd. Read 8

173

dnor Way. Slough Rutherford Wlk. Read

Way. Slough 43 F1
ock La. Read 87 D1
ock Rd. Read 86 C4
rn Way. Sand 150 B3
rn Way. Sand 150 B4
le. Bur C 111 D2
swood Cl. Read 87 E2
. Alde 135 E3
Gdns. Caver 59 E2
Mews. Caver 59 E3
ans Cl. Mar B 1 B4
ne Rd. Slough 42 C2
e. Wool 108 C1
Cl. Read 113 E4
y App. Chert 123 F1
y Rd. Newb 105 D1
y Terr. Slough 42 C3
y Terr. Stai 96 B2
ys Cotts. Gori 34 B3
orough Chase. Maid 39 D2
orth Cl. Read 114 A4
n Cl. Slough 42 A3
n Cl. Wood 87 F3
n Ct. Stai 97 D2
h Rd. Felt 98 C3
Ride. Brac 118 C3
er Cl. Burn 41 D4
er La. Slough 43 E2
ury Cl. Brac 117 F2
ons La. Silc 136 A3
ay Rd. Windl 146 C3
bury Dr. Read 87 D2
ey Cl. Winn 87 F1
s La. Woki 116 C3
ll Cl. Slough 43 F1
ll Mead. Binf 90 A1
il Cl. Black 150 C1
lph Rd. Read 59 D1
lph Rd. Slough 43 F2
igh Cres. Burl 119 E4
igh Dr. Brac 118 B3
Rd. Brac 142 A4
Ride. Sand 150 C4
View. Sand 150 C4
Way. Shepp 125 D1
wood Ave. Read 84 C2
Cl. Camb 151 F4
Green. Brac 118 B2
Cl. Read 87 E1
Cl. Yate 149 D3
dale Mews. Stai 97 D1
dale Rd. Shepp 125 F4
glass Cl. Read 87 E2
s Field. Slough 43 E2
sbourne Ave. Stan 97 F4
sbourne Dr. Wood 87 F4
scourt. Shepp 125 F4
scroft Rd. Hen-O-T 15 E1
sdale Rd. Ascot 120 A2
sfield. Eng G 95 E1
shoe Cl. Bou E 3 D2
stone Rd. Camb 152 B3
swood Ave. Crow 142 C3
swood Ave. Finch 142 C3
swood Dr. Camb 152 A3
sworth Rd. Silc 136 C3
sworth Rd. Slough 22 A1
son Rd. Camb 151 D3
r. Maid 40 A4
ea Cl. Maid 40 A4
ea Rd. Maid 40 A4
odge Mews. Maid 40 A4
ead Ct. Maid 20 B1
ead Rd. Maid 40 A4
ill Rd E. Maid 20 A1
ill Rd W. Maid 40 A4
ark Ave. Maid 40 A4
ark La. Maid 40 A4
ark Rd. Maid 40 A4
. Maid 40 A4
ond Cl. Stan 69 F3
ond Rd. Maid 39 E4
ond Rd. Slough 44 A2
rs Cl. Iver 69 E4
Ave. Wind 66 C4
ood Cl. Harl 71 E4
ng Bridge. Read 86 A4
ng Rd. Aldw 33 D1
ng Rd. Arbo 114 B2
ng Rd. Bark 140 C2
ng Rd. Black 150 A2
ng Rd. Bur C 111 E2
ng Rd. Chol 14 A4
ng Rd. Finch 140 C2
ng Rd. Gori 34 C3
ng Rd. Hen-O-T 15 F1
ng Rd. Moul 14 A4
ng Rd. Pangb 56 B3
ng Rd. Stre 34 A3
ng Rd. Woki 115 F4
ng Rd. Wood 87 E4
ation La. Shin 113 D1
ation Rd. Bou E 3 D2
ation Rd. Bur C 111 D1
ation Rd. Read 84 C4
ation Rd. Warg 36 C1
y Cl. Brac 118 B3
y Cl. Far C 22 A1
y Cl. Newb 104 C1
Rectory Cl. Sand 149 F4
Rectory Cl. Stai 125 D3
Rectory Cl. Wind 67 D3
Rectory Cl. Woki 116 B3
Rectory La. Blew 12 C4
Rectory La. Brac 118 A3
Rectory La. Windl 146 B2
Rectory Rd. Caver 59 D1
Rectory Rd. Padw 135 F4
Rectory Rd. Stre 33 E4
Rectory Rd. Tapl 20 C1
Rectory Rd. Woki 116 B3
Red Cottage Mews. Slough 43 E2
Red Cross Rd. Gori 34 B3
Red Ct. Slough 42 C3
Red Hill. Shipl 35 D3
Red House Cl. Read 114 A4
Red La. Alde 135 E3
Red Leaf Cl. Slough 43 F3
Red Lion Way. Woo G 3 F3
Red Rd. West E 152 C4
Red Rose. Binf 90 B2
Red Shute Hill. Herm 79 D2
Redberry Cl. Caver 59 E3
Redcrest Gdns. Camb 151 F3
Reddington Dr. Slough 43 F1
Redditch. Brac 118 B1
Redfield Ct. Newb 105 E2
Redford Rd. Wind 66 B3
Redhatch Dr. Read 87 D1
Redlands Rd. Read 86 B3
Redlane Hill. Alde 135 E3
Redleaves Ave. Ashf 98 A1
Redmayne. Camb 152 B2
Redriff Cl. Maid 39 E3
Redruth Gdns. Read 86 A1
Redshots Cl. Mar 1 C2
Redvers Rd. Brac 118 A2
Redwood Ave. Wood 88 A3
Redwood Dr. Camb 152 B2
Redwood Dr. Windl 121 D2
Redwood Gdns. Slough 42 B3
Redwood Way. Read 57 E2
Redwood. Burn 21 D2
Redwood. Stai 123 F4
Reed Cl. Iver 44 C4
Reed Wlk. Newb 105 E2
Reed's Hill. Brac 118 A2
Reeds Ave. Read 86 C2
Reedsfield Rd. Ashf 98 A2
Reeve Rd. Holy 65 D4
Reeves Way. Woki 116 A2
Reform Rd. Maid 40 A4
Regency Hts. Caver 58 C2
Regent Cl. Hung 100 B3
Regent Cl. Read 87 E1
Regent Ct. Bags 145 F1
Regent Ct. Maid 39 F4
Regent Ct. Read 86 A4
Regent Ct. Wind 67 E3
Regent St. Read 86 C4
Regent Way. Camb 152 A1
Regents Pl. Sand 150 B4
Regents Wlk. Ascot 120 B1
Regis Cl. Read 113 E4
Regnum Dr. Newb 105 D3
Reid Ave. Maid 39 F3
Rembrandt Way. Read 85 F3
Rembrant Cl. Woki 115 E3
Remembrance Rd. Newb 104 C1
Remenham Church La. Rem H 16 A2
Remenham La. RemH 15 F2
Renault Rd. Wood 88 A3
Renfree Way. Shepp 125 D1
Rennie Cl. Ashf 97 E3
Repton Cl. Maid 39 E2
Repton Rd. Read 87 E2
Restwold Cl. Read 85 E2
Retford Cl. Wood 60 C1
Retreat The. Eng G 95 F2
Retreat The. Holy 65 E4
Revel Rd. Woo G 3 E4
Revesby Cl. Maid 39 E2
Revesby Cl. West E 153 E3
Rex Ave. Ashf 98 A2
Reynards Cl. Winn 88 B1
Reynolds Green. Sand 150 B3
Rhodes Cl. Eng G 96 A2
Rhodes Cl. Winn 87 F2
Rhododendron Cl. Burl 92 C1
Rhododendron Rd. Camb 152 A1
Rhododendron Wlk. Burl 92 C1
Ribbleton Cl. Winn 87 F2
Ribstone Rd. Maid 39 D2
Ricard Rd. Old W 68 A1
Richards Cl. Harl 71 E4
Richborough Cl. Read 87 D1
Richfield Ave. Read 58 C1
Richings Way. Iver 44 C2
Richmond Ave. Felt 71 F1
Richmond Ave. Felt 98 C4
Richmond Cl. Camb 151 F1
Richmond Cres. Slough 43 D3
Richmond Cres. Stai 96 C2
Richmond Dr. Shepp 125 E2
Richmond Rd. Caver 58 C2
Richmond Rd. Read 85 E4
Richmond Rd. Sand 150 C4
Richmond Rd. Stai 96 C2
Richmond Rise. Woki 115 F4
Richmondwood. Went 121 D1
Rickman Cl. Arbo 114 C1
Rickman Cl. Brac 118 B2
Rickman Cl. Wood 87 E3
Rickman's La. Sto P 22 C3
Riddings La. Head 133 E1
Rider's La. Bur C 112 A2
Rideway Cl. Camb 151 D2
Ridge Hall Cl. Caver 58 C2
Ridge Mount Rd. Windl 121 D1
Ridge The. Cold A 106 B4
Ridge The. Upp B 55 F4
Ridge Way. Iver 44 C3
Ridge Way. Warg 36 C1
Ridgebank. Slough 41 F3
Ridgemead Rd. Eng G 95 D3
Ridgemount Cl. Sulh 57 D1
Ridgeway Cl. Light 153 D4
Ridgeway Cl. Mar 1 C2
Ridgeway The. Brac 118 B3
Ridgeway The. Caver 59 D2
Ridgeway The. Light 146 A1
Ridgeway The. Mar 1 C2
Ridgeway The. Wood 87 F3
Ridgeway. Iver 44 C3
Ridgeway. Shepp 125 F1
Riding Court Rd. Datch 68 C4
Riding Way. Woki 115 F3
Ridings The. Camb 152 A2
Ridings The. Caver 59 E4
Ridings The. Iver 44 C1
Ridings The. Maid 39 D3
Ridlington Cl. Winn 87 F1
Riley Rd. Mar 1 B1
Riley Rd. Read 84 C4
Ring The. Brac 118 B4
Ringmead. Brac 117 F2
Ringwood Cl. Ascot 120 A3
Ringwood Rd. Black 150 B3
Ringwood Rd. Read 58 A1
Ringwood. Brac 117 F1
Ripley Ave. Eng G 95 F1
Ripley Cl. Slough 43 F1
Ripley Rd. Read 58 A1
Ripon Cl. Camb 152 B2
Ripplesmere. Brac 118 B3
Ripplesmore Cl. Sand 150 A4
Ripston Rd. Ashf 98 B2
Risborough Rd. Maid 39 F4
Rise Rd. Sunn 120 C2
Rise The. Caver 59 D2
Rise The. Cold A 106 B4
Rise The. Crow 142 C3
Rise The. Crow 143 D3
Rise The. Finch 141 D1
Rise The. Woki 116 A4
Riseley Rd. Maid 39 E4
Rissington Cl. Read 57 F2
River Gdns. Maid 40 B2
River Gdns. Pur O T 57 E3
River Mount. Shepp 125 F1
River Park Ave. Stai 96 B2
River Park. Newb 105 D2
River Rd. Caver 58 B2
River Rd. Read 86 A3
River Rd. Stai 123 F4
River Rd. Tapl 40 B4
River Rd. Yate 149 D4
River St. Wind 67 E4
River View. Fla H 3 D4
River Wlk. Newb 105 E2
Riverbank. Stai 96 C1
Riverdene Dr. Winn 88 A2
Riverfield Rd. Stai 96 C1
Rivermead Ct. Bish 18 C4
Rivermead Rd. Camb 151 D1
Rivermead Rd. Wood 87 F3
Riverpark Dr. Mar 1 C1
Riversdale Ct. Read 86 C4
Riversdell Cl. Chert 123 F1
Riverside Ave. Light 153 E4
Riverside Cl. Stai 123 F4
Riverside Dr. Stai 96 C2
Riverside Dr. Stai 123 F4
Riverside Pl. Stan 70 C1
Riverside Rd. Stai 96 C1
Riverside Rd. Stan 70 B1
Riverside Rd. Stan 70 C1
Riverside. Bou E 3 E2
Riverside. Eng G 96 A3
Riverside. Shepp 125 F1
Riverside. Wray 95 E4
Riverview Rd. Pangb 56 B3
Riverway. Gr She 48 A2
Riverway. Stai 124 A4
Riverwoods Ave. Mar 2 A1
Riverwoods Dr. Mar 2 A1
Rixman Cl. Maid 39 E3
Rixon Cl. Slough 43 F4
Road Hill. Box 76 B2
Roasthill La. Dorn 41 E1
Roberts Cl. Stan 70 B1
Roberts Rd. Camb 151 D3
Roberts Rd. Sand 151 D3
Roberts Way. Eng G 95 E1
Robertsfield. That 105 F2
Robertson Cl. Newb 131 D4
Robin Cl. Bur C 111 D2
Robin Cl. Bur C 111 D2
Robin Hill Dr. Camb 152 A2
Robin Hood Cl. Slough 41 F3
Robin Hood Way. Winn 88 B2
Robin La. Sand 143 E1
Robin Way. Read 84 A3
Robin Way. Stai 96 C3
Robin's Bow. Camb 151 D2
Robindale Ave. Read 87 E2
Robinhood La. Winn 88 B2
Robins Cl. Newb 130 C4
Robins Grove Cres. Yate 149 D3
Robins Hill. Ink 127 F3
Robinson Ct. Read 87 D1
Rochester Ave. Felt 98 C3
Rochester Ave. Wood 60 C1
Rochford Way. Burn 41 D4
Rochfords Gdns. Slough 43 E3
Rockbourne Gdns. Read 58 A1
Rockfield Way. Sand 150 B4
Rockfield. Lamb 25 D1
Rockingham Rd. Newb 104 C1
Rockmoor La. Link 147 D1
Rodney Way. Stan 69 F3
Rodway Rd. Read 57 F1
Roebuck Estate. Binf 90 B1
Roebuck Green. Slough 41 F3
Roebuts Cl. Newb 130 C4
Rogers La. Sto P 22 C2
Rogers's La. East G 47 E3
Rogosa Rd. Camb 153 F3
Rokeby Cl. Brac 118 B4
Rokeby Cl. Newb 131 D4
Rokeby Dr. Maple 58 B4
Rokes Pl. Yate 149 D3
Rokesby Rd. Slough 21 F1
Rolls La. Holy 64 C4
Roman Fields. Silc 136 A1
Roman Lea. Cook 19 F4
Roman Ride. Finch 142 B3
Roman Way. Bou E 3 D2
Roman Way. Read 87 E2
Roman Way. That 106 A3
Romans Gate. Silc 135 F1
Romany Cl. Read 58 A1
Romany La. Read 58 A1
Romney Cl. Ashf 98 B2
Romney Ct. Mar 1 C2
Romsey Cl. Black 150 B3
Romsey Cl. Slough 43 F2
Romsey Rd. Read 58 A1
Rona Ct. Read 85 D4
Ronaldsay Spur. Slough 42 C4
Rood Hill. Wick 76 B2
Rook Cl. Woki 115 F3
Rook Rd. Bou E 3 E2
Rookery Ct. Mar 1 B1
Rookery Rd. Stai 97 D2
Rooksfield. Newt 132 A1
Rooksmead Rd. Shepp 125 F4
Rooksnest La. Kint 128 A3
Rookswood. Brac 91 D1
Rookwood Ave. Sand 143 F1
Rope Wlk. That 106 B2
Rosa Ave. Ashf 98 A2
Rosary Gdns. Ashf 98 A2
Rosary Gdns. Yate 149 E3
Rose Cl. Wood 88 A4
Rose Gdns. Stan 97 E4
Rose Hill. Binf 90 B2
Rose Hill. Burn 21 D3
Rose Kiln La. Bur C 86 A2
Rose Kiln La. Read 86 A2
Rose La. Know H 37 D4
Rose St. Woki 116 B3
Rose Wlk. Read 86 A4
Rose Wlk. Slough 42 A4
Roseacre Cl. Stai 125 D2
Rosebank Cl. Cook 19 F4
Rosebay. Woki 116 C4
Rosebery Rd. Maple 58 B4
Rosecroft Way. Shin 113 F3
Rosedale Cres. Read 87 D4
Rosedale Gdns. Brac 118 A2
Rosedale Gdns. That 106 B1
Rosedale. Binf 90 B2
Rosedene La. Sand 150 B3
Rosefield Rd. Stai 97 D2
Rosehill Park. Caver 59 E4
Roseleigh Cl. Maid 39 D4
Rosemary Ave. Read 86 C1
Rosemary Gdns. Black 150 B3
Rosemary La. Sand 150 B3
Rosemary La. Stai 123 D3
Rosemead Ave. Felt 38 C3
Rosemead Ave. Sulh 57 D2
Rosery The. Bou E 3 D2
Roses La. Wind 66 B3
Rosewood Dr. Stai 124 C2
Rosewood Way. Camb 153 F3
Rosewood Way. Far C 22 B4
Rosewood. Wood 87 E2
Rosier Cl. That 106 C1
Rosken Gr. Far C 22 A2
Roslyn Rd. Wood 87 E3
Ross Rd. Maid 39 F2
Ross Rd. Read 58 C1
Ross Rd. Read 59 D1
Rossendale Rd. Caver 59 E2
Rossett Cl. Brac 118 A3
Rossey Pl. Eton 42 B1
Rossington Pl. Read 113 E4
Rossiter Cl. Slough 43 F1
Rosslyn Cl. Ashf 98 C1
Rother Cl. Sand 150 B4
Rotherfield Ave. Woki 116 A4
Rotherfield Cl. Thea 83 F2
Rotherfield Rd. Hen-O-T 35 F4
Rotherfield Way. Caver 59 D2
Rothwell Gdns. Wood 61 D1
Rothwell Wlk. Caver 59 E1
Rotton Row Hill. Brad 81 F2
Roughgrove Copse. Binf 90 A1
Rounce La. West E 153 E3
Round Cl. Yate 149 F3
Round End. Newb 130 B3
Roundabout La. Woki 115 E4
Roundfield. Buck 107 D3
Roundhead Rd. Thea 83 E2
Roundway Cl. Camb 152 B3
Roundway. Camb 152 B3
Roundway. Stai 96 B2
Routh Ct. Felt 98 B4
Routh La. Read 84 C3
Row La. Caver 59 F4
Rowallan Cl. Caver 59 E3
Rowan Ave. Stai 96 B2
Rowan Cl. Camb 151 F4
Rowan Cl. Woki 115 F3
Rowan Dr. Brac 143 E4
Rowan Dr. Crow 143 E3
Rowan Dr. Newb 105 D3
Rowan Dr. Wood 87 F4
Rowan Way. Bur C 111 D3
Rowan Way. Slough 42 A4
Rowanhurst Dr. Far C 22 B4
Rowans Cl. Black 150 C1
Rowans The. Ashf 98 C2
Rowcroft Rd. Arbo 140 C4
Rowe Ct. Read 85 D4
Rowland Cl. Wind 66 B2
Rowland Way. Read 86 C1
Rowland Way. Stai 98 B1
Rowley Cl. Brac 118 C3
Rowley La. Sto P 23 E2
Rowley Rd. Read 86 A2
Roxburgh Cl. Camb 152 B2
Roxford Cl. Shepp 125 F2
Roxwell Cl. Slough 41 F3
Roy Cl. Herm 78 C3
Royal Ave. Read 84 B3
Royal Victoria Gdns. Ascot 120 A2
Roycroft La. Woki 141 F4
Royston Cl. Read 84 C4
Royston Way. Slough 41 E4
Rubus Cl. Camb 153 F3
Ruby Cl. Slough 42 A2
Ruby Cl. Woki 115 F4
Rudd Hall Rise. Camb 151 F2
Ruddlesway. Wind 66 B3
Rudland Cl. That 106 B1
Rudsworth Cl. Iver 69 E4
Rugby Cl. Sand 143 F1
Ruggles-Brise Rd. Ashf 97 E2
Rumsey's La. Blew 12 A4
Runnemede Rd. Eng G 96 A2
Runnymede Ct. Eng G 96 A2
Rupert Cl. Hen-O-T 15 F2
Rupert Rd. Newb 130 C4
Rupert St. Read 86 B4
Rupert's La. Hen-O-T 15 F2
Ruscombe Gdns. Datch 68 A4
Ruscombe La. Twyf 61 F3
Ruscombe Park. Twyf 61 F3
Ruscombe Rd. Twyf 61 F3
Ruscombe Way. Felt 98 C4
Rushall Cl. Read 113 F4
Rusham Park Ave. Eng G 95 F1
Rusham Rd. Eng G 95 F1
Rushbrook Rd. Wood 87 E4
Rushburn. Woo G 3 F3
Rushden Dr. Read 86 C1
Rushes The. Maid 40 A3
Rushes The. Mar 18 B4
Rushey Way. Read 87 E1
Rushington Ave. Maid 39 F3
Rushmoor Gdns. Bur C 84 A2
Ruskin Ave. Felt 71 F1
Ruskin Rd. Stai 96 C1
Ruskin Way. Woki 115 E3
Russell Ct. Maid 39 F4
Russell Dr. Stan 70 B1
Russell Rd. Maple 58 B4
Russell Rd. Newb 104 C1
Russell Rd. Shepp 125 E1
Russell St. Read 85 F4
Russell St. Wind 67 E3
Russell Way. Winn 88 A1
Russet Cl. Stan 69 F1
Russet Gdns. Camb 151 E2
Russet Glade. Bur C 111 D1
Russet Glade. Caver 59 E4
Russet Rd. Maid 39 E2
Russington Rd. Shepp 125 E2
Russley Green. Woki 116 A1
Rustington Cl. Read 87 D1
Ruston Way. Ascot 119 F4
Rutherford Wlk. Read 84 A4

Rutherwyk Rd. Chert 123 F1
Rutland Pl. Maid 39 E3
Rutland Cl. Maid 39 E3
Rutland Rd. Read 85 E4
Ruxbury Rd. Chert 123 E2
Ryan Mount. Sand 150 A4
Ryans Mount. Mar 1 B1
Rycroft. Wind 66 C2
'lydal Ave. Read 57 F1
Rydal Cl. Camb 152 B3
Rydal Dr. That 106 A3
Rydal Pl. Light 153 D4
Rydal Way. Stai 96 A1
Ryde The. Stai 124 A4
Rydings. Wind 66 C2
Rye Cl. Brac 118 B4
Rye Cl. Maid 39 D2
Rye Cl. New G 91 F1
Rye Ct. Slough 43 D2
Rye Gr. Light 146 C1
Ryecroft Cl. Warg 36 C1
Ryecroft Cl. Wood 60 C1
Ryecroft Gdns. Black 150 C2
Ryehurst La. Binf 90 C3
Ryeish La. Shin 114 C3
Ryemead La. Wink 92 B3
Rytil Way. Read 113 F4
Ryland Cl. Felt 98 C2
Rylstone Cl. Maid 39 E2
Rylstone Rd. Read 85 E4
Ryvers Rd. Slough 43 F2
Ryves Ave. Yate 149 D3

Sackville St. Read 86 A4
Saddleback Rd. Camb 151 F4
Saddlewood. Camb 151 E2
Sadler's La. Woki 115 E4
Sadlers Ct. Woki 88 B1
Sadlers Rd. Ink 127 D3
Saffron Cl. Datch 68 A3
Saffron Cl. Newb 104 C2
Saffron Cl. Read 87 E2
Saffron Rd. Brac 118 A3
Sage Cl. Read 87 D1
Sage Rd. Sulh 57 E2
Sagecroft Rd. That 106 B3
St Adrian's Cl. Maid 39 D2
St Agnes Terr. Lamb 25 D1
St Albans St. Wind 67 E3
St Andrew's Ave. Wind 66 C3
St Andrew's Cl. Old W 68 A1
St Andrew's Cl. Shepp 125 E3
St Andrew's Cl. Wray 68 C1
St Andrew's Cres. Wind 66 C3
St Andrew's Rd. Caver 58 C2
St Andrew's Rd. Hen-O-T 35 E4
St Andrew's Way. Slough 41 E3
St Andrews Cl. Woki 142 C3
St Andrews. Brac 117 F2
St Ann's Cl. Chert 123 F2
St Ann's Hill Rd. Chert 123 E2
St Ann's Rd. Chert 123 F2
St Anne's Cl. Hen-O-T 15 E1
St Anne's Rd. Caver 59 D1
St Annes Ave. Stai 97 E4
St Annes Glade. Bags 145 E2
St Anthony's Way. Harm 71 F2
St Anthonys Cl. Brac 118 A4
St Barnabas Rd. Caver 59 D3
St Barnabas Rd. Read 86 C1
St Bartholomews Rd. Read 86 C4
St Bernards Rd. Slough 43 E2
St Birinus Rd. Read 84 B3
St Catherine's Cl. Woki 88 A1
St Catherines Rd. Camb 151 F1
St Chad's Rd. Maid 39 D2
St Christophers Gdns. Burl 119 E4
St Clements Cl. Wood 87 E1
St Columba's Cl. Maid 39 D2
St David's Cl. Caver 58 C3
St David's Cl. Maid 39 D2
St David's Rd. Newb 104 C1
St Donats Pl. Newb 105 D1
St Dunstan's Rd. Felt 98 C3
St Edward's Rd. Read 87 D3
St Elizabeth Cl. Read 113 D4
St Elmo Cres. Far C 22 B1
St George's Ave. Newb 104 C1
St George's Cl. Wind 66 C3
St George's Cres. Slough 41 E3
St George's La. Ascot 120 A3
St George's La. Ascot 120 A3
St George's Rd. Read 85 E4
St George's Terr. Read 35 E3
St Georges Rd. Camb 151 E3
St Giles Cl. Read 86 A3
St Helens Cres. Sand 150 A4
St Helier Cl. Wind 116 A2
St Hilda's Ave. Ashf 97 F2
St Ives Cl. Thea 83 E1
St Ives Rd. Maid 40 A4
St James Cl. Pangb 56 B3
St James Cl. Twyf 61 F3
St James Rd. Woki 141 F4
St James Wlk. Iver 44 C2
St John's Hill. Read 86 B4
St John's Rd. Ascot 92 C1
St John's Rd. Caver 59 E1
St John's Rd. Mort 137 D3

St John's Rd. Newb 105 D1
St John's Rd. Read 86 B4
St John's Rd. Sand 150 B4
St John's Rd. That 106 B2
St John's St. Read 86 B4
St John's Cl. Eng G 96 A2
St Johns Dr. Wind 67 D3
St Johns Rd. Slough 43 D3
St Johns Rd. Wind 67 D3
St Jude's Cl. Eng G 95 E2
St Jude's Rd. Eng G 95 E2
St Katherine's Rd. Hen-O-T 35 E4
St Laurence Way. Slough 43 D2
St Leonard's Ave. Wind 67 E3
St Leonard's Hill. Wind 66 C2
St Leonard's Rd. Wind 67 E2
St Leonard's Rd. Wind 66 B1
St Leonards Wlk. Iver 44 C2
St Luke's Rd. Maid 39 F4
St Luke's Rd. Old W 68 A1
St Lukes Way. Caver 59 D2
St Margaret's Rd. Maid 39 D4
St Margarets Ave. Ashf 98 A2
St Mark's Cl. Brad 83 D3
St Mark's Pl. Wind 67 E3
St Mark's Rd. Binf 117 E4
St Mark's Rd. Hen-O-T 35 E4
St Mark's Rd. Maid 39 F4
St Mark's Rd. Wind 67 E3
St Marks Cl. That 106 B2
St Marks Cres. Maid 39 D4
St Marks Rd. Binf 90 B1
St Martin's Cir. Stai 97 E2
St Martins Cl. Wood 87 E1
St Mary's Ave. P o T 57 E3
St Mary's Ave. Stan 97 E4
St Mary's Cl. Hen-O-T 35 D4
St Mary's Cl. Maid 40 A4
St Mary's Cl. Stan 97 E4
St Mary's Cres. Stan 97 E4
St Mary's Dr. Felt 98 B4
St Mary's Gdns. Bags 145 F2
St Mary's Gdns. Bags 145 F2
St Mary's Hill. Ascot 120 B2
St Mary's Rd. Ascot 120 A2
St Mary's Rd. Camb 151 E3
St Mary's Rd. Mort 137 D3
St Mary's Rd. Newb 105 D2
St Mary's Rd. Newb 105 D2
St Mary's Rd. Slough 43 E2
St Mary's Way. Woki 88 A1
St Mary's Way. Bur C 111 D2
St Mary's Wlk. Maid 39 F4
St Marys Cl. Sand 150 B4
St Marys La. Wink 92 B3
St Michael's Cir. Slough 21 E1
St Michael's Rd. Newb 104 C1
St Michael's Rd. Read 84 B4
St Michael's Rd. Sand 149 F4
St Michaels Cl. Lamb 25 D1
St Michaels Ct. Twyf 61 F3
St Micheals Rd. Camb 151 D3
St Micheals Rd. Ashf 98 A2
St Nazaire Cl. Stai 96 B2
St Nicholas Dr. Shepp 125 D1
St Nicholas' Rd. Newb 104 C1
St Olave's Cl. Stai 96 C1
St Patrick's Ave. Char 61 D3
St Patrick's Cl. Maid 39 D2
St Paul's Cl. Ashf 98 B2
St Paul's Ct. Read 86 A3
St Paul's Gate. Woki 116 A3
St Peter St. Mar 1 C1
St Peter's Ave. Caver 58 C2
St Peter's Cl. Burn 21 D1
St Peter's Cl. Old W 68 A1
St Peter's Cl. Stai 96 C1
St Peter's Gdns. Yate 149 E3
St Peter's Hill. Caver 58 C2
St Peter's Rd. Maid 19 E1
St Peter's Rd. Read 87 D3
St Pinnock Ave. Stai 124 A4
St Ronan's Rd. Read 85 D4
St Saviour's Rd. Read 85 F3
St Sebastians Cl. Wind 142 C4
St Stephens Cl. Caver 59 D2
St Swithins Cl. Wick 75 E2
St Theresa's Rd. Harm 71 F2
St Thomas Ct. That 106 C2
Saint Catherine's Hill. Silc 136 C3
Saint-Cloud Way. Maid 40 A4
Salamanca. Finch 142 C3
Salcombe Dr. Read 87 D2
Salcombe Rd. Ashf 97 F3
Salcombe Rd. Newb 104 C1
Salcombe Rd. Read 86 B2
Sale Garden Cotts. Woki 116 B3
Saleby Cl. Winn 87 F1
Salford Cl. Read 113 E4
Salisbury Ave. Slough 42 B4
Salisbury Cl. Woki 116 A1
Salisbury Rd. Harm 71 E1
Salisbury Rd. Hung 100 B2
Salisbury Rd. Read 85 F4
Salisbury Rd. Sand 150 B3
Salmon Cl. Shin 113 D1

Salmond Rd. Read 113 E3
Salt Hill Ave. Slough 42 B3
Salt Hill Dr. Slough 42 B3
Salt Hill Way. Slough 42 B3
Salters' Rd. Maid 40 A4
Saltersgate Cl. Winn 87 E1
Salwey Cl. Brac 118 A2
Samarkand Cl. Camb 152 A2
Samian Pl. Binf 90 C1
Sampage Cl. Read 113 E3
Sampson Park. Brac 117 E4
Sampsons Green. Slough 21 F1
Sanctuary Cl. Read 84 C4
Sanctuary Rd. Stan 71 D1
Sandcroft Rd. Caver 58 C3
Sandell's Ave. Ashf 98 B2
Sanden Cl. Hung 100 B3
Sandford Down. Brac 118 C2
Sandford Dr. Wood 60 C1
Sandford La. Hurst 88 B3
Sandgate Ave. Read 57 F1
Sandhills Cl. Vir W 122 C2
Sandhills La. Vir W 122 C2
Sandhills Way. Read 84 C2
Sandhurst La. Black 150 A3
Sandhurst Rd. Brac 142 A4
Sandhurst Rd. Crow 143 D2
Sandhurst Rd. Yate 149 F4
Sandleplatt Rd. Maid 39 D3
Sandleford Cl. Read 113 E3
Sandleford Rise. Newb 131 D4
Sandlers End. Slough 22 A1
Sandown Ave. Read 84 A2
Sandown Cl. Black 150 B3
Sandown Dr. Camb 151 F1
Sandown Rd. Slough 41 F4
Sandown Way. Newb 105 E1
Sandpit Hill. Newb 130 B2
Sandpit La. Swal 140 A3
Sandringham Cl. Slough 41 E4
Sandringham Dr. Ashf 97 E2
Sandringham Rd. Maid 19 E1
Sandringham Rd. Stan 70 C1
Sandringham Way. Read 84 A2
Sands Farm Dr. Burn 21 E1
Sandstone Cl. Winn 88 B1
Sandy Cl. Herm 79 D2
Sandy Dr. Felt 98 C4
Sandy La. Asc 118 B4
Sandy La. Camb 151 F3
Sandy La. Herm 78 C2
Sandy La. Sand 143 D1
Sandy La. Sunn 121 D2
Sandy La. Vir W 122 C3
Sandy La. Woki 115 E2
Sandy Mead. Holy 40 B3
Sandy Way. Slough 125 F1
Sandygate Cl. Mar 1 B2
Sandygate Rd. Mar 1 B2
Sapgood Cl. That 106 C1
Sapphire Cl. Woki 115 F4
Sarsby Dr. Wray 96 A3
Sarum Cres. Woki 116 B4
Sarum Rd. Tad 135 D1
Sarum Way. Hung 100 B2
Sarum. Brac 117 F1
Sawtry Cl. Winn 87 F1
Sawyer's Cl. Wind 66 C4
Sawyers Cres. Whi Wa 39 D1
Sawyers Cres. Whi Wa 39 D1
Saxe Cl. Bur C 111 D2
Saxon Cl. Slough 43 F2
Saxon Gdns. Tapl 20 B1
Saxon Rd. Ashf 98 B1
Saxon Way. Harm 70 B4
Saxon Way. Old W 68 A1
Sayers Cl. Gree 131 D4
Scafell Cl. Read 57 E1
Scafell Rd. Slough 41 F4
Scania Wlk. Burl 92 A1
Scarborough Rd. Stan 70 C1
Scarborough Way. Slough 42 A2
Scarletts La. Warg 37 E1
Scholars Cl. Caver 59 D2
School Green. Shin 113 F2
School Hill. Crow 143 D2
School Hill. Sand 143 D1
School Hill. Warg 36 B1
School La. Bags 145 F1
School La. Bish 38 A2
School La. Box 76 C2
School La. Bur C 111 D1
School La. Caver 59 D1
School La. Cook 19 D4
School La. Cook 20 A4
School La. East G 47 E3

School La. Eng G 96 A2
School La. Frox 99 D1
School La. Lit M 2 B3
School La. Maid 19 F1
School La. Medm 17 D3
School La. Padw 109 F1
School La. Shepp 125 D2
School La. Sto P 23 D2
School La. W St L 62 C2
School La. Warg 36 B1
School La. Windl 146 B2
School La. Yate 149 D3
School Rd. Ascot 120 B2
School Rd. Ashf 98 A1
School Rd. Bark 114 C1
School Rd. Bis 153 F2
School Rd. Bur C 111 E3
School Rd. Chiev 78 A4
School Rd. Comp 31 F2
School Rd. Harm 70 B4
School Rd. Hurst 88 C4
School Rd. Read 84 B4
School Rd. Read 114 C1
School Rd. Swal 139 F2
School Rd. Windl 146 A3
School Rd. Woki 116 B3
School Rd. Woo G 3 F3
School Terr. Read 86 C4
Schroder Ct. Eng G 95 D2
Scotland Hill. Sand 143 D1
Scotlands Dr. Far C 22 A3
Scots Cl. Stan 97 E4
Scots Dr. Woki 115 F4
Scots Cl. Caver 59 D3
Scott Cl. Far C 22 B4
Scott Cl. Wood 88 A4
Scott Terr. Brac 118 C4
Scott's Ave. Ashf 98 C1
Scott's Way. Maid 98 C1
Scottalls La. Hamp N 52 C3
Scours La. Read 58 A1
Scratchface La. Brad 81 F3
Scriveens Mead. That 106 C2
Scylla Cres. Felt 98 A4
Scylla Rd. Felt 71 D1
Seacourt Rd. Slough 44 A1
Seaford Gdns. Wood 87 F3
Seaford Rd. Stan 70 B1
Seaford Rd. Woki 116 B3
Sealand Rd. Stan 71 D1
Searles Farm La. Bur C 85 D1
Seaton Dr. Ashf 97 F3
Seaton Rd. Camb 151 D3
Second Cres. Slough 42 C4
Sedgefield Rd. Newb 131 F4
Sedgmoor Gdns. Fla H 3 D4
Sedgmoor La. Fla H 3 D4
Sedgmoor Rd. Fla H 3 D4
Seebys Oak. Sand 150 B3
Sefton Cl. Sto P 22 C2
Sefton Cl. West E 153 F3
Sefton Paddock. Sto P 23 D2
Segsbury Gr. Brac 118 C3
Selborne Gdns. Read 58 A1
Selbourne Cl. Black 150 B3
Setley Way. Brac 119 D3
Seton Dr. Read 84 C3
Sett The. Yate 149 D3
Sevenoaks Rd. Read 87 D2
Severn Cl. Sand 150 B4
Severn Cl. That 106 A3
Severn Cres. Slough 69 D4
Severn Way. Read 84 C3
Sewell Ave. Woki 116 A4
Sewell Cl. Cold A 79 D1
Seymour Ave. Shin 113 F3
Seymour Cl. Maid 39 D2
Seymour Court Rd. Mar 1 B2
Seymour Court Rd. Mar B 1 B2
Seymour Ct La. Mar B 1 A3
Seymour Park Rd. Mar 1 B2
Seymour Plain. Mar 1 B3
Seymour Plain. Mar B 1 B3
Seymour Rd. Slough 42 B2
Seymour Way. Ashf 98 C1
Shackleton Rd. Slough 42 C3
Shackleton Way. Wood 88 A4
Shaftesbury Cres. Stai 97 F1
Shaftesbury Mount. Black 150 B2
Shaftesbury Rd. Bis 153 F2
Shaftesbury Rd. Read 85 D4
Shaftesbury Rd. Read 84 C2
Shaggy Calf La. Slough 43 D3
Shakespeare Cl. Caver 59 E3
Shakespeare Rd. That 106 B2
Shakespeare Way. Brac 118 C4
Shalbourne Cl. Hung 100 A3
Shalbourne Rise. Camb 151 E3
Sharney Ave. Slough 44 A2

Sharnwood Dr. Read
Sharpethorpe Cl. Read
Shaw Farm Rd. Newb 1
Shaw Hill. Newb 1
Shaw Park. Crow 1
Shaw Rd. Newb 1
Shaw Rd. Read
Shaw The. Cook
Sheehy Way. Slough
Sheep Leaze La. Pease
Sheep Wlk. Caver
Sheepcote La. Bou E
Sheepcote La. Holy
Sheepcote Rd. Eton
Sheepcote Rd. Wind
Sheepdrove Rd. Lamb
Sheephouse Rd. Maid
Sheephouse Way. Chadd
Sheepridge La. Bou E
Sheepridge La. Fla H
Sheepwalk. Shepp 1
Sheepwalk. Stai
Sheepwash. Newb 1
Sheepways La. Maple
Sheerlands Rd. Arbo 1
Sheerlands Rd. Bark 1
Sheerlands Rd. Bark 1
Sheet St. Wind
Sheet Street Rd. Old W
Sheet Street Rd. Wind
Sheet Street Rd. Wind
Sheffield Rd. Harm
Sheffield Way. Harm
Shefford Cres. Woki 1
Sheldon Gdns. Read
Shelgate Wlk. Wood
Shelley Ave. Brac 1
Shelley Cl. Medm
Shelley Cl. Slough
Shelley Cl. Wood
Shelley Rd. Mar
Shelley Wlk. Yate
Shelson Ave. Felt
Shelton Cl. Slough
Shenstone Cl. Woki 1
Shenstone Dr. Burn
Shenstone Park. Ascot 1
Shenstone Rd. Read
Shephards La. Brac
Shepherd's House La. Read 1
Shepherds Ave. Read
Shepherds Chase. Bags 1
Shepherds Cl. Hurl
Shepherds Cl. Shepp 1
Shepherds Hill. Brac 1
Shepherds Hill. Comp
Shepherds Hill. Wood
Shepherds La. Caver
Shepherds La. Hurl
Shepherds Mount. Comp
Shepherds Rise. Comp
Shepherds Way. Crow 1
Shepherds Wlk. Wood
Shepley Dr. Read
Shepley Dr. Went 1
Shepley End. Went 1
Shepperton Court Dr. Shepp 1
Shepperton Rd. Stai 1
Sheraton Cl. Black
Sheraton Dr. Read
Sherborne Cl. Stan
Sherborne Rd. Felt
Sherborne Dr. Wind
Sherborne Dr. Wind
Sherbourne Dr. Warg
Sherbourne Wlk. Far C
Shergold Way. Cook
Sheridan Ave. Caver
Sheridan Cres. Tad 1
Sheridan Way. Woki 1
Sherman Rd. Read
Sherman Rd. Slough
Sherrardmead. Newb 1
Sherring Cl. Read
Sherwood Cl. Brac 1
Sherwood Dr. Maid
Sherwood Gdns. Hen-O-T 1
Sherwood Rd. Winn
Sherwood Rise. Burl
Sherwood St. Read
Shield Rd. Felt
Shifford Cres. Maid
Shildon Cl. Camb 1
Shinfield Rd. Read
Shinfield Rise. Read
Shipley Cl. Wood
Shipton Cl. Read
Shire Cl. Bags 1
Shire's Head Cl. Read 1
Shires The. Woki 1
Shires Way. Yate 1
Shirley Ave. Read
Shirley Ave. Wind
Shirley Rd. Maid
Sholto Rd. Stan
Shooter's Hill. Pangb
Shop La. Leckh 1

.a. Newb ... 104 C3
.nhanger's Rd. Maid ... 39 F2
.am Rd (E). Stan ... 70 C1
.am Rd (W). Stan ... 70 C1
.a Stan ... 97 F4
.d. Stan ... 70 C1
.t. Caver ... 59 D1
.t. Pangb ... 56 B3
.t. Read ... 86 A3
.he. Pur O T ... 57 E3
.rn. Slough ... 43 E4
.ath La. Sulhd ... 110 C2
.nd. Harl ... 71 E4
.no Rd. Moul ... 13 E2
.ood Ave. Ashf ... 97 D2
.bury Rd. Harm ... 71 E1
.nham Cl. Sand ... 150 B4
.s Hill La. Went ... 121 E2
.bury Rd. Read ... 85 D2
.ands Dr. Light ... 153 D4
.nd. Woki ... 116 A3
.ck La. Tad ... 134 C1
.ark Rd. Read ... 87 D1
.. Read ... 87 E1
.Cl. Sunn ... 22 C1
.and Rd. Newb ... 130 C4
.th Grange Cl. Read ... 87 D4
.th Grange Rd. Read ... 87 D4
.th St. Read ... 86 B4
.Rd. Stai ... 97 D2
.Cl. Bur C ... 84 A2
.ter Rd. Read ... 85 E2
.er Rd. Tad ... 135 E1
.. Maid ... 39 F3
.irches. Woki ... 115 E2
.l. Maid ... 39 D3
.Dr. Camb ... 152 B2
.ox Cres. Wood ... 87 E3
.ill. Sand ... 150 C4
.a. Padw ... 136 A4
.t. Read ... 86 A3
.ale Rd. Read ... 87 E2
.ale Rd. Tad ... 135 D1
.ale Rd. Warg ... 36 C1
.ades. Yate ... 149 E2
.orne Dr. Caver ... 58 C3
.ees Dr. Maid ... 39 D3
.ood Dr. Camb ... 152 A4
.l Cl. Ascot ... 120 B4
.l Rd. Sunn ... 120 C3
.Rd. Stai ... 117 F1
.s Cl. Burl ... 92 A1
.nds Cl. Brac ... 117 F4
.nds Rd. Read ... 86 A4
.ns Cl. Slough ... 44 A1
.ns Rd. Hen-O-T ... 15 E2
.Farm La. Silc ... 136 C3
.s La. Woki ... 115 E4
.s Cl. Pur O T ... 57 E2
.Wlk. Eng G ... 95 E1
.on Cl. Maid ... 40 A4
.ham Rd. Arbo ... 114 C2
.La. Hen-O-T ... 15 F1
.Cl. Hen-O-T ... 35 F4
.l Rd. Camb ... 151 D2
.Cl. Harm ... 71 D4
.La. Harl ... 71 D4
.Way. Harm ... 71 D4
.l. Woki ... 115 F3
.e La. Ham ... 126 A3
.g Cl. Winn ... 87 F1
.rdale Way. Winn ... 87 F2
.Way. Read ... 57 E2
.n Dr. That ... 106 C2
.Rd. Read ... 57 E2
.dhill La. Brac ... 118 A4
.rs Green La. Harm ... 130 A4
.ns Cl. Newb ... 130 B3
.ore Path. Slough ... 21 F1
.l. Read ... 84 C2
.Dr. Stai ... 97 D2
.s. Newb ... 105 E2
.Dr. Harm ... 70 B4
.m Green. Brac ... 118 C1
.g Hill. Harm ... 79 D3
.ere Cl. Felt ... 98 C4
.d. Camb ... 151 D3
.Cl. Gori ... 34 B3
.The. Caver ... 59 E1
.Rd. Datch ... 68 A4
.Rd. Eton ... 42 C1
.Rd. Slough ... 42 C4
.argh Way. Slough ... 42 C4
.ead Rd. Bur C ... 85 E1
.ad Rd. Read ... 86 A4
.Sq. Brac ... 118 B4
.Hill. Let B ... 6 C3
.La. Wind ... 66 C3
.m Bridge Rd. Hung ... 100 B3
.ald Cl. Whi Wa ... 39 D2
.ald Rd. Maid ... 39 D2
.s Green. Windl ... 146 B2
.Spur. Slough ... 42 C4
.Cl. Wind ... 131 F1
.Paddock. Windl ... 146 A4
.all Hill. Whi Wa ... 64 A4
.arry Cl. Woki ... 115 F3
.Cl. Wind ... 66 B2

Snowden Dr. Read ... 84 A3
Snowdon Cl. That ... 106 B1
Snowdon Rd W. Harm ... 71 E1
Snowdon Rd. Harm ... 71 E1
Snowdrop Gr. Winn ... 88 B2
Snows Ride. Windl ... 146 A3
Soham Cl. Winn ... 114 B4
Soho Cres. Bou E ... 3 E2
Soke Rd. Alde ... 135 F2
Soke Rd. Silc ... 135 F2
Soldiers Rise. Brac ... 142 B4
Solent Rd. Stan ... 70 C1
Somerford Cl. Maid ... 40 A4
Somersby Cres. Maid ... 39 F2
Somerset Cl. Hung ... 100 B3
Somerset Cl. Woki ... 115 E3
Somerset Way. Iver ... 44 C2
Somerset Wlk. Read ... 84 A3
Somerton Gdns. Read ... 87 D1
Somerton Gr. That ... 106 B1
Somerville Cres. Yate ... 149 F3
Somerville Gr. Woki ... 115 E2
Sonning La. Eton ... 42 B1
Sonning La. Sonn ... 60 B1
Sonning Meadows. Sonn ... 60 B1
Sonninge Cl. Sand ... 150 B4
Sopwith Cl. Wood ... 88 A4
Sorrel Cl. Bur C ... 111 D2
Sorrel Cl. Newb ... 105 E3
Sorrel Cl. Woki ... 116 C4
Sorrel Dr. Light ... 152 C4
Sospel Ct. Far C ... 22 B2
South Ave. Hen-O-T ... 35 F4
South Ave. Stai ... 96 B1
South Cl. Medm ... 17 E4
South Cl. Slough ... 41 E3
South Cl. Woki ... 116 D2
South Dr. Read ... 86 C1
South Dr. Sonn ... 60 B1
South Dr. Sulhd ... 110 B4
South Dr. Went ... 122 A1
South Dr. Woki ... 116 B3
South End Rd. Brad ... 82 A1
South Field Cl. Dorn ... 41 E2
South Gate Ave. Felt ... 98 B2
South Gr. Chert ... 123 F2
South Green. Slough ... 42 C3
South Hill Rd. Brac ... 118 A2
South Lake. Wood ... 87 F3
South Lynn Cres. Brac ... 118 A3
South Meadow La. Eton ... 67 E4
South Meadow. Crow ... 143 E2
South Path. Wind ... 67 E3
South Pl. Mar ... 117 F3
South Rd. Bis ... 153 F2
South Rd. Crow ... 143 F2
South Rd. Eng G ... 95 E1
South Rd. Maid ... 39 E3
South Row. Chil ... 10 B4
South St. Blew ... 12 A4
South St. Caver ... 59 D1
South St. Read ... 86 B4
South St. Stai ... 96 C2
South View Ave. Caver ... 59 E1
South View Park. Caver ... 59 E1
South View. Hung ... 100 B3
Southampton Cl. Black ... 150 B3
Southampton Rd. Stan ... 70 C1
Southampton St. Read ... 86 A3
Southampton Way. Stan ... 70 C1
Southbourne Dr. Bou E ... 3 D2
Southbury La. Twyf ... 61 F3
Southcote Ave. Felt ... 98 C3
Southcote Dr. Camb ... 152 A3
Southcote Farm La. Read ... 85 E2
Southcote La. Read ... 85 E2
Southcote Rd. Read ... 85 E3
Southcroft. Slough ... 22 A1
Southdown Rd. Caver ... 59 D3
Southdown Rd. That ... 135 D1
Southdown Rd. That ... 105 F2
Southend. That ... 106 B3
Southern Hill. Read ... 86 B3
Southern Perimeter Rd. Harm ... 71 E1
Southern Perimeter Rd. Stan ... 70 B1
Southern Rd. Camb ... 151 E3
Southerndene Cl. Read ... 57 E1
Southfield Gdns. Burn ... 41 D4
Southfields Ave. Ashf ... 98 A1
Southlands Cl. Woki ... 116 B3
Southlands La. Woki ... 116 B2
Southlea Rd. Datch ... 68 A3
Southside. Chert ... 124 A3
Southview Cl. Twyf ... 61 F3
Southview Rd. Mar ... 1 C2
Southville Cl. Felt ... 98 C4
Southville Cres. Felt ... 98 C4
Southway. Camb ... 151 D2
Southwell Park Rd. Camb ... 151 E3
Southwick Ct. Brac ... 118 C2
Southwold Cl. Winn ... 87 E1
Southwold Spur. Slough ... 43 E2
Southwold. Brac ... 117 F1
Southwood Gdns. Bur C ... 111 D2
Southwood Gdns. Cook ... 19 F3
Southwood Rd. Cook ... 19 F3

Southwood. Woki ... 116 B2
Spackman Cl. That ... 106 B1
Spackmans Way. Slough ... 42 B2
Spade Oak Meadows. Bou E ... 2 C2
Span Hill. Caver ... 60 B4
Sparrow Cl. Woki ... 115 F3
Sparrowbill. Brig ... 28 C1
Sparvell Way. Camb ... 151 E3
Speedwell Way. That ... 106 C2
Speen Hill Cl. Newb ... 104 C2
Speen La. Newb ... 104 B2
Speen Lodge Ct. Newb ... 104 C2
Speen Pl. Newb ... 104 C2
Spelthorne Gr. Stai ... 98 C1
Spelthorne La. Stai ... 125 E4
Spencer Cl. Silc ... 135 F1
Spencer Cl. Woki ... 115 E3
Spencer Gdns. Eng G ... 95 E2
Spencer Rd. Brac ... 117 F4
Spencer Rd. Newb ... 130 B3
Spencer Rd. Read ... 113 D4
Spencer Rd. Slough ... 43 F2
Spencers Cl. Maid ... 39 E4
Spencers La. Cook ... 19 F3
Spencers Rd. Maid ... 39 E4
Spenwood Cl. Shin ... 113 D1
Sperling Rd. Maid ... 19 F1
Spey Rd. Read ... 85 D4
Spinfield La W. Mar ... 1 B1
Spinfield La. Mar ... 1 A1
Spinfield Mount. Mar ... 1 A1
Spinfield Park. Mar ... 1 B1
Spinis. Brac ... 117 F1
Spinner Green. Brac ... 118 A2
Spinners Wlk. Mar ... 1 B1
Spinners Wlk. Wind ... 67 E3
Spinney Cl. Caver ... 59 D4
Spinney Dr. Felt ... 98 B4
Spinney The. Camb ... 152 B3
Spinney The. Read ... 84 C2
Spinney The. Sunn ... 120 C2
Spinney The. Woki ... 141 F4
Spinney The. Yate ... 149 E4
Spinningwheel La. Binf ... 90 B4
Spitfire Way. Wood ... 88 A4
Spittal St. Mar ... 1 B1
Spode Cl. Read ... 84 C4
Spout La N. Stan ... 70 A2
Spout La. Stan ... 70 A2
Spray La. Brig ... 28 B1
Spray Rd. Ham ... 126 C2
Spriggs Cl. That ... 106 B1
Spring Ave. Eng G ... 95 F1
Spring Cl. Maid ... 19 F1
Spring Cl. Pangb ... 56 B3
Spring Gdns. Ascot ... 120 A3
Spring Gdns. Bou E ... 3 D2
Spring Gdns. Burl ... 92 C1
Spring Gdns. Mar ... 1 C2
Spring Gdns. Shin ... 113 D1
Spring Gdns. Woo G ... 3 F4
Spring Gr. Read ... 86 A3
Spring Hill. Maid ... 39 F2
Spring La. Alde ... 135 E4
Spring La. As T ... 12 C4
Spring La. Caver ... 60 A3
Spring La. Cold A ... 106 B4
Spring La. Cook ... 19 E3
Spring La. Far C ... 22 B3
Spring La. Mort ... 137 D3
Spring La. Slough ... 41 F3
Spring Meadow. Brac ... 118 B4
Spring Meadows. Gr She ... 48 A2
Spring Rd. Felt ... 98 C3
Spring Rise. Eng G ... 95 E1
Spring Wlk. Warg ... 36 B1
Spring Wood La. Bur C ... 111 D1
Spring Woods. Sand ... 143 E1
Spring Woods. Vir W ... 122 A3
Springate Field. Slough ... 43 F2
Springcross Ave. Black ... 150 B2
Springdale. Read ... 87 D1
Springdale. Woki ... 141 F4
Springfield Cl. Wind ... 67 D3
Springfield End. Gori ... 34 B4
Springfield Gr. Shepp ... 125 F4
Springfield Meadows. Gr She ... 48 A2
Springfield Park. Holy ... 40 B1
Springfield Park. Twyf ... 61 F2
Springfield Rd. Ashf ... 97 F2
Springfield Rd. Binf ... 117 E4
Springfield Rd. Camb ... 152 A3
Springfield Rd. Silc ... 135 F1
Springfield Rd. Slough ... 69 D3
Springfield Rd. Wind ... 67 D3
Springfield. Light ... 153 E4
Springhill Rd. Gori ... 34 B4
Springwood Cl. Woki ... 116 C3
Spruce Dr. Light ... 153 D4
Spruce Rd. Wood ... 88 A3
Spur The. Slough ... 41 E4
Spur The. Warg ... 36 C4
Spurcroft Rd. That ... 106 C1
Square The. Bags ... 145 F2
Square The. Harm ... 70 C4
Square The. Pangb ... 56 B3

Square The. Shin ... 113 D1
Squire's Bridge Rd. Stai ... 124 C3
Squires Rd. Stai ... 125 D3
Squirrels Wlk. Ashf ... 98 B1
Squirrel Cl. Sand ... 150 A4
Squirrels Drey. Crow ... 142 C3
Squirrels Way. Read ... 87 D1
Stable Cl. Bur C ... 111 D2
Stable Croft. Bags ... 145 E1
Stable Ct. Newb ... 105 D3
Stable View. Yate ... 149 E4
Stables Ct. Mar ... 1 A1
Staddlestone Cl. Read ... 57 E1
Stadium Way. Read ... 58 A1
Staff College Rd. Camb ... 124 C3
Staff College Rd. Sand ... 151 D3
Stafferton Way. Maid ... 40 A3
Stafford Ave. Slough ... 22 B1
Stafford Cl. Burn ... 41 D4
Stafford Cl. Wood ... 87 F4
Stafford Lake. Bis ... 153 F1
Staffordshire Cl. Read ... 57 F1
Staffordshire Croft. New G ... 91 F1
Stag Hill. Chil F ... 73 D1
Stainash Cres. Stai ... 97 D2
Staines By-Pass. Stai ... 97 E2
Staines La. Chert ... 124 A2
Staines Lane Cl. Chert ... 123 F2
Staines Rd W. Ashf ... 98 B1
Staines Rd. Felt ... 98 B4
Staines Rd. Stai ... 123 F2
Staines Rd. Wray ... 95 F4
Stainford Cl. Ashf ... 98 B2
Stamford Ave. Camb ... 151 F1
Stamford Rd. Maid ... 39 E3
Stanbrook Cl. Brad ... 82 A1
Stanfield. Tad ... 135 D1
Stanham Rd. Read ... 84 C4
Stanhope Heath. Stan ... 70 B1
Stanhope Rd. Read ... 86 B2
Stanhope Rd. Sand ... 150 C2
Stanhope Rd. Slough ... 41 E4
Stanhope Way. Stan ... 70 B1
Stanlake La. Twyf ... 61 F2
Stanley Cl. Mar ... 1 C2
Stanley Cotts. Slough ... 42 C3
Stanley Gr. Read ... 85 F4
Stanley Green E. Slough ... 43 F1
Stanley Green W. Slough ... 43 F1
Stanley Rd. Ashf ... 97 F2
Stanley Rd. Newb ... 105 D1
Stanley Rd. Woki ... 116 C3
Stanley St. Read ... 85 F4
Stanmore Cl. Ascot ... 120 A3
Stanmore Gdns. Mort ... 136 C3
Stanmore Rd. Beed ... 30 B1
Stanmore Rd. East I ... 30 C4
Stanshawe Rd. Read ... 86 A4
Stanstead Rd. Stan ... 70 C1
Stanton Cl. Read ... 87 E2
Stanton Way. Slough ... 43 F1
Stanwell Cl. Stan ... 70 B1
Stanwell Gdns. Stan ... 70 B1
Stanwell Moor Rd. Harm ... 70 A2
Stanwell Moor Rd. Stan ... 70 A2
Stanwell New Rd. Stai ... 97 D3
Stanwell Rd. Ashf ... 97 F2
Stanwell Rd. Felt ... 71 D1
Stanwell Rd. Hort ... 68 C4
Stanwell Rd. Hort ... 69 E2
Stapleford Rd. Read ... 85 E2
Staplehurst. Brac ... 117 F1
Stapleton Cl. Mar ... 1 C2
Stapleton Cl. Newb ... 130 B3
Star La. Know H ... 37 F2
Star La. Read ... 86 A4
Star Post Rd. Camb ... 151 F4
Star Rd. Caver ... 59 E1
Starling Cl. Woki ... 115 F3
Starlings Dr. Read ... 84 A3
Starmead Dr. Woki ... 116 C3
Starting Gates. Newb ... 105 E1
Starts La. Cook ... 19 E3
Starwood Ct. Slough ... 43 E2
Statham Ct. Brac ... 117 F4
Station App. Ashf ... 97 F2
Station App. Mar ... 1 C1
Station App. Read ... 86 A4
Station App. Shepp ... 125 E4
Station App. Slough ... 42 C2
Station App. Vir W ... 122 B3
Station App. Woki ... 116 B3
Station Cres. Ashf ... 97 F2
Station Hill. Ascot ... 120 A3
Station Hill. Cook ... 19 F4
Station Hill. Read ... 86 A4
Station Par. Vir W ... 122 B3
Station Rd. Ashf ... 97 F2
Station Rd. Bags ... 145 F2
Station Rd. Bell H ... 130 A2
Station Rd. Bou E ... 3 D2
Station Rd. Brac ... 118 A4
Station Rd. Camb ... 151 E1
Station Rd. Chert ... 124 A2
Station Rd. East G ... 47 E3
Station Rd. Eng G ... 96 A2
Station Rd. Gori ... 34 B3

Station Rd. Gr She ... 48 A2
Station Rd. Hen-O-T ... 15 F1
Station Rd. Hung ... 100 B3
Station Rd. Kint ... 102 A1
Station Rd. Lamb ... 25 D1
Station Rd. Mar ... 1 C1
Station Rd. Newb ... 104 B3
Station Rd. Newb ... 105 D1
Station Rd. Pangb ... 56 B3
Station Rd. Read ... 86 A4
Station Rd. Shepp ... 125 E2
Station Rd. Shipl ... 36 A2
Station Rd. Slough ... 41 F4
Station Rd. Sunn ... 121 D2
Station Rd. Tapl ... 40 C4
Station Rd. That ... 106 C1
Station Rd. Twyf ... 61 E2
Station Rd. Warg ... 36 B1
Station Rd. Woki ... 116 A3
Station Rd. Wool ... 108 B1
Station Rd. Wray ... 69 D1
Station Rise. Mar ... 117 F3
Staunton Rd. Slough ... 42 B4
Staveley Rd. Ashf ... 98 B1
Staverton Cl. Woki ... 116 C3
Staverton Rd. Read ... 86 B2
Stayne End. Went ... 122 A3
Steam Farm La. Harm ... 71 F2
Steeple Wlk. Read ... 113 F4
Steerforth Copse. Crow ... 143 F1
Stepgates. Chert ... 124 A1
Stephen Cl. Stai ... 96 B1
Stephen Rd. Mort ... 136 C3
Stephen's Cl. Mort ... 136 C3
Stephens Firs. Mort ... 136 C3
Stephenson Cl. That ... 106 B2
Stephenson Rd. Bark ... 141 D4
Stephenson Rd. Wind ... 67 D4
Sterling Way. Read ... 58 A1
Stevens Hill. Yate ... 149 F3
Stevenson Dr. Binf ... 90 B2
Stewart Ave. Slough ... 42 C4
Stewart Ave. Stai ... 125 D3
Stewart Cl. Holy ... 65 E3
Stewarts Dr. Far C ... 22 A4
Stewarts Way. Mar B ... 1 B4
Stile Rd. Slough ... 43 E2
Stilton Cl. Winn ... 87 F1
Stilwell Cl. Yate ... 149 F3
Stirling Cl. Camb ... 151 F1
Stirling Cl. Caver ... 59 E3
Stirling Cl. Wind ... 66 B3
Stirling Rd. Slough ... 42 A3
Stirling Rd. Stan ... 70 C1
Stockbridge Way. Yate ... 149 E2
Stockbury Cl. Read ... 87 D1
Stockdales Rd. Eton ... 41 F1
Stockton Rd. Read ... 86 B1
Stockwells. Tapl ... 20 B1
Stockwood Rise. Camb ... 151 F3
Stoke Common Rd. Fulm ... 23 D4
Stoke Common Rd. Sto P ... 23 D4
Stoke Court Dr. Sto P ... 22 C2
Stoke Gdns. Slough ... 42 C3
Stoke Green. Sto P ... 23 D2
Stoke Park Ave. Far C ... 22 A1
Stoke Poges La. Slough ... 42 C4
Stoke Rd. Slough ... 42 C4
Stoke Wood. Sto P ... 22 C4
Stokeford Cl. Brac ... 118 C2
Stokes View. Pangb ... 56 B3
Stokesay. Slough ... 42 A3
Stokesley Rise. Woo G ... 3 F4
Stomp Rd. Burn ... 21 E1
Stomp Rd. Slough ... 41 D4
Stompits Rd. Holy ... 65 E4
Stone Cres. Felt ... 98 C4
Stone House La. Cook ... 2 C1
Stone St. Read ... 58 A1
Stoney La. Winn ... 114 B4
Stonecroft Ave. Iver ... 44 C4
Stonefield Park. Maid ... 39 E4
Stonegate. Camb ... 152 B3
Stoneham Cl. Read ... 85 D3
Stonehaven Dr. Wood ... 88 A3
Stonehill Rd. Light ... 146 A1
Stonehouse Rise. Camb ... 151 F1
Stoneleigh Cl. Camb ... 151 F1
Stoney Cl. Yate ... 149 E2
Stoney La. Burn ... 22 A2
Stoney Meade. Slough ... 42 A3
Stoney Rd. Brac ... 118 A4
Stoney Ware Cl. Bish ... 18 C4
Stoney Ware. Bish ... 18 C4
Stoneyfield. Been ... 109 D3
Stoneyland Cr. Eng G ... 95 F2
Stoneylands Rd. Eng G ... 95 F2
Stookes Way. Yate ... 149 D2
Stour Cl. Read ... 84 C4
Stour Cl. Slough ... 42 A2
Stovell Rd. Wind ... 66 C2
Stowe Rd. Slough ... 41 F3

Straight Bit. Fla H 3 D4
Straight La. Lamb 46 C3
Straight Mile The. Hurst 89 E3
Straight Mile The. W St L 62 C1
Straight Rd. Old W 68 A1
Strand La. Cook 19 F3
Strand Way. Wood 87 E1
Stranraer Rd. Stan 70 C1
Stratfield Rd. Slough 43 D2
Stratfield. Brac 117 F1
Stratford Cl. Read 85 D4
Stratford Dr. Bou E 3 E2
Stratford Gdns. Maid 39 E2
Stratford Rd. Harm 71 E1
Stratford Way. Read 84 A3
Strathcona Cl. Fla H 3 E4
Strathcona Way. Fla H 3 E4
Strathearn Ave. Read 71 F4
Stratheden Pl. Read 85 F4
Strathmore Dr. Char 61 D2
Strathy Cl. Read 85 D4
Stratton Gdns. Read 86 B1
Stratton Rd. Shepp 125 F4
Strawberry Hill. New G 91 F1
Strawberry Hill. Newb 104 C2
Streatley & Goring Bridge. Gori 34 A3
Streatley Hill. Stre 33 F3
Street The. Alde 135 D4
Street The. Brad 83 D3
Street The. Mort 137 E3
Street The. Moul 14 A3
Street The. Sou S 14 A2
Street The. Swal 139 E4
Street The. Tidm 56 B1
Street The. W St L 63 D3
Streets Heath. West E 153 F4
Stretton Cl. Brac 82 A1
Strode St. Eng G 96 A2
Strode's Cres. Stai 97 E2
Stroller Cl. That 105 F2
Strongrove Hill. Hung 100 B3
Stroud Cl. Wind 66 B2
Stroud Farm Rd. Holy 65 D4
Stroud Way. Ashf 98 A1
Stroude Rd. Vir W 122 C3
Stroude Rd. Vir W 123 D4
Strouds Meadow. Cold A 106 B4
Strouds The. Been 108 C3
Stuart Cl. Caver 59 D3
Stuart Cl. Wind 66 C3
Stuart Rd. Newb 130 B3
Stuart Way. Stai 97 D1
Stuart Way. Vir W 122 A3
Stuart Way. Wind 66 C3
Stubbles La. Cook 19 D3
Stubbs Folly. Sand 150 B4
Studios Rd. Stai 124 C3
Studland Cl. Read 113 E4
Sturbridge Cl. Wood 87 E1
Sturdee Cl. Camb 151 F1
Sturges Rd. Woki 116 B3
Sturt Green. Holy 64 C4
Styventon Pl. Chert 123 F1
Suck's La. Asham 54 B2
Suffolk Cl. Slough 41 F4
Suffolk Cl. Woki 115 E3
Suffolk Rd. Maid 39 E2
Suffolk Rd. Read 85 E4
Suffork Cl. Bags 145 F1
Sulham La. Pangb 56 C2
Sulham La. Pur O T 56 C2
Sulham La. Suih 56 C2
Sulham Wlk. Read 85 D2
Sulhamstead Hill. Sulhd 110 B3
Sulhamstead La. Sulhd 110 B2
Sulhamstead Rd. Bur 111 D3
Sulhamstead Rd. Sulhd 111 D3
Sullivan Rd. Camb 151 D3
Summer Gdns. Camb 152 B3
Summerfield Cl. Woki 88 C1
Summerfield Rise. Gori 34 B4
Summerhouse La. Harm 70 B4
Summerlea. Slough 42 A3
Summerleaze Rd. Maid 20 A1
Summers Rd. Burn 21 E1
Summit Cl. Woki 141 F4
Sun Gdns. Bur C 111 D1
Suｎ La. Maid 39 F4
Sun La. Swal 139 D1
Sun Pas. Wind 67 E3
Sun Ray Estate. Sand 150 A4
Sun St. Read 86 B4
Sunbury Cres. Felt 98 C3
Sunbury Rd. Eton 67 E4
Sunbury Rd. Felt 98 C3
Sunderland Cl. Wood 88 A4
Sunderland Rd. Maid 39 D4
Sundew Cl. Camb 153 E4
Sundew Cl. Woki 116 C4
Sundon Cres. Went 122 B2
Sundown Rd. Ashf 98 B2
Sunley Cl. Newb 130 B3
Sunmead Rd. Shepp 125 F3
Sunning Ave. Sunn 120 C1
Sunninghill Cl. Ascot 120 B3
Sunninghill Rd. Ascot 120 B3
Sunninghill Rd. Windl 146 A4
Sunninghill Rd. Wink 93 E1
Sunnybank. Mar 1 B2

Sunnyside. Newb 104 C3
Surbiton Rd. Camb 145 D1
Surley Row. Caver 59 D3
Surly Hall Wlk. Wind 66 C3
Surrey Ave. Camb 151 D2
Surrey Ave. Slough 22 B1
Surrey Rd. Read 86 A2
Surridge Ct. Bags 145 F1
Sussex Cl. Slough 43 D2
Sussex Gdns. Wood 87 F4
Sussex La. Shin 113 E1
Sussex Pl. Slough 43 D2
Sutcliffe Ave. Read 87 E2
Sutherland Ave. Shepp 125 F4
Sutherland Chase. Ascot 119 F4
Sutherland Gdns. Shepp 125 F4
Sutherland Gr. Read 84 C2
Sutherlands Ave. Read 86 B3
Sutherlands. Newb 130 C4
Sutton Ave. Slough 43 E2
Sutton Cl. Cook 20 A4
Sutton Cl. Maid 39 E3
Sutton La. Slough 44 B1
Sutton Pl. Slough 69 D4
Sutton Rd. Camb 145 D1
Sutton Rd. Cook 20 A3
Sutton Rd. Newb 104 B3
Sutton Wlk. Read 86 B3
Suttons Park Ave. Read 86 C4
Swabey Rd. Slough 44 A1
Swainstone Rd. Read 86 A3
Swaledale. Brac 118 A2
Swallow Cl. Read 84 B3
Swallow Cl. Stai 96 C2
Swallow Cl. Yate 149 D3
Swallow St. Iver 44 B4
Swallow Way. Woki 115 F3
Swallowfield Dr. Read 113 E3
Swallowfield Gdns. Thea 83 F2
Swallowfield Rd. Arbo 114 B1
Swallowfield. Eng G 95 D1
Swan La. Sand 150 A4
Swan Pl. Read 86 A4
Swan Rd. Iver 44 C4
Swancote Green. Brac 118 A2
Swangate. Hung 100 B4
Swanholm Gdns. Read 84 C2
Swanmore Cl. Winn 87 F1
Swanscourt T 61 F2
Swansdown Wlk. That 106 A2
Swansea La. Harm 71 E1
Swansea Rd. Read 59 D1
Swansea Terr. Read 57 E1
Swanston Field. Whi-O-T 56 B4
Sweeps La. Eng G 95 F2
Sweet Briar Dr. Bur C 84 B2
Sweetbriar. Brac 143 D4
Sweetzer's Piece. Silc 136 C3
Sweqstone Cl. Read 87 E1
Swift Cl. Woki 115 F3
Swift La. Windl 145 F2
Swinbrook Cl. Read 57 E2
Swindon Rd. Harm 71 E1
Swinley Rd. Brac 119 E2
Swiss Cottage Cl. Read 84 B4
Switchback Cl. Maid 19 E1
Switchback Rd N. Cook 19 F2
Switchback Rd N. Maid 19 F2
Switchback Rd S. Maid 19 E1
Switchback Rd. Cook 19 F2
Switchback The. Maid 19 E3
Sycamore Cl. Bur C 111 D2
Sycamore Cl. Camb 151 F1
Sycamore Cl. Sand 150 A4
Sycamore Cl. Wood 87 E3
Sycamore Cl. Wind 67 E2
Sycamore Dr. Camb 151 F1
Sycamore Dr. Mar B 1 B3
Sycamore Dr. Twyf 61 E3
Sycamore Rd. Read 86 C1
Sycamore Rise. Brac 118 B3
Sycamore Rise. Newb 105 E3
Sycamore Wlk. Eng G 95 D1
Sycamore Wlk. Slough 43 F4
Sycamores The. Black 150 A3
Sydings The. Newb 130 B3
Sydney Cl. Brac 143 E4
Sydney Cres. Ashf 98 A1
Sydney Gr. Slough 42 B4
Syke Cluan. Iver 44 C2
Syke Ings. Iver 44 C2
Sykes Rd. Slough 42 A4
Sylvan Ridge. Sand 143 D1
Sylvan Wlk. Read 85 E2
Sylvanus. Brac 117 F1
Sylverns Ct. New G 91 F1
Sylvester Cl. Newb 104 C3
Sylvester Rd. Maid 19 F1
Symondson Mews. Binf 90 B2
Sympson Rd. Tad 135 E1

Tachbrook Rd. Felt 98 C4
Tadcroft Wlk. Read 84 C2
Tadham Pl. That 106 B1
Tadley Common Rd. Tad 135 E1
Tadley Common. Shepp 125 F3
Taff Way. Read 86 D4
Tag La. Warg 37 D1
Talbot Ave. Slough 43 F2

Talbot Cl. Caver 59 E1
Talbot Cl. Newb 104 C3
Talbot Cl. Read 86 A4
Talbot Pl. Bags 145 F2
Talbot Pl. Datch 68 B3
Talbot Rd. Ashf 97 F2
Talbot Way. Sulh 57 E2
Talbots Dr. Maid 39 D3
Talfourd Ave. Read 87 D3
Talisman Cl. Woki 142 B3
Tall Trees. Stan 69 F3
Tallis La. Read 84 B3
Tamar Gdns. Read 86 B2
Tamar Way. Slough 44 A1
Tamar Way. Woki 115 F4
Tamarind Way. Read 86 C1
Tamarisk Ave. Read 86 C1
Tamarisk Rise. Woki 116 B4
Tamarisk Way. Slough 42 A2
Tamworth Cl. Wood 87 E1
Tamworth. Brac 118 B1
Tandem. Brac 117 E4
Tangier La. Eton 67 E4
Tanglewood Ride. West E 153 F4
Tanglewood. Woki 142 A4
Tangley Dr. Brac 116 A2
Tanglyn Ave. Stai 125 D2
Tanhouse La. Woki 116 A3
Tank Rd. Sand 150 C3
Tanner Cl. Newb 105 D2
Tanners La. Maple 58 C4
Tanners Yd. Bags 145 F2
Tape La. Hurst 88 C4
Taplow Common Rd. Burn 21 D2
Taplow Common Rd. Tapl 21 D2
Taplow Rd. Burn 41 D4
Tarbat Ct. Sand 150 B4
Tarbay La. Oak G 66 B2
Target Cl. Felt 71 F1
Targett Cl. Winn 88 A1
Tarlton Ct. Read 84 C3
Tarn Way. Harm 70 A4
Tarn La. Newb 130 C4
Tarnbrook Way. Brac 118 C1
Tarragon Cl. Read 86 C1
Tarragon Way. Bur C 111 D2
Tarrants Hill. Hung 100 B3
Tasker Cl. Harl 71 E4
Tatchbrook Cl. Maid 40 A4
Tattersall Cl. Woki 116 C3
Tavistock Cl. Maid 39 D4
Tavistock Cl. Stai 97 E1
Tavistock Rd. Read 86 A2
Tawfield. Brac 117 F1
Tay Rd. Read 85 D4
Taylor's Cl. Mar 1 C1
Tazewell Ct. Read 85 F3
Tebbit Ct. Brac 118 B4
Teesdale Rd. Slough 41 F4
Tekels Ave. Camb 151 E2
Tekels Way. Camb 151 F2
Telford Cres. Wood 60 C1
Telford Dr. Slough 42 A2
Telston Cl. Bou E 3 D3
Tempest Rd. Stai 96 B1
Templar Ct. Sand 150 A4
Templars Pl. Mar 1 C1
Temple Gdns. Stai 123 F4
Temple La. Bish 18 B3
Temple Mill Island. Bish 18 B3
Temple Park. Hurl 17 F2
Templecroft. Ashf 98 B1
Templedene Ave. Stai 97 E1
Templeton Gdns. Read 86 B1
Templewood La. Far C 22 B4
Ten Acre La. Stai 123 E4
Tenaplas Dr. Upp B 54 C3
Tenby Ave. Caver 59 E3
Tenby Dr. Ascot 120 B2
Tennyson Rd. Ashf 97 F2
Tennyson Rd. Read 86 B2
Tennyson Rd. Wood 87 F2
Tennyson Way. Slough 21 F1
Terrace Rd N. Binf 90 B2
Terrace Rd S. Binf 90 B1
Terrace The. Ascot 120 B2
Terrace The. Crow 143 E3
Terrace The. Maid 40 B2
Terrace The. Woki 116 A3
Terrington Hall. Mar 1 C1
Terry's La. Cook 19 F4
Tesimond Dr. Yate 149 D3
Tessa Rd. Read 58 C1
Test Cl. Read 85 D4
Testwood Rd. Wind 66 B3
Teviot Rd. Read 84 C4
Thakerays The. That 106 B1
Thames Ave. Chert 124 A3
Thames Ave. Pangb 56 B3
Thames Ave. Read 59 D1
Thames Ave. Wind 67 E4
Thames Cl. Bou E 3 D2
Thames Cl. Chert 124 B1

Thames Cres. Maid 20 A1
Thames Dr. Char 60 C4
Thames Ind Est. Mar 1 C1
Thames Mead. Wind 66 C3
Thames Rd. Gori 34 A3
Thames Rd. Slough 44 A2
Thames Rd. That 106 B3
Thames Reach. Medm 17 E4
Thames Reach. Pur O T 55 E3
Thames Side Prom. Read 59 D1
Thames Side. Chert 124 B1
Thames Side. Hen-O-T 15 F1
Thames Side. Read 59 D1
Thames Side. Stai 96 C1
Thames Side. Wind 67 E4
Thames St. Shepp 125 F1
Thames St. Sonn 60 B2
Thames St. Stai 96 C2
Thames St. Wind 67 E4
Thamesfield Ct. Shepp 125 E1
Thamesfield Gdns. Mar 1 C1
Thanington Way. Read 87 D1
Thatchers Dr. Maid 39 D3
Theal Cl. Sand 150 B4
Theale Rd. Bur C 111 E3
Theobald Dr. Read 57 E2
Theobalds Way. Camb 152 B2
Thetford Mews. Caver 59 E3
Thetford Rd. Ashf 97 F3
Thibet Rd. Sand 150 B4
Thicket Gr. Maid 38 C4
Thicket Rd. Read 84 C4
Thickthorne La. Stai 97 E1
Third Ave. Mar 1 C1
Third Cres. Slough 42 B4
Thirkleby Cl. Slough 42 B3
Thirlmere Ave. Read 57 F1
Thirlmere Ave. Slough 41 E4
Thirlmere Cl. Stai 96 A1
Thirtover. Cold A 79 D1
Thistledown. Read 57 E1
Thistleton Way. Winn 87 F1
Thomas Dr. New G 91 F1
Thomas La. Woki 141 F4
Thomas Rd. Bou E 3 E2
Thompkins La. Burn 22 A3
Thompson Cl. Herm 78 C3
Thompson Cl. Slough 44 A1
Thompson Dr. That 106 C1
Thomson Wlk. Bur C 84 C2
Thone Cl. Brac 143 D4
Thorburn Chase. Sand 150 B3
Thorn Dr. Slough 43 F4
Thorn La. Read 86 A4
Thorn St. Read 86 A4
Thornaby Pl. Woo G 3 F4
Thornbank Cl. Stan 70 A1
Thornbers Way. Char 61 D3
Thornbridge Rd. Read 113 D4
Thornbury Cl. Crowt 143 D3
Thorncroft. Eng G 95 E1
Thorndike. Slough 42 A4
Thorndown La. Windl 146 B2
Thorndown La. Windl 146 B2
Thorne Cl. Stai 98 B1
Thorne Cl. Woki 115 E2
Thorney Cl. Winn 87 F1
Thorney La N. Iver 44 C3
Thorney La S. Iver 44 C3
Thornfield Green. Black 150 C2
Thornfield. Head 132 B2
Thornford Rd. Gree 132 B2
Thornford Rd. Head 132 C2
Thornford Rd. That 132 B2
Thornhill Way. Stai 125 D2
Thornhill. Brac 118 C3
Thorningdown. Chil 10 B4
Thornton Mews. Read 85 E4
Thornton Rd. Read 85 E4
Thorp Cl. Binf 90 B2
Thorpe By Pass. Stai 123 D3
Thorpe Cl. Woki 115 E2
Thorpe Lea Rd. Stai 96 A1
Thorpe Rd. Chert 123 E2
Thorpe Rd. Stai 96 B2
Thorpe Rd. Stre 123 E2
Thrale Mews. Read 85 D4
Three Acre Rd. Newb 130 C4
Three Firs Way. Bur C 124 B3
Three Gables La. Stre 34 A4
Three Post La. Lamb 25 D1
Threshfield. Brac 118 A2
Thrift La. Holy 64 B4
Throgmorton Rd. Yate 149 D3
Thrush Cl. Bur C 111 D2
Thurlby Way. Maid 39 D4
Thurlestone Cl. Shepp 125 E2
Thurlestone Gdns. Read 86 B1
Thurnscoe Cl. Read 113 F4
Thurso Cl. Read 85 D4
Thurston Rd. Slough 42 A4
Thyme Cl. Read 87 D1
Tichborne Cl. Black 150 C2
Tichbourne Cl. Camb 151 F2
Tickenor Dr. Woki 141 E4
Tickhill Cl. Read 113 F4
Tidmarsh La. Pangb 56 A1
Tidmarsh La. Sulh 56 A1
Tidmarsh Rd. Pangb 56 B2

Tidmarsh Rd. Tidm ......
Tidmarsh St. Read ......
Tiffany Cl. Woki ......
Tiger Cl. Wood ......
Tigerseye Cl. Woki ......
Tilbury Cl. Caver ......
Tile Barn Row. Ball H ......
Tilecotes Cl. Mar ......
Tilehurst La. Binf ......
Tilehurst Rd. Read ......
Tilling Cl. Read ......
Tilly's La. Stai ......
Tilney Way. Read ......
Tilstone Ave. Eton ......
Tilstone Cl. Eton ......
Timbers Wlk. Maid ......
Timline Green. Brac ......
Timsway. Stai ......
Tindal Cl. Yate ......
Tinkers La. Wind ......
Tinkers La. Windl ......
Tinsey Cl. Stai ......
Tinsley Cl. Read ......
Tintagel Dr. Camb ......
Tintagel Rd. Brac ......
Tintern Cl. Slough ......
Tintern Cres. Read ......
Tinwell Cl. Winn ......
Tippett Rise. Read ......
Tippings La. Wood ......
Tippits Mead. Brac ......
Tiptree Cl. Read ......
Titcombe Way. Kint ......
Tite Hill. Eng G ......
Tithe Barn Dr. Holy ......
Tithe Cl. Holy ......
Tithe Ct. Slough ......
Tithe La. Wray ......
Tithe Meadows. Went ......
Tithebarn Gr. Read ......
Titlarks Hill Rd. Went ......
Tiverton Cl. Wood ......
Toad La. Black ......
Tockley Rd. Burn ......
Tofrek Terr. Read ......
Tokers Green Rd. Maple ......
Tokersgreen La. Caver ......
Tokersgreen La. Maple ......
Toll Gdns. Brac ......
Tollgate. Maid ......
Tolpuddle Way. Yate ......
Tomlin Cl. That ......
Tomlin Rd. Slough ......
Tomlins Ave. Camb ......
Tomlinson Dr. Brac ......
Top Common. New G ......
Topaz Cl. Slough ......
Topaz Cl. Woki ......
Tope Cres. Bark ......
Tope Rd. Bark ......
Torcross Gr. Bur C ......
Torin Ct. Eng G ......
Torquay Spur. Slough ......
Torridge Rd. Slough ......
Torrington Rd. Read ......
Toseland Way. Winn ......
Totnes Rd. Read ......
Tottenham Wlk. Crow ......
Totterdown. Bur C ......
Toutley Cl. Woki ......
Toutley Rd. Woki ......
Tower Cl. Caver ......
Tower Cl. Fla H ......
Tower Hill. Chadd ......
Towers Dr. Crow ......
Town Farm Way. Stan ......
Town La. Bou E ......
Town La. Stan ......
Town Sq. Brac ......
Town Square. Camb ......
Town Tree Rd. Ashf ......
Townsend Cl. Brac ......
Townsend Rd. Aldw ......
Townsend Rd. Read ......
Townsend Rd. Stre ......
Townsend. Shepp ......
Tozer Wlk. Wind ......
Trafalgar Cl. Woki ......
Trafalgar Ct. Read ......
Trafalgar Way. Sand ......
Trafford Rd. Read ......
Travis Ct. Slough ......
Travis Ct. Wood ......
Travis La. Sand ......
Tredegar Rd. Caver ......
Tree Cl. Read ......
Tree Tops Ave. Camb ......
Trees Rd. Bou E ......
Treesmill Dr. Maid ......
Treeton Cl. Read ......
Trefoil Cl. Woki ......
Trelawney Ave. Slough ......
Trelawney Dr. Read ......
Trelleck Rd. Read ......
Tremayne Wlk. Camb ......
Trenchard Rd. Holy ......
Trenches La. Slough ......
Trent Cl. Woki ......

res. That 106 A3
ld. Slough 69 D4
n Cl. Camb 152 A1
m Cres. Yate 149 D3
an. Brac 117 F1
e The. Read 84 B4
down. Brac 91 D1
id. Read 57 E1
Ave. Mar 1 B2
Cl. Stan 70 B1
Cl. Sunn 121 D2
Rd. Read 85 F4
Pl. Wind 67 E3
Rd. Mar 1 B1
Crow 143 F1
h Cl. Harl 71 E3
orth Ave. Vir W 122 C3
od Cl. Crow 143 F1
l. Mar 18 B4
Wlk. Newb 105 E2
eck Cl. Twyf 61 E3
s La. Bee H 138 B2
s La. Swal 138 B3
ull Rd. Brac 91 D1
s Green Cl. Vir W 122 C2
s Mill La. Went 122 C2
sgreen Ave. Went 122 B2
sgreen Rd. Went 122 B2
Cl. Maid 39 D4
Hill Rd. Ascot 120 B2
Cnr. Hen-O-T 35 F4
orge Cl. Winn 87 F1
Farm Cl. Lamb 25 D1
Rd. Sto P 23 D2
Cl. Ashf 97 F2
Cl. Woki 116 C3
Dr. Woo G 3 E4
Dr. Yate 149 E2
Gdns. Slough 41 E4
La. Old W 95 E4
Rd. Ashf 98 B1
Rd. Newb 105 D1
Rd. Read 86 A4
ric Cl. Read 86 C1
l Link Rd. Stan 71 D1
l Rd E. Harm 71 D3
l Rd W. Harm 71 D3
Hill Cotts. Read 87 D3
La. Hen-O-T 15 F1
La. Slough 42 B2
y Rd. Read 85 F4
ill Rd. Camb 151 F4
La. Silc 137 D2
ric Cl. Read 86 C1
erry. Brac 117 F1
ridge Cl. Read 114 A4
r Pl. Sand 150 B3
r Rd. Slough 43 E2
rs Cl. Stai 97 D2
rs Dr. That 106 C1
y The. That 106 B2
elds. That 106 B2
ak Park. Wind 66 C2
ke Rd. Brac 117 F4
ke Rd. Newb 130 C4
ke Rd. That 105 F2
one Cl. Winn 88 A2
one End. Yate 149 D3
ille Cl. Light 146 A1
n Rd. Felt 71 F1
s Cr. Maid 39 D3
s Rise. Windl 146 A3
s Way. Slough 42 B2
m Way. Sand 150 C2
rd Cl. Read 57 F1
rd Mews. Read 85 D4
d Ct. Read 85 D4
d. Slough 69 D4
Oaks. Caver 59 D3
hes La. Slough 42 A3
Tree Hill. Hen-O-T 35 D4
rd Rd. Binf 89 D1
rd Rd. Binf 90 B4
rd Rd. W St L 62 C3
ham Rd. Maid 39 D4
ton Pl. Read 86 F3
hams. Newb 130 C4
Pl. Old W 68 A1
Rd. Read 84 B4
Cl. Caver 58 C3
s La. Buck 84 C4
s Pl. Read 84 C4
Way. That 106 A3
Gdns. Wind 66 C2
rton. Brac 118 B4

gton Cl. Read 84 B4
ton Dr. Brac 118 C3
t Cl. Read 113 F4
ater Cl. Light 146 A1
ater Cl. Slough 41 E4
ater Cl. That 106 A2
ater Rd. Read 57 E2
ater Rd. Light 146 A1
ater. Brac 117 F1
r Cl. Caver 58 C3
erville Way. Slough 21 F1
rhill Cl. Maid 39 F3
rhill. Moul 14 A2

Underwood Rd. Read 85 D2
Underwood. Brac 117 F2
Union Cl. Sand 143 F1
Union Rd. Brad 82 B2
Union St. Read 86 A4
Unity Cl. Caver 59 D3
Unwin Ave. Harm 71 E1
Upavon Dr. Read 85 F3
Upavon Gdns. Brac 118 C2
Upcroft. Wind 67 D2
Updown Hill. Windl 146 B2
Upland Rd. Camb 151 E4
Uplands Cl. Sand 150 A4
Uplands Rd. Caver 58 C3
Uplands. Hung 100 B3
Uplands. Mar B 1 B3
Upper Bray Rd. Maid 40 B2
Upper Broadmoor Rd. Crow . 143 E3
Upper Charles St. Camb .. 151 F3
Upper Chobham Rd. Camb . 152 A2
Upper College Ride. Camb .. 151 F4
Upper Crown St. Read ... 86 A3
Upper End. Chadd 49 D4
Upper Gordon Rd. Camb . 151 E3
Upper Halliford Rd. Shepp . 125 F3
Upper Lambourn Rd. Lamb .. 25 D2
Upper Lees Rd. Slough ... 22 A1
Upper Meadow Rd. Read .. 86 B1
Upper Nursery. Sunn 121 D2
Upper Park Rd. Camb ... 151 F3
Upper Red Cross Rd. Gori . 34 B3
Upper Redlands Rd. Read . 86 C3
Upper Village Rd. Ascot . 120 B2
Upper Warren Ave. Caver .. 58 B2
Upper Woodcote Rd. Caver . 58 B3
Uppingham Dr. Wood 60 C1
Uppingham Gdns. Wood .. 60 C1
Upshire Gdns. Brac 118 C3
Upton Cl. Hen-O-T 15 F1
Upton Cl. Slough 42 C2
Upton Court Rd. Slough ... 43 D1
Upton Lea Par. Slough 43 D3
Upton Park. Slough 42 C2
Upton Rd. Read 85 D4
Upton Rd. Slough 43 D2
Urquhart Rd. That 106 C1
Usk Rd. Read 84 C3
Uxbridge Rd. Slough 43 E3

Vachel Rd. Read 86 A4
Vale Cres. Read 57 F1
Vale Cr. Slough 42 C2
Vale Rd. Camb 151 D2
Vale Rd. Felt 98 C2
Valentia Rd. Read 85 E4
Valentine Cres. Caver 59 E2
Valeview Dr. Bee H 138 B3
Valley Cl. Caver 59 D2
Valley Cl. Gori 34 B3
Valley Cres. Woki 116 A4
Valley End. Iver H 23 E1
Valley Rd. Bur C 111 D2
Valley Rd. Camb 152 B1
Valley Rd. Hen-O-T 35 D4
Valley Rd. Newb 130 C4
Valley Way. Silc 135 F1
Valon Rd. Arbo 140 C4
Valpy St. Read 86 A4
Valroy Cl. Camb 151 E3
Vandyke. Brac 117 F2
Vanlore Way. Read 84 B3
Vanners La. Ham M 129 E3
Vansittart Rd. Bish 18 C4
Vansittart Rd. Wind 67 D3
Vantage Rd. Slough 42 A3
Vanwall Bsns Park. Maid . 39 E3
Vanwall Rd. Maid 39 E2
Vastern Rd. Caver 59 D1
Vaughan Copse. Eton 42 B1
Vaughan Way. Slough 21 F1
Vauxhall Dr. Wood 88 A3
Vegal Cres. Eng G 95 E2
Venetia Cl. Caver 59 E4
Venning Rd. Bark 140 C4
Ventnor Rd. Read 57 E1
Venus Cl. Woki 115 F3
Verey Cl. Twyf 61 F2
Vermont Rd. Slough 21 F1
Vermont Woods. Woki .. 141 F4
Verney Cl. Mar 1 B1
Verney Mews. Read 85 D4
Verney Rd. Slough 44 A1
Vernon Cres. Read 113 D4
Vernon Dr. Ascot 119 F4
Vernon Rd. Felt 98 C3
Verran Rd. Camb 151 E2
Viburnum St. Camb 153 F3
Vicarage Cl. Caver 59 E4
Vicarage Cr. Cook 20 A4
Vicarage Cres. Stai 96 A2
Vicarage Cl. Felt 98 B4
Vicarage Dr. Stai 96 A1
Vicarage Dr. Maid 40 B2
Vicarage Gdns. Ascot 120 A2
Vicarage La. Cold A 108 B3
Vicarage La. Stai 124 B3
Vicarage La. Wray 95 F4
Vicarage La. Yate 149 E4
Vicarage Rd. Ashf 98 C1

Vicarage Rd. Bags 145 E2
Vicarage Rd. Black 150 C2
Vicarage Rd. Hen-O-T 35 F4
Vicarage Rd. Maid 39 F4
Vicarage Rd. Read 86 B3
Vicarage Rd. Stai 96 A1
Vicarage Rd. Stai 96 C3
Vicarage Rd. Yate 149 E4
Vicarage Way. Iver 69 E4
Vicarage Wlk. Maid 40 B2
Vickers Cl. Shin 113 F2
Vickers Cl. Wood 88 A4
Victor Rd. That 106 C2
Victor Rd. Wind 67 E2
Victor Way. Wood 88 A4
Victoria Ave. Camb 151 D3
Victoria Cres. Iver 44 C3
Victoria Ct. Bags 145 F1
Victoria Dr. Black 150 B2
Victoria Rd. Ascot 120 A2
Victoria Rd. Caver 59 D2
Victoria Rd. Eton 41 F1
Victoria Rd. Far C 22 B3
Victoria Rd. Mar 1 C1
Victoria Rd. Mort 136 C3
Victoria Rd. Read 84 B4
Victoria Rd. Sand 143 F1
Victoria Rd. Slough 43 D3
Victoria Rd. Stai 96 C3
Victoria Rd. Warg 36 C1
Victoria St. Eng G 95 E1
Victoria St. Read 86 B4
Victoria St. Wind 67 E3
Victory Rd. Chert 124 A1
Vigo La. Yate 149 E3
Vigo La. Yate 149 E2
Viking. Brac 117 F2
Village Cl. Read 113 D3
Village Rd. Dorn 41 E2
Village Rd. Stai 123 D3
Village The. Finch 141 F2
Village The. Old W 94 A3
Village Way. Ashf 98 A2
Villiers Mead. Woki 116 A3
Villiers Rd. Slough 42 B4
Villiers Way. Newb 130 B3
Villiers Wlk. Newb 130 B3
Vincent Cl. Chert 123 F1
Vincent Cl. Wood 87 F3
Vincent Dr. Shepp 125 F3
Vincent Rd. Chert 123 F1
Vincent Rd. That 106 C2
Vincent Rise. Brac 118 C3
Vine Cl. Stan 70 A1
Vine Cres. Read 85 D2
Vine Rd. Sto P 22 C3
Vineries Cl. Harm 71 D4
Vines The. Warg 36 B1
Viney The. Woki 115 E2
Vineyard Dr. Bou E 3 D3
Viola Ave. Stan 97 F4
Virginia Ave. Vir W 122 B2
Virginia Beeches. Vir W .. 122 A1
Virginia Cl. Stai 124 B3
Virginia Dr. Stai 124 B3
Virginia Way. Read 85 E4
Viscount Rd. Stan 97 F4
Viscount Way. Harm 71 F2
Viscount Way. Wood 88 A4
Vivien Cl. Cook 19 F3
Voller Dr. Read 84 B3
Vulcan Cl. Sand 150 A4
Vulcan Way. Sand 150 A4

Wabone Rd. Bou E 3 D2
Wade Dr. Slough 42 A3
Wadham Cl. Shepp 125 E1
Wadham. Crow 143 F1
Wagbullock Rise. Brac . 118 B2
Waggoners Hollow. Bags . 145 F1
Wagner Cl. Whi Wa 38 C2
Wagtail Cl. Twyf 61 F2
Waingels Rd. Char 61 D1
Waingels Rd. Wood 61 D1
Wakefield Cres. Sto P 22 C3
Wakeford Cl. Silc 135 F1
Wakelins End. Cook 19 F4
Wakeman Rd. Bou E 3 D2
Wakemans. Pangb 55 E2
Walbury. Brac 118 C2
Waldeck Rd. Maid 40 A4
Waldeck St. Read 86 A3
Waldegrave Pl. Newb 130 C2
Walden Ave. Arbo 114 B2
Waldens Cl. Bou E 3 D2
Waldorf Hts. Black 150 B2
Waldron Hill. Brac 118 C4
Walgrove Gdns. Whi Wa .. 63 F4
Walk The. Ashf 98 C1
Walk The. Eton 42 A1
Walker Rd. Maid 40 A2
Walker's La. Lamb 25 D2
Walker's Ridge. Camb .. 151 F3

Walkers Pl. Read 85 E4
Wall La. Silc 136 B1
Wallace Cl. Mar 1 C2
Wallace Cl. Shepp 125 E3
Wallace Cl. Wood 87 E3
Walled Gdn The. Warg 36 B1
Waller Dr. Newb 105 F3
Wallingford Cl. Brac 118 C3
Wallingford Rd. Comp ... 31 F3
Wallingford Rd. Gori 14 B3
Wallingford Rd. Sou S 14 B3
Wallingford Rd. Stre 34 A4
Wallington Rd. Camb 145 D1
Wallington's Rd. Kint 101 F1
Wallis Ct. Slough 43 D2
Wallner Way. Woki 116 C3
Walmer Cl. Crow 143 E3
Walmer Cl. Read 85 D3
Walmer Rd. Wood 60 C1
Walnut Cl. Woki 115 F3
Walnut Cl. Yate 149 E2
Walnut Tree Cl. Bou E 3 D1
Walnut Tree Cl. Twyf 61 F3
Walnut Tree Ct. Gori 34 B3
Walnut Tree Rd. Stai 125 E3
Walnut Tree Rd. Stai 125 E4
Walnut Way. Bou E 3 D1
Walnut Way. Read 84 B4
Walpole Rd. Old W 95 D4
Walpole Rd. Slough 41 E4
Walrus Cl. Wood 88 A4
Walter Rd. Woki 115 F4
Walters Cl. Cold A 106 B4
Waltham Cl. Crow 143 E1
Waltham Cl. Whi Wa 38 C1
Waltham Rd. Twyf 61 F2
Waltham Rd. Whi Wa 38 C3
Walton Ave. Hen-O-T 35 F4
Walton Bridge Rd. Shepp . 125 F1
Walton Cl. Wood 87 E4
Walton Dr. Ascot 119 F4
Walton Gdns. Felt 98 C2
Walton La. Burn 21 F2
Walton La. Shepp 125 F1
Walton Way. Newb 105 E2
Wandhope Way. Read 57 E1
Wanstraw Gr. Brac 118 C1
Wantage Cl. Brac 118 C2
Wantage Rd. Gr She 48 B3
Wantage Rd. Lamb 25 E3
Wantage Rd. Read 85 E4
Wantage Rd. Sand 150 B4
Wantage Rd. Stre 33 F4
Wapshott Rd. Stai 96 C2
War Memorial Pl. Hen-O-T . 35 F4
Waram Cl. Hung 100 C4
Warbler Cl. Read 84 A3
Warborough Ave. Read 84 A4
Warborough Rd. Let B 7 D4
Warbreck Dr. Sulh 57 D2
Warbrook La. Finch 141 D1
Ward Cl. Iver 44 C3
Ward Cl. Woki 116 B4
Ward Gdns. Slough 41 F3
Ward Royal. Wind 67 E3
Ward Stone Park. Brac .. 118 C1
Wardle Ave. Read 57 E1
Wardle Cl. Bags 145 F2
Wareham Rd. Brac 118 C2
Warfield Rd. Brac 91 E1
Warfield Rd. Felt 98 C4
Wargrave Hill. Warg 36 B1
Wargrave Rd. Rem H 36 A4
Wargrave Rd. Twyf 61 E3
Wargrove Dr. Sand 150 B4
Waring Cl. Winn 116 C4
Warley Rise. Sulh 57 E2
Warner Cl. Harl 71 E4
Warner Cl. Slough 41 F3
Warners Hill. Cook 19 E4
Warnford Rd. Read 84 C4
Warnsham Cl. Read 87 D1
Warren Cl. Bur C 111 D2
Warren Cl. Sand 150 A4
Warren Down. Brac 117 F4
Warren End. Newb 130 B3
Warren House Rd. Bint 89 E1
Warren House Rd. Woki . 116 B4
Warren La. Woki 141 F3
Warren Rd. Ashf 98 C1
Warren Rd. Newb 60 B1
Warren Rise. Camb 151 F2
Warren Row Rd. Know H .. 37 E3
Warren Row. Burl 119 F4
Warren The. Caver 58 C2
Warrington Ave. Slough .. 42 B4
Warrington Spur. Old W .. 95 D4
Warwick Ave. Slough 22 A1
Warwick Ave. Stai 97 E1
Warwick Cl. Camb 151 E4
Warwick Cl. Maid 39 D2
Warwick Cl. Wood 88 A4
Warwick Rd. Ashf 97 F2
Warwick Rd. Read 86 C2
Warwick. Brac 118 C2

Wasdale Cl. Crow 143 E1
Wash Hill Lea. Bou E 3 E2
Wash Hill. Bou E 3 F2
Wash Water. Ham M 130 A4
Wash Water. Newb 130 A2
Washing La. Brim 134 B3
Washington Ct. Mar 2 A2
Washington Dr. Slough 41 E3
Washington Dr. Wind 66 C2
Washington Gdns. Woki . 116 C3
Washington Rd. Caver 59 D1
Watchetts Dr. Camb 151 E1
Watchetts Lake Cl. Camb . 151 E2
Watchetts Rd. Camb 151 D2
Watchmoor Rd. Camb ... 151 D2
Water La. Gree 131 E4
Water Rd. Read 85 D3
Water St. Hamp N 52 C3
Waterbeach Rd. Slough ... 42 B4
Waterfall Cl. Vir W 122 A3
Waterford Way. Woki ... 116 B3
Waterham Rd. Brac 118 A2
Waterhouse Mead. Sand . 150 C4
Waterloo Cres. Woki 116 C3
Waterloo Rd. Crow 143 D2
Waterloo Rd. Read 86 A3
Waterloo Rd. Woki 116 C3
Waterman Pl. Read 59 D1
Waterman's Rd. Hen-O-T . 35 F4
Waterman's Way. Warg ... 36 B1
Watermead. Felt 98 C4
Watermill Ct. Wool 108 B1
Waters Dr. Stai 96 C2
Watersfield Cl. Read 87 D1
Waterside Cl. Newb 105 D2
Waterside Dr. Pur O T 57 E3
Waterside Dr. Slough 44 A2
Waterside Dr. Thea 83 F2
Waterside Gdns. Read 86 A4
Waterside Park Ind Est. Brac . 117 F4
Waterside. Woo G 3 F4
Waterplash La. Asc 120 C4
Watersplash La. Wink ... 120 C4
Watersplash Rd. Stai 125 D3
Watery La. Chert 123 E1
Watery La. Kint 128 C3
Watery La. Woo G 3 F4
Watkins Cl. Woki 141 F4
Watlington St. Read 86 B4
Watmore La. Winn 88 B1
Watson Cl. Woki 115 F1
Watt's La. Blew 12 A4
Wavell Cl. Read 85 D4
Wavell Gdns. Slough 21 F1
Wavell Rd. Maid 39 D3
Wavendene Ave. Stai 96 B1
Waverley Cl. Camb 151 F2
Waverley Dr. Camb 151 F2
Waverley Dr. Vir W 122 A3
Waverley Rd. Bags 145 F2
Waverley Rd. Read 85 E4
Waverley Way. Woki 116 B4
Waverley Way. Woki 115 F1
Waverley. Brac 117 F2
Waverleys The. That 106 B2
Waybrook Cres. Read 86 C2
Wayland Cl. Brac 118 C3
Waylen St. Read 85 F4
Ways End. Camb 151 F2
Wayside Mews. Maid 39 F4
Weald Rise. Read 57 F1
Wealden Way. Read 84 C4
Wealden Way. Read 84 C4
Weavers La. Ink 127 E3
Weavers Wlk. Newb 105 D2
Webb Cl. Bags 145 F1
Webb Cl. Binf 90 C1
Webb Cl. Slough 43 E1
Webbs Acre. That 106 C1
Webbs La. Bren 109 D4
Webster Cl. Maid 39 D3
Wedderburn Cl. Winn 88 B1
Wedgewood Way. Read .. 57 F1
Weekes Dr. Slough 42 A2
Weighbridge Row. Read .. 59 D1
Weir Cl. Camb 151 D2
Weir Pl. Stai 123 E3
Weir Rd. Chert 124 A1
Welbeck Rd. Maid 39 D2
Welbeck. Brac 117 F2
Welby Cl. Maid 39 D2
Welby Cres. Winn 88 A1
Welford Rd. Wood 88 A4
Well Cl. Camb 151 D2
Well House La. Swal 140 B2
Well Meadow. Newb 105 D3
Welland Cl. Read 57 E1
Welland Cl. Slough 42 C1
Wellbank. Tapl 20 C1
Wellcroft Rd. Slough 42 B3
Weller Dr. Bark 141 D3
Weller Dr. Camb 151 F2
Weller's La. New G 91 E4
Wellesley Ave. Iver 44 C2
Wellesley Cl. Bags 145 E2

Wellesley Dr. Brac

Wellesley Dr. Brac 142 C3
Wellesley Dr. Finch 142 C3
Wellesley Rd. Slough 43 D2
Welley Ave. Wray 68 C2
Welley Rd. Hort 68 C1
Welley Rd. Wray 68 C1
Wellfield Cl. Read 84 B4
Wellhill Rd. Fawl 27 E3
Wellhouse La. Buck 79 F3
Wellhouse La. Herm 79 F3
Wellhouse Rd. Maid 19 F1
Wellington Ave. Read 86 B2
Wellington Ave. Vir W 122 A2
Wellington Ave. Went 122 A2
Wellington Busn Park. Maid 142 C2
Wellington Cl. Newb 105 E3
Wellington Cl. Sand 150 B4
Wellington Cl. Shepp 125 F1
Wellington Cres. Tad 134 B1
Wellington Dr. Brac 118 C2
Wellington Rd. Ashf 97 F2
Wellington Rd. Crow 143 E2
Wellington Rd. Harm 71 F1
Wellington Rd. Maid 39 E4
Wellington Rd. Sand 150 B4
Wellington Rd. Woki 116 A3
Wellington St. Slough 43 D2
Wellingtonia Ave. Finch 142 B2
Wells Cl. Wind 67 D4
Wells La. Ascot 120 A3
Welsh La. Swal 139 D1
Welshman's Rd. Silc 136 A3
Welwick Cl. Winn 87 F1
Welwyn Ave. Felt 71 F1
Wendan Rd. Newb 130 C4
Wendover Dr. Camb 152 B2
Wendover Pl. Stai 96 B2
Wendover Rd. Bou E 3 D3
Wendover Rd. Burn 41 D4
Wendover Rd. Slough 41 D4
Wendover Rd. Stai 96 B2
Wendover Way. Read 84 B4
Wenlock Edge. Char 61 D2
Wenlock Way. That 106 B1
Wensley Cl. Twyf 61 E3
Wensley Rd. Read 85 F3
Wensleydale Dr. Camb 152 B3
Wentworth Ave. Burl 119 E4
Wentworth Ave. Read 113 E4
Wentworth Ave. Slough 22 A1
Wentworth Cl. Ashf 98 A2
Wentworth Cl. Brac 142 C3
Wentworth Cl. Yate 149 E3
Wentworth Cres. Maid 39 E3
Wentworth Ct. Newb 105 D1
Wentworth Dr. Vir W 122 A2
Wentworth Way. Burl 119 E4
Wescott Rd. Woki 116 B3
Wosley Dr. Eng G 96 A1
Wessex Cl. Hung 100 B3
Wessex Gdns. Twyf 61 F2
Wessex Rd. Bou E 3 D1
Wessex Rd. Harn 70 C2
Wessex Way. Maid 39 D2
Wessons Hill. Cook 19 E4
West Cl. Ashf 97 F2
West Cl. Medm 17 E4
West Cres. Wind 66 C3
West Dean. Maid 39 F4
West Dr. Read 84 C3
West Dr. Sonn 60 C1
West Dr. Went 121 F1
West Dr. Went 122 A1
West End Ct. Sto P 22 C2
West End La. Hart 71 E4
West End La. Sto P 22 C2
West End Rd. Silc 136 C3
West Fryerne. Yate 149 E4
West Green Ct. Read 85 F3
West Green. Yate 149 D4
West Hill. Read 86 A3
West Mead. Maid 19 F1
West Mills. Newb 104 C2
West Point. Slough 41 E3
West Ramp. Harm 71 D3
West Rd. Camb 151 E3
West Rd. Felt 98 B4
West Rd. Maid 19 F1
West Ridge. Bou E 3 D2
West Sq. Iver 44 C4
West St. Hen-O-T 15 E1
West St. Maid 39 F4
West St. Mar 1 B1
West St. Newb 104 C2
West St. Read 86 A4
West View. Felt 98 B4
West View. Pease 50 B4
West Way. Shepp 125 E2
Westacott Way. Bur G 38 B2
Westborough Cl. Maid 39 E3
Westborough Rd. Maid 39 E3
Westbourne Rd. Felt 98 C3
Westbourne Rd. Sand 150 C4
Westbourne Rd. Stai 97 D1
Westbourne Terr. Read 85 E4
Westbrook Cl. Hung 100 B3
Westbrook Gdns. Brac 118 B4
Westbrook Green. Blew 11 F4
Westbrook Rd. Read 58 B1

Westbrook Rd. Stai 96 C2
Westbrook St. Blew 11 F4
Westbrook. Holy 40 C1
Westbury Cl. Crow 143 D3
Westbury Cl. Shepp 125 D2
Westbury La. Pur O T 57 D3
Westcombe Cl. Brac 118 C1
Westcote Rd. Read 85 E3
Westcotts Green. New G 91 F1
Westcroft. Slough 22 A1
Westdene Cres. Caver 58 C2
Westerdale Dr. Camb 152 A2
Westerdale. That 106 B2
Western Ave. Chert 124 A3
Western Ave. Hen-O-T 35 F4
Western Ave. Newb 104 C2
Western Ave. Stai 123 D3
Western Ave. Wood 60 C1
Western Cl. Chert 124 A3
Western Dr. Bou E 3 F3
Western Dr. Shepp 125 E2
Western Elms Ave. Read 85 F4
Western End. Newb 104 C1
Western Oaks. Read 57 F1
Western Perimeter Rd. Harm . 70 A2
Western Perimeter Rd. Stan ... 70 A2
Western Rd. Brac 117 F4
Western Rd. Hen-O-T 35 F4
Western Rd. Read 85 F3
Westfield Cotts. Medm 16 C3
Westfield Cres. Shipl 36 A2
Westfield Cres. That 106 A2
Westfield Rd. Camb 151 D1
Westfield Rd. Caver 59 D1
Westfield Rd. Chol 13 E4
Westfield Rd. Maid 39 D4
Westfield Rd. Slough 22 A1
Westfield Rd. That 106 A3
Westfield Rd. Winn 88 A1
Westfields. Comp 31 E2
Westgate Cres. Slough 41 F3
Westgate Rd. Newb 104 C1
Westhatch Cnr. New G 91 E3
Westhatch La. New G 91 E3
Westhope Rd. Mar 1 C2
Westland Cl. Stan 70 C1
Westland. That 106 A2
Westlands Ave. Read 86 C1
Westlands Ave. Slough 41 E4
Westlands Cl. Slough 41 E4
Westlands Rd. Newb 131 D4
Westley Mill. Binf 90 C4
Westley Mill. Holy 63 F1
Westlyn Rd. Silc 135 F1
Westmacott Dr. Felt 98 C4
Westmead Dr. Newb 130 C4
Westmead. Wind 67 D2
Westminster Way. Wood 87 E1
Westmorland Cl. Woki 115 E3
Westmorland Dr. Camb 152 A2
Westmorland Dr. New G 91 F1
Westmorland Rd. Maid 39 E3
Weston Gr. Bags 145 F1
Weston Rd. Slough 41 F4
Westonbirt Dr. Caver 58 C2
Westons. Beed 51 E4
Westridge Ave. Pur O T 57 E3
Westview Dr. Twyf 61 F3
Westward Rd. Woki 115 F4
Westwates Cl. Brac 118 B4
Westway. Gori 34 B4
Westwood Glen. Read 57 E1
Westwood Green. Cook 19 F3
Westwood Rd. Mar 1 B1
Westwood Rd. Newb 105 E1
Westwood Rd. Read 57 E1
Westwood Rd. Windl 146 C3
Westwood Row. Read 57 E1
Wetherby Cl. Caver 59 E3
Wethered Dr. Burn 41 D4
Wethered Rd. Mar 1 A1
Wetton Pl. Eng G 96 A2
Wexham Park La. Iver H 23 E1
Wexham Park La. Sto P 23 E1
Wexham Rd. Slough 43 D3
Wexham St. Sto P 23 D2
Wexham Woods. Slough 43 E4
Wey Ave. Chert 124 A3
Wey Cl. Camb 151 D3
Weybridge Mead. Yate 149 F4
Weycrofts. Brac 90 C1
Weymead Cl. Chert 124 B1
Whaley Rd. Woki 116 B4
Wharf La. Bou E 3 D2
Wharf La. Hen-O-T 15 F1
Wharf Rd. Newb 105 D2
Wharf Rd. Wray 95 E4
Wharf St. Newb 105 D2
Wharf The. Newb 105 D2
Wharfdale Rd. Winn 88 A2
Wharfside. Padw 109 E2
Whatley Green. Brac 118 A2
Whatmore Cl. Stan 70 A1
Wheatash Rd. Chert 124 A1
Wheatbutts Meadow. Eton 41 F1
Wheatfield Cl. Maid 39 D2
Wheatfields Rd. Shin 113 F3
Wheatlands Cl. Read 84 C2

Wheatlands La. Ham M 130 A3
Wheatlands Rd. Slough 43 E2
Wheatley Cl. Read 86 C1
Wheatley. Brac 117 F2
Wheatsheaf La. Newb 105 D2
Wheatsheaf La. Stai 96 C1
Wheble Dr. Wood 87 E4
Wheeler Cl. Bur C 111 D2
Wheelers Green Way. That 106 C1
Wheelton Cl. Winn 87 F2
Whins Cl. Camb 151 D2
Whins Dr. Camb 151 D2
Whinshill Ct. Went 121 D1
Whistler Gr. Sand 150 B3
Whistley Cl. Brac 118 C3
Whitamore Row. Hen-O-T 35 F4
Whitby Dr. Read 86 B3
Whitby Green. Caver 59 E3
Whitby Rd. Slough 42 B3
Whitchurch Cl. Maid 19 F2
Whitchurch Rd. Pangb 56 B3
White Bridge Cl. Felt 71 F1
White City. Crow 143 E3
White Cl. Newb 78 C3
White Cl. Slough 42 B3
White Gates. Wick 75 E3
White Hart Rd. Maid 39 F4
White Hart Rd. Slough 42 B2
White Hart Row. Chert 124 A1
White Hill. Beac 3 F4
White Hill, Rem H 16 A1
White Hill. Shipl 35 D3
White Hill. Windl 146 A3
White Hill. Woo G 3 F4
White Horse La. Finch 141 E3
White Horse Rd. Wind 66 B3
White House Gdns. Yate 149 E4
White Lilies Island. Wind 67 D4
White Lion Way. Yate 149 E4
White Lodge Cl. Sulh 57 D2
White Lodge. Mar B 1 B3
White Paddock. Whi Wa 39 D1
White Rd. Chil 10 B4
White Rd. Sand 150 C3
White Rock. Maid 20 A1
White Shoot. Blew 12 A3
White's La. Been 109 D4
Whitebeam Cl. Woki 115 E2
Whiteford Rd. Slough 42 C4
Whitegate La. Read 113 E4
Whitegates La. Read 87 D4
Whitehall Dr. Arbo 140 C4
Whitehall Farm La. Vir W 122 C3
Whitehall La. Eng G 95 F1
Whitehall La. Eng G 69 D1
Whitehall La. Mar B 1 B3
Whitehall Pk. Vir W 122 C2
Whitehill Rd. Camb 151 E4
Whitehills Green. Gorl 34 B3
Whiteknights Rd. Read 86 C3
Whitelands Dr. Burl 119 E4
Whitelands Rd. That 106 B2
Whiteley. Wind 66 C4
Whitemoor La. Upp B 54 C3
Whitepit La. Fla H 3 E4
Whites Hill. Sulhd 110 C3
Whites La. Datch 68 A4
Whitestone Cl. Winn 87 F2
Whitewalls Cl. Comp 31 F3
Whitewalls Cl. Stai 97 D1
Whitley Cl. Stan 70 C1
Whitley Park La. Read 86 B2
Whitley Rd. Yate 149 E2
Whitley St. Read 86 A3
Whitley Wood La. Read 113 E4
Whitley Wood Rd. Read 113 E4
Whitmoor Rd. Bags 145 F1
Whitmore Cl. Sand 143 E1
Whitmore La. Sunn 121 D2
Whitstone Gdns. Read 86 B1
Whittaker Rd. Slough 21 F1
Whittenham Cl. Slough 43 D3
Whittle Cl. Crow 143 D1
Whittle Cl. Woki 141 F4
Whittle Parkway. Slough 41 E4
Whitton Cl. Brac 118 C3
Whitton Cl. Winn 87 E1
Whitworth Rd. Bark 141 D4
Whurley Way. Maid 19 F1
Whynstones Rd. Ascot 120 A2
Whyteladyes La. Cook 19 F3
Wick Hill La. Woki 142 A3
Wick La. Eng G 94 C1
Wick Rd. Eng G 95 D1
Wick's Green. Binf 90 A2
Wickford Way. Read 113 F4
Wickham Cl. Bags 145 F3
Wickham La. Eng G 96 A1
Wickham Rd. Camb 151 F4
Wickham Rd. Winn 87 F1
Wickham Vale. Brac 117 F2
Widbrook Rd. Maid 20 A2
Widecombe Pl. Read 86 A1
Widecroft Rd. Iver 44 C4
Widmere La. Mar B 1 A4
Wield Ct. Winn 87 F1
Wiggett Gr. Binf 90 B1
Wigmore La. Read 58 A1
Wigmore La. Read 58 B1
Wigmore La. Thea 83 E1

Wigmore Rd. Tad 134 C1
Wilberforce Way. Brac 118 B2
Wilcox Gdns. Stai 124 C3
Wild Briar. Woki 141 F4
Wild Cl. Winn 114 B4
Wildcroft Dr. Woki 116 A1
Wilder Ave. Pangb 56 C3
Wilderness Ct. Read 87 D2
Wilderness Rd. Camb 151 F1
Wilderness Rd. Read 87 D2
Wilders Cl. Brac 91 D1
Wilders Cl. Camb 151 F2
Wildgreen N. Slough 44 A1
Wildgreen S. Slough 44 A1
Wildridings Rd. Brac 118 A3
Wildridings Sq. Brac 118 A3
Wildwood Dr. Tad 134 B1
Wildwood Gdns. Yate 149 E2
Wilford Rd. Slough 43 F1
Wilfred Way. That 107 D2
Wilfrids Wood Cl. Bou E 3 D3
Willats Cl. Chert 124 A2
William Cl. That 106 B1
William Ellis Cl. Old W 68 A1
William Slim Wood. Burl 92 A1
William St. Read 85 F4
William St. Slough 42 C3
William St. Wind 67 E3
Williant Cl. Whi Wa 38 C1
Willington Cl. Camb 151 D3
Willoners. Slough 42 A4
Willoughby Rd. Brac 117 F3
Willoughby Rd. Slough 44 A2
Willow Cl. Bur C 111 D3
Willow Cl. Fla H 3 E3
Willow Cl. Iver 69 E4
Willow Cl. Newb 104 C1
Willow Ct. Camb 151 E1
Willow Dr. Brac 118 B4
Willow Dr. Maid 40 A1
Willow Dr. Twyf 61 E3
Willow Gdns. Read 86 C1
Willow Green. West E 153 F3
Willow La. Black 150 B2
Willow La. Warg 36 B2
Willow Park. Sto P 23 D3
Willow Pl. Eton 67 E4
Willow Rd. Newt 131 F1
Willow Rd. Stan 69 F3
Willow St. Read 86 A3
Willow Tree Glade. Bur C 84 B2
Willow Way. Sand 142 C1
Willow Wlk. Chert 124 A1
Willow Wlk. Eng G 95 E2
Willowbrook Rd. Stan 97 F3
Willowbrook. Eton 42 B1
Willowdale. Woki 141 F4
Willowford. Yate 149 E3
Willowmead Cl. Mar 1 C2
Willowmead Cl. Newb 130 B3
Willowmead Gdns. Mar 1 C2
Willowmead Rd. Mar 1 C2
Willowmead Sq. Mar 1 C2
Willows End. Sand 150 A4
Willows Rd. Bou E 3 D2
Willows The. Caver 59 D1
Willows The. Light 146 B1
Willowside. Wood 60 C1
Wilson Rd. Eng G 95 D2
Wilmington Cl. Wood 87 F4
Wilmot Cl. Binf 90 B1
Wilmot Rd. Burn 21 D1
Wilmot Way. Camb 151 F2
Wilmot Wlk. Newb 130 B3
Wilmott Cl. Winn 88 A1
Wilsford Cl. Read 113 F4
Wilson Ave. Hen-O-T 35 F4
Wilson Cl. Comp 31 F2
Wilson Ct. Winn 88 A1
Wilson Rd. Read 85 E4
Wilton Cl. Harm 70 B4
Wilton Cres. Wind 66 B2
Wilton Rd. Camb 151 D2
Wilton Rd. Read 85 E4
Wiltshire Ave. Crow 143 D3
Wiltshire Ave. Slough 22 B1
Wiltshire Dr. Woki 116 B4
Wiltshire Gr. New G 91 F1
Wiltshire Rd. Mar 1 C2
Wiltshire Rd. Woki 116 B4
Wiltshire Wlk. Read 84 A3
Wilwood Rd. Brac 117 F4
Wilwyne Cl. Caver 59 E2
Wimbledon Cl. Camb 144 C1
Wimbledon Rd. Camb 144 C1
Wimblington Dr. Winn 114 B4
Wimborne Gdns. Read 58 A1
Wimbushes. Woki 141 E3
Winbury Ct. Maid 39 F4
Wincanton Rd. Read 113 E4
Winch Cl. Binf 90 B2
Winchcombe La. Lit M 2 A3
Winchcombe Rd. Newb 105 D1
Winchcombe Rd. Twyf 61 F2
Winchester Cl. Stan 70 B4
Winchester Dr. Maid 39 D2
Winchester Rd. Harl 71 F4
Winchester Rd. Read 86 A2

Wolsey Rd.

Winchester Way. Black ....
Winchgrove Rd. Brac ....
Winchstone Cl. Stai ....
Wincroft Rd. Caver ....
Windermere Cl. Felt ....
Windermere Cl. Read ....
Windermere Cl. Light ....
Windermere Rd. Read ....
Windermere Way. Slough ....
Windermere Way. That ....
Winding Wood Dr. Camb ....
Windle Cl. Windl ....
Windlebrook Green. Brac ....
Windlesham Cl. Windl ....
Windlesham Rd. Brac ....
Windlesham Rd. West E ....
Windmill Ave. Woki ....
Windmill Cl. Stai ....
Windmill Cl. Wind ....
Windmill Cl. Woki ....
Windmill Cnr. Mort ....
Windmill Field. Windl ....
Windmill La. Buck ....
Windmill La. Wool ....
Windmill Rd W. Stai ....
Windmill Rd. Brac ....
Windmill Rd. Cook ....
Windmill Rd. Felt ....
Windmill Rd. Mort ....
Windmill Rd. Slough ....
Windmill Rd. Stai ....
Windrush Ave. Slough ....
Windrush Hts. Sand ....
Windrush Way. Maid ....
Windrush Way. Read ....
Windsor Dr. Ashf ....
Windsor Hill. Bou E ....
Windsor La. Burn ....
Windsor Park. Rd. Harl ....
Windsor Rd. Ascot ....
Windsor Rd. Chob ....
Windsor Rd. Eng G ....
Windsor Rd. Holy ....
Windsor Rd. Maid ....
Windsor Rd. Oak G ....
Windsor Rd. Oak G ....
Windsor Rd. Slough ....
Windsor Rd. Sto P ....
Windsor Rd. Wray ....
Windsor Ride. Sand ....
Windsor Ride. Woki ....
Windsor Rise. Newb ....
Windsor Way. Read ....
Wingate Rd. Wood ....
Wingfield Gdns. Camb ....
Wingrove Rd. Read ....
Winkfield Cl. Woki ....
Winkfield La. Wink ....
Winkfield Rd. Ascot ....
Winkfield Rd. Wink ....
Winkfield St. Burl ....
Winnersh Gate. Winn ....
Winnersh Gr. Winn ....
Winscombe. Brac ....
Winser Dr. Read ....
Winston Cl. Shin ....
Winston Way. Pur O T ....
Winston Way. That ....
Winter Hill. Cook ....
Winter Hill. Cook ....
Winter Hill. Cook ....
Winter Hill. Maid ....
Winterbourne Rd. Box ....
Winterborne Rd. Wint ....
Winterton Dr. Newb ....
Winton Cres. Yate ....
Winton Rd. Read ....
Wintoun Path. Slough ....
Wintringham Way. Pur O T .....
Winvale. Slough ....
Winwood. Slough ....
Wise's Firs. Sulhd ....
Wishmoor Cl. Camb ....
Wishmoor Rd. Camb ....
Wispington Cl. Winn ....
Wistaria La. Yate ....
Wisteria Cl. Woki ....
Wiston Terr. Read ....
Witcham Cl. Winn ....
Withey Cl. Wind ....
Witheygate Ave. Stai ....
Withy Cl. Light ....
Withy Cl. Read ....
Withy Croft. Slough ....
Withybed La. Kint ....
Wittenham Ave. Read ....
Wittenham Rd. Brac ....
Woburn Cl. Camb ....
Woburn Cl. Caver ....
Wokingham Rd. Brac ....
Wokingham Rd. Hurst ....
Wokingham Rd. Read ....
Wokingham Rd. Sand ....
Wolf La. Wind ....
Wolseley St. Read ....
Wolsey Rd. Ashf ....

Rd. Caver 59 D1
ham Way. That 106 B1
ford Dale. Binf 90 B2
n Manor Park. Bou E ... 3 F3
n Mews. Bou E 3 F3
il. Wind 67 E2
nd. Crow 142 C2
reen Cl. Read 85 F4
a. Arbo 114 C2
a. Binf 90 B1
a. Iver 44 B4
a. Slough 42 A2
loor. Finch 14 F1
d. Camb 151 D1
d. Stai 125 D3
ne Cl. Sand 150 B4
ne Cl. Winn 87 E1
ne La. Newt 130 C1
urne Cl. Yate 149 E3
idge Rd. Black 150 A3
idge Rd. Read 84 A3
ary. Lamb 25 E1
r Dr. Sunn 120 C1
ite Rd. Caver 58 C2
ite Rd. Sou S 14 B2
ite Way. Caver 58 B3
d. Stai 39 E3
d Cl. Burl 119 F4
d Dr. Ascot 120 A2
hill. Brac 117 F1
ld Dr. Maid 39 D3
ild Way. Thea 83 F2
rd Cl. Caver 58 C2
rd Green. Brac 118 C3
rd Way. Slough 22 A1
all La. Windl 146 C4
aw. Stai 96 A3
ouse La. Head 133 E1
ouse St. Brac 90 C1
ouse St. Brac 117 F4
urst La. Woki 115 F4
urst Rd. Maid 20 A1
s Cl. Binf 90 B1
nd Ave. Slough 42 B3
nd Ave. Wind 66 C2
nd Ave. Woki 115 F4
nd Cl. Mar 1 C2

Woodland Cres. Brac 91 E1
Woodland Dr. Read 84 B4
Woodland Way. Mar 1 C2
Woodlands Ave. Bur C 111 D2
Woodlands Ave. Wood 87 E4
Woodlands Busn Park. Maid .. 39 D1
Woodlands Cl. Ascot 119 F2
Woodlands Cl. Black 150 C1
Woodlands Cl. Herm 78 C3
Woodlands Ct. Crow 143 F1
Woodlands Gr. Caver 59 F2
Woodlands La. Windl 146 C2
Woodlands Parade. Ashf 98 B1
Woodlands Park Ave. Whi Wa . 39 D1
Woodlands Park Rd. Maid 39 D2
Woodlands Park Rd. Whi Wa .. 39 D2
Woodlands Rd E. Vir W 122 B3
Woodlands Rd W. Vir W 122 B3
Woodlands Rd. Camb 151 D3
Woodlands Rd. Shipl 35 F2
Woodlands Rd. Tad 134 B1
Woodlands Rd. Vir W 122 B3
Woodlands Ride. Ascot 120 A2
Woodlands The. Woki 115 E2
Woodlands Wlk. Black 150 C1
Woodlands. Yate 149 E2
Woodlee Cl. Vir W 122 B4
Woodley Green. Wood 87 F4
Woodman Cl. Read 113 E3
Woodman's La. Bur C 110 C2
Woodmancott Cl. Brac 118 C2
Woodmere Cl. Read 87 D1
Woodmere. Brac 118 C3
Woodmoor End. Cook 20 A4
Woodpecker Cl. Twyf 61 F2
Woodridge Cl. Brac 118 B3
Woodrow Dr. Woki 116 C3
Woods Rd. Caver 59 F2
Woodsend Cl. Read 113 E4
Woodshore Cl. Vir W 122 A2
Woodside Ave. Fla H 3 E4
Woodside Cl. Buck 107 E3
Woodside Cl. Woki 141 F4
Woodside La. Wink 93 E2
Woodside Rd. Ascot 93 D1
Woodside Way. Read 113 E4
Woodside Way. Vir W 122 A3
Woodside. Black 150 B2
Woodside. Fla H 3 E3

Woodside. Newb 130 B4
Woodside. Sand 150 C4
Woodstock Ave. Slough 43 E1
Woodstock Cl. Maid 19 F1
Woodstock St. Read 86 C4
Woodthorpe Rd. Ashf 97 E2
Woodthorpe Rd. Stai 97 E2
Woodview Rd. Pangb 56 B3
Woodville Cl. Black 150 A3
Woodward Cl. Winn 88 B1
Woodway Rd. Blew 12 A4
Woodway. Camb 151 D3
Woodwaye. Wood 87 E4
Woodyer Cl. Wood 87 F3
Woolacombe Dr. Read 86 C1
Woolford Cl. Burl 92 B1
Woolhampton Hill. Wool 108 B2
Woolhampton Way. Brac 118 B2
Woosehill La. Woki 115 F3
Woosehill La. Woki 115 F4
Woosehill. Woki 115 F3
Wootton Cl. Read 84 B4
Wootton Dr. Woo G 3 F4
Wootton Rd. Hen-O-T 35 E4
Wootton Way. Maid 39 E3
Worcester Cl. Maid 39 E2
Worcester Cl. Read 85 D3
Worcester Dr. Ashf 98 A2
Wordsworth Ave. Yate 149 D2
Wordsworth Ct. Caver 59 E4
Wordsworth Rd. Slough 21 E1
Wordsworth Rd. That 106 B2
Wordsworth. Brac 117 F2
Worlds End Hill. Brac 118 C2
Worple Ave. Stai 97 D1
Worple Rd. Stai 97 D1
Worple The. Wray 68 C1
Worrall Way. Read 113 F4
Worster Rd. Cook 19 F3
Worton Dr. Read 113 D4
Wrabness Way. Stai 124 A4
Wraysbury Rd. Stai 96 B3
Wraysbury Rd. Wray 96 B3
Wren Cl. Bur C 111 D2
Wren Cl. Woki 115 F3
Wren Cl. Yate 149 D3
Wren Ct. Slough 44 A2
Wren's Ave. Ashf 98 B2
Wrenfield Dr. Caver 58 C3

Wrensfield. Mar 1 B1
Wrenswood Cl. Read 113 D4
Wright Cl. Wood 88 A4
Wright. Oak G 66 B2
Wroxham Rd. Wood 87 E4
Wroxham. Brac 117 F2
Wurford Dr. That 106 C2
Wyatt Rd. Stai 97 D2
Wyatt Rd. Wind 66 B2
Wychcotes. Caver 58 C2
Wychelm Rd. Light 153 E4
Wychelm Rd. Shin 113 F3
Wychwood Ave. Brac 118 C3
Wychwood Cl. Read 86 C1
Wychwood Cres. Read 86 C2
Wychwood Pl. Camb 145 D1
Wychwood Pl. Camb 152 A4
Wycombe La. Woo G 3 F4
Wycombe Rd. Mar 1 C2
Wycombe Rd. Mar B 1 C3
Wye Cl. Ashf 98 A2
Wye Cl. Read 84 C3
Wye Rd. Woo G 3 E4
Wykeham Cl. Harm 71 D4
Wykeham Rd. Read 87 D3
Wylam. Brac 117 F2
Wylands Rd. Slough 44 A1
Wyld Court Hill. Hamp N 53 E3
Wymers Cl. Burn 21 D2
Wymers Wood Rd. Burn 21 D2
Wyncote Cl. Read 86 C1
Wyndale Cl. Hen-O-T 15 F1
Wyndham Cl. Yate 149 E4
Wyndham Cres. Burn 21 D2
Wyndham Cres. Wood 60 B1
Wyndham Rd. Newb 105 E3
Wynford Cl. Read 85 E2
Wynnstay Gdns. Mar B 1 C3
Wynsham Way. Windl 146 A3
Wyre Ct. Sulh 57 E2
Wyres Dale. Brac 118 C1
Wythe Mead. Binf 90 A1
Wyvern Cl. Brac 118 A3

Yale Cl. Crow 143 F1
Yard Mead. Eng G 96 A3
Yardley. Brac 117 F2
Yarnold Cl. Wood 116 C4
Yarnton Cl. Caver 59 E3

Yateley Dr. Yate 149 D1
Yateley Rd. Sand 149 F4
Yattendon La. Asham 54 B1
Yattendon La. Yatt 54 B1
Yattendon Rd. Herm 79 D4
Yaverland Dr. Bags 145 E1
Ye Meads. Tapl 40 C3
Yelverton Rd. Read 86 B2
Yeomans La. Newt 131 D1
Yeomans Way. Camb 151 F3
Yeosfield. Swal 139 E2
Yeoveney Cl. Stan 96 B3
Yeovil Rd. Burn 41 F4
Yeovil Rd. Sand 143 F1
Yew Cl. Woki 115 F3
Yew Gate. Newb 104 C3
Yew La. Read 85 F3
Yew Tree Cl. Maid 39 F4
Yew Tree Ct. Gori 34 B3
Yew Tree Rd. Slough 43 D2
Yew Tree Rise. Read 84 B3
Yew Tree Wlk. Camb 151 F1
Yewhurst Cl. Twyf 61 E3
Yewtrees. Stai 123 E3
Yield Hall La. Read 86 A4
Yield Hall Pl. Read 86 A4
Yockley Cl. Camb 152 B2
Yoreham Cl. Winn 87 F1
York Ave. Slough 42 B4
York Ave. Wind 67 D3
York Cl. Newb 105 D1
York Rd. Binf 90 B2
York Rd. Camb 151 E4
York Rd. Hen-O-T 15 E1
York Rd. Hung 100 B2
York Rd. Maid 40 A4
York Rd. Mar 1 B1
York Rd. Newb 105 D1
York Rd. Read 59 D1
York Rd. Wind 67 D3
York Way. Sand 150 A4
Yorktown Rd. Sand 150 B4
Youlden Cl. Camb 152 A3
Youlden Dr. Camb 152 A3

Zealand Ave. Harm 70 C4
Zinnia Cl. Woki 115 E4
Zinzan St. Read 85 F4

Ordnance Survey

COUNTY STREET ATLASES

Berkshire	**East Kent**
Buckinghamshire	**West Kent**
East Essex	**Oxfordshire**
West Essex	**Surrey**
North Hampshire	**East Sussex**
South Hampshire	**West Sussex**
Hertfordshire	**Warwickshire**

The whole series is available from all good bookshops or by mail order direct from the publisher. Payment can be made by credit card or cheque/ postal order in the following ways

By phone
Phone through your order on our special *Credit Card Hotline* on **0933 410511**. Speak to our customer service team during office hours (9am to 5pm) or leave a message on the answer machine, quoting your full credit card number plus expiry date and your full name and address.

By post
Simply fill out the order form opposite and send it to:
Cash Sales Department, Reed Book Services, PO Box 5, Rushden, Northants, NN10 9YX

I wish to order the following titles:

		Price	Quantity	Total
Berkshire	ISBN 0 540 05596 4 hardback	£10.99		
	ISBN 0 540 05835 1 pocket	£4.99		
Buckinghamshire	ISBN 0 540 05660 X hardback	£10.99		
	ISBN 0 540 05711 8 pocket	£4.99		
East Essex	ISBN 0 540 05590 5 hardback	£10.99		
West Essex	ISBN 0 540 05591 3 hardback	£10.99		
North Hampshire	ISBN 0 540 05610 3 hardback	£10.99		
South Hampshire	ISBN 0 540 05611 1 hardback	£10.99		
Hertfordshire	ISBN 0 540 05720 7 hardback	£10.99		
	ISBN 0 540 05840 8 pocket	£4.99		
East Kent	ISBN 0 540 05661 8 hardback	£10.99		
West Kent	ISBN 0 540 05662 6 hardback	£10.99		
Oxfordshire	ISBN 0 540 05665 0 hardback	£10.99		
Surrey	ISBN 0 540 05694 4 hardback	£10.99		
	ISBN 0 540 05624 3 pocket	£4.99		
East Sussex	ISBN 0 540 05663 4 hardback	£10.99		
West Sussex	ISBN 0 540 05664 2 hardback	£10.99		
Warwickshire	ISBN 0 540 05642 1 hardback	£10.99		

Postage and packing free   Grand Total ☐

Name _____ (block capitals)

Address _____

_____ Postcode _____

I enclose a cheque/postal order for £ ☐ made payable to **Reed Book Services** or

Please debit my ☐ Access ☐ Visa ☐ American Express account number

☐☐☐☐ ☐☐☐☐ ☐☐☐☐ ☐☐☐☐

by £ ☐ Expiry date ☐☐ / ☐☐

_____ signature

* Free postage and packing * While every effort is made to keep prices low, the publisher reserves the right to increase prices at short notice. ***** Your order will be dispatched within 28 days, subject to availability.

STREET 1